Letts study aids

A-Level Economics
Course Companion

Ray Powell MA, MSc

Lecturer in Economics, Kingston College of Further Education

Charles Letts & Co Ltd
London, Edinburgh & New York

First published 1982
by Charles Letts & Co Ltd
Diary House, Borough Road, London SE1 1DW
Reprinted 1983 (twice)

Design: Ben Sands
Illustrations: Tek-Art
Editor: Jeremy Lawrence

ISBN 0 85097 413 5

Printed and bound by
Charles Letts (Scotland) Ltd

Preface

This book is written for all students taking the Advanced Level examination in economics. In recent years, both the style of the examination and the knowledge and skills required of candidates have undergone significant and sometimes fundamental change. As an experienced teacher and assistant Chief Examiner who has worked for two of the larger examining boards, I have written this book to acquaint students with the standards and skills now required by all the examining boards.

The core of the book comprises twenty eight topic units, which I have chosen after a careful analysis of the syllabuses of the examining boards and the subject areas on which questions have been set most frequently in recent years. At the end of each topic unit I have discussed a number of representative questions, many of which are selected from recent examination papers.

At all times in writing the book, I have tried to help students to make the most of the information and skills learned in a taught course but which, sadly, many students fail to reproduce amidst the pressures and stresses of an examination. Answering an examination is not merely a matter of learning and displaying a factual knowledge, important though that can be. Conventional textbooks, excellent as they are, seldom provide guidance on how to develop and make use of the wider range of skills that modern examinations seek to test. The purpose of this book is to provide exactly such an aid to students. It has **not** been designed **either** as **an examination crammer, or** to provide **a simple means of spotting questions**, nor does it contain model answers to be learned parrot-fashion. The questions at the end of each unit are there to provide guidance on the different approaches to a particular topic area, and the type of skills required to answer a question satisfactorily. In any case, spotting questions is a dangerous business: Chief Examiners change frequently, and in a discipline such as economics different issues become fashionable and topical.

The following examination boards have given permission to reproduce questions set by them in previous examinations, for which I am most grateful:

AEB : Associated Examining Board for the General Certificate of Education

JMB : Joint Matriculation Board

London : University of London University Entrance and School Examination Council

Cambridge : University of Cambridge Local Examinations Syndicate

Oxford : Oxford Delegacy of Local Examinations

Southern : Southern Universities Joint Board for School Examinations

O & CSEB : Oxford and Cambridge Schools Examination Board

WJEC : Welsh Joint Education Committee

SEB : Scottish Examination Board

The answers to the questions are my own and none of the above boards can accept any responsibility whatsoever for the accuracy or method of working in the answers given.

I wish to express my special thanks to Keith West who wrote the larger parts of Units 17, 18, 26 and 27 and who contributed many ideas to other units throughout the book. I am also most grateful to Bill Stevenson who read through the manuscript and suggested many improvements, to Jeremy Lawrence for editing the typescript, to the staff at Charles Letts Limited for their support and patience during the preparation of the book, and to my wife Christine for her encouragement and for all the hard work and long hours spent typing the manuscript in a form fit for the printer. However, any shortcomings the book may possess are entirely my own responsibility.

Ray Powell

iv

Contents

Introduction and guide to using this book

This book has been written specifically to prepare candidates for the Advanced Level examinations in economics set by the various GCE examining boards. It should also prove useful as a preparation for the many business studies and professional examinations in economics of a comparable standard to A-Level. The book is organized in a series of Topic Units chosen both to represent the subject areas with which examination questions deal, and also to prepare candidates for answering questions on 'new' subject areas as yet not well covered in existing textbooks. Thus, while the topic units are conventionally ordered, proceeding from micro- to macro-economics, units are included on such topics as the determination of agricultural prices, market 'failures', the Public Sector Borrowing Requirement, and areas of controversy between Keynesian and monetarist economists.

Since the book does not attempt to cover every aspect of the Advanced Level syllabuses of the various examining boards, it should not be regarded as a substitute for the many excellent and detailed textbooks that are available, or for sources of up-to-date information such as the *British Economy Survey* and *Treasury Economic Progress Reports*. It is designed for use throughout a taught economics course, and it should prove especially useful in preparing examination technique in the period immediately before an examination. Each topic unit contains two distinct but complementary parts. The first section provides a detailed summary of the underlying concepts used by economists of different schools of thought and points of perspective in approaching the topic, together with a summary of essential, largely factual, information, and a note on how the topic links with the other units in the book. The last part contains a selection of representative questions chosen largely from the examination papers set in recent years by the principal examining boards. Each question is discussed in detail, and suggestions are made on examination technique and on how to avoid the pitfalls that may be present in the question.

The book's aim is to help examination candidates gain the knowledge, techniques and skills, not only to be sure of passing at Advanced Level, but also to realize what is required to achieve the highest possible grades. At all times the book tries to explain in a clear but precise way the new developments taking place in the subject, and to show how these are reflected in recent examination questions and in the answers expected by the examiners.

THE DIFFERENCE BETWEEN O AND A LEVEL STUDY

The majority of students who start an Advanced Level course in economics are completely new to the subject; only a minority have studied Ordinary Level economics. For this reason, no mention is made in the individual topic units of the difference between what is required at O and A Level. There is in fact little difference in the range of subjects included in the 'straight' economics syllabuses at O and A Level, though the A Level syllabus tends to be rather wider. However, some examination boards offer 'combined subject' syllabuses at Advanced Level, or subjects such as social economics and family economics (both offered by the Associated Examining Board) as alternatives to 'straight' economics at Ordinary Level. At Advanced Level, the Oxford and Cambridge Board allows the combination of economic principles and British economic and social history in a single examination, as an alternative to the 'straight' economic combination of economic principles and applied economics. Similarly, economics can be combined with English social and economic history, or the structure and working of British government, or world affairs since 1945, in the Economic and Public Affairs option offered by the Cambridge Local Examinations Syndicate. Again, this is an alternative to the 'straight' economics Advanced Level syllabus available through the Cambridge Board.

The principal difference between O and A Level economics lies not in the syllabus content but in the order of the skills that the examinations try to test. The Ordinary Level examination is largely concerned with testing the 'lower order' skills of factual recall and description together with the understanding and application of simple ideas. In contrast, at Advanced Level much more emphasis is placed on the 'higher order' skills involved in theoretical analysis and evaluation. Although the practice of each examining board is slightly different, students should derive useful guidance from the introductions to the syllabuses of the Joint Matriculation Board and the Associated Examining Board, the two boards that publish in detail the aims of their economics syllabuses. By the end of the AEB course, candidates are expected to show:

(a) a factual knowledge of the institutional framework and main features of the economy of the United Kingdom (some examination boards allow candidates taking examinations at overseas centres to illustrate their answers with examples from their own economy – overseas students should carefully check the requirements of the board for which they are entered);

(b) a knowledge and understanding of basic concepts used by economists and an ability to apply these to the analysis of economic problems;

(c) a competence in organizing, interpreting and presenting economic information;

(d) the ability to evaluate the reliability of evidence and its relevance to the economic problem.

Most helpfully, the JMB syllabus specifies **six areas of knowledge and skill** which the A-Level examination is designed to test, providing a guide which should prove very useful to all students of Advanced Level economics, irrespective of examination board:

1 Knowledge (30% of total marks)

(i) Knowledge in the terminology of economics.

(ii) Knowledge of specific facts relating to economics and economic institutions.

(iii) Knowledge of general and specific methods of enquiry and of the main sources of information about economic matters and ways of presenting economic information.

(iv) Knowledge of the main concepts, principles and generalizations employed within the field of economics and of the major economic theories held.

2 Comprehension (25%)

(i) The ability to understand and interpret economic information presented in verbal, numerical or graphical form and to translate such information from one form to another.

(ii) The ability to explain familiar phenomena in terms of the relevant principles.

(iii) The ability to apply known laws and principles to problems of a routine type.

(iv) The ability to make generalizations about economic knowledge or about given data.

3 Application (15%)

The ability to select and apply known laws and principles to problems which are unfamiliar or presented in a novel manner.

4 Analysis and synthesis (15%)

(i) The ability to recognize unstated assumptions.

(ii) The ability to distinguish between statements of fact, statements of value and hypothetical statements.

(iii) The ability to make valid inferences from material presented.

(iv) The ability to examine the implications of a hypothesis.

(v) The ability to organize ideas into a new unity and to present them in an appropriate manner.

(vi) The ability to make valid generalizations.

5 Evaluation (15%)

(i) The ability to evaluate the reliability of material.

(ii) The ability to detect logical fallacies in arguments.

(iii) The ability to check that conclusions drawn are consistent with given information and to discriminate between alternative explanations.

(iv) The ability to appreciate the role of the main concepts and models in the analysis of economic problems.

6 Expression

The ability to organize and present economic ideas and statements in a clear, logical and appropriate form.

The Board notes also that questions frequently overlap these broad objectives, and that although no specific allocation of marks is given to the skill of **expression**, candidates will inevitably penalize themselves if they fail to express themselves clearly.

AN ANALYSIS OF QUESTION STYLES

In order to test a range of skills such as those illustrated in the extract from the JMB syllabus, most examining boards have recently introduced new examination papers and new types of question. A typical A Level economics examination now includes (i) an **essay paper**, (ii) a **multiple choice** (or **objective test**) **paper** and (iii) a **data response** (or **stimulus**) **paper**. However, there are variations from board to board which you are advised to check, particularly concerning the type of data response material the board includes in its examination.

1 Essay questions

There is little doubt that Advanced Level economics has become a more difficult and testing examination over the twenty years since the day when, with fear and trepidation, the author faced the JMB examination in the subject. In those days it was common practice for the examining boards to set just two essay papers which allowed candidates a fair degree of scope in choosing the parts of the syllabus to revise, and which included a number of questions testing factual recall and description.

Since the introduction of multiple choice and data response questions, the essay paper has become rather more specialized. Questions answerable simply by factual recall may allow candidates to do well simply by 'rote-learning' pages of notes. Such questions have fallen out of favour with examiners because they fail to discriminate between 'good' and 'bad' candidates on the basis of the ability of a good candidate to practise the higher order skills we have listed. Some, but not all, examining boards have shifted the testing of factual knowledge to the multiple choice paper, leaving the essay paper free to test analytic evaluation and similar skills.

Most boards which have not as yet introduced a separate data response paper have kept two essay papers supplemented by a multiple choice paper. Where two essay papers are set, it is usual for the first paper to cover **micro-economics** and for the second paper to test the **macro-economic** topics in the syllabus, though the papers of the Oxford and Cambridge Board divide between **economic principles** and **applied economics**. Among the boards which have only one examination paper, the JMB and the AEB place a strong emphasis on **'applied' questions** (questions related to current economic problems and government policy), a feature which is much less marked in the London paper. Most boards allow a candidate the 'free choice' of selecting questions (usually five) from any part of the essay paper. The London paper is the most restrictive, including only ten or twelve questions (compared with as many as sixteen set by some other boards), divided into two sections corresponding roughly to the division between micro- and macro-economics. Candidates are required to answer five questions, choosing at least two from each section.

Because of these differences in both the structure of the essay paper and in the 'house style' of questions set by each board, it is vital for a candidate to study the precise regulations of the examination for which he or she is sitting, and also to analyse a selection of recent papers or specimen papers set by the board. When important changes are made in the syllabus, or when the method of examination is changed, it is usual for the examining board to publish a specimen paper or papers. Each year your teacher should get an **Examiner's Report** which discusses the previous year's examination. He should go through the report with you as it will provide a useful insight into the Chief Examiner's approach and demands. Increasingly, via the publications of the **Economics Association** and schools conferences, the chief examiners are becoming better known and more accessible. If the chief examiner gives a lecture in your area, go and listen! If your teacher does not know who the Chief Examiner is, get him or her to find out and study any textbook he may have recently written.

2 Multiple Choice Questions

Almost all the examining boards now either set a separate multiple choice paper or include multiple choice questions in a separate section of one of their other papers. Candidates are usually required to answer about fifty or sixty compulsory questions within an hour and a quarter or an hour and three-quarters. (The length of the examination depends upon the number of questions in the paper and the 'house style' of questions – the questions in the common paper set by the Cambridge Local, Oxford Local, Welsh, and Oxford and Cambridge Boards involve more calculation than is usual in the papers set by the other boards, so more time is allowed.)

The multiple choice paper tests the whole range of the syllabus and it can also test certain types of numerical and logical skills that essay questions cannot adequately do. The AEB and the London Board use their multiple choice papers to test descriptive knowledge, but this is not a noticeable feature of the JMB paper or of the common paper shared by the other boards.

The structure of the multiple choice paper also varies between boards. Four main types of question are used: (i) **single completion**; (ii) **multiple completion**; (iii) **assertion/reason**; and (iv) **matching pairs**. We provide many examples and a detailed explanation of most of these types of question in the main part of this book. Most **single completion** questions contain a **stem** (the question itself) and **five possible answers** (a single **correct** answer and four incorrect **distractors**), though the AEB now sets questions with only four possible answers. **Multiple completion** questions are similar, but one or more of the possible answers may be correct. (In some multiple completion questions, all the suggested possible answers may be incorrect; however, no examples of this type of question have been included in this book.) **Assertion/reason** questions are perhaps the most difficult type of question. The candidate must first decide whether the two statements in the question are correct when considered as separate statements. If both are correct, he must then decide whether the second statement provides an explanation of the first. A **matching pairs** question requires the candidate to select items from one list to match up with items from a second list provided in the question.

Some multiple choice papers include only single completion questions, whereas others are divided into separate sections with each section devoted to a different type of question. (The common paper shared by many of the boards is of the first type, whereas the London Board, the AEB and the JMB favour the latter approach.) Subject-areas listed at the beginning of the board's published syllabus are usually tested first, with the questions then proceeding through the remaining syllabus topics. (If the paper is divided into different types of question, it is usual for each section to cover the syllabus in this manner; the largest section of the paper contains single completion questions which thoroughly cover the syllabus, but the coverage of the other sections may be rather sketchy.) Some of the examining boards publish details of the number of questions they intend to set on each broad division of the syllabus, together with the skills the questions are designed to test.

3 Data Response Questions

Most of the examining boards have now introduced a new **data response** or **stimulus** paper, or have incorporated questions of this type into one or other of their existing papers. Data response or statistical questions have been introduced in response to a growing dissatisfaction felt by many teachers, universities and employers that economics students have lacked the ability and confidence to handle empirical data, whether in written, numerical or graphical form. However, there are considerable differences in both the stimulus material that the boards include in their questions, and in the skills which the questions are designed to test.

The Cambridge and Southern Boards set statistical questions which require a considerable amount of calculation to work out a correct answer. In contrast many of the questions set by the London Board are not noticeably different from essay questions—they may simply require the candidate to discuss the significance of a passage selected from a book or newspaper. The JMB sets a single, hour-long compulsory question containing perhaps two or three detailed sources of data which may be in either numerical or written form. Both the JMB and the AEB appear to favour the **'incline of difficulty' approach** to the setting of data response questions: the question is structured into separate parts, each succeeding part becoming more difficult, in order to test the 'higher order' skills. Thus the first part of a JMB or AEB data response question may require the candidate to **describe** some aspect of the data, while later parts require an **explanation of the data in terms of economic theory and an evaluation**. Properly constructed questions of this type discriminate well between good and bad candidates.

We have noted only some of the differences between the style of questions set by the examining boards. It is vitally important that a candidate should be familiar with the 'house style' of a board's data response questions. Some boards set a compulsory data response question or questions; with other boards there is free choice. The Southern Board includes both statistical and essay questions in the same paper, offering candidates a 'free choice' of questions. Thus candidates can avoid the statistical questions if they so wish. The Oxford and Cambridge Board offers perhaps the most interesting range of choice; data response questions form an optional section within the Board's applied economics paper, a paper which also includes a **Documents and Commentaries** option. This option, which is the only one of its type offered by any of the examining boards, contains questions which resemble data response questions, the principal difference being that questions are set on government publications and other documents which are similar to 'set books'. The Oxford and Cambridge Board notifies schools and colleges some time before the examination about the publications that candidates are expected to read.

THE EXAMINATION

Once you have prepared for the examination as thoroughly as time allows, the most daunting task still remains to be faced: to do yourself justice when presented with unseen questions amid the stresses and strains of the examination room. In this section of the book we shall discuss some 'golden rules' that, if followed, should stand you in good stead and make your task rather easier, providing of course that that most useful ingredient, luck, is also at least a little on your side.

1 Revision technique

You can reduce the need for luck by preparing a revision programme. Since you will have to face a multiple choice paper containing compulsory questions covering the whole of the syllabus, plan a thorough programme and begin it several weeks before the examination, time-tabling periods of each day when you know you can work for up to two or three hours completely free of distraction. It is a good idea, however, to allow yourself a brief relaxation period every half hour or so to facilitate the absorption of the knowledge, ideas, and concepts intensively revised in the previous period. Although you must cover the whole syllabus, concentrate on key concepts and on essential economic theory rather than on detailed historical and descriptive fact.

There are various methods of revising, and not all may suit every candidate. Generally it is not a good idea to read through sheaves of notes or chapters from a textbook, and certainly it is not good practice to 'rote-learn' pages of notes. Nevertheless, you must learn key definitions, though it is even more important to learn how and when to use them. Remember that, as a properly prepared candidate, you will only be able to use a small fraction of your total economic knowledge in a single essay or data response paper. Provided that you have revised in a reasonably structured way in the weeks before the examination, it is certainly not a good idea to work late into the night on the day preceding the examination. Answering an examination paper is a tiring task, especially if you are to display the type of skill the paper is testing; you need to arrive in the examination room as refreshed as possible and capable of thinking clearly not just for a few minutes, but for up to three hours.

If you decide to arrange your revision programme around the use of this book, we suggest that you select one or at most two topic areas for coverage at each revision session. Quickly read the first half of a topic unit, making a mental note of key definitions or concepts. Then try to write your own answer plans to two or more questions at the end of the unit. Check your completed answer plan against the one included in the book and read through the notes on understanding the question. Go back over the topic unit to make sure you understand the most important definitions and concepts, which you should now write out in a revision list. Several hours later or on the next day, write **in your own words** the meaning of the concepts and key definitions. Check what you have written against the explanations given in the topic unit. Repeat this exercise frequently throughout your revision period until you feel confident that you **thoroughly understand** all the concepts and definitions. You might also attempt on later dates to write answer plans to the questions omitted when you first revised the topic unit.

2 Essay technique

Most examination boards require a candidate to answer five questions in a three-hour essay paper, allowing about thirty-five minutes for each question. (The JMB requires that only four questions are answered.) It is vital to arrange your time so as to answer all five questions, since all carry equal marks and no allowance is made for answering too few. Spend at least a couple of minutes at the beginning of the examination in carefully reading the paper, paying close attention to the wording of each question. Carefully select five and read each through again; subconciously you will be thinking about the other questions while working on your first answer! Choose the easiest question to answer first, but remember again to divide your time equally. When a question contains more than one section it is also important to divide your time between each part, assuming, unless the question specifies otherwise, that each carries equal marks. Examiners frequently complain that the second section of a question is either ignored or treated in cursory fashion, with the answer being little more than a footnote.

Nevertheless, if you find that you have allocated your time badly you must take action to remedy the situation. It may be a good idea to answer one or both of the last two questions with an elongated though carefully written essay plan. In general, marks are awarded for relevant points made. It follows that you should make as many relevant points as possible and avoid dwelling on any single point. Of course in a properly developed essay you should have time to elaborate appropriately the points you make, but even so it is easy to spend too much time on a single argument – a variation of the 'law of diminishing returns' applies to economics essays written under examination conditions! The marking scheme may allocate perhaps two, three, or four marks for a particular relevant argument, and a brief mention of the argument can earn you at least half and possibly all the allocated marks if it is properly related to the question. Candidates frequently waste valuable time by unnecessarily elaborating one argument, while failing even to mention a range of others. It is surprising how often an answer written as a series of points by a candidate pressed for time at the end of an examination earns more marks than the answer the candidate attempted first! Examiners *always* prefer short, well-structured and concise answers to long, rambling and repetitive essays.

Whether your essay is long or short, it must always be addressed to the set question. You will earn no marks at all for writing a 'model answer' to a question not on the examination paper! Long introductory and concluding paragraphs are generally inadvisable since they seldom pick up many marks. Nevertheless, it is good practice to use the first paragraph both to define precisely the terms mentioned in the question and also to state any assumptions you are making in interpreting the meaning of the question. If you think the question is open to more than one interpretation, then tell the examiner and explain why you are favouring a particular interpretation. Many questions are capable of different interpretations and there may be no 'single correct answer'. At all times try to 'get behind the question' to the underlying assumptions and economic theories necessary for a proper development of the answer.

While diagrams and particularly graphs are often appropriate, they should complement rather than simply repeat the information you are providing in written form. Diagrams are often included which fail to earn any extra marks yet which waste valuable examination time. If you cannot correctly remember a particular graph or diagram, then leave it out. A wrongly drawn graph will serve no purpose other than to signal to the examiner in the clearest possible way that a candidate has not understood the essential theory required for answering a question! Draw your graphs large rather than small, and pay careful attention to how you label the axes and all curves.

Every essay question includes at least one key instruction, calling for a discussion, evaluation, comparison or contrast. Very few questions can be answered simply by factual description or by an uncritical historical account. Most examination questions test whether you can introduce basic economic theory in a simple but clear way in order to cast light on the specified problem. We include difficult or more advanced theories in this book where relevant to specific examination questions, though as a general rule simple theories used well are always preferable to the latest, most advanced theories obviously misunderstood by the candidate.

Questions asking for comparisons or contrasts should not be answered with two separate accounts. Strictly, a 'comparison' notes points of similarity whereas a 'contrast' notes points of difference, though in practice examiners are unlikely to be pedantic about this distinction. However, it is important to avoid confusing questions asking for a discussion of **causes** with those concerned with the **economic effects** resulting from a particular government policy or change in the economy. When discussing causes and effects it is as well to remember the central importance in economics of the **price mechanism** and of the concept of the **margin**. Most economic changes occur at the margin in response to movements in relative price or income, when an economic agent decides it is no longer worthwhile to engage in its earlier pattern of economic behaviour.

Small adjustments rather than **massive structural changes** are the rule; even the 1973 oil crisis, an event regarded as cataclysmic at the time, produced rather slow adjustments that are still taking place. Changes usually take a time to work through; a **trigger event**, **event A** (such as the 1973 oil crisis or a change in government policy), may directly cause **event B**, which in turn causes **event C** and so on. In general the immediate direct effects of A on B are easier to predict than the later indirect effects further down the 'causal chain'. The chain of direct and indirect effects may be either **dampened** or **explosive**; in the former case event B is smaller than event A, and C is smaller than B, and so on. In contrast, a causal chain is explosive if each succeeding event is more powerful than the previous one. Because most economic changes are eventually 'absorbed' through relative price changes and minor adjustments at the margin, economic chains may often be dampened.

Nevertheless a further complication may be caused by the existence of **feed-backs**, when for example event B feeds back to change the variable associated with the original event A. In terms of essay technique, you should at all times avoid being dogmatic when discussing economic cause and effect, and remember that in economics it is often the case that 'everything depends upon everything else'.

3 Data Response technique

Many of the examination techniques relevant to essay questions are also applicable to the data response paper. It is perhaps even more important to read through the questions to make sure that you thoroughly understand both the data content and the questions. Where a choice is allowed, the rubric at the beginning of the paper will usually advise you to spend at least fifteen minutes reading through the paper; take this instruction seriously and carefully read through each question before you make your final choice.

We have already noted how stimulus questions frequently start by asking for the extraction of simple facts from the data. Avoid the temptation to elaborate your answer to this part of the question since it is unlikely that more than a couple of marks will be allocated for simple description. Conversely, you must not simply describe or **paraphrase** the data when tackling the parts of a question that require the 'higher order' skill of interpreting or evaluating. Search for the conclusions that can reasonably be **inferred** from the data, and the more tentative conclusions that really require stronger supporting evidence. Sometimes a question will explicitly ask for a statement of the **assumptions** upon which the arguments in the data are based or upon which you are making your inferences. It may also ask for a discussion of **other sources of information or data** that might allow you to draw **stronger inferences** and conclusions.

Very often the limited amount of data included in a stimulus question is consistent with more than one interpretation, not by itself either proving or refuting a particular **economic theory** or **hypothesis**. Nevertheless, the examiner is hoping that candidates will be able to handle basic economic method by stating the assumptions being made in interpreting the data and by discussing how far the data appear consistent with at least one economic theory. So even if a question does not formally ask for a statement of basic assumptions or for a discussion of the limitations of the data, a good answer will show that a candidate is thinking about these issues. You should clearly show the examiner when you are drawing conclusions based solely on the data, and when you are bringing in 'outside knowledge', either in the form of economic theory or descriptive fact, to help in its interpretation.

Numerical questions may be based upon various forms of data including tabulated schedules, charts and different types of graph. They may also involve either data extracted from **real-world sources** or **simulated data** made up specially for the question. Whereas data from real world sources may contain various inaccuracies, being an estimate of what has happened in the real world, simulated data are completely fictitious. Simulated data on such topic areas as supply and demand, the theory of the firm, the multiplier and comparative advantage may be included to test whether candidates can use basic economic theory to perform simple **calculations**. Most examining boards now allow the use of electronic calculators in the data response paper (but not as yet in the multiple choice paper). Nevertheless it is vital to show all your workings, and you should also explain to the examiner what you are trying to do at each stage in the manipulation of the data. Stimulus questions try to test economic knowledge rather than arithmetical skills, though there will usually be a single correct answer to a question or part of a question involving a calculation. However, an arithmetic slip should not be heavily penalized, providing that you have clearly shown that you are using the correct economic method to answer the question.

When answering questions based on real-world data sources, it is useful to know the difference between **time-series** and **cross-sectional** data, and to be aware of the uses and limitations of data expressed in such forms as **index numbers** and **percentages**. **Time-series data** observe how economic variables change over time, from year to year, quarter to quarter, or month to month. For example, British national income figures for 1981, 1982, and 1983 would form a short time-series. Whereas time-series data are often highly **aggregated, cross-sectional data** divide up or disaggregate the data into its various components. (The division of annual national income data into wages, profits and rent provides a simple example. Cross-sectional and time-series data can of course be combined together, in which case they are known as **pooled data**.)

Time-series data measuring changes in economic variables such as national income, output, and expenditure usually fluctuate both **seasonally** and also with the upswings and downswings of the **business cycle**. Seasonal fluctuations cannot of course be detected unless the data are presented in **quarterly** or **monthly** form, in which case they may be presented in either **seasonally adjusted** or **unadjusted form**. Adjusted data pick up the long-term trend from year to year whereas unadjusted data show the fluctuations occurring from season to season.

If the data contain observations for only two or three years, great care must be taken in interpretation. It is very easy to confuse the **long-term trend** of the data with relatively **short-term fluctuations** associated with the business cycle. As a general rule, a time-series must extend over at least five or six years to allow a long-term trend to be detected, and even then there is a danger that structural changes taking place in the economy may have altered the trend. Where it is possible to detect a long-term trend in the data, it may also be possible to **extrapolate** the trend in order to **predict** the future. Beware, however, of basing a forecast upon data subject to violent fluctuations, and always be prepared for the possibility that a structural change or 'outside shock' occurring in the future may upset the forecast.

Many economic variables measured in money units are affected by inflation, which can seriously distort time-series data. Check whether data are unadjusted for inflation, in the **current prices** of each year, or whether the data have either been converted to the **constant prices** of a particular year, or been expressed in **index numbers**. Index numbers, which are usually based on 100, can sometimes be confused with data expressed in **percentages** which must, of course, add up to 100. Cross-sectional data are often expressed in percentages, sometimes in the form of a chart or pie graph. Great care must be taken in interpreting both index numbers and percentages, particularly if absolute totals are not included in the data. A 1% change is seldom exactly equivalent to a one-point movement in an index, and the percentage share of, for example, income tax in total government revenue can fall yet the absolute total of income tax revenue may still be rising.

As a final word of warning, be especially wary of reading economic interpretations into the apparent steepness or flatness of curves when data are presented in graphical form. By altering the scales on the vertical and horizontal axes it is possible to show changes in an economic variable either by a steep or a flat curve (providing that the variable is rising or falling). So look carefully at the chosen scales whenever a question requires graphical interpretation.

4 Multiple choice technique

A multiple choice paper allows candidates to spend only a minute or two on each question. Some questions can usually be answered in a few seconds, but others which involve calculation or deep thought may require several minutes. It is important to avoid being delayed by such questions occurring early in the paper, in which case you may never reach some 'easier' questions in the later sections. Try to go through the paper three times in all. On the first occasion, quickly move on from any question proving difficult or involving a calculation, making sure to draw a heavy pencil line around all the questions you do not attempt. Similarly, place a question mark against any question you do attempt, but which gives you serious cause for doubt. If one and a quarter hours are allowed for the paper, try to complete your first run-through in about fifty minutes. On the second run, return to the questions you have placed a mark against, and be prepared to spend several minutes on each. If time allows, scan through the paper a third time, checking whether you have correctly interpreted the wording of each question. If you have second thoughts about any of your answers, take great care to erase completely your initial mark on the answer sheet. Indeed, make sure that all your marks are in the correct positions on the answer sheet since the computer which checks the sheet cannot award credit for any slips on your part.

Finally, allow at least half a minute to guess the answers to any questions still unanswered. Your aim is to maximize your marks, so do not leave any questions unattempted. There is always at least a twenty per cent chance that your guess will turn out to be correct!

GUIDANCE FOR SCOTTISH HIGHER STUDENTS

The Scottish Examination Board offers two certificates in Economics for the post sixteen year old age group.

The Certificate of Sixth Year Studies which is based largely on an in-depth study of one selected topic and is only open to students with previous examination success in Economics, and the Higher Grade which is normally a one year post-Ordinary Grade course intended for seventeen year olds, although often taken by older or Further Education candidates, for which this book is more suited. The course covers the same range of economic theory and analysis as most A level courses, but, because of its shorter duration, the questions set may require less depth or development in order to reach a pass standard. A and B passes are required for university entrance. There are few differences between this course and a typical A level course in the field of Economic analysis covered by the syllabus. However, here there is not the same emphasis on factual knowledge recall nor on the memorising of traditional theory. More time is spent on the acquisition of numerate and interpretive skills and the application of key concepts and principles to real world problems (similar to JMB).

The syllabus aims to develop in candidates:

1 An understanding of the basic concepts and principles of economics;
2 The capacity to apply this understanding to the analysis of economic problems;
3 An understanding of the nature and extent of economic inter-dependence;
4 An appreciation of the economic dimension of life and of the changing economic framework of the United Kingdom;
5 Economic literacy and numeracy;

6 An appreciation of the applicability and limitations of economic theory in contemporary society.

The Examination has three papers. A multiple choice objective test consisting of thirty items of the four-response type and worth thirty per cent of the total marks. These items do not specifically test the knowledge of economic facts and figures but concentrate on the understanding and application of concepts and principles. Paper two is a one hour interpretation paper similar to the data-response type. Here skills tested are mainly those of number and interpretation. The higher skills of evaluation and synthesis are tested along with the others in a two and a half-hour essay paper which breaks down to two analysis questions and two questions of applied economics from a total of twelve. Contemporary and, where possible, Scottish examples are used, and study is normally confined to the decade prior to the examination. Comparative and development economics are largely excluded at this level, but the effects of EEC membership on the British economy are studied.

The Scottish Board has several key marking principles which stress the positive and tolerant approach to candidates' work. In general the aim is to give credit to what is correct and relevant and to ignore all else, that is, wrong statements carry no weight and marks are not deducted. The whole emphasis of the examination is on the testing of economic understanding rather than on strict factual accuracy from the candidates.

TABLE OF ANALYSIS OF EXAMINATION SYLLABUSES

The table which follows shows how the topic units that make up the main body of the book relate to the specific syllabuses set by the examining boards. As we have already noted, there is a common core to most of the syllabuses. The main differences lie in the style of the examination papers and in the questions they contain, rather than in the coverage of the syllabus. Syllabuses change from time to time, so some of the information provided in this guide may already be out of date. If in doubt consult either your teacher or an up-to-date syllabus provided by your examining board.

Summary of Examination Papers set by The Examining Boards

Board	AEB	London	JMB	WJEC	Southern
Syllabus	618	120		0011	9076
Subject Name	Economics	Economics	Economics	Economics	Economics
Number of Papers	3	3	2	2	2
Paper 1	1¼ Hours Multiple Choice 50 compulsory questions (30%)	3 Hours Essays 5 questions to be answered from a choice of approximately 10 or 12; with at least two from each section of the paper (40%)	*Part 1* 1½ Hours Multiple Choice approximately 50 compulsory questions (35%) *Part 2* 1 Hour Data Response 1 compulsory question (15%)	3 Hours Essays (Largely Micro-economics) 5 questions to be answered from a choice of 12 (50%)	3 Hours Essays and questions based on numerical data (largely micro-economics) 5 questions to be answered from a choice of 12 (50%)
Paper 2	1½ Hours Data Response 1 or more compulsory questions (20%)	1¼ Hours Multiple Choice 50 compulsory questions (30%)	3 Hours Essays 4 questions to be answered from a choice of 12 (50%)	*Part 1* 1¾ Hours Multiple Choice ● 50 compulsory questions (25%) *Part 2* 1½ Hours Essays (Largely Macro-economics) 2 questions to be answered from a choice of 6 (25%)	3 Hours Essays and questions based on numerical data 5 questions to be answered from a choice of 12 (50%)
Paper 3	3 Hours Essays 5 questions to be answered from a choice of 12 (50%)	1¾ Hours Data Response 3 questions to be answered, including at least one based on numerical data from a choice of approximately 5 (30%)			
Paper 4					

Key: ● Common Shared Multiple Choice Paper

Table of topics common to the syllabuses of all the Boards

Topic Area	Comments
1 The central problem of all economic societies The problem of scarcity, choice, opportunity cost, allocation of resources; the market mechanism; free goods, economic goods, private and public goods; types of economic system.	All boards set questions asking for a comparison of market and command economies and a discussion of their virtues and disadvantages, together with those of mixed economies. See Unit 9, and also Units 1 and 8.
2 Demand Theory Individual and market demand curves; consumer behaviour; utility theory, movements along and shifts of demand curves; price, income and cross elasticities of demand; substitution and income effects; complementary and competing demand; consumer surplus.	The London and Associated Examining Boards do not require a knowledge of indifference curves, a topic on which most of the other Boards set specific questions. See Units 2 and 4, and also Unit 5.
3 Cost and Supply Theory Firm and industry supply curves; the behaviour of firms; the law of returns and the economic short run; increasing returns to scale and the economic long run; economies and diseconomies of scale; the derivation of marginal total and average cost curves; price elasticity of supply in the market period, short run and long run; movements along and shifts of supply curve.	There is a tendency for all the Boards to set questions best answered with some knowledge of alternative theories of the firm (managerial and behavioural). However, the syllabuses only specify the orthodox profit maximizing theory of the firm. Most Boards expect a knowledge of the structure of industry in the British economy, the size and growth of firms, the capital market, etc., but there has been a movement away from expecting a a detailed descriptive knowledge of topics such as the various types of business enterprise in the British economy. For theory: Units 3, 4 and 5. For an institutional approach: Units 10 and 11.
4 Market Equilibrium and the Equilibrium Firm The concept of equilibrium in economics; the interaction of supply and demand and industry (or market) equilibrium; marginal, total and average revenue; short- and long-run equilibrium. The determination of a firm's equilibrium price and output in different market structures (perfect competition, monopolistic competition, oligopoly, and monopoly).	Questions are being increasingly set on 'market failures' and the circumstances in which goods and services are provided outside the market (public goods, merit goods, externalities); the recently revised syllabus of the AEB explicitly recognizes this new topic area. Also questions increasingly require an evaluation of equilibrium in different market structures in terms of their desirable and undesirable properties – productive and allocative efficiency, etc. For market equilibrium see Units 1 and 9. For the equilibrium firm: Units 6 and 7, and for market failures Unit 8.
5 The Theory of Distribution Demand for and supply of factors of production; the determination of wages, interest, profits and rent; economic rent, quasi-rent and transfer earnings; wage determination and bargaining in the British economy; the role and effectiveness of trade unions.	See Unit 15.

Oxford	Cambridge	Cambridge	Oxford & Cambridge	Oxford & Cambridge	SEB
9840	9070	9072	9633	9635	
Economics	Economics	Econ. & Public Affairs	Economics	Econ. & Polit. Studies	Economics
2	3	4 (any 2 of the papers to be taken)	3 (Paper 1 compulsory Papers 2 & 3 are options)	4 (Paper 1 compulsory Papers 2, 3 & 4 are options)	3
3 Hours Essays 5 questions from a choice of approximately 14 (50%)	1¾ Hours Multiple Choice ● 50 compulsory questions (40%)	3 Hours Economics Essay Paper (50%)	*Part 1* 1¾ Hours Multiple Choice ● 50 compulsory questions *Part 2* 1½ Hours Essays 2 questions from a choice of 6	3 Hours Principles of Economics Essays	1 Hour Multiple Choice 30 compulsory questions (30%)
1¾ Hours Multiple Choice ● 50 compulsory questions (50%)	¾ Hour Statistical Questions 1 question to be answered, usually from a choice of 2 (10%)	3 Hours Structure and working of British Government Essay Paper (50%)	3 Hours Applied Economics (4 sections, questions to be answered from at least three sections. 4 questions to be answered.) *Section A* The British Economy *Section B* Documents and Commentaries *Section C* Economic Numeracy *Section D* Comparative Economics	3 Hours Political Thought Essays	1 Hour Interpretation (Data Response) 2 compulsory questions a) prose interpretation b) statistical material interpretation (20%)
	3 Hours Essays 4 questions to be answered from a choice of approximately 12 (50%)	3 Hours World Affairs since 1945 Essay Paper (50%)	3 Hours British Economic and Social History since 1780 Essays, Documents and commentaries, and statistical questions.	3 Hours Representative Government Essays	2½ Hours Essay Paper 4 Questions to be answered; 2 from Section A covering economic theory and 2 from Section B covering government policy and the external economic relations of the UK (50%)
		3 Hours English Social and Economic History, 1915-1973 Essay Paper (50%)		3 Hours British Constitutional History since 1830	

Topic Area	Comments
6 The System of National Income Accounts The definition and measurement of income expenditure and output; net and gross; national and domestic; market prices and factor cost; relationship between measures; problems of comparison over time and between countries; the Balance of Payments as a part of the National Accounts.	Questions frequently ask for a discussion of the extent to which National Income figures provide a useful measure of economic welfare. Scottish candidates may be required to analyse National Income Accounts in the Interpretation paper. See Unit 20.
7 The Theory of Income and Output Determination The circular flow of income; injections into and withdrawals from the flow; the consumption function; the multiplier; theories of investment; the accelerator; the equilibrium level of income; inflationary and deflationary gaps; the determinants of the aggregate levels of employment and prices (inflation theory).	The syllabus content of this topic area reflects the 'Keynesian orthodoxy' of the 1950s and 1960s. Increasingly however, the questions being set require a knowledge of the theoretical issues separating Keynesians and monetarists and their different views of 'how the economy works'. Look mainly at Units 21, 22 and 23, but also at Units 24 and 25.
8 Money and Banking The nature and functions of money and credit; the demand for and supply of money; the money market; the functions of the Bank of England and commercial banks; reserve ratios and the operation of monetary policy; interest rates, open market operations and special deposits.	Questions are now set which require a knowledge of Keynesian and monetarist views on the role of money, the demand for money, interest rate theory and the role and effectiveness of monetary policy. See Units 16, 17, 18 and 25.
9 International Economics The theory of specialization and trade; the gains from trade and the principle of comparative advantage; the case against trade; the theory of the Balance of Payments and fixed and flexible exchange rates; the terms of trade; the UK Balance of Payments; international economic institutions including the International Monetary Fund, World Bank, General Agreement on Tariffs and Trade and the European Economic Community; free trade areas and customs unions.	Questions are frequently set requiring an application of the principle of comparative advantage to a discussion of the regional problem or division of labour and specialization *within* a country. Other questions require some knowledge of the operation of macro-economic policy within an open economy; the effects of the foreign trade multiplier, the Balance of Payments and the money supply, exchange rates and inflation, etc. Use Units 26, 27 and 28.
10 The Economic Role of the Government Public provision and distribution of goods and services; the distinction between private and social costs; the management of national, regional and local economies; policy instruments and objectives; fiscal policy; monetary policy; incomes policy; direct controls; micro-economic policies; industrial, regional and employment policies; competition policy; the nationalized industries; the determinants of government revenue and spending; the National Debt and the Public Sector Borrowing Requirement.	In recent years, questions have increasingly reflected the Keynesian v monetarist debate on the correct role of the government in the economy, demand management v 'supply side' policies, fiscal v monetary policy, the implications of taxation, public spending and the Public Sector Borrowing Requirement, etc. Questions on 'the mixed economy' are a key feature of Scottish Higher Grade papers. For micro-economic policy use Units 5, 7, 12, 13 and 14. For macro-economic policy use Units 17, 18, 19, 22, 24, 25, 27 and 28.

Examination Boards

AEB Associated Examining Board
Wellington House, Aldershot, Hampshire GU11 1BQ

Cambridge University of Cambridge Local Examinations Syndicate
UCLES Syndicate Buildings, 17 Harvey Road, Cambridge CB1 2EU

JMB Joint Matriculation Board, Manchester M15 6EU
(For JMB Publications contact John Sherratt & Son Ltd,
78 Park Road, Altrincham, Cheshire)

London University Entrance & Schools Examination Council
University of London, 66–72 Gower Street, London WC1E 6EE
Publications Office: 52 Gordon Square, London WC1H 0PJ

Oxford Oxford Local Examinations
Delegacy of Local Examinations, Ewert Place, Summertown, Oxford OX2 7BX

Oxford & Oxford & Cambridge Schools Examination Board
Cambridge 10 Trumpington Street, Cambridge & Elsfield Way, Oxford

SUJB Southern Universities Joint Board for School Examinations
Cotham Road, Bristol BS6 6DD

WJEC Welsh Joint Education Committee
245 Western Avenue, Cardiff CF5 2YX

SEB Scottish Examination Board
Ironmills Road, Dalkeith, Midlothian EH22 1BR
(For SEB Publications contact Robert Gibson & Son Ltd,
17 Fitzroy Place, Glasgow G3 7SF)

NIGCEEB Northern Ireland General Certificate of Education Examinations Board
Beechill House, 42 Beechill Road, BT8 4RS

1 Price Determination

1.1 POINTS OF PERSPECTIVE

According to Professor Lionel Robbins's well-known and long-established definition, economics is 'the science which studies human behaviour as a relationship between ends and scarce means which have alternative uses'. Although by no means all economists agree that this is the best definition of the subject, it does emphasize the importance (except perhaps in Marxist economics) of **resource allocation** as the central problem to be studied. Economics is literally the study of economizing, with consumption as the ultimate end to which economic activity is directed.

Production converts the primary resources of the earth's surface into **economic goods**, which are then consumed to satisfy human wants or needs. Some goods, such as air, are known as **free goods** because no scarcity exists and nobody can charge a price for them. Most goods and all services, however, are economic goods. Scarce resources are used up and costs are incurred in the production of economic goods. The cost involved is an **opportunity cost**, which to economists means rather more than just a money cost. Resources which are allocated to one particular end-use cannot simultaneously be used elsewhere; the opportunity cost of using resources in a particular way is the value of the alternative uses foregone. For example, the opportunity cost of a visit to the theatre might be the sacrificed opportunity to spend the same time and money at a football match.

In all forms of society or economic system, some mechanism must exist to allocate or ration economic goods (and the resources contained in them) between competing uses. In a market economy, the **price mechanism** operating in a system of interrelated markets acts as the rationing device, determining **what** is produced, **how** it is produced and **for whom** it is produced.

Examination candidates at Advanced Level are often rather better at discussing the relative advantages and disadvantages of economic systems – market economies, mixed economies and planned economies – than they are at showing a detailed understanding of how a single market operates. In particular, **market plans** and **market action** are almost always confused. The objective of this first topic unit is to explain, from basic principles, how market price is determined in a single market – leaving the 'market versus planned economy' issue for consideration rather later in the book, after other important aspects of market behaviour have been introduced in the intervening units.

1.2 UNDERLYING CONCEPTS

1 The nature of a market

A market is a meeting of buyers and sellers in which goods or services are exchanged for other goods or services. The exchange is usually indirect, by means of money; in modern economies goods are seldom bartered for each other. Instead, one good is exchanged for money which is then traded a second time for other goods, usually after a time delay. The exchange must be voluntary; a forced transaction is not a market transaction.

A market need not exist in a single geographical location, although transport costs and lack of information may create barriers which separate markets. Markets are decentralized and usually unorganized in the sense that there is no central authority, such as the government, to decide how much is going to be traded and how much each buyer and seller in the market must trade. Price is the only information which needs to be known by each trader in the market.

2 The functions of price

If the price mechanism is to work efficiently in a market economy, it must simultaneously fulfil two functions:

(i) The signalling function. Prices must convey sufficient information to all traders in the market for their economic activities and plans to be co-ordinated. Markets will function inefficiently if prices signal wrong or misleading information, leading in extreme cases to complete market failure or breakdown (see Unit 8).

(ii) The incentive function. Markets will only operate in an orderly and efficient manner if the buyers and sellers in the market respond to the incentives provided by the price mechanism. If demand rises relative to supply, the price will tend to rise. This provides the incentive for firms to shift resources into producing goods and services whose relative price has risen, and to demand more resources such as specialized labour in order to increase production. This may bid up wages and other input prices, causing households to switch their supply of labour into industries where relative wages are rising.

3 The 'Goods Market' and the 'Factor Market'

You will have noticed from the preceding section that both households and firms are simultaneously operating within two sets of markets. On the one hand, consuming households face business enterprises in the retail or goods market, where households are the source of demand. For this demand to be an **effective demand** (demand backed up by money), the households must sell their labour services in the labour market, where it is now the firms who exercise demand. Although a market economy will usually be made up of a vast number of different and often specialized markets, for many purposes we can generalize and consider just a **'goods' market** and a **'factor' market** (one where households sell the services of the labour and capital they own) – the two markets being linked together through the decisions of both households and firms.

1.3   ESSENTIAL KNOWLEDGE

1 Demand and Supply curves

For the rest of the unit we shall ignore the factor market and restrict ourselves to exploring in greater detail the process of price determination within a single market in the goods market. Figure 1.1a illustrates the essential features of such a market.

A **demand curve** D_1 represents household or consumer behaviour in the market, while the **supply curve** S_1 maps out the supply decisions of firms. You will notice that the downward-sloping demand curve shows that consumers demand more of a good at low prices than at high prices. Be very careful of how you interpret this. It is insufficient to say that a demand curve slopes downward because more is demanded at low prices than at high prices; we need to go further than this and to 'get behind' the demand curve by developing a theory of consumer behaviour to explain demand. This is done in Unit 2. In a similar way, Unit 3 develops a theory of the behaviour of firms to 'get behind' the supply curve and explain supply. For the time being, however, we shall accept that normal demand curves slope downwards and normal supply curves slope upwards.

2 Market Plans and Market Action

The distinction between market plans and market action is of crucial importance to a proper understanding of the way a market works, yet it is a distinction which appears unknown to a significant proportion of candidates at Advanced Level. A demand curve, such as D_1 in Figure 1.1a, shows how much of a good all the consumers in the market intend to demand at the various

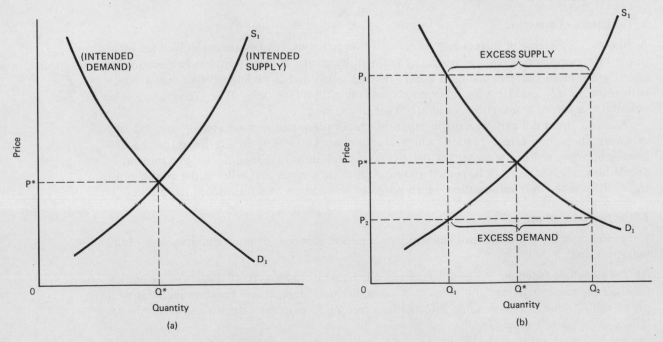

Fig 1.1 The determination of equilibrium price in a single market: (a) equilibrium requires intended demand to equal intended supply; (b) the price mechanism ensures convergence towards equilibrium

possible prices. **Intended demand** is also known as **planned demand** or **ex ante demand**. Similarly, the supply curve S_1 shows **intended supply** (**planned supply** or **ex ante supply**). It is easy to show that, at almost all prices, it is impossible for both the firms and the consumers to fulfil their plans simultaneously. Suppose that for some reason the price in the market is P_1, as represented in Figure 1.1b. Firms would like to supply quantity Q_2 at this price, but households are only willing to purchase Q_1: intended supply is greater than intended demand and **excess supply** results.

You should now ask yourself what will be the quantity actually traded if the price remains at P_1. The answer is quantity Q_1. The amount bought is Q_1, and the amount sold is Q_1; the two are the same, as indeed they must be. Now the amount bought is just another name for **realized demand** (**actual demand** or **ex post demand**), and the amount sold is another name for **realized supply** (**actual supply** or **ex post supply**). It follows that realized demand will always equal realized supply whatever the price. This represents an **identity**.

3 The equilibrium price

The concept of equilibrium is of the utmost importance in economic theory and analysis. Equilibrium is a **state of rest**, when there is no reason for anything to change unless disturbed by an outside shock. Households and firms will be in equilibrium if they can both fulfil their market plans. In Figure 1.1b, the price P_1 is not an equilibrium price because the firms are unable to fulfil their plans at this price. Realized demand, of course, equals realized supply at Q_1, but this is largely irrelevant: the crucial point is that intended supply is greater than intended demand at this price.

We now introduce a very important assumption about economic behaviour, which will recur throughout the book: if any economic agent (such as a household or firm) is unable to fulfil its market plans, a reason exists for it to change its plans. At the price of P_1 in Figure 1.1b, the firms are unable to fulfil their market plans. If firms react to their unsold stocks (or excess supply) by reducing the price that they are prepared to accept, then the market will **converge** towards the equilibrium price.

Similarly, if the initial price is P_2 in Figure 1.1b it may be supposed that the households, who are unable to fulfil their market plans at this price, will bid up the price to eliminate the **excess demand** in the market.

The equilibrium price, P^*, is the only price which is **consistent** with the market plans of both households and firms, who consequently have no reason to change their plans. At the equilibrium price, intended demand = intended supply. This is often known as the **equilibrium condition** to clear the market; it must not be confused with the **identity**: realized demand = realized supply.

In Figure 1.1b, the market mechanism ensures a **convergence** towards the equilibrium price of P^*. Consider, however, Figure 1.1c, which includes a (theoretically possible) downward-sloping supply curve. We leave it as an exercise for the reader to work out why this is a **divergent**

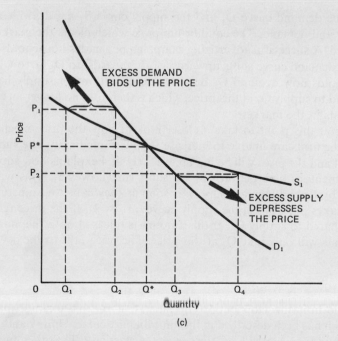

Fig 1.1 (c) Different assumptions about supply would cause a divergence away from equilibrium

equilibrium. What will happen if excess supply $(Q_4 - Q_3)$ or excess demand $(Q_2 - Q_1)$ exists in the market? Would the same events happen if the supply curve is drawn steeper than the demand curve?

To summarize the main conclusions of this very important section of the unit:
  (i) if intended supply > intended demand, price will fall (disequilibrium condition);
 (ii) if intended supply < intended demand, price will rise (disequilibrium condition);
(iii) if intended supply = intended demand, price stays the same (equilibrium condition);
(iv)   realized supply ≡ realized demand, at all prices (identity).

4 Shifts in demand and supply

When we draw a demand curve to show how much of a product households intend to demand at the various possible prices, it is assumed that all the other variables which may also influence intended demand are held unchanged or constant. This is known as the *ceteris paribus* assumption. (In economic shorthand we write: $Q = f(P)$, ceteris paribus.) In a similar way, all the other variables which may influence supply are held constant when a supply curve is drawn. Common sense suggests that household income and fashion will influence demand, and costs of production will affect supply decisions, but you should refer to Units 2 and 3 for a more detailed explanation. In this section, we shall restrict the analysis to a brief investigation of a change in the **conditions of demand**, when one of the variables which influences demand is assumed to change. The reader should have little difficulty in extending the analysis to a change in the conditions of supply.

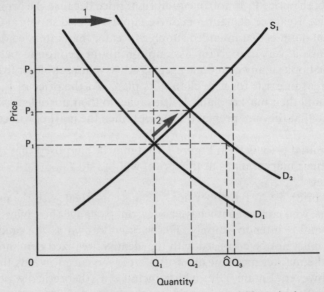

Fig 1.2 The effect of a shift in the demand curve within a single market

In Figure 1.2, the demand curve D_1 and the supply curve S_1 are drawn to show the initial condition of supply and demand. The equilibrium price which clears the market is at P_1, where quantity Q_1 is traded. A successful advertizing campaign persuades households to demand more at all prices and the demand curve shifts upwards (or rightwards) to D_2 (arrow 1). At the existing price of P_1, households now demand $\hat{Q}$. But because conditions of supply have not changed, firms still only intend to supply Q_1 at this price, which is therefore no longer an equilibrium price. Excess demand exists in the market.

It is worthwhile at this point to take a closer look at how the price mechanism eliminates excess demand. If the firms are unable to increase supply immediately, the supply curve will be temporarily vertical and the price will be bid up to P_3. (Unit 4 explains how supply is completely **inelastic** in the momentary time period.) In the short run, however, firms will respond to the incentive provided by P_3 and increase supply as soon as they can. An adjustment in supply, in response to price, takes place along the supply curve (arrow 2). If the price remained at P_3, the firms would be prepared to supply Q_3. If this amount is released onto the market the price will fall, as the consumers will only take Q_1 at this price. The price falls to the new market-clearing equilibrium at P_2.

1.4   LINKS WITH OTHER TOPICS

The next nine topic units develop important aspects of the basic single-market supply and demand model which has been described in this unit. In particular, Units 2 and 3 explain demand and supply curves, and Unit 4 introduces the concept of elasticity. The other units investigate how markets may function when different assumptions are made about market circumstances – time-lags in the supply of agricultural products, producer power, barriers to entry, perfect and imperfect information, etc. Finally, Unit 10 draws the threads together and assesses the advantages and disadvantages of the market economy as an economic system.

1.5 QUESTION PRACTICE

Essay Questions

Question 1 Give a brief explanation of the term 'economic model'. Outline a model of price and output determination in a free market and explain how a rise in real income can result in a new level of market price.

(JMB. June, 1976)

Understanding the Question The existence and use of economic models have not been mentioned in the main body of the topic unit. Nevertheless, the unit does serve to illustrate the importance of model-building as a technique used by economists firstly to understand the working of the economy and secondly to predict what might happen in the future. Models are small-scale replicas of real-world phenomena. An economic model, however, is better thought of as a simplification of the real world in which the essential features of an economic problem are explained using diagrams, words, or perhaps algebra.

In the widest sense, a market economy (or 'free' economy) is itself an economic model of resource allocation, since no real-world economy is a pure market economy. A **general equilibrium** model of a market economy investigates the conditions necessary for the simultaneous determination of price and output in every market within the market economy. General equilibrium analysis is rather complicated and beyond the scope of Advanced Level economics. Examiners will, however, expect you to understand a **partial equilibrium** model of a market economy. In partial equilibrium analysis, the basic model is the **'supply and demand model'** of a single market upon which this unit has concentrated. The model explains the conditions necessary for determining price and output in a single market, assuming that conditions in all other markets are held constant – the ceteris paribus assumption.

Answer plan

1 Explain the meaning of an economic model as a simplification of the real world.

2 Scarcity is the central problem of interest to economists. Economists create models of market economies to explain how markets and the price mechanism deal with the problem of scarcity.

3 Explain in some detail how price and output are determined within the 'supply and demand model' of a single market.

4 You could then go on to show how such a model can be used for predictive purposes – e.g. the model predicts that if price is held below the market-clearing equilibrium price, excess demand will occur and black markets may arise.

5 Show how a change in real income violates a basic assumption of the model, the ceteris paribus assumption, and results in a movement to a new equilibrium price and output.

Question 2

(a) Explain the role of the price mechanism.

(b) Explain why each of the following phenomena is the result of either the absence of, or restrictions on, the use of the price mechanism:

  (i) the necessity for students to obtain certain minimum Advanced Level grades as a condition of entry to particular universities;

  (ii) the emergence of 'black' markets in tickets for major sporting events;

  (iii) traffic congestion in major cities.

(WJEC.: June, 1979)

Understanding the Question You must avoid the temptation to write too much on the first part of a multi-part question, thus relegating the other answers to being little more than footnotes. Restrict yourself in your first answer to a brief explanation of how the price mechanism allocates scarce resources between competing uses, with resources being switched between markets in response to the signals and incentives provided by prices.

The price mechanism may be inappropriate for allocating *merit goods* such as education (see Unit 8). In some circumstances, only people who could afford to pay would gain access to higher education, and this might be socially undesirable. One alternative is to replace the price mechanism completely and to finance universities out of general taxation. In this case, a minimum academic requirement acts as a rationing or screening device. You should note that rationing by price and by minimum entrance-qualification can be combined together.

To answer the question on black markets, you should draw on the section of the unit that deals with excess demand. Black markets are likely to emerge under two sets of circumstances: a) when the market for a good such as heroin is made illegal, and b) when a government or sporting authority creates excess demand by imposing a maximum price which is below the equilibrium price. In this latter case, 'lucky' customers are able to buy the good at the imposed price, but 'unlucky' customers have to go without. In a normal market, the price would rise to clear the market, but if this is prevented a black market can come into existence. In the black market the 'lucky' customers, who would be prepared to re-sell at a higher price, meet 'unlucky' customers, who are prepared to pay more than the imposed price. Black markets are usually characterized by very imperfect information which enables 'spivs' or ticket-touts to act as middlemen.

The last part of the question illustrates the concept of **market failure**, and for an explanation you should refer to the coverage of **externalities** and economic **'bads'** in Unit 8. The basic problem is that the person who is inconvenienced by traffic congestion is unable to charge a price to the motorists who generate it. Nevertheless, the government can use the price mechanism to discourage congestion by charging a price to motorists for access to city centres – though it may well be that such a policy is neither practical nor politically feasible.

Answer plan

1 Briefly describe the role of the price mechanism in allocating scarce resources in a market economy. Stress the role of prices as signals and incentives.
2 Explain how the price mechanism can, in principle, provide higher education, but it might underprovide and fail to provide for the poor.
3 Black markets result both from restrictions on the price mechanism and from its absence. A black market in the allocation of council houses amongst those on council waiting-lists is an example of the latter.
4 It may be impossible for the price mechanism, operating in the private market, to ration traffic congestion.
5 Inelastic supply is a common feature of the three phenomena.

Question 3 'Price controls are an inefficient method of helping poor people because they always lead to shortages.' Discuss.

(AEB.: June, 1980)

Understanding the Question The starting-point in understanding and answering this question is the analysis of imposed prices and excess demand which we have explained in the context of the previous question. One way of developing the answer is to explain how the rationing systems and black markets, which result from the excess demand and apparent shortages, are inefficient – you should refer to Unit 6 for a discussion of efficiency in economics. An alternative approach (which can be combined with these arguments) is to state that price controls are also inefficient for a reason not mentioned in the question. If price controls are imposed on goods and services such as electricity and gas to help the poor, they will also help the rich, who individually will benefit more. A more efficient way to help the poor may be to allow market prices to rule in each market and to give selective subsidies directly to the poor as cash benefits.

Answer plan

1 In theory, price controls may not always cause shortages, but excess demand and shortages will result if a maximum price is fixed below the equilibrium price in a market.
2 Price controls may lead to allocative inefficiency, administrative costs and the costs of queuing and waiting.
3 The controls may benefit the rich more than the poor and fail to achieve the intended distributional benefits.
4 Nevertheless, there may be some advantages, including political and counter-inflation benefits – though many economists would disagree.

Multiple Choice Questions

Question 4 Which of the following statements that refer to the price mechanism is NOT true?
(a) In a private enterprise system the sovereignty of the consumer is not always complete.
(b) Lack of information may prevent the price mechanism from working perfectly as an allocative device.
(c) Exchange can only take place at equilibrium prices in a market economy.
(d) A rise in the relative price of a good tends to attract resources from markets where relative prices have fallen.

Understanding the Question These are all general statements about the nature of a market economy. All are true except for the third statement. If a private enterprise system conformed to the conditions of perfect competition, then consumer sovereignty would follow from the basic assumptions of the model, but perfect competition seldom, if ever, exists. Information problems, which prevent the price mechanism from working, have been referred to in the unit, which has also shown that trading can take place at disequilibrium prices.

Question 5 Which of the following will cause the demand curve of butter to shift to the right?
(a) A fall in the price of butter.
(b) A rise in the costs of producing butter.
(c) A subsidy granted to milk producers.
(d) A successful advertizing campaign by the dairy industry.

Understanding the Question This type of question is testing whether you can correctly identify the variables which are responsible for the positions of the supply and demand curves. It also tests whether you can distinguish between a shift in the demand curve and an adjustment in response to a price change along a curve (statement (a)). The correct answer is (d).

1.6   FURTHER READING

Lipsey, R. G., *An Introduction to Positive Economics*, 5th edition (Weidenfeld & Nicolson, 1979) Chapter 8: The theory of the behaviour of individual competitive markets

Lancaster, K., *Modern Economics, Principles and Policy*, 2nd edition (Rand McNally, 1979) Chapter 4: Supply, Demand and the Market

2 Demand

2.1 POINTS OF PERSPECTIVE

In this unit we 'go behind' the market demand curve in order to demonstrate how its shape and essential characteristics are derived from basic economic principles, and from a set of initial assumptions about how consumers behave. Different assumptions about consumer behaviour lead to differently shaped demand curves, so that although conventional downward-sloping demand curves are normally to be expected, it is best to avoid describing this characteristic as a 'law' of demand (which suggests a misleading inevitability about the existence of downward-sloping demand curves).

1 Market Demand and Individual Demand

Students often confuse the **market** (or industry) demand curve, which shows how much of a commodity all the consumers in the market intend to buy at all possible prices, and the **individual** demand curve of a single consumer or household in the market. The relationship between the two is very simple: the market demand curve is obtained by adding up all the individual demand curves for every consumer in the market. Henceforth in this unit, 'demand' will mean individual demand rather than market demand. It will also mean **effective demand** – a demand backed by purchasing power or money.

2 The Utility Approach and the Indifference Curve Approach

Two different methods can be used to derive demand curves from a set of initial assumptions – the **utility** approach and the **indifference curve** approach. While both approaches lead to the same conclusions, the indifference curve method is preferred at a university level because it is more rigorous and the technique can be extended to other aspects of advanced economic theory. However, at the school or college level, our experience is that students are far better advised to learn simple theories well rather than risk fouling up a more complicated, if academically respectable, theory. For this reason, only the utility approach is explained in this unit.

Nevertheless, you should check whether or not the syllabus of your particular examining board requires a knowledge of indifference curves. The books which are recommended for further reading at the end of this unit include a thorough coverage of indifference curve analysis.

2.2 UNDERLYING CONCEPTS

1 Utility maximization

The basic or fundamental assumption of demand theory is that consumers always seek in the market place to maximize the total *utility* they obtain from the set of goods they buy. Utility cannot be seen, touched, or even properly measured. It is sometimes defined as the pleasure which a consumer obtains from using a good or service. However, it really means rather more than this. Some goods, such as medicine for example, are consumed because they **fulfil a need** rather than because they give the consumer direct pleasure. The assumption of utility maximization also implies that consumers act **rationally**, which in the sense used here means that people act in their own self-interest.

2 The existence of constraints

If consumers had unlimited income, or if all goods were free, a consumer would maximize utility by obtaining those goods which gave him utility up to the point of **satiation**. However, all but a few lucky and very wealthy consumers face a number of **constraints** which limit their freedom of action in the market place. The principal constraints are:

(i) **Limited Income.** Consumers do not possess unlimited means with which to purchase all the goods which would give them utility. The **opportunity cost** to a consumer of choosing one good is the lost opportunity to choose the next best alternative. (Note that the assumption of rationality implies that the 'best' alternative will always be chosen!) A limited income constrains a consumer's freedom of choice, and so it imposes a **budget constraint** on his market action.

(ii) **The consumer faces a given set of prices.** A single consumer is unable to influence the market prices of any of the goods he might wish to buy: he is a '*price-taker*' rather than a '*price-maker*'.

(iii) **Tastes and preferences are fixed.** A consumer who prefers Good A to Good B today will also prefer Good A tomorrow: the consumer is said to behave *consistently* if his preferences are stable over time.

3 Maximizing v minimizing behaviour

Demand theory is thus essentially concerned with the way in which a consumer with a limited income and fixed tastes behaves in the face of changing prices. The consumer attempts to maximise a desired objective (utility), subject to a set of constraints. The assumption of maximizing or minimizing behaviour (on the part of consumers, firms, workers and even perhaps the government) is central to orthodox micro-economic theory. You should note that a **maximizing objective** can always be rewritten in minimizing terms. Thus, we can rewrite the consumer's assumed objective 'to maximize the utility obtained from a purchased bundle of goods' as: 'to minimize the outlay, expenditure or cost of obtaining the same set of goods'. They are different sides of the same coin.

Whether we set up an assumed objective in maximizing or minimizing terms depends upon our convenience; we can do either. The reader will find further examples of 'maximizing and minimizing behaviour' in later units, for example in distribution theory and in the theory of the firm.

2.3   ESSENTIAL INFORMATION

1 Diminishing Marginal Utility

The principle of diminishing marginal utility states that although the total utility derived from a good increases with the amount consumed, it does so at a decreasing rate. It is quite possible that a person may experience increasing marginal utility when more of a good is consumed, at least for the first few units of that good. This is why we refer to diminishing marginal utility as a **'principle'** rather than as a **'law'**. The principle is illustrated in Figure 2.1. The upward (or positive) slope of the total utility curve in Figure 2.1a indicates that **total utility** rises with consumption. The last unit purchased is always the **marginal unit**, so the utility derived from it is the **marginal utility**. (Formally, the marginal utility derived from the n'th unit = the total utility of n units minus the total utility of $(n-1)$ units. If 20 units are produced, n = 20.) You will notice that the principle of diminishing marginal utility is shown by the **diminishing rate of increase** of the slope of the total utility curve in Figure 2.1a. The marginal utility derived from each unit of consumption is plotted separately in Figure 2.1b. The principle of diminishing marginal utility is represented by the negative or downward slope of the curve in this diagram.

Figure 2.1 illustrates an important lack of rigour in the utility approach to demand analysis. The vertical axes are measured in degrees of utility, 'utils' or 'subjective units of pleasure', which are not really measurable because a 'unit of pleasure' will vary from person to person.

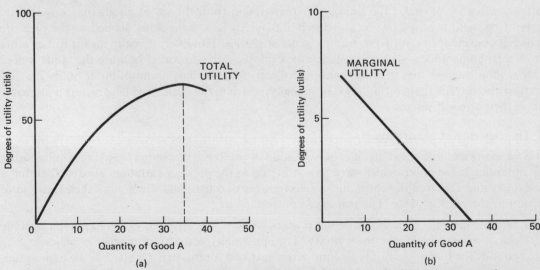

Fig 2.1 Utility curves (a) total utility rises at a diminishing rate as an individual's consumption of Good A increases (b) this can also be shown by a marginal utility curve—note that at the peak of the total utility curve marginal utility drops to zero.

2 Consumer Equilibrium and the derivation of the demand curve

A consumer, constrained by limited income, fixed tastes and the prices which he faces in the market place, will continue to buy units of a commodity until the marginal utility which he gains is the same as that he could have obtained by spending a similar amount of money on another commodity. The equilibrium condition with respect to a single commodity is, therefore, where Marginal Utility = Price. It is an easy matter to extend the analysis to the case where a consumer buys many commodities. Successive units will be bought of each commodity to the point where its marginal utility equals its price. The multi-commodity equilibrium condition is:

$$\frac{\text{Marginal Utility of Good A}}{\text{Price of A}} = \frac{\text{Marginal Utility of Good B}}{\text{Price of B}} = \frac{\text{Marginal Utility of any Good}}{\text{Price of any Good}}$$

Suppose that a consumer can only choose between Good A and Good B and he starts off from a position of consumer equilibrium. At existing prices he is satisfied with the combination of Goods A and B that he buys. The price of Good A now falls, and the situation can now be represented by:

$$\frac{\text{M.U. of Good A}}{\text{Price of A}} > \frac{\text{M.U. of Good B}}{\text{Price of B}}$$

The consumer is no longer in equilibrium; he would be better off substituting more of the good whose relative price has fallen for a good whose relative price is now higher. He is not now maximizing utility, and so he has a motive for changing his market behaviour.

When he consumes more of Good A, he moves 'down' the marginal utility curve for Good A, and 'back up' the marginal utility curve for Good B. As he substitutes more of Good A for less of Good B, the marginal utilities adjust until he is once again in equilibrium, when no alternative reallocation will increase his total utility. The equilibrium is achieved at a point of **equi-marginal utility**, where the marginal utility derived from each good as a ratio of its price is the same for all goods. The essential point is that more is demanded of the good whose relative price has fallen. The **substitution effect**, whereby consumers substitute more of a good whose relative price has fallen for goods whose relative price has risen, helps to explain the downward-sloping demand curve.

3 The Substitution Effect and the Income Effect

If consumer behaviour was determined only by the substitution effect of a price change, demand curves would only slope downwards. This is provided that customers are utility maximizers who experience diminishing marginal utility, and assuming also that they are uninfluenced by future uncertainty and status. However, if consumers expect even higher prices in the future, they may demand more at high prices for speculative reasons. Similarly, if a high price indicates status, 'status maximizers' may be expected to demand more of a good at higher prices.

When we introduce the **income effect** of a price change, matters become rather more complicated. If the price of one good falls, a consumer's **real income** rises. The nature of this income effect depends upon whether the good is a **'normal' good** or an **'inferior' good**. If expenditure on a good rises when a consumer's real income rises, then the good is a normal one. Conversely, if expenditure on the good falls when income rises, then that good is classed as inferior. It is important to stress that the same good can, for a particular individual, switch from being normal to inferior as his income rises. Suppose that the Income-Expenditure graph in Figure 2.2a represents an individual's expenditure on bus travel at different levels of real income. When the

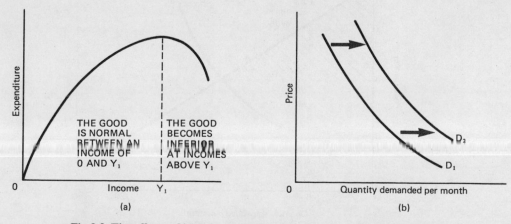

Fig 2.2 The effects of income on demand (a) an income expenditure curve for a good which is inferior at high levels of income (b) a shift in the price demand curve for a normal good following an increase in income

person is poor, his expenditure on bus travel rises as his income rises: bus travel is a normal good. But beyond the level of income Y_1, bus travel becomes an inferior good, presumably because the person can now afford to travel by car.

For normal goods, the substitution effect of a price change is reinforced by the income effect, and the two effects together explain the downward-sloping demand curve. But in the case of inferior goods, the income effect works in the opposite direction to the substitution effect. The income effect is, however, likely to be much smaller than the substitution effect, because expenditure on a single good is probably only a tiny proportion of a consumer's total spending; real income hardly alters at all if the price of a single good changes. Nevertheless, a theoretical possibility exists that the income effect of a price change will not only be in the opposite direction to the substitution effect but that it will also be stronger. This is the special case of an inferior good known as a **'Giffen' good** – less of a Giffen good is demanded as the price falls, hence the demand curve slopes upward.

4 Shifts of demand

In the previous section, the analysis explains how a change in real income, resulting from a change in the price of a good, influences the shape of the demand curve. It is important to separate this effect from the effects of a change in real income which is independent of a change in the good's own price. If a person's real disposable income rises as a result of a wage increase or a cut in income tax, then the demand curve of each of the goods that the person buys may shift. If the good is a normal one, the demand curve will shift to the right (or upwards) and more will be demanded at every price. This is illustrated in Figure 2.2b. In the case of an inferior good, however, a rise in real income causes the demand curve to shift to the left (or downwards).

A change in real disposable income is only one of the possible causes of a shift in the demand curve. In general, a change in any of the constraints facing the consumer (sometimes known as the **conditions of demand**) will shift the demand curve. The good's own price is not listed as one of the conditions of demand because the demand curve is itself a 'map' showing how demand responds to price changes. However, changes in the price of a **complementary** or **substitute** good will normally shift a demand curve. Most people in Britain regard bread and butter as complementary goods. If the price of bread rises, the demand curve of butter will probably shift to the left and less butter will be demanded at all prices. Conversely, a rise in the price of a substitute for butter, such as margarine, will normally cause the demand curve for butter to shift rightwards.

The time-period under consideration will also influence demand. Strictly speaking, the horizontal axis of a demand graph should specify the time-period for which demand is being measured. If the time-period is changed, for example from monthly to yearly demand, the ability of consumers to respond to a change in price will also alter. This aspect of demand theory will be investigated in Unit 4 on elasticity.

5 Consumer Surplus

The concept of consumer surplus is illustrated in Figure 2.3, which shows the market demand curve of all the consumers in the market. You should refer to Question 5, at the end of the unit, for an example of consumer surplus in the context of an individual consumer.

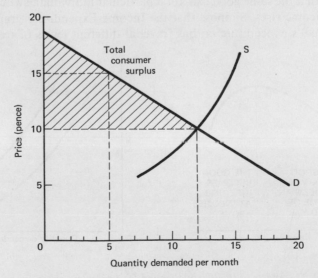

Fig 2.3 Consumer Surplus: the shaded area shows total consumer surplus when the market price is 10 pence

In Figure 2.3, the equilibrium price of 10 pence is the price which every consumer in the market pays for the good in question. It is also the price which the marginal consumer is only just prepared to pay in order to obtain the good. If the price rose above 10 pence, the marginal consumer would either drop out of the market or reduce his demand. However, some consumers, who value the good more highly, would be prepared to pay 15 pence for it. They gain a consumer surplus (or **surplus utility**) equal to the difference between what they would be prepared to pay and what they actually need to pay. The total consumer surplus, the utility which consumers enjoy but do not pay for, is shown by the shaded area of the graph.

2.4 LINKS WITH OTHER TOPICS

Although the determination of the shape of the demand curve has been the central theme of this unit, we have largely ignored a very important aspect of the shape and slope of demand curves: the concept of **elasticity of demand**. Unit 4 on elasticity should be regarded as a very useful follow-up to this unit.

In this unit we have dealt only with the **micro-economic theory of consumer behaviour** – how consumers choose between alternative goods and services. The **macro-economic theory of consumption** (covered in Unit 21) explains how consumers divide their limited income between **aggregate consumption** on all goods and **saving**. Although economists agree that a sound macro-economic theory should be based firmly on micro-economic foundations, students are often confused by the parallel existence of micro- and macro- consumption theory. Think carefully about the context of the question, when you decide how to structure and plan your answer to a question on consumer behaviour.

2.5 QUESTION PRACTICE

Essay Questions

Question 1 Explain, with examples, the nature and purpose of economic theory and outline the characteristics of a useful theory. Discuss how far the theory of consumer behaviour with which you are familiar possesses these characteristics.

(JMB.: June, 1980)

Understanding the Question Most economic theories claim to be **positive theories**: they attempt to **explain** how the economy works, and to predict what will happen in the future if certain actions are taken now. However, some economic theories are **normative theories** about what ought to happen: a theory of optimal government policy is a 'normative' theory because it is essentially concerned with how a government should make value judgements when choosing between different policy options.

The theory of demand (or consumer behaviour) is a positive theory: the problem or puzzle to be explained is how consumers make decisions when faced with the choice of how to spend their incomes. (The theory does not say how they ought to spend their incomes.) Restricting ourselves to positive theories, the usefulness of a theory may be judged by three criteria: (i) relevance, (ii) realism of assumptions, and (iii) ability to survive empirical tests.

(i) *How relevant is a theory?* If a 'good' theory explains a trivial problem of no interest to anybody, then it is hardly a useful theory. This, for instance, is the basic Marxist criticism of orthodox economics. Marxists argue that orthodox economics is dominated by the study of the 'uninteresting' problem of individual behaviour in a 'timeless' economy, thereby ignoring or side-stepping the 'interesting' problems (to a Marxist) of how a capitalist economy comes into existence and changes over time, and the economic relations between **classes** (as distinct from relations between **individuals**).

(ii) *How realistic are the theory's assumptions?* All economic theories involve a set of simplifying assumptions about economic relationships or how people behave. Thus, in demand theory, economists assume that consumers have the single aim of utility maximization. This is obviously a simplifying assumption as sometimes people will have other aims, but it may still be a useful way of simplifying.

(iii) *Can a theory survive empirical tests?* The predictions (or implications) of a theory follow logically from its initial assumptions. Thus, demand theory predicts a downward-sloping demand curve, but if the initial assumptions of the theory had been that people are status maximizers and that status is indicated by high price, then the theory would be unlikely to survive an empirical test. Empirical testing means that the predictions of a theory are tested against observed behaviour in the real world. Useful theories survive the process of empirical testing, whereas theories whose predictions are plainly at odds with observed behaviour are discarded.

Answer plan

1 Base your answer to the first part of the question on the concepts discussed in the previous section: the distinction between positive and normative theories, and how a theory simplifies – yet explains – the real world.

2 The characteristics of a useful (positive) theory are its relevance, the realism of its assumptions, and its ability to stand up to empirical testing. Often the mechanism of a theory can be expressed with the use of mathematics in an economic model.

3 Assess the usefulness of demand theory in terms of these three characteristics. Do downward-sloping demand curves conform to observed behaviour?

Question 2 Outline and explain the conditions for a consumer to be in equilibrium when faced with a given income and relative prices. How will this equilibrium be altered:
(a) by a rise in the price of one good;
(b) by a rise in the general price level while the consumer's income remains unchanged?

(AEB.: June, 1980)

Understanding the Question Although this question can be answered with either indifference curve analysis or utility theory, we shall restrict ourselves to the latter. To obtain a very good grade, you must show that you understand the meaning of equilibrium in economics. It is sensible to base your answer on the equilibrium condition for a utility-maximizing consumer, showing how the events specified in (a) and (b) will disturb an existing equilibrium and cause the consumer to alter his market actions until he is back in equilibrium once again. One of the aims of the question is to test whether you are able to introduce the concepts of substitution and income effects into your answers to (a) and (b).

Answer plan
1 Define equilibrium as a state of rest. A consumer will be in equilibrium when he spends his limited income in such a way as to maximize the utility obtained from the bundle of goods purchased.
2 This can be written as the equilibrium condition:

$$\frac{\text{M.U. of Good A}}{\text{Price of Good A}} = \frac{\text{M.U. of Good B}}{\text{Price of Good B}} = \frac{\text{M.U. of any Good}}{\text{Price of any Good}}$$

Briefly explain why this is the equilibrium condition.
3 Explain how event (a), involving a change in relative prices, disturbs an initial equilibrium through both a substitution effect and an income effect, though the substitution effect is likely to be greater.
4 Event (b) involves only an income effect because relative prices do not change. Total spending on normal goods will now fall, but spending on inferior goods might increase.

Question 3 What is meant by the 'substitution effect'? Why is this not sufficient to determine the actual shape of the demand curve for a specific good or service?

(O & CSEB.: June, 1981)

Understanding the Question Although the question only specifies the substitution effect of a price change, an aim of the question is to test your understanding of the relative importance of the substitution effect and the income effect. The substitution effect always causes a consumer to substitute more of a good whose relative price has fallen for a good whose relative price has risen. In the case of normal goods, the income effect reinforces the substitution effect, and the result is a downward-sloping demand curve. The demand curve for most inferior goods will also slope downwards because the 'perverse' income effect is insufficient to offset the much stronger substitution effect. Finally, you must introduce the example of a Giffen good as the extreme special case of an inferior good for which the perverse income effect is greater than the substitution effect.

Answer plan
1 The market demand curve for a good is the addition of all the individual demand curves.
2 Explain the meaning of the substitution effect and its influence on a demand curve.
3 Introduce the income effect in the context of (a) normal goods; (b) inferior goods; (c) Giffen goods.
4 Conclude that a knowledge of the direction and relative strength of the income effect is necessary in order to determine the shape of a demand curve.

Multiple Choice Questions

Question 4 The Law of Diminishing Marginal Utility states that the more you consume of a commodity:
1 the higher the price you will be prepared to pay;
2 the slower the rate of increase in the total utility you derive from it;
3 the less the pleasure that you get from having an additional unit of it.

Directions

A	B	C	D
1, 2, 3 are all correct	1, 2 only correct	2, 3 only correct	1 only correct

Understanding the Question The objective questions included in Unit 1 are examples of **simple completion questions** where there is a straightforward choice between four or five possible answers, of which only one is correct. The second type of question is a **multiple completion question** where, although there is only one correct response you can make, this can depend on one or more of the completion items being correct. In this particular example, completion item 1 is wrong because it has nothing whatever to do with diminishing marginal utility, but items 2 and 3 are both correct. Thus the answer to the question is C.

Data Response Questions

Question 5 Given below are the daily utility functions for three cold drinks for a man arriving at a desert oasis with a budget of £28.

Price	DRINK A £2	DRINK B £4	DRINK C £6
Quantity	Total utility	Total utility	Total utility
1	8	8	14
2	14	13¼	27
3	18	18¼	39
4	21	23	49
5	22	27½	55
6	24	31¾	60
7	25	35¾	62

Assuming that holding money has no utility for him and that he seeks to maximize his satisfaction, answer the following:

(a) On his first visit the only drink for sale is B. How many drinks does he buy, and why?

(b) In the circumstances of (a), calculate the consumer's surplus.

(c) On a return visit, with another £28, all the drinks are available. How will he now allocate his budget between the three drinks?

(d) What is unlikely about the total utility figures for drink A?

(London: June, 1980)

Understanding the Question This is an example of a data response question based on simulated data which the Chief Examiner will have made up himself. (You can usually tell when the data are simulated since no reference is made in the question to a statistical source.) In most questions of this type, the data are constructed so that a single correct answer can be calculated without too much difficulty – after all, the question is testing your economic ability and not your mathematics! You are unlikely to lose many marks for a wrong answer which is the obvious result of an arithmetical slip, as long as the examiner believes that your economic reasoning is sensible and relevant.

This particular question is testing your knowledge of the condition for a utility-maximizing consumer to be in equilibrium and your ability to apply the equilibrium condition to the data.

Answer plan

1 To answer (a) you must state the fundamental assumption that consumers are utility maximizers. It should be obvious from the data that the man will spend all his income on good B as long as each extra drink gives him some extra utility.

2 Part (b) is the most difficult part of the question. The price the consumer pays (£4) equals the marginal utility he obtains from the last drink consumed (4 units of utility). You can measure the total cost of the drinks, in units of utility, by multiplying the number of drinks consumed by the price (4 utility units). Finally, to measure consumer surplus, subtract the total cost of the drinks, measured in utility units, from the total utility obtained.

3 For (c) apply the equilibrium condition:

$$\frac{\text{M.U. of A}}{\text{Price of A}} = \frac{\text{M.U. of B}}{\text{Price of B}} = \frac{\text{M.U. of C}}{\text{Price of C}},$$ subject to the budget constraint of £28.

4 Use the principle of diminishing marginal utility to answer the last part of the question.

2.6 FURTHER READING

Lipsey, R. G., *An Introduction to Positive Economics*, 5th edition (Weidenfeld & Nicolson, 1979) Chapter 14: Theories of household demand

Burningham, D., editor, *Understanding Economics, an Introduction for Students* (Macmillan, 1978)

3 Cost and Supply

3.1 POINTS OF PERSPECTIVE

In much the same way that the characteristics of demand curves depend upon the typical behaviour of consumers, so the properties of supply curves depend upon the behaviour of **producers** or **firms**. The **market supply curve**, which shows how much all the firms in an industry intend to supply at various possible prices, is obtained by adding up the separate supply curves for individual firms. For the rest of this unit, we shall assume that there are a large number of firms within a well-defined industry and that each firm is a passive **'price-taker'**, unable to influence the market price by its own decisions on how much to supply. We are really constructing the theory of supply within a **perfectly competitive** industry, though a more comprehensive treatment of perfect competition is delayed until Unit 6.

3.2 UNDERLYING CONCEPTS

1 The Firm

A firm is a **productive unit** or business enterprise which sells its output at a price, within the market economy. In the **private sector** of the economy, firms may range from a one-man window-cleaning business (a **sole trader** or **individual proprietor**) to huge 'multinational' public joint-stock companies, such as ICI, with branches and plants in many countries. Most **public corporations** or nationalized industries in the **public sector** of the economy are also considered as firms because they sell their output within the market economy. It is not usual, however, to regard **public services**, such as the National Health Service, as firms or business enterprises. Although the NHS is a major customer or market for firms which supply it from within the market economy, most of its own activities take place outside the market economy.

2 Profit-maximizing behaviour

In constructing a theory of supply we are not especially interested in the organizational complexities of firms, such as the different forms of ownership and control and the existence of multi-product and multi-plant enterprises. These are aspects of the **internal** structure of firms, which is the subject matter of Unit 10. In this unit we **abstract** from the internal organization of firms and concentrate instead upon the **external** behaviour of firms when they make decisions on the production and sale of a good or goods within the market. In the context of this unit, it does not matter who makes the decisions within the firm, as long as the decisions are consistent with a desired goal or objective which is assumed to exist for all firms. In the traditional theory of the firm it is assumed that all firms, whatever their internal structure and whatever the form of market in which they exist, share the common goal of profit maximization.

3 Factors of Production

Economists conventionally divide all the inputs necessary for production to take place into four categories, or **'factors of production'**. These are land, labour, capital and enterprise (or the entrepreneurial factor). For the rest of this unit we shall simplify and assume that just two inputs, labour and capital, are all that is needed for production to take place.

4 The Short Run and the Long Run

The economic short run is defined as a period of time in which at least one factor of production is fixed. Thus, in the short run a firm can only increase output or supply by adding more of a variable factor, in this case labour, and combining it with the fixed input, capital. In the long run it is assumed that all factors of production are variable. The **scale** of the fixed factors can only be altered in the economic long run. From a firm's point of view, the short run is thus a time-period in which its ability to increase supply is **constrained** by the size of its fixed capital. We must distinguish between a firm's short-run or constrained supply curve, and its long-run supply curve, which is unconstrained except by factors such as the available technology and the prices it must pay to obtain the services of labour and capital.

3.3   ESSENTIAL INFORMATION

1 The Principle of Diminishing Returns

If a firm attempts to increase output or supply in the economic short run by adding a variable input, such as labour, to a given amount of fixed capital, then eventually diminishing marginal returns to labour will set in: an extra worker will add less to total output than the previous worker. (Diminishing marginal **output** and diminishing marginal **product** are alternative expressions of the same principle.) You should note that the principle of diminishing marginal returns refers to the physical productivity of labour and not to either the money cost of employing labour (the wage) or to the money value of the output which labour produces. The principle of diminishing returns is sometimes known as a 'law', but it must be stressed that when the first units of labour are added to fixed capital **increasing marginal returns** are likely to be experienced. This is because the employment of an extra worker allows greater **specialization** and **division of labour** to take place, with the result that total output increases more than proportionately as workers are added to the labour force.

There are two useful ways of illustrating the principle of diminishing returns in a diagram. In Figure 3.1, a **production possibility curve** has been drawn to show how many cars or bicycles a labour force of 100 men can produce if combined with fixed amounts of capital in either the car or

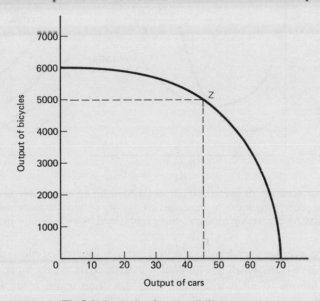

Fig 3.1 A production possibility curve

the bicycle industry. If all the men are employed in the bicycle industry, the maximum output is 6000 bicycles and no cars. Similarly, seventy cars and no bicycles can be produced if all the men are switched to the car industry. The production possibility curve, drawn between these two extremes, represents all the combinations of bicycles and cars which are possible if some of the men are employed in one industry and some in the other. The point Z on the production possibility curve shows that the total possible output is 5000 bicycles and forty-five cars if fifty men are employed in each industry.

Now ask yourself what will happen if workers move out of the car industry into the bicycle industry (or vice versa). Whereas the first fifty workers in the bicycle industry produce a total of 5000 bicycles, the addition of a second fifty workers only increases output by an extra 1000 bicycles. The slope of the production possibility curve, which is concave to origin, is evidence of diminishing marginal returns in both industries.

Figure 3.2a again illustrates the principle of diminishing returns to labour, but in this example within a single industry. You will notice that the diagram distinguishes between diminishing **marginal** returns to labour and diminishing **average** returns – a source of confusion to many students. The concept of marginal returns refers to the addition to output attributable to the last worker added to the labour force. (Formally, the marginal returns of the n'th worker = total returns of n workers minus total returns of (n-1) workers.) The average return per worker is simply the total output divided by the number of workers employed (total returns/n).

The mathematical relationship between any marginal variable and the average to which it is related is:

(a) if the marginal > the average, the average will rise;
(b) if the marginal < the average, the average will fall;
(c) if the marginal = the average, the average will neither rise nor fall.

This is a universal mathematical relationship with a host of economic applications. It is essential for students to understand what it means and to avoid the very common error of misrepresenting the relationship. It does *not* state that an average will rise when a marginal is rising, or that an average will fall when the marginal is falling. Figure 3.2a clearly shows that the marginal returns curve begins to fall as soon as the point of diminishing marginal returns is reached. Nevertheless, the average returns curve continues to rise as long as the marginal output of an extra worker is greater than the existing average output – thereby, 'pulling up' the average curve. The point of diminishing average returns is reached only when the output of an extra worker falls below the existing average.

2 Short-run cost curves

The total cost of producing a particular output is made up of the cost of employing both the variable and the fixed factors of production. This can be expressed as the identity:

$$TC \equiv TVC + TFC$$

Likewise, average total cost can be written as:

$$ATC \equiv AVC + AFC$$

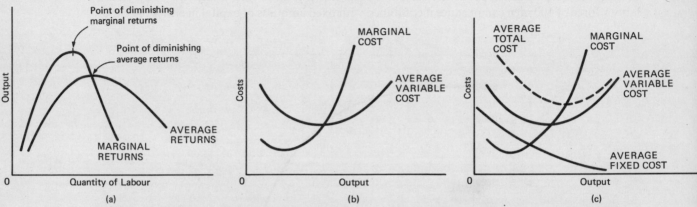

Fig. 3.2 The derivation of the firm's short-run cost curves (a) diminishing marginal returns and diminishing average returns to labour set in (b) these can be translated into money costs as the marginal cost curve and the average variable cost curve (c) the average total cost curve is obtained by including average fixed costs in the diagram

In Figure 3.2b, the average variable cost (AVC) curve is illustrated alongside (in Figure 3.2a) the average returns curve from which it is derived. Variable costs are the wage costs of employing the variable factor, labour. If all workers are paid the same wage, total wage costs will rise proportionately with the number of workers employed. However, while increasing average returns are being experienced, workers on average are becoming more efficient. It follows that average variable costs per unit of output will fall as output rises, but once diminishing average returns set in, average variable costs will rise with output.

In a very similar way, the marginal cost (MC) curve is derived from the nature of marginal returns to the variable inputs. If an extra worker adds more to total output than the previous worker, yet the wage cost of employing him remains the same, then the MC of producing an extra unit of output must fall. When diminishing marginal returns set in, however, the MC curve will rise.

While the nature of average and marginal returns to the variable factors of production determines the shapes of the AVC and MC curves, a separate, but very simple, explanation is needed for the average fixed cost (AFC) curve. Because total fixed costs do not vary with output in the economic short run, AFC per unit of output will fall as the fixed costs or 'overheads' are spread over larger and larger outputs. A falling AFC curve is drawn in Figure 3.2c, which also includes the average total cost curve obtained by adding up the AVC and AFC curves. The short-run ATC curve is typically U-shaped, showing that average total costs first fall and later rise as output is increased. You should note that the MC curve cuts both the AVC and the ATC curves at their lowest points. Check back to the preceding section to make quite sure that you know why this must be so. However, the point where the MC curve cuts the AFC curve is of no significance because the MC curve is derived only from variable costs and not from fixed costs.

3 The firm's short-run supply curve

We are now in a position to show how the short-run supply curve of a firm in a perfectly competitive industry is derived from its marginal cost curve. (The characteristics of perfect competition as a **market form** are examined in Unit 6.) A perfectly competitive firm, being a price-taker, will sell its output at the same market-determined price or **average revenue**, whatever the output it decides to supply to the market. This means that **total revenue** will always rise by the amount of price or average revenue when the firm decides to release an extra unit of output on the market. Now, **marginal revenue** is defined as the addition to total revenue resulting from the sale of an extra unit of output. It follows that **marginal revenue equals average revenue** for a perfectly competitive firm and is represented by a horizontal price-line such as P_1 in Figure 3.3.

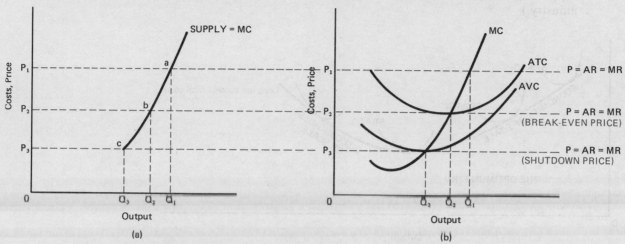

Fig 3.3 (a) The derivation of the firm's short-run supply curve from its MC curve (b) only the part of the MC curve above AVC is the firm's supply curve

It can easily be shown that any profit-maximizing firm, whatever the market form or structure, will produce the output where $MR = MC$. (We are now using MR as the economic shorthand for marginal revenue and not marginal returns!)

(a) If $MR > MC$, the firm is sacrificing the profit it could make from an extra unit of output. Therefore, it should increase output.

(b) If $MR < MC$, the firm is making a loss on at least the final unit of output produced. Therefore, it should decrease output.

(c) If $MR = MC$, there is no incentive to increase or decrease output. This is the **equilibrium condition** for a profit-maximizing firm.

Returning to Figure 3.3, let us suppose that the market-determined price is P_1. Using the equilibrium condition, the firm will choose to supply Q_1 onto the market, but if the price falls to P_2, supply will be reduced to Q_2. This is the **break-even price**, since the firm will start to make a loss if the price falls below the ATC curve. Nevertheless, if the price falls below P_2 it may still be consistent with profit-maximizing behaviour for the firm to continue to supply an output, in the short run at least, even though it is making a loss. As long as the price covers AVC, the size of the loss will be less than the fixed costs the firm would still incur if it produced zero output. The **shut-down price** is P_3, at which the firm just covers its variable costs.

Our conclusion is that the firm's MC curve, above AVC, is its short-run supply curve. The curve maps out how much the firm is prepared to supply to the market at each price. We have shown that the MC curve slopes upwards because of diminishing marginal returns to the variable factors of production. It is extremely useful to remember that the slope of the supply curve is derived from the principle of diminishing marginal returns and the assumption of profit-maximizing behaviour by firms. You should note the parallel between this analysis and the derivation, in Unit 2, of the demand curve from the principle of diminishing marginal utility and the assumption of utility-maximizing behaviour by households.

4 Shifts in supply

In the preceding analysis, the productivity of labour reflected in the principle of diminishing returns, and the wage or money costs of hiring labour determined the position of the firm's MC curve or short-run supply curve. If either productivity or wage costs change, the position of the supply curve will shift. Generalizing, a change in any of the **conditions of supply** will shift the supply curve. If labour becomes more productive, if wage costs fall, or if taxes on the firm are cut, then the supply curve will shift rightwards (or downwards), showing that the firm is prepared to supply more at existing prices.

5 Long-run costs and supply

In the long run, a firm can change the **scale** of the fixed factors of production and move to a new size of productive unit (or new short-run situation). The long-run average cost curve, which is illustrated in Figure 3.4, is a mathematical line drawn as a tangent to a 'family' or set of short-run cost curves, each representing a feasible size of productive unit. A firm can thus move in the long run from one short-run supply curve to another, which is associated with a different scale of fixed capacity. (It is useful to remember that firms can also enter or leave the industry in the long run. This means that the **industry** short-run supply curve, obtained by adding the individual supply curves of each firm, can shift its position in the long run when firms enter or leave the industry.)

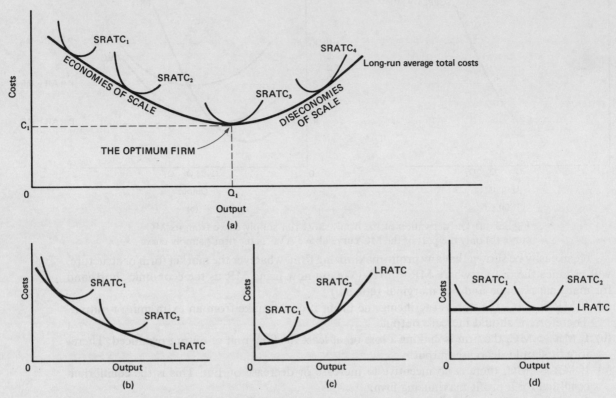

Fig 3.4 Long-run average total cost curves (a) economies of scale followed by diseconomies of scale (b) an industry with economies of large scale production (c) an industry with diseconomies of large scale production (d) an industry without economies or diseconomies of scale

The shape of the long-run ATC curve depends upon whether economies or diseconomies of scale are experienced. Long-run costs may be falling, rising, or constant. If an increase in all the inputs or factors of production results in falling long-run average total costs, **economies of scale** exist. Eventually **diseconomies of scale** may set in when the long-run ATC curve begins to rise. The textbook example of a U-shaped long-run ATC curve is drawn in Figure 3.4a. There is no reason, however, why the curve must be U-shaped. An industry, such as the automobile industry, with **economies of large-scale production** is represented in Figure 3.4b, while Figure 3.4c illustrates the **economies of small-scale production** which might be more typical of agriculture. (Further explanation of industries with economies of large- and small-scale production and a description of the main economies and diseconomies of scale are included in Unit 10.) Statistical studies have suggested an absence of significant economies and diseconomies of scale in many industries, in which case the correct long-run ATC curve would be the horizontal line in Figure 3.4d

If the firm's long-run marginal cost curve is also its **long-run supply curve**, this would imply a horizontal (or perfectly elastic) long-run supply curve in industries with constant long-run average costs. Firms of many different sizes could co-exist without significant differences in costs.

6 Returns to Scale

Many textbooks confuse economies of scale with the closely related concept of **increasing returns to scale**. Economies of scale refer to long-run **money costs** of production, whereas long-run returns to scale relate only to the **physical output** of the factors of production or inputs. If physical output increases more than proportionately as the scale of all the inputs is changed, **increasing returns to scale** occur. (**Decreasing returns to scale** and **constant returns to scale** are other possibilities.) Increasing returns to scale contribute to economies of scale (in the form of **technical economies**), but some economies of scale are not explained by increasing returns to scale – for example, '**bulk-buying' economies**, when a firm uses its market power to buy inputs at low prices.

While it is useful to understand the difference between economies of scale and increasing returns to scale, it is much more important for the student at Advanced Level to be absolutely clear about the difference between short-run returns, explained earlier in the unit, and the long-run returns to scale described in this section. It is the impact of diminishing marginal returns on the costs and profits of a firm in the economic short run that encourages the firm to change the scale of its operations in the long run.

3.4 LINKS WITH OTHER TOPICS

In this unit it has been assumed that a firm exists within a perfectly competitive industry. Further aspects of the supply and output decisions of firms in conditions of perfect competition and monopoly are developed in Unit 6, while Unit 7 extends the analysis to imperfect competition. Elasticity of supply is explained in Unit 4, which is followed in Unit 5 by a survey of the special problems of agricultural supply.

3.5 QUESTION PRACTICE

Essay Questions

Question 1 How would you use the law of variable proportions to explain the conventional theoretical shapes of a firm's cost curves?

(O & CSEB.: June, 1981)

Understanding the Question The law of variable proportions is another name for the 'law' or principle of diminishing marginal returns, which states that when a variable factor of production is added to a fixed factor, eventually the marginal output of the variable input will fall. As the unit explains, the shape of a firm's short-run MC curve is derived from the principle of diminishing marginal returns and, in a similar way, diminishing average returns is the basis of the AVC curve. You would be expected to explain at least one of these 'laws' to earn a pass grade at Advanced Level. Higher grades would require a clear exposition of both marginal and and average returns and an explanation of how the short-run ATC curve also depends on a separate phenomenon, the spreading of fixed costs. Finally, a very good answer should distinguish between short-run and long-run cost curves and explain, perhaps briefly, how the 'laws' of returns to scale differ from the short-run law of variable proportions.

Answer plan
1 Explain the law of variable proportions.
2 Show how the short-run MC and AVC curves are derived.
3 Introduce the AFC curve as a necessary part of the short-run ATC curve.
4 Distinguish between short-run and long-run cost curves, stressing that the law of variable proportions is only applicable to the short run.

Question 2 The scope for cost reduction from (a) internal economies of scale and (b) external economies is greater under some circumstances than others.' Comment.

(London: January, 1978)

Understanding the Question The question is deliberately open and vague, inviting you, the candidate, to give your own interpretation. However, a good answer must include a discussion of both internal and external economies. An *internal economy* is simply an economy of scale. Examiners are used to weaker candidates restricting themselves to a descriptive list of economies of scale – the managerial, technical and capital-raising economies described in Unit 10. This approach is adequate, provided that the various economies of scale are critically discussed. A better and more analytical approach is to introduce a diagram similar to Figure 3.4 in the unit, and to discuss the existence of industries with either economies of small-scale production or constant long-run average costs.

The essential characteristic of an **internal** economy of scale is that a firm's long-run average costs of production are reduced as a direct result of the firm itself growing larger. In contrast in the case of an **external** economy (a concept not explained in the unit) the firm's average costs of production are reduced as a result of the activities of an external economic agent, such as another firm or the government. For example, a farmer benefits from an external economy if the yields of his crops improve and production costs fall as a result of a drainage system installed by his neighbour. A good answer to the question would include a few examples selected from different types of industry, and it might also suggest the possibility of **external diseconomies**. (External economies and diseconomies are explained in greater detail in Unit 8.)

Answer plan
1 Define and distinguish between internal and external economies.
2 Discuss the possible occurrence of industries with economies of large-scale production, small-scale production, or constant long-run average costs.
3 Briefly describe different types of economy of scale, assessing their importance in different industries.
4 Introduce some examples of external economies and the possibility of external diseconomies.

Multiple Choice Questions

Question 3 A firm's total fixed costs are £1200. If at a certain output its average total costs per unit are £10 and the average variable cost per unit is £7, then that level of output is:

    (a) 200 units
    (b) 300 units
    (c) 400 units
    (d) 500 units

Understanding the Question The correct answer (c) is obtained in two stages:
(i) calculate average fixed costs per unit by using the identity:
    average total costs $\equiv$ average fixed costs + average variable costs;
(ii) the level of output = total fixed costs $\div$ average fixed costs.

Question 4 Diminishing returns occur in the short run when there is a reduction in:
    (a) the average product of the fixed factor
    (b) the total product of the variable factor
    (c) the marginal product of the fixed factor
    (d) the marginal product of the variable factor

Understanding the Question This is a straightforward question on the short-run 'laws' of returns. Although average and total returns will eventually diminish as more and more of a variable factor is added to fixed capacity, the principle of diminishing returns usually refers to the **marginal** returns of a variable input – alternative (d).

Data response Questions

Question 5 An economy has a working population of 800 men who can only produce two goods, X and Y. There are no differences in skill between the workers whether they produce good X or good Y. All other resources are specific to the production of only one of the goods. The potential outputs of each good are as follows:

Good X		Good Y	
No. of men	*Weekly output*	*No. of men*	*Weekly output*
100	60	100	25
200	120	200	65
300	190	300	110
400	260	400	160
500	330	500	200
600	380	600	235
700	420	700	260
800	450	800	275

(a) Sketch a diagram showing the production possibility curve (transformation curve).
(b) State the output level for good X and for good Y at which the marginal return to labour would begin to diminish.
(c) What would be the effects of some of the labour force becoming more efficient at the production of good X while the remainder became more efficient at the production of good Y?
(d) Assume that X is an investment good and Y is a consumption good and that, in 1976, 260 X and 160 Y were produced weekly. What would be the consequences if, in 1977, 330 X and 110 Y were produced weekly?

(London: June, 1977)

Understanding the Question

1 Parts (a) and (b) of the question require an understanding of Figure 3.1 in the unit. You will find that the production possibility curve which you draw is not the neat 'concave to origin' textbook example of Figure 3.1. This is because the data in the question are not a simple case of diminishing marginal returns in each industry: increasing and constant returns to labour complicate things!

2 It is impossible to calculate the marginal returns of a single worker from the data, so you must calculate the amount that each unit of 100 men adds to total output in each industry.

3 When a production possibility curve is drawn, it is assumed that the variable inputs, in this instance workers, are completely interchangeable: it does not matter which industry any individual worker is employed in. Question (c) violates this assumption: there are now two types of workers and it is no longer possible to draw a single production possibility curve. Two separate curves could be constructed, although the question does not require you actually to draw them. One curve would be for 'Type X' workers and the other for 'Type Y' workers. Total possible output would now increase. If you refer to Unit 26, you will see how the principle of comparative advantage is based on workers, or countries, specializing in what they do best.

4 Both combinations of X and Y specified for 1976 and 1977 fully employ the labour force of 800 men. This represents a move along the production possibility frontier. You could consider:
(i) Whether the switch in supply was in response to a change in demand.
(ii) If not, and if the demand for Y remained at the 1976 level, what might happen to the price of Y.
(iii) The effects on growth, and the position of the production possibility frontier.

3.6 FURTHER READING

Lipsey, R. G., *An Introduction to Positive Economics*, 5th edition (Weidenfeld & Nicolson, 1979)
Chapter 16: Background to the theory of supply.
Chapter 17: The theory of costs.
Chapter 18: The equilibrium of a profit-maximizing firm.

Samuelson, P., *Economics*, 11th edition (McGraw-Hill, 1980)
Chapter 23: Competitive Supply.
Chapter 24: Analysis of Costs and Long-run supply.

4 Elasticity

4.1 POINTS OF PERSPECTIVE

Consider the demand curves which are drawn in Figure 4.1 and which show the demand for a product such as electronic calculators in two separated markets, the London area market and a market for the rest of the United Kingdom. Demand curve D_2 is quite clearly flatter than D_1. Students are often tempted to use the flatness or steepness of a demand or supply curve to describe its elasticity – the responsiveness of demand or supply to a change in price. However, a careful inspection of Figure 4.1 reveals that the slope of the curves is misleading and that flatness or steepness is not a proper indicator of elasticity. In each market a twenty per cent reduction in price from £20 to £16 results in a doubling of the quantity which households intend to buy: despite their different slopes, the demand curves display identical elasticities whenever the price changes. In this example we could calculate the **average elasticity** when the price changes from £20 to £16. Strictly, however, elasticity is a measure of the response of demand to a price change at a **specific point** on a curve, and the concept should not be used to describe quite large changes in price.

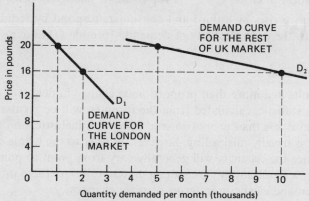

Fig 4.1 Demand curves with the same elasticities but different slopes

Whenever one variable responds to another variable, an elasticity can be estimated. Elasticity is an especially useful **descriptive statistic** of the relationship between any two variables because it is independent of the units, such as quantity and price units, in which the variables are measured. A knowledge of supply and demand elasticities is particularly useful to decision-makers both in firms and in government. If we are told, for example, that the demand elasticity of Scotch whisky is 2, then this single statistic contains the information that a one per cent price-rise causes a two per cent fall in quantity demanded. (Strictly, the elasticity is −2 as the price-rise causes a fall in quantity demanded, but the minus sign is frequently omitted.) The size of the elasticity will indicate the extent to which sales may drop when a tax is imposed upon Scotch whisky: the more elastic the demand (and supply) curves, the greater will be the fall in sales. Since the government's tax-revenue equals the amount of the tax multiplied by the after-tax quantity of sales, the government will experience the least loss in tax-revenue when it imposes a tax on goods with low demand and supply elasticities.

4.2   UNDERLYING CONCEPTS

1 The estimation of elasticity

Suppose that a businessman wishes to estimate how his customers will respond when the price of his product is increased. If he possesses perfect market information, as in perfect competition, there will be no problem: he simply reads off, from a chart or graph displayed on his office wall, the quantities that would be demanded at all possible prices. Unfortunately, many students at Advanced Level seem to think that all business decisions are made in this way! Businessmen, however, seldom if ever possess perfect information and this means that they cannot be sure how their customers will react to price changes. One method of estimating the elasticity of demand for a good is to collect data on the quantities actually bought at different prices in previous years – but the elasticity statistic which is obtained from such an exercise must be treated with caution. It will have been calculated on **ex post** rather than **ex ante** data: the amount **actually bought** may not have been the same as the quantity that households had planned or intended to buy. Also, conditions of demand and the general price-level may have changed over the years. To overcome these problems, a businessman could hire a market research team to go into the street with questionnaires, to ask people how much they would buy at various prices.

4.3   ESSENTIAL INFORMATION

1 Elasticity Formulae

When an examination question requires you to discuss the measurement and interpretation of elasticity statistics, you must bear in mind the data-collecting problems described in the preceding section: measurement of elasticity involves more than just a textbook formula. Nevertheless, once the information on the planned demand of households or the supply intentions of firms has been collected, a simple formula is used to estimate the elasticity:

(i) Price elasticity of demand $= \dfrac{\text{Proportionate change in quantity demanded}}{\text{Proportionate change in price}}$

(ii) Price elasticity of supply $= \dfrac{\text{Proportionate change in quantity supplied}}{\text{Proportionate change in price}}$

(iii) Income elasticity of demand $= \dfrac{\text{Proportionate change in quantity demanded}}{\text{Proportionate change in income}}$

(iv) Cross-elasticity of demand for Good A with respect to Good B $= \dfrac{\text{Proportionate change in quantity of A demanded}}{\text{Proportionate change in price of B}}$

For example, if the price rises by a third and consumers respond by reducing the quantity demanded by two-thirds, the price elasticity of demand – formula (i) above – is 2 (strictly -2).

2 Price elasticity of demand

If a price change results in a more than proportionate change in demand, demand is said to be **elastic**. The elasticity statistic, calculated from the formula, will be greater than 1. Similarly, if the change in demand is less than proportionate, demand is **inelastic**, and the elasticity statistic will be less than 1. It is usually misleading, however, to refer to the whole of a demand curve as elastic or inelastic since the elasticity will generally vary from point to point along the curve.

Before we show how the elasticity varies along the curve, it is useful to introduce an alternative way of describing demand elasticity in terms of price changes:

(i) If total **consumer expenditure increases** in response to a **price fall**, demand is relatively elastic.
(ii) If total **consumer expenditure decreases** in response to a **price fall**, demand is relatively inelastic.
(iii) If total **consumer expenditure remains constant** in response to a **price** fall, elasticity of demand = unity.

Figure 4.2 illustrates some possible changes in consumer expenditure which might follow a reduction in price. When the price falls from P_1 to P_2 in Figure 4.2a, total consumer expenditure **increases** by the shaded area k, but **decreases** by the area h. The area k, which represents the proportionate increase in the quantity demanded, is clearly larger than area h, which represents the proportionate change in price. Demand is thus elastic at all points on the demand curve between a and b on curve D_1. However, if the price falls from P_3 to P_4 on the same demand curve, the shaded area k′ is smaller than the area h′. Total consumer expenditure falls, and demand is inelastic at all points between c and d on the demand curve.

We are now in a position to explain the misleading generalization that a 'flat' demand curve is elastic and a 'steep' curve is inelastic. Moving along all linear (straight-line) demand curves

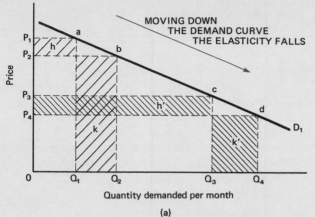

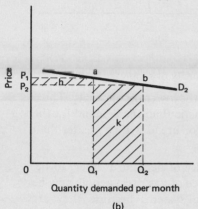

(a)

Fig 4.2 Price elasticity of demand (a) elasticity varies from point to point along a linear downward sloping curve (b) demand is elastic along this stretch of a 'flat' demand curve (c) demand is inelastic along this stretch of a steep demand curve (d) a rectangular hyperbola shows unit elasticity at all points on the curve

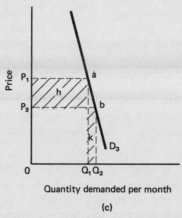

(b)

(c)

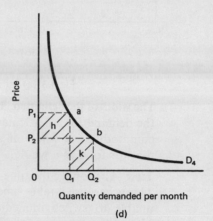

(d)

that slope down from left to right, elasticity of demand falls from point to point along the curve. The 'flat' demand curve illustrated in Figure 4.2b is really only the upper part of a curve which, if extended far enough rightwards or downwards, would eventually become inelastic in its lower reaches. Similarly, the 'steep' inelastic demand curve in Figure 4.2c is the lower part of a curve which would become elastic in its upper reaches if these could be included in the diagram.

Intuition suggests that if elasticity varies from point to point along a downward-sloping *linear* curve, then we require a *non-linear* curve to show a constant elasticity at all points. The rectangular hyperbola illustrated in Figure 4.2d is the special case of a non-linear demand curve which shows a unit elasticity at all points on the curve.

3 Infinite elasticity and zero elasticity

Infinitely elastic (or perfectly elastic) demand or supply can be represented by a horizontal curve, such as those drawn in Figure 4.3a. The diagram illustrates a trap awaiting the unwary student. In the case of the perfectly elastic demand curve, consumers demand an infinite amount at a price of P_2 or below; if the price rises above P_2, demand falls to zero as consumers switch to the perfect substitutes which are assumed to be available. In the case of the perfectly elastic supply curve, however, firms are prepared to supply an infinite amount at a price of P, or above. If the price falls below P_1, the firms refuse to supply any output onto the market!

Figure 4.3b illustrates a completely inelastic supply curve: whatever the price, the same amount is supplied onto the market. Similarly, completely inelastic demand would be shown by a vertical demand curve.

4 The determinants of demand elasticity

Substitutability When a perfect substitute for a product exists, consumers can respond to a price-rise by switching their expenditure to the substitute product. Commodities – for example, British motor-cars – which have close substitutes available tend to be in more elastic demand than those that do not.

Percentage of income Items on which many people spend a large proportion of their income, such as summer holidays, tend to be in more elastic demand than goods such as matches, on which only a fraction of income is spent.

Necessities v luxuries Necessities tend to be in inelastic demand, luxuries in elastic demand. Salt is often cited as a commodity with a very inelastic demand: it is a necessity, with no close substitutes, and expenditure on it is only a small part of most households' total spending.

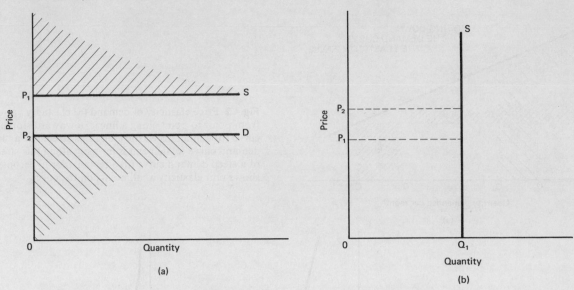

Fig 4.3 (a) Infinitely elastic supply and demand (b) zero elasticity of supply

The width of the definition The wider the definition of a commodity, the lower the elasticity. Thus, the demand for a particular brand of a commodity will be more elastic than the demand for the commodity as a whole. In a similar way, the elasticity of demand for bread will be greater than that for food as a whole.

Time The longer the time-period involved, the greater the elasticity of demand is likely to be. This is because it takes time to adjust to a change in price. If the price of gas rises, people may be unable to switch immediately to alternative household heating systems because they are 'locked in' to their existing investments in gas-fired appliances. However, the opposite may be true in certain circumstances: some consumers might react to a sudden increase in the price of cigarettes by giving up smoking altogether, and then gradually drift back to their old habits.

5 Price elasticity of supply

Supply curves normally slope upwards from left to right, and the mathematical properties of upward-sloping (or positive) curves are different from those of downward-sloping (or negative) curves. The key points to note are:

(i) **Any** straight-line (linear) supply curve drawn from the origin (point O) will display unit elasticity of supply **at all points** along the curve. This is illustrated in Figure 4.4a, where a doubling of the price causes an exact doubling of the quantity supplied.

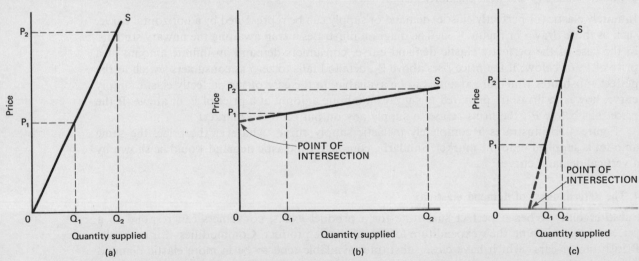

Fig 4.4 Price elasticity of supply (a) unit elasticity of supply (b) elastic supply (c) inelastic supply

(ii) The 'flat' supply curve drawn in Figure 4.4b is *elastic* at all points along the curve, since any price-change would result in a more than proportionate change in supply. But the elasticity *falls towards unity*, moving from point to point up the curve to the right.

(iii) Similarly, the 'steep' curve in Figure 4.4c is *inelastic* at all points, since any price-change results in a less than proportionate change in supply. But in this case the elasticity *rises towards unity*, moving from point to point up the curve.

(iv) However, as in the case of demand curves, the 'flatness' or 'steepness' of a supply curve is a misleading guide to its elasticity. The key point is not the flatness or steepness of the curve, but **whether the supply curve intersects the price axis or the quantity axis.**

The rule is:

(a) If a linear supply curve intersects the price axis, the curve is elastic at all points.

(b) If a linear supply curve intersects the quantity axis, the curve is inelastic at all points.

(c) If a linear supply curve intersects the origin, the elasticity is unity at all points along the curve.

In the case of non-linear supply curves, it is possible to use the rule to check the elasticity at a particular point on the supply curve by drawing a **tangent** to the point, and by noting the axis which the tangent intersects. We leave it as an exercise for the reader to do this, and also to draw a 'steep' supply curve intersecting the price axis. You will find that the curve is elastic at all points, showing that a 'steep' curve can be elastic!

6 The determinants of supply elasticity

Suppose that the demand for a good such as a car-component suddenly doubles at all prices. The factors which may determine whether supply is able to respond include:

(i) **The number of firms in the industry** Generally, the greater the number of firms in an industry, the more elastic is the industry supply.

(ii) **The length of the production period** If production converts inputs into outputs in the space of a few hours, supply will be more elastic than when several months are involved, as in agriculture.

(iii) **The existence of spare capacity** If spare capacity exists and if variable inputs such as labour and raw materials are available, it should be possible to increase production quickly in the short run.

(iv) **The ease of accumulating stocks** If it is easy to store unsold stocks at low cost, firms will be able to meet a sudden increase in demand by running down stocks. Likewise, they can respond to a sudden fall in demand and price by taking supply off the market and by diverting production into stock-accumulation.

(v) **The ease of factor substitution** Many firms produce a range of different products and are able to switch machines and labour from one type of production to another. If factors of production can be switched in this way, then the supply of one particular product will tend to be elastic.

(vi) **Time** The longer the time-period under consideration, the greater the ability of firms to adjust to a price-change. It is useful to distinguish three separate time-periods, the short run, the momentary period, and the long run:

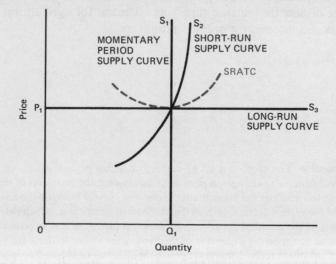

Fig 4.5 The elasticity of the supply curve varies with the time period

(a) **The short-run supply curve** The short-run supply curve of an individual firm is its short-run marginal cost curve. In Unit 3 it is explained how the impact of diminishing marginal returns to the variable inputs determines the shape of the MC curve.

(b) **The momentary period supply curve** Figure 4.5 illustrates the case of a firm on its short-run supply curve, S_2, producing an output Q_1 at price of P_1. If the price doubles, the firm will respond as soon as possible by increasing supply along S_2. However, in the momentary period the firm is unable to adjust at all. A vertical supply curve S_1, drawn through the existing output Q_1, represents the completely inelastic momentary supply curve.

(c) **The long-run supply curve** The perfectly elastic long-run supply curve, S_3, drawn in Figure 4.5 represents the special case of a firm in an industry with constant long-run average costs. In the special circumstances of Figure 4.5, a firm can increase output beyond Q_1 either by moving in the short run up S_2, or by moving in the long run along S_3 to a new size or scale of fixed capacity. The precise shape of the long-run supply curve will depend upon whether economies or diseconomies of scale are experienced, but in general we may expect long-run supply to be more elastic than short-run supply.

7 Income elasticity of demand

The income elasticity of demand – which measures how demand responds to a change in income – is always **positive** for a **normal** good and **negative** for an inferior good. The quantity demanded of an inferior good **falls** as income **rises**. Normal goods are sometimes further subdivided into **luxuries** or **superior goods**, for which the income elasticity of demand is greater than unity, and **essential** or **basic** goods with an elasticity of less than one. Although the quantity demanded of normal goods always rises as income rises, it rises more than proportionately with income for superior goods (such as dish-washers). Conversely, demand for a basic good such as soap rises at a slower rate than income.

8 Cross-elasticity of demand

This is a statistic which describes the complementary or substitute relationship between two commodities. A cross-elasticity of demand of -0.1 for bread with respect to the price of butter indicates that a ten per cent rise in the price of butter is associated with a one per cent fall in the demand for bread. In contrast, a cross-elasticity of $+0.8$ for margarine with respect to the price of butter shows that a ten per cent rise in the price of butter will result in an eight per cent increase in the demand for margarine. Whereas the mathematical sign of a cross-elasticity statistic depends on the nature of the relationship between the two commodities, the absolute size of the statistic indicates the strength of the relationship. Cross-elasticities are negative for complementary goods, and positive for substitutes. A cross-elasticity statistic very close to zero is likely when there is no complementary or close substitute relationship between two goods.

4.4   LINKS WITH OTHER TOPICS

There are three important applications of the elasticity concept in public finance, exchange-rate policy, and agriculture. The possible effects of the elasticity of supply and demand on government tax revenue are explained in Unit 17. Elasticity of demand for exports and imports has an important effect upon exchange-rate policy, which is the subject of Unit 28. Meanwhile, Unit 5 develops the theme of how the inelastic supply and demand for agricultural products results in very unstable prices and incomes for primary producers.

4.5   QUESTION PRACTICE

Essay Questions

Question 1 Define 'price elasticity of demand' and outline the factors which determine its value. Show the relevance of price elasticity in analyzing the effects of a rise in the price of petrol on the demand for different forms of transport.

(JMB: June 1980)

Understanding the Question You must start off by correctly defining price elasticity of demand as a measure of the responsiveness of demand to changes in **price only**. Briefly describe problems of measurement, but avoid the temptation to write too much on the mathematics of demand curves! Develop the answer by drawing on the coverage in the unit of the various factors, such as the existence of substitutes, which determine the value of the elasticity. The last part of the question is particularly important because it is impossible to rely on textbook definitions and formulae in answering a question of this type: your ability to think for yourself is being tested. Because of the lack of substitute fuels, demand for petrol for all forms of motor transport tends to be inelastic, though under some circumstances cycling, walking, and trains powered by electricity will provide alternatives. Demand for a particular form of motor transport, such as that provided by private cars, will be rather more price-elastic, as motorcycles and buses are substitutes. In each case, the effects of a petrol price-rise will vary with the percentage cost increase that this has on each form of transport.

A general rise in the price of petrol and oil-based products, resulting from a rise in the price of imported oil, would probably cause real incomes to fall. Some of the effects on the demand for different forms of transport might be the result of the income effect, as for example when people who feel poorer give up cars and switch to bus travel. It is of course completely impossible to analyse *all* the effects and 'feedbacks' in an examination answer. The examiner will be hoping that you can make intelligent use of the concept of price elasticity of demand in developing *some* of the possible lines of argument – perhaps noting at the same time that income and cross-elasticity of demand will also be involved.

Answer plan This question is in two fairly equal parts. The first requires recall of knowledge and explanation of a key economic concept. A fair attempt at the second part would be needed to secure a pass grade.

1 Define price elasticity of demand, stating the formula.
2 Explain, with diagrams, the main determinants.
3 Analyze the effects of a petrol price-rise. Credit is unlikely to be given for a detailed consideration of the *causes* of the price rise. The types of transport to consider would seem to be car, bus, train, aeroplane, cycling and walking. Choose perhaps two or three forms and look at the immediate direct effects, bringing in elasticity.
4 Finally, consider the more difficult indirect effects, for example the income effects and feedbacks.

Question 2

(a) Discuss briefly what is measured by the concept of 'the price elasticity of demand'.
(b) Explain how the value of the relevant price elasticity will play a critical role in determining the degree of success of the following policies:
    (i) An increase of 0.5 pence per unit in the price of electricity intended to reduce consumption by 10 per cent.
    (ii) An increase in admission charges by Football League clubs intended to increase gate receipts.
    (iii) The introduction of subsidies paid to producers of certain foods intended to reduce the cost of living.

(WJEC: June 1980)

Understanding the Question We have included this question as an example of some of the policy-making applications of the elasticity concept. In the first of the examples specified in the question, the success of the increase in the price of electricity is measured by the fall in the quantity demanded. If the price-rise represents a 20 per cent increase, for example, then the elasticity would have to be 0.5 in order to achieve the required fall in demand. If the true elasticity is 1.0, the policy would 'overshoot', causing a 20 per cent drop in demand.

In the second example, success is measured by the change in revenue (which equals **consumer expenditure**) rather than by the change in the quantity traded. This is a simple application of the rule which states that demand must be inelastic if a **rise** in consumer expenditure is to result from a **rise** in price.

The effects of a subsidy on the price of food are illustrated in Figure 4.6. Because demand for **all foods** is inelastic, a general food subsidy would result in a substantial fall in food prices. This is shown in Figure 4.6a. According to the question, however, only certain foods are to be subsidized. If consumers are able to switch from unsubsidized substitute foods, demand is likely to be elastic. Figure 4.6b shows how the main effect will be on sales and on producers' revenue rather than on the price of food and the cost of living.

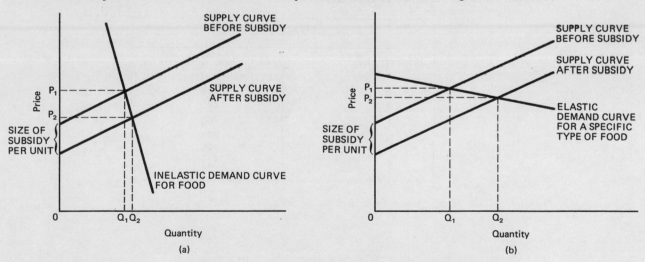

Fig 4.6 Food subsidies and the price of food (a) a substantial fall in the price of food when demand is inelastic (b) the main effect of the subsidy is on producer's revenue when demand is elastic

Answer plan

1 Describe how the elasticity is a descriptive statistic measuring the responsiveness of demand to a change in price.
2 A precise knowledge of the elasticity is required by the electricity board in order to reduce demand by an exact amount.
3 A general knowledge of the elasticity or inelasticity of demand is sufficient for the Football League clubs.
4 Whether a subsidy will reduce food prices and the cost of living will depend upon the range and type of foods being subsidized.

Question 3 Why would you expect the short-run supply of artificial flowers to be more price-elastic than that of potted plants? In what circumstances would you expect the reverse?

(London: June 1978)

Understanding the Question Generally, the elasticity of supply of agricultural products will be lower, in the short run at least, than the elasticity of supply of manufactured products. It is quite usual for an examination question to ask for a comparison of what determines the elasticity of supply of some manufactured product, in this case artificial flowers, and an agricultural product such as potted plants. You must be very careful to avoid falling into a trap which the Chief Examiner has prepared for you! On the demand side, potted plants and artificial flowers are close substitutes, but this is not a question about elasticity of demand. Having avoided this trap, the main body of the question is quite straightforward. You are expected to explain why the shorter length of the production period and the ease of stocking a non-perishable manufactured product most likely account for the greater ability of manufacturers to respond to a price change. However, you should be able to think of an ad hoc list of circumstances when the opposite might be true. There might be a single monopoly supplier of artificial flowers while a large number of small horticulturalists produce potted plants. Shortages of labour or raw materials, and the existence of full capacity, could prevent a manufacturer from increasing supply.

Answer plan

1 Define price elasticity of supply as the responsiveness of supply to a change in price.
2 Explain that artificial flowers are a manufactured product whereas a potted plant is an example of an agricultural product.
3 Introduce the determinants of elasticity of supply and suggest how they account for different short-run elasticities for manufactured and agricultural products.
4 The reverse may be true if different time-periods are considered, or if factors such as raw material shortages or full capacity affect manufacturers of artificial flowers.

Multiple Choice Questions

Question 4 If there is a free market in potatoes and if demand is completely inelastic, the most likely effect of an outstandingly good crop will be:
(a) to increase the total income of potato farmers
(b) to increase the price of potatoes
(c) to increase the quantity demanded
(d) to reduce the total income of potato farmers

Understanding the Question The correct answer (d) is obtained from simple supply and demand analysis. The demand curve is vertical, showing that the same quantity is demanded at all prices – so alternative (c) is clearly wrong. The new equilibrium will be where a 'lower' supply curve intersects the vertical demand curve. The new equilibrium price is lower than the old price, and farmers' income falls.

Questions 5 and 6 are based on the table below.

Demand Schedule for carrots	
Price in pence	Quantity demanded per week (tons)
3	600
4	480
5	400
6	300
7	280
8	245

Question 5 If the price increases from 5p to 6p the demand is
(a) inelastic
(b) of unit elasticity
(c) elastic
(d) perfectly elastic

Question 6 Between which prices is the elasticity of demand unitary?
(a) 4p and 5p
(b) 5p and 6p
(c) 6p and 7p
(d) 7p and 8p

Understanding the Questions You may encounter a problem if you use the elasticity formula to answer these questions. The elasticity statistic calculated for a price **rise** from 5p to 6p will differ from the statistic calculated for a price **fall** from 6p to 5p. This is because the formula calculates the **average elasticity** between two points on the demand curve and the answer obtained depends upon whether the upper or lower point is used as the base for the calculation. It is better, and much quicker, to use the simple rule described in the unit, to obtain the answers. Firstly calculate the total consumer expenditure at each price. The answer to question 5 is (c) because a **rise** in price is associated with a **fall** in consumer expenditure. Total consumer expenditure remains the same at 1960 pence between a price of 7p and 8p, so the answer to question 6 is (d).

Question 7 Which of the following statements concerning supply is (are) correct?
(1) The momentary period is that period in which supply is completely inelastic.
(2) In the short run, part of a firm's marginal cost curve is also its supply curve.
(3) Supply is usually more elastic in the short run than in the long run.

(a)	(b)	(c)	(d)
1, 2, 3 correct	1, 2 only	2, 3 only	1 only

Understanding the question This is a straightforward question which is testing your understanding of the supply curve and elasticity of supply. The correct answer is (b). Sometimes the **momentary period** may be called the **market period**: it is the period in which firms cannot bring extra supplies onto the market, or remove supply from the market.

Data Response Questions

Question 8 Comment on the significance for the British economy of the figures shown below and on the difficulties in interpreting them.

Industries with a money income elasticity of demand for imports greater than 2, and export elasticities of the same commodities, 1963–74.

	U.K. income elasticity of demand for imports	World income elasticity of demand for U.K. exports
Motor vehicles	3.7	0.9
Linoleum, leather cloth, etc.	3.5	1.2
Men's and boys' tailored outerwear	3.2	1.7
Radio and other electronic apparatus	2.9	1.8
Cans and metal boxes	2.8	0.6
Motor-cycles	2.7	0.9
Plastics moulding and fabricating	2.6	1.7
Domestic electrical appliances	2.6	1.1
Insulated wires and cables	2.6	1.0
Iron castings, etc.	2.6	1.3
Furniture and upholstery	2.5	2.2
Tobacco	2.5	1.1
Bedding, etc.	2.4	0.6
Overalls and men's shirts, underwear, etc.	2.4	2.0
Other textile industries	2.4	1.1
Pharmaceutical and toilet preparations	2.3	1.4
Women's and girls' tailored outerwear	2.3	1.1
Weatherproof outerwear	2.3	0.7
Miscellaneous manufacturing industries	2.3	1.8
Metal industries not elsewhere specified	2.2	1.2
Cardboard boxes, etc.	2.2	1.3
Dresses, lingerie, infants' wear, etc.	2.2	1.3
Telegraph and telephone apparatus	2.2	1.0
Production of man-made fibres	2.1	1.3
Other drink industries	2.1	1.0
Glass	2.1	1.2
Wire and wire manufactures	2.1	0.9
Miscellaneous stationers' goods	2.1	1.1
Biscuits	2.1	1.3
Other electrical goods	2.1	1.3

(Source): A. P. Thirlwall, *National Westminster Quarterly Bank Review*, February 1978.)

(London: June 1980)

Understanding the Question An income elasticity of demand of 2 for imported goods means that a one per cent increase in United Kingdom income results in a two per cent increase in imports. The data do not distinguish between an increase in **real income** and an increase in **money income** caused by a general price-rise. In the first case, people could have a high income elasticity of demand for foreign goods because they regard them as superior to British-made equivalents. However, if real income in Britain remains unchanged but money income rises with inflation, a high income elasticity of demand for imports may indicate the falling relative prices of imports. It may well be that the high income elasticity of demand for a product such as imported motor vehicles is due to both factors, superior quality and falling relative price. It would be helpful for the data to specify whether the elasticities are calculated for changes in money income or real income. You could also develop the point that it is difficult to compare like with like when making comparisons of income changes across different countries.

It is explained in the unit that the income elasticities of demand for luxuries are greater than unity. It is misleading, however, to class all the goods listed in the table as luxuries. The data do not tell us what the income elasticity of demand is, in the United Kingdom, for the British-made product. Nevertheless, British people may regard the imported products as superior substitutes for the home-made product.

The obvious conclusion to draw from the data is that if British income rises at the same rate as world income, then imports will rise faster than exports. However, the data do not tell us whether there are other industries with low U.K. income elasticities of demand for imports and high world income elasticities of demand for U.K. exports. It will also be the case that exports will rise faster than imports for the listed industries if British income remained unchanged at a time when world income is growing. Without further information, we cannot tell what will happen to the actual balance of trade.

Answer plan

1 Explain the meaning of income elasticity of demand.
2 If British income grows at the same rate as world income, imports will grow faster than exports in the listed industries, provided that supply is available.
3 Whether the balance of trade would improve or deteriorate in these circumstances will depend on the elasticities and relative importance of industries not included in the list.
4 Explain how other results might occur if United Kingdom and world income grow at different rates.
5 The elasticities may also change as other factors, such as price and quality, change with time.
6 The data do not indicate whether the elasticities are calculated for changes in money income or real income. It would also be useful to know how the elasticities have changed over time.

4.6 FURTHER READING

Marshall, B. V., *Comprehensive Economics,* 2nd edition (Longman, 1975)
Part Two: Chapter II: Theory of Value or Price. Stage 1: Section II Elasticity (or Responsiveness) of Supply and Demand

Burningham, D., editor, *Understanding Economics, an Introduction for Students* (Macmillan, 1978)
Chapter 5: Consumer Behaviour

Lipsey, R. G., *An Introduction to Positive Economics*, 5th edition (Weidenfeld & Nicolson, 1979)
Chapter 9 Elasticity of demand and supply

5 Agricultural Prices

5.1 POINTS OF PERSPECTIVE

Agriculture is an industry in which there are thousands of producers, few of whom can influence the market price by individual decisions to supply or not to supply. At the same time many agricultural products, for example soft wheat, are relatively uniform or **homogeneous** commodities for which the world price is a ruling market price. In other words, it would seem that agriculture approximates to the economist's abstraction of **perfect competition** as a market form. Yet, if we look more closely, we also see that agriculture is the industry in which governments of a variety of political persuasions have consistently intervened in order to support farm prices and agricultural incomes. In this unit we examine the causes of fluctuating prices and incomes, and compare some of the ways in which governments can intervene to create greater stability.

5.2 UNDERLYING CONCEPTS

Throughout history, agriculture has experienced two closely related problems. Firstly, there has been a **long-run downward trend in agricultural prices** relative to the prices of manufactures and services, and secondly, **agricultural prices and incomes have been unstable from year to year**. The long-run trend is largely explained by **shifts** in agricultural supply and demand curves through time, while the short-run instability results from the **inelastic nature** of agricultural supply and demand, and the effects of good and bad harvests on the position of the short-run supply curve from one year to another.

5.3 ESSENTIAL KNOWLEDGE

1 The long-run downward trend in the relative price of agricultural products

In Figure 5.1, the equilibrium price and output of food in an earlier historical period is shown at point E_1. Over time, both the supply and the demand for foodstuffs have increased, but the supply curve has shifted further to the right. Thus the new long-run equilibrium at E_2 represents a larger output at a lower price. The shift in the demand curve for food is explained mainly by an increase in the population and higher incomes. However, food is a necessity with a low income elasticity demand: when real income doubles, food consumption also increases, but by a smaller proportionate amount. Meanwhile, improvements in agricultural technology, such as the introduction of machinery and fertilizers, have rapidly increased farm yields, thereby causing the much greater long-run shift in supply.

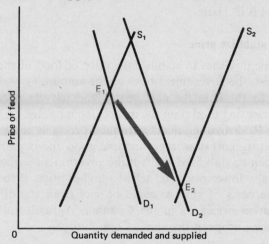

Fig 5.1 The long-run fall in agricultural prices

2 Price instability

The year-to-year instability in farm prices is caused by **low short-run elasticities of supply and demand** combined with **random fluctuations** in the harvest. Because of the length of the production period between planting and harvesting a crop, it is often appropriate to depict the short-run supply curve as a vertical or completely inelastic line. We are assuming that once the crop is harvested, it will be sold for whatever it will bring. The supply curve S_1, drawn in Figure 5.2a, represents supply in a 'normal' year. However, weather conditions and other factors outside the

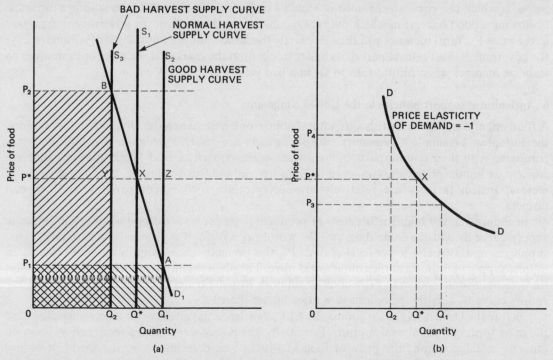

Fig 5.2 Short-run price instability of agricultural products (a) without government intervention, both prices and farm incomes fluctuate (b) target prices to stabilize farm incomes

farmers' control will shift the position of the supply curve from year to year. The size of the resulting price fluctuations will depend upon the price elasticity of demand. Demand for food-stuffs in general is inelastic because food is a necessity, so significant fluctuations in price occur as the vertical supply curve shifts up or down the relatively inelastic demand curve.

3 Fluctuations in agricultural incomes

From a farmer's point of view, fluctuations in his income are more serious than fluctuations in price. If demand is elastic, a **fall** in price causes a **rise** in farm income, but when demand is inelastic the opposite is true: income **falls** when price falls. Following a bad harvest, the supply curve in Figure 5.2a shifts to S_3 and agricultural incomes are represented by the rectangle OP_2BQ_2. In the event of a good harvest, the diagram shows that farm incomes decline to the area OP_1AQ_1. Paradoxically, therefore, a farmer may benefit more from a bad harvest than from a good one, when demand is inelastic.

4 Government policy to stabilize price

Suppose that a government wishes to stabilize the price of food at the 'normal' year price, P^*. Following a good harvest, the government buys up the amount $Q_1 - Q^*$ to prevent the market price falling below P^* to P_1. If in the next year a bad harvest occurs, the government will supplement supply by releasing food onto the market from its stocks; this will prevent the price from rising above P^* to P_2. Providing that agricultural products can be stored, that the government is prepared to meet the cost of storage, and that good and bad harvests are roughly evenly divided, then the price can be stabilized at P^*. If the government wished to make the policy self-financing, it could buy at a lower price and sell at a higher price. Price would now be stabilized within a range, and the costs of storage could be met from the difference between the two **intervention** or **stabilization** prices, as in the Common Agricultural Policy of the European Common Market (i.e. the European Economic Community).

5 Government policy to stabilize agricultural incomes

The policy described in the previous section is an example of a **buffer stock policy**. Although such a policy may successfully stabilize price, it does not necessarily stabilize agricultural incomes. In the event of a good harvest, farmers' income will be the rectangle OP^*ZQ_1 if the price is stabilized at P^*. Incomes will decline to the area OP^*YQ_2 following a bad harvest. Farm incomes thus vary directly with the size of production, the exact opposite of the situation in which prices are left free to fluctuate in conditions of inelastic demand.

How then can a government use a buffer stock policy to stabilize incomes rather than prices? The answer is provided by Figure 5.2b. The curve DD, with a unit elasticity, is drawn through X, the point which determines farm incomes in a normal year. DD shows the complete range of prices at which the government must operate its buffer stock policy if it is to stabilize incomes. Following a good harvest in which output Q_1 comes onto the market, the government must buy at the price P_3: farm incomes will then be exactly the same as in the normal year. Symmetrically, the government must release part of its buffer stocks onto the market at the price of P_4 in order to stabilize incomes when output falls to Q_2 in a bad year.

6 Agricultural support policies in the United Kingdom

A fundamental change in British agricultural policy took place when the United Kingdom joined the **European Economic Community**. British farmers are relatively high-cost producers when compared with their counterparts in areas such as the American Mid-West, although they are efficient within the constraints imposed by farm size and the British climate. In most agricultural sectors, British farmers are relatively low-cost producers when compared with European farmers.

In Figure 5.3, the high British costs of production are represented by the long-run domestic supply curve S_1. On the same diagram, the world price of food is shown by a perfectly elastic supply curve drawn at a lower level of costs P_1; this perfectly elastic supply curve represents an infinite supply of imports at the ruling world price. The diagram implies (perhaps unrealistically) that, without some system of protection or support, British farmers would produce no food: the supply curve S_1 cuts the price axis at a price higher than P_1.

Before the United Kingdom joined the EEC, **deficiency payments** or **producer subsidies** were the main form of agricultural support. Essentially, the policy was a **'cheap food' policy**, financed out of general taxation: the price of food in Britain was determined by the world price and subsidies were paid to British farmers to keep them in business. This is illustrated in Figure 5.3a. British farmers were guaranteed a price of P_2 at which they supplied Q_2. Nevertheless, domestic

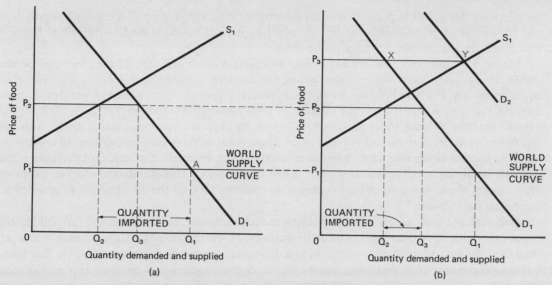

Fig 5.3 Farm price support systems (a) A deficiency payment system (b) A buffer stock system plus an external tariff

production was sold to the consumer at the world price P_1, the difference in the two prices being the deficiency payment to the farmers provided by the government. Under this system, the total demand Q_1 was determined at A. Quantity Q_2 was domestically produced and the remainder was imported.

In contrast, the **Common Agricultural Policy** (CAP) of the EEC has dealt with the problem of cheap imports by imposing an external **tariff** or **levy** which brings the price of imports up to the level of cost, plus normal profits, of European farmers. Suppose that the tariff is fixed at P_2 in Figure 5.3b. The total amount demanded will be reduced to Q_3 as compared to Q_1 in the deficiency payment scheme. Quantity Q_2 will still be domestically produced and the rest imported.

The external tariff on food imports is only one part of the CAP. As earlier indicated, the Community also operates a buffer stock policy with upper and lower stabilization prices. The problem has been that for many products the lower of these two intervention prices has been set too high, at a level such as P_3 in Figure 5.3b. An excess supply of XY is encouraged and the price can only be sustained if the Community continuously intervenes to purchase the over-production. This is represented by the shift in the demand curve to D_2. The effects of bad harvests in causing temporary leftward shifts in the short-run supply curve have been insufficient to reverse the accumulation of the butter 'mountains' and wine 'lakes' which have resulted from the policy.

7 Dynamic causes of price instability

Because of the length of the production period, there may be a **supply lag** between the decision to produce and the actual supply coming onto the market. We can assume that this year's price has

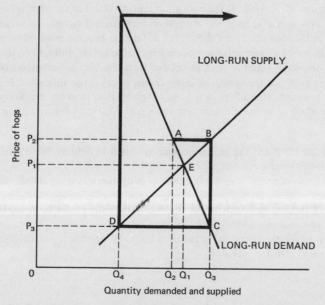

Fig 5.4 Dynamic causes of price instability: the cobweb theory

no effect on this year's supply but instead determines next year's supply. Year-long supply lags can be typical of crops such as wheat, though the original **'cobweb' model** – described below – was based on the market for hogs in the USA.

Figure 5.4 illustrates how the **adjustment mechanism** from one year to the next may be **unstable**, being associated with ever-increasing fluctuations in price and output. Suppose that equilibrium is at E where long-run supply and demand intersect. An outbreak of pig disease now disturbs the system and reduces the number of hogs coming onto the market to Q_2. Within the current year, an inelastic short-run supply curve can be depicted by a vertical line drawn through Q_2. A new price P_2, determined at point A on this vertical line, encourages farmers to supply Q_3 onto the market in the next year. Again, a vertical line can be drawn through Q_3 to represent the inelastic short-run supply curve next year. When the supply Q_3 comes onto the market, the price drops to P_3. Price and output then continue to oscillate around the equilibrium in a series of increasing fluctuations.

Although in the above example the cobweb model is associated with increasing instability, this is not inevitable. Try drawing a cobweb diagram in which the long-run supply curve is steeper than the long-run demand curve. Following a disturbance, price and output will again fluctuate, but the adjustment mechanism will now be stable, converging towards the long-run equilibrium at E.

5.4 LINKS WITH OTHER TOPICS

In recent years it has become fashionable to talk of **'supply side economics'**, which covers government **micro-economic policy**. This aims to improve the structure of the economy and the performance of industry. Government policy to support agricultural incomes and prices can be considered as a part of this wider micro-economic policy, other aspects of which are developed in Units 12, 13, and 14. Subsidies to the agricultural sector form part of public spending (Unit 17), whilst external tariffs influence trade (Unit 26) and the Balance of Payments (Unit 27).

5.5 QUESTION PRACTICE

Essay Questions

Question 1 'The Common Agricultural Policy (CAP) of the EEC operates in the interests of producers rather than of consumers'. Discuss.   *(London: June 1979)*

Understanding the Question In order to answer the question properly, you must firstly describe the main elements of the CAP and then go on to evaluate the policy. A brief description of the system of intervention prices and the external tariff is included in the earlier part of this unit, though you could also mention other aspects of the policy such as internal free trade and the financing of the policy. In evaluating the policy, one approach is to compare the CAP as a 'dear food policy' with a deficiency payments scheme as a 'cheap food policy'. The CAP uses the external tariff or levy to raise the price of imports to the guaranteed intervention price based on the higher costs of European farmers. A deficiency payments scheme would bring the price of European food down to the world price of imports. Although a deficiency payments system would appear to be in the interests of consumers, you should remember that many consumers are also the tax-payers who would finance the policy.

It does not matter whether you agree or disagree with the statement in the question, but it is advisable to set out both sides of the argument. In so far as the policy attempts to stabilize farmers' incomes it operates in the interests of producers. This may also be in the interest of consumers if conditions of greater certainty allow farmers to plan ahead: in the long run prices should fall as farmers become more efficient. Consumers should also benefit from conditions of greater certainty caused by stable prices, though, as the unit explains, intervention prices cannot completely stabilize both prices and farm incomes simultaneously. However, the main criticism of the CAP has been that the system of intervention prices is too inflexible. In particular, the lower intervention price is set too high: consumers have to pay higher prices than are necessary, and they also pay a second time through taxation to finance the over-production and the ever-accumulating buffer stocks.

Answer plan
1 Describe the aims of the CAP and the policy instruments used to achieve these aims – the external tariff, intervention prices, buffer stocks, etc.
2 Discuss whether a 'dear food policy' is in the interests of consumers. A diagram similar to Figure 5.3 could be included.
3 Explain how price and income stabilization can operate in the interests of both consumers and producers through the creation of conditions of certainty.
4 Evaluate the extent to which the intervention prices in the CAP operate against the interests of consumers because the prices are too high and inflexible.

Question 2 How and for what reasons is the behaviour of the prices of agricultural products likely to differ from those of manufactures?

(JMB: June 1977)

Understanding the Question This question provides a good test of your ability to apply the theoretical analysis explained in this unit. You will be expected to include the key analysis on how inelastic short-run supply and demand and random fluctuations in supply cause year-to-year fluctuations in agricultural prices and output. You could then go on to explain the long-run downward trend in agricultural prices and, if you have the time, the cobweb theory.

Answer plan

1 Agriculture is dominated by a large number of small producers who are 'price-takers'. In contrast, industrial firms are more likely to be monopolists or 'price-makers', with the market power to stabilize prices if they wish.

2 The agricultural production period is usually longer and individual farmers may be unable to accumulate stocks. Explain how an inelastic short-run supply curve results. Conversely, as manufacturers produce more durable goods, their supply curve tends to be more elastic.

3 Analyze year-to-year price instability in conditions of inelastic supply and demand.

4 Explain the long-run downward trend in agricultural prices relative to the price of manufactured goods. Manufactured goods are more income-elastic and producers may have the ability to create demand.

5 Supply lags in agriculture, illustrated by the cobweb theory, may also cause fluctuating prices.

Multiple Choice Questions

Question 3 When the demand for agricultural products is *elastic*
(a) a price fall results in a fall in a farmer's receipts
(b) a price fall makes no difference to a farmer's receipts
(c) a price rise makes no difference to a farmer's receipts
(d) a price rise results in a fall in a farmer's receipts.

Understanding the question Figure 5.2a in the unit illustrates the effect on a farmer's income when the price changes in conditions of **inelastic** demand. This question tests your ability to extend the analysis to conditions of elastic demand. The correct answer is (d). Alternatives (b) and (c) would only be correct if elasticity was unity at all points on the demand curve, and (a) would be correct if demand was inelastic.

Question 4

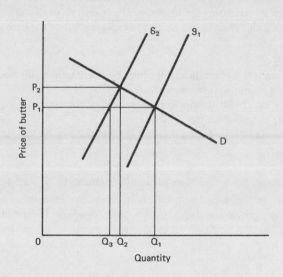

In the above diagram, the demand curve for butter is constant but the supply curve has been shifted to S_2. The European Commission uses its butter mountain stockpile to stabilize the price at P_1. Thus the change in the butter mountain will be:

(a) $Q_1 - Q_3$
(b) OQ_2
(c) $Q_2 - Q_3$
(d) $Q_1 - Q_2$

Understanding the question This is a straightforward case of excess demand at the fixed price of P_1. The quantity supplied of Q_3 is less than the quantity demanded Q_1, thus the difference $Q_1 - Q_3$ is the reduction in the butter stockpile. This quantity is put on the market by the European Commission to satisfy the excess demand. Thus (a) is the correct alternative.

OQ_2 shows market quantity without price controls.

$Q_2 - Q_3$ is the difference between quantity supplied at different prices on the new supply curve.

$Q_1 - Q_2$ shows the reduction in quantity demanded when price rises to P_2.

Data Response Questions

Question 5

'Cocoa traders were puzzled yesterday by news from Brazil that Cacex, the state-controlled export agency, had freed for export 300 000 bags (of 60 kilos) of new-crop cocoa-beans and a further 300 000 bags of cocoa products.

'The announcement comes at a time when the leading cocoa-exporting countries, including Brazil, are supposed not to be selling until prices reach an unspecified minimum level. In fact the Cocoa Producers' Alliance is to meet in Accra from February 25–29 to discuss the progress of the decision to withhold supplies from the market and consider setting up a support fund.

'Meanwhile, it now appears that the producers are willing to resume selling if prices exceed £1510 a tonne, according to an official of the Ghana Cocoa Marketing Board speaking to Reuter.

'On the London market the shipment price for Ghana cocoa was £1524 a tonne, but Brazilian cocoa is somewhat cheaper and still below £1510. On the futures market the May position was marginally higher yesterday at £1462, after falling to £1447.

'Cocoa prices have been sustained recently by the decision of the Ivory Coast to stockpile the new crop until the market rises to a more "reasonable" level. Other producers, notably Brazil, have declared they will not be selling either. But traders noted that, while Brazil had sold a considerable percentage of its main crop before withdrawing from the market, there was a considerable quantity of West African cocoa, including that held by the Ivory Coast, yet to be sold.'

(Source: Financial Times, 16 January 1980.)

(a) Explain what the Cocoa Producers' Alliance was attempting to do, and the likely consequences of the Brazilian action. (8)

(b) What aspects of the primary products market encourage the producers to behave in this way? (12)

(SUJB: June 1981)

Understanding the Question Although some of the ways in which a government can intervene in the market to stabilize agricultural prices have been explained in the unit, no mention has been made of producers' *cartels*. A cartel is a price ring in which all the producers, with the encouragement of their respective governments, agree to behave as a single monopolist. Output is restricted below demand in order to force up the price. Usually, the main purpose of an agricultural cartel is to increase producers' incomes, though prices may also be stabilized. However, as the unit explains, the ability of a price-rise to increase incomes depends upon demand being inelastic. In a world recession, demand in industrial countries is likely to be elastic and in these conditions the members of the cartel will accumulate large unsold stocks and experience falling incomes. An individual member of the cartel may then be tempted to renege on the agreement. It will release its unsold stocks onto the market at a lower price, thereby increasing the income of the country's producers. As a result the cartel may collapse. It is worth noting that this analysis can be used to explain some of the behaviour of the oil-producers' cartel OPEC.

Answer plan

1 The aim of the Alliance is to increase producers' incomes by restricting supply and forcing up the price.

2 The Brazilian action would appear to undermine the cartel.

3 The formation of the cartel may be an attempt to reverse the long-run downward trend in agricultural prices. It is also a reaction to year-to-year price instability.

4 The Brazilian action is encouraged by falling incomes in conditions of elastic demand.

5.6 FURTHER READING

Marshall, B. V., *Comprehensive Economics,* 2nd edition (Longman, 1975) Part I: Chapter 3: Some Major Industries

Swann, D., *The Economics of the Common Market,* 4th edition (Penguin, 1978) Chapter 6: Common Policies

6 Perfect Competition and Monopoly

6.1 POINTS OF PERSPECTIVE

1 Market structure and the theory of the firm

Perfect competition and monopoly are examples of **market structures** or **market forms**. They are opposite or polar extremes which separate a spectrum of market structures known as **imperfect competition**. Figure 6.1 illustrates the main types of market structure, including monopolistic competition and oligopoly which we shall examine in Unit 7 on imperfect competition. Monopoly itself can be considered to be the most extreme form of imperfect competition, since there is no competition at all within an industry if a single firm produces the whole of an industry output.

Nevertheless, monopoly is usually a relative rather than an absolute concept. This is because a firm will almost always experience some competition from substitute products produced by firms in other industries, even when it has an absolute monopoly in the production of a particular good or service.

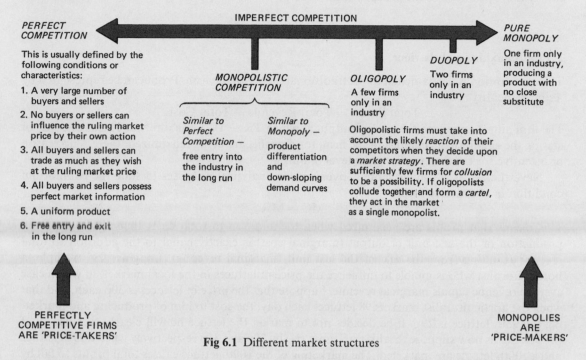

Fig 6.1 Different market structures

Although the analysis in this unit is restricted to perfect competition and pure monopoly, you must avoid the temptation to consider either of these two market structures as typical or representative of the real world. Pure monopoly is exceedingly rare; the **public monopolies** or nationalized industries, such as the electricity industry, provide perhaps the best examples. Perfect competition is actually non-existent – it is a **theoretical abstraction** or model, defined by the conditions which are listed in Figure 6.1. Some economists argue that the emphasis given to perfect competition encourages students to adopt a false perspective in the belief that a perfect market is an attainable 'ideal'. This view will be explored in rather greater depth in Unit 9. As you proceed through this unit, remember how perfect competition is essentially an unrealistic market structure, but note how it provides a 'bench-mark' by which we may judge the desirable or undesirable properties of the imperfectly competitive market structures of the world we live in.

2 The traditional theory of the firm

For many years the theory of the firm was principally concerned with the nature of perfectly competitive markets. The development of this theory owes much to the great nineteenth century British economist, Alfred Marshall. During Marshall's lifetime the British economy was still dominated by a large number of small firms, for many of which a single owner/decision-maker, or **entrepreneur**, could be identified. Thus, perfect competition may have been a reasonable approximation to what the economy was like in the late nineteenth century.

3 Alternative theories of the firm

During the first half of the twentieth century, many economists became dissatisfied with perfect competition as *the* theory of the firm. Their dissatisfaction was a response to the growth in the size of firms and the increasing domination of markets by a small number of large business enterprises. Theoretical models of monopoly and imperfect competition were developed by Edward Chamberlin and Joan Robinson in an attempt to give a greater realism to the theory of the firm. More recently, some economists have attacked the **profit-maximizing** assumption that is fundamental to the traditional theories of monopoly, imperfect competition and perfect competition. The 'new' theories of the firm are called **managerial theories** and **organizational** (or **behavioural**) **theories**: both claim to be more *realistic* and hence better at explaining actual behaviour than the traditional profit-maximizing theories of the firm. Managerial theories, popularized by J. K. Galbraith in his book *The New Industrial State* (1967), take as their starting point the split between shareholders as owners and managers as decision-makers in large modern business corporations. It is argued that managers aim to maximize **managerial objectives**, such as sales, growth, and managerial career prospects, rather than shareholders' profits. In contrast, organizationalists such as Professor Herbert Simon, a winner of the Nobel Prize for Economics, see the firm as an organization or **coalition** of different groups, such as managers, production workers, research scientists, etc. The firm is a **'satisficer'** rather than a **maximizer**, attempting to satisfy the aspirations of the groups which make up the coalition.

6.2 UNDERLYING CONCEPTS

1 Profit-maximizing behaviour

This assumption is fundamental to the traditional theory of the firm. Profit can be represented by a simple identity:

$$\text{Total Profits} \equiv \text{Total Revenue} - \text{Total Cost.}$$

The firm aims to produce the level of output at which TR − TC is maximized. This is one way of stating the **equilibrium condition** of the firm, for if profits are being maximized, there is no reason or incentive for the firm to change its level of output.

Nevertheless, it is usually more convenient for analytical purposes to state the equilibrium condition in alternative form:

$$\text{MC} = \text{MR}$$

This means that profits are maximized when the addition to total costs that results from the production of the last unit of output (marginal cost) is exactly equal to the addition to total revenue resulting from the sale of the last unit (marginal revenue). Imagine, for example, a horticulturalist who is unable to influence the price of lettuces in the local market, in which case average revenue equals marginal revenue. Suppose that the price of lettuces is 30p each, and that when the horticulturalist markets 98 lettuces each day, the cost to him of producing and marketing the 98th lettuce is 29p. If he decides not to market the lettuce he will clearly sacrifice 1p of profits. Let us now suppose that his total costs rise by 30p and 31p respectively when a 99th lettuce and a 100th lettuce are marketed. The marketing of the 100th lettuce causes total profits to fall by 1p, but the 99th lettuce neither adds to nor subtracts from total profits: it represents the level of output at which profits are exactly maximized. To sum up:

1 If MC < MR, it pays to increase output (disequilibrium condition)
2 If MC > MR, it pays to decrease output (disequilibrium condition)
3 If MC = MR, it pays to keep output unchanged (equilibrium condition) provided that the MC curve cuts the MR curve from below.

2 The concept of normal profit

The concepts of normal and abnormal (or supernormal) profit are completely abstract concepts, which have nothing to do with how an accountant will measure a company's profits. **Normal profit** is defined as the minimum level of profit required to keep existing firms in production, yet being insufficient to attract new firms into the industry. As such, normal profit is regarded as a necessary cost of production, which is included in the average cost curve. **Abnormal profit** is defined as any extra profit over and above normal profit. We shall now examine what happens to abnormal profits in conditions of perfect competition and monopoly.

6.3 ESSENTIAL INFORMATION

1 Short-run equilibrium in conditions of perfect competition

Perfect competition can be defined in terms of the **conditions of perfect competition**, which are listed in Figure 6.1. While you must learn the conditions of perfect competition, it is seldom relevant to an examination question merely to repeat the list. Instead, you must learn to use the conditions to analyze the essential properties of a perfectly competitive firm and industry in equilibrium, compared with those of a monopoly in equilibrium. For example, the assumptions that a perfectly competitive firm can sell as much as it wishes at the ruling market price, and that it cannot influence the ruling market price by its own actions, allow us to say that the firm is a **'price-taker'**. The perfectly competitive firm faces an **infinitely elastic demand curve**, determined by the ruling market price in the industry as a whole. This horizontal demand curve or price line is also the perfectly competitive firm's **average revenue** and **marginal revenue curve.**

To show the equilibrium output of a perfectly competitive firm in the short run, we superimpose this horizontal average and marginal revenue curve upon the average and marginal cost curves which were derived in Unit 3. Using the equilibrium condition MC = MR, the resulting equilibrium output is illustrated at Q_1 in Figure 6.2a. Total abnormal profits at this output are represented by the shaded area obtained by subtracting the total cost area ($OC_1 \times Q_1$) from the total revenue area ($OP_1 \, y \, Q_1$).

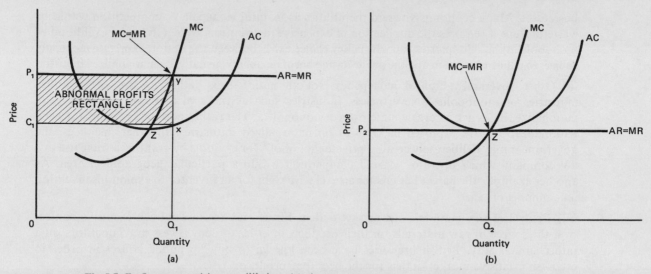

Fig 6.2 Perfect competition equilibrium (a) short-run equilibrium (b) long-run equilibrium

2 Long-run equilibrium in conditions of perfect competition

In order to distinguish between short-run and long-run equilibrium in perfect competition, we assume complete freedom of entry and exit by firms in and out of the industry in the economic long run. The market price signals to firms whether abnormal profits, normal profits or losses can be made. The existence of abnormal profits will provide the **incentive** for new firms to enter the industry, and, in a similar way, existing losses will create the incentive for firms to leave. As illustrated in Figure 6.3, the entry of new firms causes the industry supply curve to shift rightwards and the ruling market price falls. Symmetrically, the departure of firms causes the industry supply curve to shift leftwards and the price line rises. Long-run equilibrium will occur when there is no incentive for firms to enter or leave the industry: this is represented by the output Q_2 at the price of P_2 in Figures 6.3 and 6.2b. The total revenue area now equals the total cost area, illustrating the fact that abnormal profits have been competed away. It must be stressed at all times that it is **impersonal market forces** and individual self-interest, operating in conditions of freedom of entry and exit, which bring about this long-run equilibrium outcome.

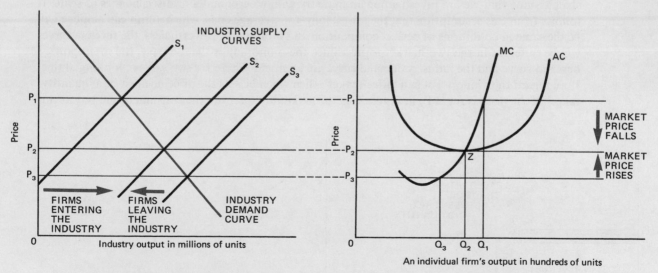

Fig 6.3 Perfect competition long run equilibrium: the entry and exit of firms produces a long-run equilibrium for an individual firm output Q_2 and price P_2

3 The causes of monopoly

An effective monopoly must be able to exclude competitors from the market through **barriers to entry**. However, the closer the substitutes that competitors can produce, and the more elastic the demand curve facing the firm, the weaker the monopoly position. A monopoly is strongest when it produces an essential good for which there are no substitutes. Monopoly is likely to exist under the following circumstances:

(i) Public utility industries Utility industries such as the gas, electricity, water and telephone industries experience a particular marketing problem. They produce a service which is delivered through a distribution grid or network of pipes or cables into millions of separate homes and businesses. Many economists regard the utilities as **'natural monopolies'**: competition would be wasteful since it requires the duplication of expensive distribution grids. Given the likelihood of monopoly in these industries, a **public policy choice** exists between the option of **private monopoly subject to public regulation** and the **public ownership of monopoly**, usually as a **nationalized industry.**

(ii) Other government-created monopolies Not all nationalized industries are either utility industries or monopolies. Nevertheless, industries such as the coal and rail industries were nationalized in order to create state-owned monopolies. The rather complex reasons for such nationalizations are explored in Unit 14 on nationalized industries. In other instances, the government may deliberately create a private monopoly, for example by granting a **franchise** to a TV company which operates without competition within a particular geographical area. As another example, the **patent law** creates an exclusive right for an inventor to exploit his invention for a number of years.

(iii) Control of raw materials and market outlets Firms may try to establish exclusive control over the source of raw materials for their products in order to deny access to competitors. In a rather similar way, British breweries have been known to buy up public houses in order to establish exclusive market outlets for the beer they produce.

(iv) Advertizing as a barrier to entry It is sometimes argued that small firms are prevented from entering an industry because they cannot afford the minimum level of advertizing which is necessary to persuade retailers to stock the goods they produce. Their products are 'crowded out' of the market by the mass advertizing, brand-imaging, and other marketing strategies of much larger established firms.

(v) Economies of scale Many industries, for example the aircraft-building industry, are **'decreasing cost' industries** with scope for perhaps unlimited economies of scale. In most circumstances, however, the **market size** will limit the number of firms that can exist in an industry and simultaneously benefit from full economies of scale. The existence of economies of scale is a major cause of the growth of large firms and monopoly in manufacturing industry. It may also explain how a large supermarket can monopolize the grocery trade in the limited market of a small town or suburb as a result of driving small grocery stores out of the business.

4 Monopoly equilibrium

Despite the likelihood of economies of scale in conditions of monopoly, for the time being we shall assume that we are investigating an industry with **no economies or diseconomies of scale**. It follows from this assumption that the lowest long-run average costs which a firm can achieve will be the same in conditions of perfect competition and monopoly. Nevertheless, the **revenue curves** will be different in the two market forms. Since the monopoly is the industry, the monopolist's demand curve and the industry demand curve are identical. There are two ways of looking at this. If we regard the monopolist as a **'price-maker'**, then when he sets the price he must be a **'quantity-taker'**. If the price is set at P_1 in Figure 6.4a the maximum quantity the consumers will buy at this

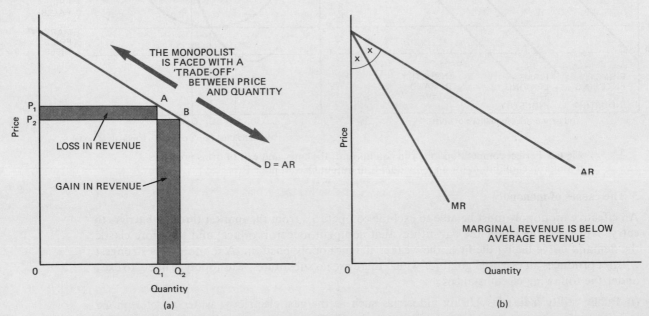

Fig 6.4 The relationship between average revenue and marginal revenue in monopoly. (a) MR equals the gain in revenue minus the loss in revenue (b) the MR curve is always below the AR curve

price is Q_1. Alternatively, if the monopolist acts as a **'quantity-setter'**, the demand curve determines the maximum price the monopolist can charge in order successfully to sell the chosen quantity. This is an example of a **'trade-off'**, an important economic concept which is closely related to **opportunity cost**. A problem of choice exists because the monopolist does not possess the freedom to set both price and quantity: if he acts as a price-maker, the demand curve determines the maximum output he can sell, and vice versa.

Since the demand curve shows the price the monopolist charges for each level of output, it is also the monopolist's average revenue curve. The demand curve is not the marginal revenue curve, which must be below the average revenue curve. We can use Figure 6.4 to explore the relationship between the AR and MR curves in conditions of monopoly. If the monopolist decides to produce output Q_1 in Figure 6.4a, the area OQ_1AP_1 will represent total revenue. When output is increased by one unit to Q_2, total revenue changes to the area OQ_2BP_2. Two shaded areas are drawn on the diagram. The area marked as the **'gain in revenue'** represents the extra unit sold multiplied by the new price – or the average revenue per unit at the new level of output. The other shaded area shows the **'loss in revenue'** which results from the fact that all the units of output comprising the previous level of output, Q_1, must now be sold at the price of P_2 rather than P_1. The marginal revenue associated with Q_2 is obtained by subtracting the loss in revenue from the gain in revenue (or average revenue). The resulting MR curve which is drawn in Figure 6.4b is twice as steep as the AR curve. This will always be the case providing that the monopolist's demand or AR curve is linear (a straight line), though this mathematical property will not apply if the AR curve is non-linear.

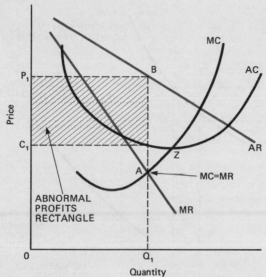

Fig 6.5 Monopoly equilibrium

The equilibrium output in conditions of monopoly is illustrated in Figure 6.5. Equilibrium is determined at point A, where MC = MR. It is worth repeating that the equilibrium condition MC = MR applies to **any firm**, whatever the market structure, as long as the firm is a profit-maximizer. You must avoid the temptation to read off the equilibrium price at point A: point B on the AR curve locates the monopolist's equilibrium price.

As in the case of short-run equilibrium under perfect competition, the monopolist makes abnormal profits, represented by the shaded area of Figure 6.5. However, the existence of barriers to entry allows the **abnormal profits to persist into the long run**, whereas in perfect competition abnormal profits are essentially temporary.

5 The meaning of economic efficiency

Before we attempt a comparison of the desirable or undesirable properties of perfect competition and monopoly, it is necessary to explain *some* of the meanings which economists attach to the word efficiency:

(i) Productive efficiency This is often called **technical efficiency**, although in fact the two concepts are slightly different. A technically efficient oil-fired engine may be economically inefficient if the cost of oil greatly exceeds the cost of fuel for a less technically efficient engine. To achieve productive efficiency, or **cost efficiency**, a firm must use the techniques which are available **at the lowest possible cost**. Productive efficiency is measured by the **lowest point on a firm's average cost curve**.

(ii) Allocative efficiency This rather abstract concept is of crucial importance to the understanding of economic efficiency. Allocative efficiency occurs when **marginal cost is equated to price in**

all the industries in the economy. If all industries are perfectly competitive and if equilibrium prices prevail, allocative efficiency will automatically occur (providing that we ignore the existence of **externalities** discussed in Unit 8). If you check back to Figures 6.2 and 6.3, you will see that P = MC in conditions of perfect competition. Let us look more closely at this. The price, P, indicates the **value in consumption** placed by buyers on an extra unit of output. At the same time, MC measures the **value in production** of the resources needed to produce the extra unit of output. Suppose that P > MC, as is the case in monopoly: households will pay for an extra unit an amount greater than the cost of producing it. Allocative inefficiency results. Total consumer satisfaction can be increased by transferring resources out of industries in which they are currently employed, into this particular industry, up to the point where P = MC. Resources will be allocated efficiently, for a given distribution of income, when it is no longer possible to change the allocation of resources without reducing the total utility obtained in consumption.

(iii) Distributional efficiency is achieved when the goods produced in the economy are distributed to the consumers who actually want them. Any reduction in choice, for example from a rationing scheme, will reduce this kind of efficiency. No one should be forced to accept one commodity if he prefers a different commodity which is also available. If a reallocation of commodities between consumers would increase the consumers' total utility, given the existing income distribution, then the initial allocation must have been distributionally inefficient.

6 Evaluating perfect competition and monopoly

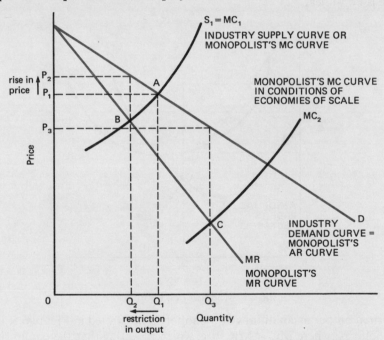

Fig 6.6 The effects of economies of scale on price and output in monopoly

If you refer back to Figures 6.2b and 6.3, you will see that a perfectly competitive firm achieves both productive and allocative efficiency in long-run equilibrium. (The productively efficient output is the lowest-cost output, shown at point Z in Figures 6.2 and 6.3 – it is often called the **optimum output** of the firm.) Strictly speaking, however, the firm will be allocatively efficient only if all other industries are perfectly competitive and if there are no externalities present. In contrast, in conditions of monopoly, average cost is above the minimum possible level, and price is not equated to marginal cost. In Figure 6.6, the analysis is extended to compare monopoly with the whole of a perfectly competitive industry, rather than with a single firm within the industry. The curve S_1 represents the supply curve of a perfectly competitive industry or the MC curve of a monopoly if all the firms aggregate together to form a monopoly. In conditions of perfect competition, industry price P_1 and output Q_1 are located at point A. In contrast, monopoly price P_2 and output Q_2 are determined at point B where MR = MC. The diagram neatly illustrates the standard case against monopoly that it **restricts output** and **raises the price**. Furthermore, this restriction of output is at a point above minimum average cost, resulting therefore in productive inefficiency.

Consider, however, the possibility that a monopoly, but not a perfectly competitive firm, can **benefit from economies of scale**. The curve MC_1 is no longer relevant to the analysis of monopoly price and output, which is now determined at point C. The monopoly price P_3 is now lower and output Q_3 is higher than those achieved in perfect competition. It is possible that the benefits which result from economies of scale may exceed the productive and allocative efficiency losses which occur in monopoly. In these circumstances, monopoly may be viewed as being preferable to perfect competition.

6.4 LINKS WITH OTHER TOPICS

Various other aspects of the behaviour or conduct of monopolies, such as price discrimination towards different groups of customers, are examined in Unit 7 on imperfect competition. Because the market price conveys misleading information in conditions of monopoly, the existence of monopoly provides a very important form of market failure, the subject of Unit 8. Some descriptive aspects of the growth of monopoly are introduced in the context of the size and growth of firms (Unit 10), while Unit 12 examines government policy towards monopoly and some possible justifications for the existence of monopoly, additional to the economies of scale argument introduced in this unit.

6.5 QUESTION PRACTICE

Essay questions

Question 1 Discuss the circumstances under which a firm, operating in a perfectly competitive industry, would continue to produce at a loss.

(AEB: November, 1978)

Understanding the Question The question is testing whether you can apply the logic of the profit-maximizing behaviour assumed in the theory of the firm to loss-making situations. It is also testing your competence in distinguishing between short-run and long-run equilibrium in perfect competition.

Answer plan

1 State the aim of the firm in terms of **either** profit maximization **or** loss minimization.
2 Define the economic short run and explain how a firm will incur losses equal to total fixed costs if it chooses to produce a zero output in the short run.
3 Explain how it is possible to reduce the loss below the level of TFC by producing the output for which MR = MC, if price or average revenue is greater than average variable cost. This is explained in Unit 3.
4 Introduce the economic long run and explain that if the loss continues into the long run, the firm should close down. It will never be consistent with profit-maximizing behaviour for a firm to produce at a loss in the long run. Perhaps add a sentence or two on whether the firm expects the loss to be temporary or to persist into the long run.

Question 2 Comment on the significance of the main distinctions between perfect competition and monopoly as market forms.

(London: June 1978)

Understanding the Question You must avoid the temptation to write separate accounts of perfect competition and monopoly or simply to list the conditions of perfect competition. Nevertheless, you can use the conditions of perfect competition to explain the main distinctions between perfect competition and monopoly. For example, the lack of barriers to entry in perfect competition is significant in explaining how market forces compete away abnormal profits, thereby resulting in productive efficiency. Similarly, the perfectly elastic price-line or demand curve facing the individual firm in perfect competition is significant in explaining why allocative efficiency occurs in this market form.

It would be difficult to obtain a good grade without some evaluation of perfect competition and monopoly in terms of productive and allocative efficiency. However, there is another approach to the question which would earn some marks. Some economists believe that the really important distinction between the two market forms is the extent to which they realistically model the actual behaviour of firms and the structure of industries. According to this view, important parts of the economy are increasingly dominated by monopoly, whereas perfect competition is merely a theoretical and unreal abstraction. Other economists might reply that an abstract model may still be useful, particularly if it exposes the undesirable features of monopoly. There might be advantages in attempting to break up monopolies and in shifting the system towards the supposed 'ideal' state of perfect competition.

Answer plan

1 List the major distinctions between perfect competition and monopoly as market forms.
2 Explain the significance of barriers to entry, comparing long-run equilibrium in perfect competition and monopoly in terms of productive efficiency.
3 Explain the significance of the completely elastic price-line in perfect competition, and the concept of allocative efficiency.
4 Introduce the possible benefits of economies of scale in conditions of monopoly.
5 Discuss the significance of the realism of the two market forms.

Question 3 What is meant by 'freedom of entry'? From the cases of ship-building, legal practice, and retailing illustrate the kinds of limitation on the freedom of firms to enter markets. Discuss whether the complete freedom of entry to any market is either possible or desirable.

(JMB: June 1978)

Understanding the Question Markets do not necessarily have a stable membership: both buyers and sellers may enter or leave over time. The ease with which sellers are able to move in or out is determined by the 'freedom of entry'. Perfect competition, which assumes perfect mobility of factors of production, has complete freedom of entry, except in the short run. Conversely, in imperfect competition there is **restricted entry** and in pure monopoly **no entry**. The limitations on entry vary between different markets, as the three cases illustrate:

1 Shipbuilding: Economies of scale and capital costs are the main entry barriers. They demonstrate the general importance of cost and the availability of inputs as a limitation. **Indivisibilities** may also reduce freedom of entry. An indivisibility occurs when particular types of capital can only be feasibly employed in certain minimum units. In recent British experience, the **nationalization** of shipbuilding considerably reduced freedom of entry, though the unprofitable state of the industry made it unlikely that large operators would wish to enter even if they were free to do so.

2 Legal practice: The length of the training period, an ability requirement, and the need to pass professional examinations are the principal barriers to entry. In the case of barristers, the cost of financing the training period is an important consideration. Some people argue that the training period and the required entrance qualifications act as a restrictive practice to deliberately restrict entry and competition.

3 Retailing: Retailing is not a single market but a series of separated markets with barriers of various types between the markets. The time and cost involved in travelling between shops and other retail outlets may prevent consumers from obtaining information about market conditions; this important barrier to competition explains why a shop may be an effective monopoly in a particular local area. In multiple retailing and department stores, economies of scale may provide a barrier. **Exclusive outlets**, such as petrol-stations which only sell one brand of petrol, **price-cutting, advertizing**, and **brand-imaging**, are **market strategies** which are also used to prevent effective competition.

In the last part of the question, candidates must distinguish clearly between possibility and desirability: in essence, the distinction between positive and normative economics. Professional qualifications which restrict entry may be desirable if they preserve standards or promote public safety. In utility industries, such as gas or electricity, competition might be wasteful.

Answer plan
1 Define freedom of entry in the context of different market forms.
2 Discuss barriers to entry in the three specified cases.
3 Explain that the possibility of complete freedom of entry depends upon the assumptions underlying perfect competition as a separate market form.
4 Consider the desirability of entry barriers in terms of their economic consequences. What is desirable for an established firm may not be desirable for a firm attempting to gain entry to the market, or to the community in general.

Multiple Choice Questions

Questions 4, 5 and 6
(a) Both the assertion and the reason are true statements, and the reason is a correct explanation of the assertion.
(b) Both the assertion and the reason are true statements, but the reason is not a correct explanation of the assertion
(c) The assertion is true but the reason is a false statement
(d) The assertion is false but the reason is a true statement

Assertion		*Reason*
Question 4 A profit-maximizing monopolist will charge the lowest possible price for his product	because	the monopolist may benefit from economies of scale.
Question 5 In long-run equilibrium firms in perfect competition make only normal profits	because	firms in perfect competition always act in the public interest.
Question 6 The demand curve facing a perfectly competitive firm is infinitely elastic	because	perfect substitutes exist for the firm's output.

Understanding the Questions These are examples of the **'assertion/reason'** type of question set by the London and Joint Matriculation examining boards. Alternative (d) is the correct answer to question 4. The second statement is true, but the first statement is false because the lowest possible price would require the sacrifice by the monopolist of his abnormal profits; this course of action would be inconsistent with profit-maximization. In question 5, the first statement is true and the second statement is false. The desirable properties of perfect competition result from impersonal market forces, not from an assumption that entrepreneurs are any less motivated by self-interest! Question 6 provides an example of both statements being true with the second statement being the reason for the truth of the first statement. If a perfectly competitive firm charged a price above its demand curve, all the customers would switch to the identical goods produced by other firms in the industry.

Data Response Questions

Question 7 'The classical theory of the firm relied heavily on the notion that firms are small, owner-managed organizations operating in highly competitive markets whose demand functions are given and where only normal profits can be earned. If the firm did not therefore maximize profits it would fail to survive under those conditions. Setting aside the question as to whether this ever was a valid description … it is certainly far removed from the actual characteristics of firms in many branches of economic activity today. It is only when the main features of the organization of modern corporations are taken into account that the questions of the goals of the firm and its decision processes can be effectively discussed.'

(J. F. Pickering, *Industrial Structure and Market Conduct*, Martin Robertson & Co. Ltd., 1974)

(a) Explain, within the context of classical theory, how profit maximization is crucial for a firm's survival.

(b) What 'main features of modern corporations' would you consider the author had in mind when he questioned the adequacy of the traditional theory of the firm? Giving your reasons, state whether you would agree that such theory is now obsolete. *(London: January 1980)*

Understanding the Question You should be able to infer from the passage that the author is using the classical theory of the firm as a label for perfect competition, though, as the next unit explains, the profits of firms in monopolistic competition are also competed away in the long run. You must show how long-run equilibrium in perfect competition comes about and how high-cost firms are competed out of existence. An understanding of the meaning of normal profit is important. In answering the second part of the question, one approach is to argue that alternative theories, such as the managerial and behavioural theories of the firm, are more realistic because they model the split between owners and managers, which is a 'main feature of modern corporations'. Alternatively, you could argue that the most significant feature is the fact that large corporations exist in monopolistic markets and that barriers to entry prevent the competing away of abnormal profits. To earn a very high grade, you must attempt to answer the final point in the question. Perfect competition is regarded by some economists and politicians as an 'ideal' towards which the system should be shifted. Milton Friedman has defended perfect competition by arguing that it does not matter if the assumptions of a theory are unrealistic. The managers of large corporations need not be consciously profit-maximizing, but in a competitive world only the firms which operate close to the profit-maximizing path will survive.

Answer plan

1 Explain what the author means by the classical theory of the firm.
2 Show how surviving firms make only normal profits in perfect-competition long-run equilibrium. It is **not** necessary to write a list of the conditions of perfect competition.
3 Discuss what is meant by a modern corporation.
4 The main features of modern corporations may be monopoly power, survival of inefficient firms, and different market behaviour and goals. Develop some of these points.
5 State whether you regard the traditional theory to be obsolete. Offer some reason for your view point.

Question 8 A firm hires a machine costing £500 per day, which can only be combined with units of 10 men, and wage rates are £20 per day. There are no other costs of production. Output and average revenue are estimated to be as follows:

Number of men	Output per day	Average Revenue
10	1	70
20	5	65
30	10	60
40	20	55
50	45	50
60	70	45
70	90	40
80	110	35
90	125	30
100	130	25

(a) Calculate
 (i) the profit-maximizing level of price and output; (6)
 (ii) the level of profits. (4)
(b) Wage rates now rise to £30 per day. Calculate the new
 (i) profit-maximizing level of price and output; (6)
 (ii) level of profits. (4)

(SUJB: June 1979)

Understanding the Question This is a straightforward data response question in which you are expected to perform simple, if repetitive, calculations. You must clearly show your workings so that you can avoid losing more than a mark or two if you make an arithmetical error. It is easier to calculate the profit-maximizing output by subtracting total cost from total revenue than by using the MR = MC rule.

Answer plan

1 Set out TFC and TVC schedules on your answer sheet. TFC will be the same at every level of output. Calculate TVC by multiplying the labour force by the wage.
2 Set out a TC schedule. TC = TFC + TVC.
3 Calculate the TR schedule by multiplying output by AR.
4 Calculate the level of profits at each output by subtracting TC from TR.
5 Read off the highest level of profits. Note the output and price (AR).
6 Repeat the process for the second part of the question.

Question 9 A producer of rubber goods manufactures its own rubber sheet, which is subsequently used in the manufacture of a wide range of products, at a cost of £6 per square metre. The cost is allocated as follows:

Raw materials	£2
Labour	£2
Depreciation of buildings and machinery	£2

The current market price for rubber sheet is £5.50 per square metre.

Should the firm continue to manufacture its own rubber sheet or should it buy from an outside supplier? (Carefully state the reasons for your decision.)

(London: January 1979)

Understanding the Question The calculations required to answer this question are simpler than those needed for the previous question, but the question requires a deeper understanding of the theory of the firm. It is easy to show that the firm will be making a loss on its rubber sheet manufacturing operations. If you assume that depreciation is a fixed cost which must be borne in the short run, then you can argue that the firm should continue to produce its own sheeting in the short run. The firm will be better off buying in from outside in the long run **unless** you assume that the outside supplier is a monopolist who might raise his prices, or that the firm will experience falling average costs in the future.

Answer plan
1 Explain why the firm will make a loss if it manufactures its own sheeting.
2 Show that if some of the costs are treated as fixed costs, the firm should still produce in the short run.
3 Specify some circumstances in which the firm may still be better off in the long run if it produces its own sheeting.

6.6   FURTHER READING

Burningham, D., editor, *Understanding Economics, an Introduction for Students* (Macmillan, 1978)
Chapter 6: Determination of Price: Perfect Competition and Monopoly.
Chapter 8: Markets and Efficiency.

Lipsey, R. G., *An Introduction to Positive Economics*, 5th edition (Weidenfeld & Nicolson, 1979).
Chapter 19: The theory of perfect competition.
Chapter 20: The theory of monopoly.

7 Imperfect Competition

7.1   POINTS OF PERSPECTIVE

Imperfect competition is the label attached to the wide variety of market structures between the extremes of perfect competition and pure monopoly. A great many theoretical models of imperfect competition have been devised, each model pertaining to a precisely defined market structure and a set of assumptions about how the member firms behave. In this unit we shall examine just three of the possible market structures:
1 **monopolistic competition**, in which it is assumed that firms act independently of each other.
2 **competitive oligopoly**, an example of a market structure in which **interdependent** firms must take account of the reactions of one another when forming a **market strategy**.
3 **collusive oligopoly**, which occurs when firms attempt to overcome the **uncertainty** associated with guessing how competitors will react by colluding together and forming a cartel.

7.2   UNDERLYING CONCEPTS

As in the theories of perfect competition and monopoly, the **profit-maximizing assumption** is fundamental to the models of imperfect competition considered in this unit. If you refer back to the introduction to Unit 6, you will see how **managerial** and **behavioural theories** of the firm attack the assumption of profit-maximizing behaviour as being an **unrealistic** objective for large modern business corporations.

Even if imperfectly competitive and monopolistic firms aim to maximize profits, they may simply not possess the accurate information about their market situation needed to equate marginal cost and marginal revenue. For this reason, imperfectly competitive firms are often modelled as **price-searchers**, seeking by trial and error the price which will maximize profits. In some circumstances, firms may produce a wide variety of differentiated products and services, for which the marginal cost of producing each particular good or service is different. In these conditions, imperfectly competitive firms commonly resort to 'rule of thumb' pricing, without ever consciously setting MC equal to MR. Businessmen may ask their accountants to estimate the cost of one unit of output when producing at near to full-capacity. This estimate is called a **standard cost** and is used for price setting. On the basis of this standard cost, firms may adopt 'cost-plus' or 'mark-up' pricing, by adding a profit margin to the standard cost. The choice of the profit margin may itself be based on rule of thumb, or historical experience, or what a firm thinks it can charge without falling foul of a governmental monopoly investigation.

Nevertheless, many economists argue that the gap between the MC = MR rule and actual business pricing-behaviour can be bridged. When cost-plus pricing gets businessmen too far out of line with what they would achieve with profit-maximizing pricing, they will modify their pricing. Firms which stray too far from the profit-maximizing path will experience low profits and falling share-prices. While such firms are unlikely to be competed out of business in a highly imperfect market, they may become vulnerable to **'discipline by the capital market'**. This means that firms which perform badly are vulnerable to **take-over** by managers who believe that they can manage the firms' assets more successfully.

7.3   ESSENTIAL KNOWLEDGE

1 The theory of monopolistic competition

The theory of monopolistic competition was introduced by Edward Chamberlin in 1933 as an early attempt to model the characteristics of imperfect competition. As the name implies, monopolistic competition resembles both perfect competition and monopoly in some respects. Each firm's product is assumed to be a little different from those of its competitors; if it raises its price slightly, it will not lose all its customers. Thus a firm faces a **downward-sloping demand curve**, rather than the horizontal or infinitely elastic demand curve of perfect competition. Nevertheless, the **absence of barriers to entry** allows market forces, through the entry of new firms, to shift the demand curve and to **compete away abnormal profits** in the long run.

The short-run equilibrium in monopolistic competition is little different from the monopoly equilibrium illustrated in Figure 6.5, except that the demand or average revenue curve is likely to be rather more elastic. Figure 7.1 shows the long-run equilibrium, achieved after the entry of new firms has eliminated abnormal profits. As in the case of monopoly, monopolistic competition involves both **productive inefficiency** (the lowest-cost output is not produced) and **allocative inefficiency** (P > MC). However, the consumer is presented with a **considerable choice between differentiated goods**. There may be circumstances in which consumers prefer a wider choice at the expense of an improvement in productive efficiency.

Nevertheless, it is also possible that firms are using advertizing and brand-imaging to present the consumer with a false choice between essentially similar goods, in which case advertizing is an unnecessary cost and a waste of resources. Advertizing may manipulate consumer 'wants' by persuading people to buy products through the association of the product with other desirable properties such as social success. Many economists distinguish between **informative advertizing**, which helps the consumer to make a more rational choice between products, and **persuasive advertizing**, which distorts the choice.

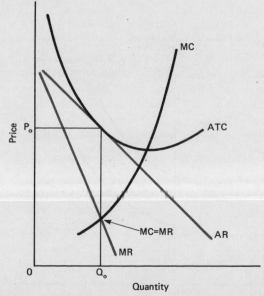

Fig 7.1 Long-run equilibrium of a firm in monopolistic competition

2 Competitive oligopoly

Monopolistic competition shares with perfect competition and monopoly the characteristic that member-firms choose their market strategy in a way which is completely **independent** of the likely **reactions** of other firms. However, this may not be very realistic, particularly when there are only a few large firms competing within an industry. An **oligopoly** is sometimes defined in terms of an industrial **concentration ratio**: for example, a four-firm concentration ratio of 70% means that the four largest firms account for 70% of sales. Alternatively, an oligopoly can be defined in relation to the behaviour or market strategy of the member-firms. Oligopolists are **mutually interdependent** since each firm is concerned about the reactions of its competitors. There are a great many separate theories of oligopoly, each modelling a different set of assumptions about how the rivals react. Many of these theories are examples of **games theories**, in which each oligopolist is regarded as a player in a game, choosing a best strategy subject to retaliations.

3 Reasons for the existence of oligopoly

In many industries there are economies of large-scale production, but diseconomies of scale begin to set in while output is still well below the total market size. The result is a **natural oligopoly** in which a few firms can produce the total industry output and simultaneously benefit from full economies of scale. In other circumstances, **countervailing power** may explain the existence of an oligopoly: large duopolists such as Unilever and Procter & Gamble may each possess sufficient **market power** in the detergent industry to prevent the other emerging as a sole monopolist. **Government monopoly legislation** may also deter the creation of an outright monopoly.

4 Price stability and the kinked demand curve

Although oligopolistic markets are characterized by competitive behaviour, the competition often takes the form of **non-price competition** such as:

  (i) advertizing competition, packaging, brand-imaging and product differentiation;
 (ii) marketing competition, including the attempt to obtain **'exclusive outlets'** through which to sell the product;
(iii) quality competition, including the provision of after-sales servicing.

Figure 7.2 illustrates the theory of the kinked demand curve, a theory originally proposed in 1939 by Paul Sweezy as an explanation of price rigidity and the absence of price wars in conditions of oligopoly. Suppose that an oligopolist, for whatever reason, produces an output Q_0 at a price P_0, determined at point X on the diagram. He perceives that **demand will be relatively elastic in response to an increase in price**, because he **expects** his rivals to **react** to the price rise by keeping their prices stable, thereby gaining customers at his expense. Conversely, he **expects** his rivals to react to a decrease in price by cutting their prices by an equivalent amount; he therefore expects demand to be relatively inelastic in response to a price fall, since he cannot hope to lure many customers away from his rivals. In other words, the oligopolist's initial position is at the junction of two demand curves of differing relative elasticity, each reflecting a different assumption about how the rivals are expected to react to a change in price. If the oligopolist's expectations are correct, sales revenue will be lost whether the price is raised or cut. The best policy may be to leave the price unchanged.

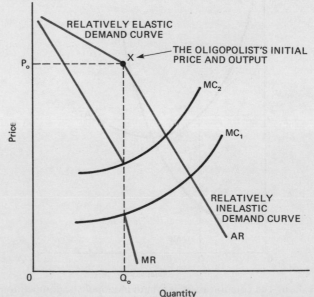

Fig 7.2
The 'kinked'
oligopoly theory

A second explanation of price rigidity is also suggested by Figure 7.2. In mathematical terms, a **discontinuity** exists along a vertical line above output Q_0, between the marginal revenue curves associated with the relatively elastic and inelastic demand (or average revenue) curves. Costs can rise or fall within a certain range without causing a profit-maximizing oligopolist to change either price or output. At output Q_0 and price P_0, MC = MR as long as the MC curve is between an upper limit of MC_2 and a lower limit of MC_1.

Although the kinked demand curve theory provides a neat and perhaps plausible explanation of price rigidity, it has been subject to many attacks. It is an **incomplete theory** because it does not explain how and why an oligopolist chooses to be at point X in the first place. **Empirical evidence** casts great doubt on whether oligopolists respond to price changes in the manner assumed. Oligopolistic markets often display evidence of **price leadership**, which provides an alternative explanation of orderly price behaviour. Firms come to the conclusion that price-cutting is self-defeating and decide that it may be advantageous to follow the firm which takes the first step in raising the price. If all firms follow, the price rise will be sustained to the benefit of all the firms.

5 Collusive oligopoly

The theory of the kinked demand curve illustrates an important characteristic of competitive oligopoly: the existence of **uncertainty**. An oligopolist can never be sure how his rivals will respond, yet he must take their **expected reactions** into account when determining his own market strategy. An incentive may exist for oligopolists to **collude** together in order to **reduce uncertainty**. Also, by acting collectively the firms may achieve an outcome which is better for all of them than if they had remained a competitive oligopoly. This can be shown by the principle of **joint profit maximization**, which is illustrated in Figure 7.3. We shall assume that there are three firms with similar cost curves in an industry. The cost curves of one of the firms are drawn in the left-hand panel of Figure 7.3. Suppose that the firms now decide to get together and act as a single monopolist, yet at the same time maintaining their separate identities. The monopoly MC curve, which is illustrated in the right-hand part of the diagram, is obtained by adding up the identical MC curves of the three separate firms. Monopoly output of 750 units is determined where MC = MR, and each firm charges a price of £10. You should notice that the monopoly output is well below 1000 units, which would be the output if the industry was perfectly competitive. The shaded area in the right-hand panel represents the **efficiency loss** which is caused by the cartel raising the price to £10 and restricting the industry output to 750 units.

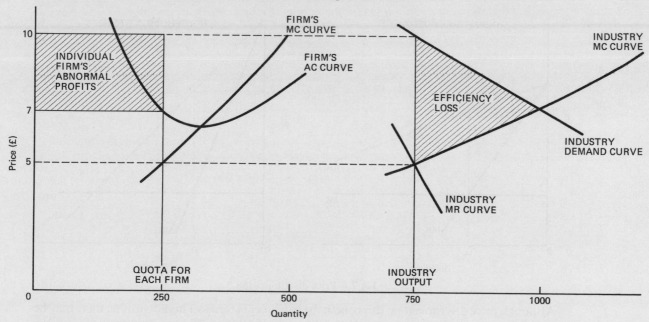

Fig 7.3 Joint profit maximization by a three firm cartel in which the market is shared equally by the three firms

If the firms decide to split the output of 750 units equally between themselves, each firm will be allocated a **quota** of 250 units to produce. In this situation, the shaded area in the left-hand part of the diagram shows the abnormal profits made by an individual firm. Other forms of market-sharing, based for example on geography or historical tradition, are of course possible.

It is important to stress that the formation of a cartel does not completely eliminate uncertainty. Each member of the cartel has an **incentive to cheat** on the other members: this is because the marginal cost of producing the 250th unit is only £5, yet the marginal revenue received, which equals the price, is £10. A firm can increase its total profit at the expense of the other members of the cartel by **secretly** selling an output over and above its quota at a price which is less than £10 but greater than the marginal cost incurred. This is an example of a **divergency** between **collective and individual interest**. The firms' collective interest is to maintain the cartel so as to keep sales down and the price up. Nevertheless, an individual firm can benefit if, while the other members maintain the cartel, it secretly undercuts the agreement by selling more than its allotted market share.

6 The possibility of price discrimination

Monopolies, and other firms in highly imperfect markets, regularly charge a number of different prices to different groups of customers. Sometimes more than one product is involved, as in the case of first- and second-class rail travel; in other instances the prices may reflect the different transport and handling costs which are incurred in delivering the good or service to the customer. You must not confuse these examples of differentiated prices with the concept of monopoly or oligopoly **price discrimination**. Price discrimination occurs when a firm is able to charge different prices for an **identical** product. The costs of production must be the same, irrespective of the type of customer to whom the product is sold. Price discrimination will benefit a firm if it increases the firm's total profits. The necessary conditions for successful price discrimination are:

(i) It must be possible to identify different groups of customers or markets for the product.

(ii) There must be a different elasticity of demand in each market.

(iii) Total profits will be increased by selling at a higher price in the market where demand is **less** elastic. (Demand will **never** be inelastic, since this would imply that marginal revenue is negative.) The markets must be **separated** to prevent **seepage**, which occurs when customers buy at the lower price in one market in order to resell in the other market at a price which undercuts the monopolist.

Figure 7.4 illustrates the simplest case of price discrimination, when a firm's MC curve is assumed to be constant. Profits are maximized by equating MR to the constant MC curve in each market. Output Q_1 is sold at a price of P_1 in the industrial market, while household customers buy Q_2 at price P_2. Marginal revenue is the same in each market at these outputs. If this was not the case, the firm would be able to increase profits by reallocating its output between the markets.

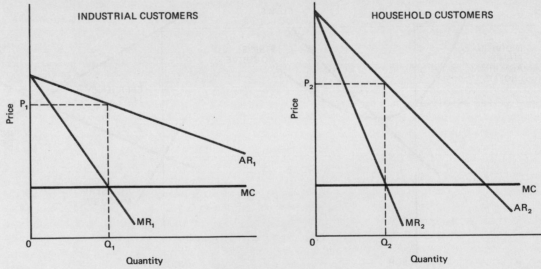

Fig 7.4 Price discrimination

Although price discrimination can benefit the producer in terms of higher profits, there may be circumstances in which it is also in the interest of consumers. The classic case concerns the demand for the services of a doctor in an isolated small town. If all the townspeople are charged the same price for health care, the town's doctor is unable to make a sufficient income to cover his opportunity cost: it is in his interest to move to a larger city, thus leaving the townspeople without any medical care. If, however, the doctor is permitted to charge a higher price to the few rich citizens who can afford to pay, he may be able to earn sufficient income to make it worth his while to treat the poorer people at a lower price. Everybody ends up by getting some benefit from the introduction of price discrimination – though, as the next unit explains, **collective provision** of a **merit good** such as health care **outside the market** may be judged more desirable than **private provision through the market**.

7.4 LINKS WITH OTHER TOPICS

This unit has followed on from Unit 6 in extending the coverage of market structures to include the main forms of imperfect competition. Certain aspects of the behaviour or conduct of large firms which have been examined in some depth in this unit are equally applicable to the case of pure monopoly. Likewise, the descriptive aspects of the growth of firms covered in Unit 10, and the policy-making implications of industrial concentration (Unit 12), relate to the highly imperfect market structures introduced in this unit as well as to conditions of pure monopoly.

7.5 QUESTION PRACTICE

Essay questions

Question 1 Explain the equilibrium of the firm under conditions of monopolistic competition. What would be the consequences for the firm of
(a) an increase in interest rates
(b) a successful advertizing campaign for the firm's products?

(Cambridge: June 1981)

Understanding the Question You must define the essential characteristics of monopolistic competition, namely product differentiation, a relatively large number of firms, and the existence of freedom of entry in the long run. The question does not specify whether the equilibrium to be explained is the **short-run** or the **long-run** equilibrium. It is best to explain both, preferably with the use of diagrams. You must certainly explain the long-run equilibrium, as this is the 'true' equilibrium.

In order to earn a pass grade, a competent attempt at the second and third parts of the question is necessary; this is because these parts of the question test your ability to use economic analysis, whereas the first part can be answered by recall knowledge. An increase in interest rates will raise production costs, shifting the average and marginal cost curves upwards. If the firm is in a position of long-run equilibrium, losses will result. You can then extend the analysis to show the effects on the demand or AR curve if some of the firms leave the industry. This will allow you to introduce the effects of the advertizing campaign into the analysis since this will also shift the AR curve. The advertizing campaign may also raise costs a little, and it is additionally possible that the rise in interest rates will reduce consumption, thereby shifting the AR curve inwards.

Answer plan

1 Briefly explain what is meant by monopolistic competition.
2 Illustrate short-run and long-run equilibrium with the use of diagrams.
3 The increase in interest rates will raise costs and cause losses.
4 Firms will leave the industry and the AR curve will shift upwards until remaining firms are just making normal profits.
5 The advertizing campaign shifts the AR curve upwards. Existing firms now make abnormal profits. New firms are attracted in until a new long-run equilibrium is reached.

Question 2 Discuss the benefits to the consumer of an oligopolistic market structure.

(London: June 1979)

Understanding the Question You can interpret oligopolistic market structures as including both competitive and collusive oligopoly. A discussion of benefits must include an assessment of the disadvantages to the consumer as well as the advantages. One approach to the question is to argue that consumers benefit from relatively stable prices in conditions of oligopoly. However, you must be careful to direct your answer to the **set question**: although it is worthwhile to mention the theory of the oligopolist's 'kinked' demand curve, this is **not** a question on the **causes** of price stability. Price stability reduces uncertainty for both consumers and producers, allowing both to plan ahead. Once consumers have obtained correct information about prices they can make use of this information for a longer period; this reduces the costs of collecting information about what is available and at what price. On the other hand, oligopolists may market a wide range of branded products which are all essentially identical. For example, almost all detergents marketed in the United Kingdom are produced by just two firms, Unilever and Procter & Gamble. This increases the costs of obtaining correct information and it may also be an example of 'wasteful competition', which the consumer pays for in the form of higher prices. However, it is also true that consumers can benefit from forms of competition, such as advertizing and after-sales servicing, which oligopolists use instead of price competition. Since price stability allows producers to plan ahead, consumers may benefit in the long run from better products and lower-cost methods of production. Nevertheless, it will generally be the case that consumers will benefit from **low and stable** prices and that **high and stable** prices are no substitute for low, if more variable, prices.

Answer plan

1 Define an oligopolistic market structure.
2 Explain how consumers may benefit from stable prices.
3 Discuss other benefits *e.g.* benefits from other forms of competition and benefits from falling production costs, economies of scale, etc.
4 In some circumstances, the members of the oligopoly may form a cartel or collude together. Disadvantages may result from inefficiency, price-rigging, etc.
5 Disadvantages may also result from wasteful competition.

Multiple Choice Questions

Question 3

(A)	(B)	(C)	(D)
1, 2 and 3	1 and 2 only	2 and 3 only	1 only

The market conditions necessary for a producer to successfully undertake price discrimination include:
(1) different price elasticities of demand in different market sectors
(2) different marginal cost conditions in different market sectors
(3) demand must be price-inelastic in at least one market sector.

Understanding the Question It is possible for a firm to be monopolist in one market whilst competing in a wider market where demand is more elastic. Indeed, there must be different elasticities of demand in the different markets to make price discrimination profitable to the firm. Alternative (D) is therefore correct. The remaining statements are incorrect yet students regularly fail to see why. If different marginal costs are incurred, then we are really dealing with two slightly differentiated products. The **service** provided in delivering coal to a consumer in London is **not the same service** as that provided in delivering coal to a consumer who lives near the coal-mine. Firms can obviously charge different prices for different products or services, but this is **irrelevant** to the question. Price discrimination refers to the charging of different prices for the same good or service, produced at identical cost.

We assume that a discriminating monopolist is a profit-maximizer. Therefore it is illogical for the firm to produce an output for which demand is inelastic, since MR will be negative. **Profit-maximizing firms must always produce in the elastic section of their demand curve where MR is positive!**

Question 4

Output (units)	Total Revenue (pence)	Total Cost (pence)
1	15	5
2	27	12
3	36	21
4	42	32
5	45	45

The firm described in this table is operating under conditions of:
(a) Imperfect competition and decreasing marginal cost.
(b) Imperfect competition and increasing marginal cost.
(c) Perfect competition and increasing marginal cost.
(d) Perfect competition and decreasing marginal cost.

Understanding the Question You must carefully distinguish between average and marginal cost and revenue. In this example, the extra cost of producing one more unit of output is increasing (by 7, 9, 11 and 13 pence); thus alternatives (a) and (d) must be wrong. The changes in total revenue indicate the nature of the market. In order to sell more units of output, the firm has to accept a price which falls from 15 to $13\frac{1}{2}$ to 12 to $10\frac{1}{2}$ to 9 pence; this implies a downward-sloping demand curve. Hence the firm is in some form of imperfect competition. Alternative (b) is clearly the correct answer.

Data Response Questions

Question 5

Price (pence)	Quantity demanded (000s)
15	250
14	320
13	400
12	450
11	480
10	500

The market for a homogeneous product is shared equally among three producers, each of which has an average total cost (excluding normal profit) of 10 pence per unit at all levels of output. Given the above market demand schedule, what would be the profit-maximizing price? Explain what would be likely to happen to the profit-maximizing price and output if a fourth producer, with the same costs as the existing three producers, were to enter the industry.

(London: January 1978)

Understanding the Question The question is a test of your ability to apply straightforward profit-maximizing rules in an unconventional market structure. The question states that the market is shared between three firms; you can assume from this that the firms are engaged in some form of collusion. It is easiest to assume that the three firms have formed a cartel which is engaged in **joint profit maximization**. Industry price and output will be the same as for a single monopolist, the firms dividing up the output between themselves. Each firm has a horizontal average cost curve, so AC = MC = 10p for all firms. You must calculate the monopolist's MR curve from the data and then read off the average revenue or equilibrium price at the output where $MC = MR = 10p$. If a fourth producer enters the market as an 'invited' member of the cartel, the industry output and price will remain the same, but output will now be divided between four firms rather than three. However, another possibility is that the newcomer is 'uninvited'. In these circumstances the new firm can gain a market share by charging a lower price than the cartel; it may for example, choose a price of 11p, thus allowing perhaps 1p for normal profits, thereby undercutting the cartel and attracting customers away from the cartel. In this event, the cartel is likely to break up. If the price falls to 11p, then the entry of the fourth firm provides an example of market forces serving to compete away abnormal profits.

Answer plan
1 Assume that the three firms are a cartel engaged in joint profit maximization.
2 Explain how $AC = MC = 10p$.
3 Determine the monopoly output and price where $MC = MR$.
4 Explain how the answer to the last part of the question depends upon whether the newcomer joins the cartel or acts as a competitor.

7.6 FURTHER READING

Burningham, D., editor, *Understanding Economics, an Introduction for Students* (Macmillan, 1978).
Chapter 7: Oligopoly.

Samuelson, P., *Economics,* 11th edition (McGraw-Hill, 1980).
Chapter 26: Imperfect Competition and Antitrust Policy.

8 Market Failures

8.1 POINTS OF PERSPECTIVE

1 Failure associated with market structure
Monopolistic and **imperfectly competitive** market structures provide the best-known examples of **market failure.** The 'wrong' quantity is produced and sold at the 'wrong' price. In comparison with perfect competition, too little is produced at too high a price, and the market outcome is neither **allocatively efficient** nor **productively efficient**. Nevertheless, the market can still function in conditions of imperfect competition, producing at least **some** of the good or service.

2 Failure associated with the market mechanism
Even when most of the conditions of perfect competition are met, **informational problems** may prevent the market mechanism from working properly. A certain **minimum level of organization** of a market is required to allow information about market prices to be transmitted to all the participants. A lack of sufficient information about prices in other parts of the market may cause a market to degenerate into **bilateral bargaining**, where a buyer and seller enter into an exchange in a state of ignorance about prices in other parts of the market.

In other instances, the adjustment process towards equilibrium may be **too slow** or **unstable**, and equilibrium may never be reached. As a result, trading may always take place at disequilibrium prices.

3 Market failure and the 'New' Micro-economics
In this unit, attention is concentrated upon some examples of market failure which have been largely ignored, at least until fairly recent times, in the more traditional textbooks designed for Advanced Level students. In particular we shall investigate **public goods** (and **'bads'**), **merit goods** and **externalities**. Traditionally, micro-economics has been concerned with the manner in which markets function smoothly, relegating the coverage of market breakdown to something of a footnote, if indeed the subject was mentioned at all. In contrast, a modern micro-economic approach is to acknowledge that markets may function inadequately, perhaps more often than they function smoothly, and that in certain situations the market may completely fail to provide

any quantity at all of a desired good or service. In response to this change of emphasis, questions on market failure are regularly appearing in the Advanced Level papers of all the examining boards.

8.2   UNDERLYING CONCEPTS

1 Market failure v market inadequacy

A market fails completely when there is no incentive for firms to produce a good or service, even though utility would be gained from its consumption. We shall show why markets fail to provide **pure public goods** such as national defence, which by its nature has to be consumed **collectively** rather than individually. Markets also fail to regulate the production and consumption of **externalities**, with the result that too much of an external **'bad'** such as pollution and too little of an external **good** such as a beautiful landscape may be produced.

In other circumstances, markets will provide some of the good or service, but an inadequate quantity: monopoly and imperfect competition have already been mentioned in this respect. The market mechanism may provide too little of a **merit good**, such as education or health care, and too much of a 'good' such as a narcotic drug or alcoholic drink–goods which are sometimes classed as **demerit goods**.

2 The problem of self-interest

We shall see that the case of a merit good provides an example of the possible conflict between an individual's judgement of his self-interest and the judgement of an outside authority, such as the state, as to what is in his interest. A rather different conflict can emerge in the case of externalities. **Divergencies** arise between the **private cost and benefit** to the firm or individual generating the externality, and the **social costs and benefits** received by the wider community. We shall explore some of the interesting **public policy implications**, when for example the social costs of pollution conflict with the self-interest of the polluter.

8.3   ESSENTIAL KNOWLEDGE

1 Pure public goods and quasi-public goods

A **pure** public good such as national defence is defined by the properties of **non-exclusion** and **non-diminishability**. A person can benefit from national defence without having to pay for it. Furthermore, if an extra person benefits from defence, this in no way diminishes the benefits available to others. Most public goods, for example roads, street lighting and broadcasting, are **quasi-public** goods or **non-pure** public goods. Markets could, in principle provide the goods, but for various reasons they do not. Instead, the goods or services are usually **collectively** provided by the state, often at zero price, and financed out of general taxation.

The essential properties of a public good can be explained with the use of the well-known example of a lighthouse. This is illustrated in Figure 8.1.

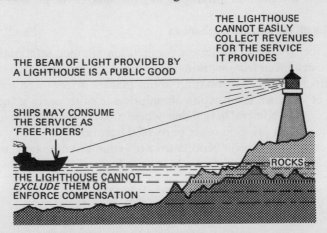

Fig 8.1 The essential features of a public good

The lighthouse provides a service (a beam of light) for which there is a need; if the service is not provided more ships will be wrecked and transport costs will rise. Lighthouses could be provided through the market if entrepreneurs were able successfully to charge a price to passing ships. Now, most goods are called **private goods** because an entrepreneur who provides them can **enforce private property rights** and exclude people who do not wish to pay from consuming the goods. In the case of quasi-public goods, it is theoretically possible to exercise private property rights and to exclude **free-riders** – people who consume without paying. A motor toll-road provides an example. However, in many cases the difficulty and cost of collecting revenue may prove prohibitive. A lighthouse company might try moral persuasion in order to collect revenue from passing ships, relying on the fact that it is in the interest of all ship-owners for the service to be provided; an incentive nevertheless exists for any individual ship-owner to become a free-rider, providing that the other ship-owners still pay up. In these circumstances, most ship-owners may be expected to become free-riders, thereby destroying the incentive for the private provision of the lighthouse.

2 Public goods and government goods

A public good is sometimes defined as any good or service provided by the public sector. This is not a very satisfactory definition. A good such as coal produced by a nationalized industry should be regarded as a private good provided through the market. Other goods and services such as education and health care are merit goods rather than public goods, though they share with public goods the characteristic of being collectively provided at zero price, and being financed out of taxation. It is useful to note that **public collective provision** is **not inevitable** in the case of public goods: in some instances, **private collective provision** is possible. A co-operative of ship-owners could provide lighthouses, though it might be necessary to make membership legally compulsory. **Modified market provision** is another alternative. For example, the difficulty of charging a price to consumers of commercial TV and radio programmes is circumvented by charging advertizers for access to the public good!

3 Merit goods

An incentive certainly exists for merit goods to be provided through the market, but the government may take the paternalistic view that people are not always the best judges of what is good for them. The government can try to encourage the consumption of merit goods and to discourage and sometimes outlaw the consumption of harmful products or demerit goods. Demerit goods must not be confused with nuisance goods or economic 'bads'. Most products and services are economic **goods** that yield utility in consumption – people are prepared to pay a price in order to obtain them, unless of course they can consume the goods as public goods without paying. The consumption of a demerit good, such as a narcotic drug, may not be in the consumer's best interest but it certainly gives pleasure to the person who consumes it, as it fulfils a need. In contrast a 'product' such as garbage is an economic **'bad'** because it yields only unpleasantness or disutility: people are prepared to pay a price in order to have an economic bad taken away.

4 Merit goods and the informational problem

Uncertainty of information may partially explain why people choose to consume too little of a merit good such as health care if it is privately provided at market prices. For example, a person does not know in advance when, if ever, he is going to need the services of a specialist surgeon: sudden illness may lead to a situation in which he is unable to afford the surgeon's services. One market-orientated solution is for a private insurance market to come into being, in which case health care would be collectively provided through the market. However, this may still fail to provide a service for the chronically ill or the very poor. **Public collective provision** through a compulsory state insurance scheme is therefore another solution. It is interesting to note that both private and public collective schemes are a response to the fact that the demand or need for medical care is much more predictable for a large group of people than for an individual – an application of the 'Law' of large numbers.

5 Externalities

An externality is a special type of **public good** or **'bad'**, its crucial characteristic being that it is generated and received **outside the market**. This can be demonstrated by considering the well-known example of pollution as an **external cost**. Figure 8.2 illustrates the generation of pollution by a brickworks. The nearby laundry is an **unwilling free-rider** receiving the pollution as a nuisance good or economic 'bad'.

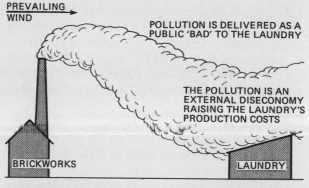

PREVAILING WIND →

POLLUTION IS DELIVERED AS A PUBLIC 'BAD' TO THE LAUNDRY

THE POLLUTION IS AN EXTERNAL DISECONOMY RAISING THE LAUNDRY'S PRODUCTION COSTS

BRICKWORKS

LAUNDRY

THE MONEY COST OF MAKING BRICKS IS LESS THAN THE REAL COST, WHICH INCLUDES THE COST OF POLLUTION

THE LAUNDRY IS AN UNWILLING FREE-RIDER: IT CANNOT CHARGE A PRICE FOR THE POLLUTION IT RECEIVES

Fig 8.2 Case study of an externality: Pollution

The different types of externality

	External costs	External benefits
Generated in production and received in production.	Pollution discharged by a brickworks and received by a nearby laundry. (External diseconomies)	Warm water discharged by a power-station and received in the form of bigger fish catches by nearby commercial fishermen. (External economies)
Generated in production and received in consumption.	Pollution discharged by a brickworks and received by nearby households.	Warm water discharged by a power-station and received in the form of bigger fish catches by private anglers.
Generated in consumption and received in production	Congestion caused by private motorists increasing production costs for firms. (This is another type of external production diseconomy.)	Commercial bee-keepers benefiting from the private gardens of nearby households. (This is another type of external production economy.)
Generated in consumption and received in consumption.	Congestion caused by private motorists causing a utility loss to other private motorists, pedestrians and households.	Passers-by enjoying the view of nearby private gardens.

External costs such as pollution, which increase the production costs of the firms that receive them, are examples of **external diseconomies**. Symmetrically, a firm may generate **external benefits** which are **external economies** if they lower the production costs of other firms. The laundry is unable to charge a price through the market to the brickwork for the pollution it unwillingly consumes. In a similar way, a power-station discharging warm water into a lake cannot charge a price to fishermen for the external benefit they receive in the form of larger catches of fish. The market thus **fails to provide an incentive** for the brickworks to generate **less** pollution and for the power-station to discharge **more** warm water. Without such an incentive, **too much** of an external cost and **too little** of an external benefit are likely to be generated. Thus governments may become involved in adjusting markets via taxes and subsidies in order to discourage economic bads and to encourage external benefits.

Externalities are essentially **'spin-offs'** which are generated by one economic agent in the pursuit of its private self-interest and received outside the market by other agents. **Divergencies** are likely to arise between the **private cost and benefit** of the generator of the externality and the **social cost and benefit** to all who receive them. An external cost such as pollution can be regarded as part of the production cost of bricks which is evaded by the brickworks by being 'dumped' on others. The **real cost** of bricks is greater than the **money cost** at market prices because the real cost includes the cost of pollution; bricks are therefore **underpriced** at market prices, price being less than the true marginal cost. Too many bricks are produced, causing a **misallocation of resources** (allocative inefficiency).

In this example, pollution is an externality which is both **generated** and **received in production**, thereby increasing the production cost of the firms receiving the pollution. Externalities may also be generated and received in consumption. This, and the other possibilities, are summarized in the table at the top of the page.

6 Public policy and market failure

Public goods are usually provided 'free' by the state since otherwise they would not be provided at all. This is an example of public provision **replacing** the market. In the case of merit and demerit goods, the government can either **replace** or **modify** the market. A demerit good such as heroin may be judged so harmful that its consumption and sale are made illegal. A complete ban on a good is the ultimate **quantity control** which a government can use to regulate sale or consumption. Nevertheless a market may still exist in the form of an illegal **black market.** Black markets emerge when free markets are severely regulated or suppressed. In other circumstances, a government may decide that less severe quantity controls are more appropriate, such as the creation of no-smoking areas and restrictions on the sale of tobacco and alcohol. The symmetrical equivalent to a complete ban on heroin is to make the consumption of a merit good such as education or vaccination compulsory.

At the same time, price controls provide another form of regulation which can be used to modify the market. **Minimum price legislation** can discourage the consumption of demerit goods, whereas **maximum price legislation** increases the demand for merit goods – though problems of excess supply and demand are likely to result. For this reason governments may prefer to influence demand by **taxing** demerit goods and by **subsidizing** merit goods. If a 100% subsidy is given to the private producers of a merit good, it becomes effectively 'free', in the sense that it is available at zero price. An example occurs when free places in private schools are financed by the state. Alternatively, the state can provide the merit good itself at zero or token price, similarly financed out of general taxation.

The problem of externalities can be tackled in a rather similar way with a combination of quantity controls or regulations, and taxes and subsidies to influence price. Discharge of pollution may be made illegal or restricted to certain times of the day or year. Maximum emission limits can be imposed. Since the central problem is the failure of the market to provide incentives to generate fewer external costs and more external benefits, taxes and subsidies can be used to provide the desired incentives. The government could, in principle, calculate the money cost of pollution and impose this as a **pollution tax** upon the polluter. The imposition of such a tax **internalizes** the externality! More controversially, subsidies can be paid to encourage external benefits, for example those which result from the planting of trees.

8.4   LINKS WITH OTHER TOPICS

In this unit we have investigated in some depth the circumstances in which the **signalling** and **incentive** functions of prices (described in Unit 1) may break down, resulting in the failure of markets to function smoothly. In some situations markets may fail to function at all. The relative merits of the market economy and the planning mechanism (the subject of Unit 9) link directly to the question whether individual markets function smoothly or badly. Units 8 and 9 are thus very closely related. If a case exists for the public provision of public goods and some merit goods, then this will influence the level and pattern of both government spending and government revenue. These examples of market failure are reintroduced in Unit 17 on taxation and public spending.

8.5   QUESTION PRACTICE

Essay Questions

Question 1 Why do governments supply certain goods and services at zero prices whereas other commodities and services are supplied via the market mechanism?

(WJEC: June 1980)

Understanding the Question The goods and services which are usually provided at zero price by governments are public goods and merit goods. You should explain the reasons why the market mechanism fails to provide any quantity at all of a pure public good and underprovides for merit goods, giving examples of each. A good provided 'free' through public spending must not of course be confused with a true **free good**, for example air. You might also draw on some of the arguments which are developed in the next unit, such as the advantages of the market mechanism in providing for private goods. Public provision of merit goods may also be justified for **distributional reasons,** as a means of increasing the real income or living standards of low-income groups if the provision of the merit goods is financed by taxing better-off sections of the population. The provision of free merit goods is a part of the **'social wage'** of the community.

Answer plan

1 Most goods are private goods which may be efficiently provided through the market.
2 Explain why the market fails to provide pure public goods, and may fail to provide quasi-public goods. Public collective provision replaces the market.
3 Merit goods are underprovided by the market. The state can provide them free or, alternatively, it can subsidize private provision.
4 Explain the distributional reasons for the free provision of merit goods.

Question 2 What are the economic advantages and disadvantages of State provision of education?

(AEB: November 1978)

Understanding the Question You must restrict your answer to the **economic** advantages and disadvantages and avoid the temptation to write more generally. It might be useful to distinguish between a situation in which state education is compulsory and private education is abolished, and the system operating in Britain for many years in which state and private provision exist side by side. In the first case, a disadvantage might be the restriction of consumer choice to those with the ability to pay, though advocates of a state-only system argue that private schools cream resources away from the state sector.

Education is a merit good, so you should construct your answer around the disadvantages of the private provision of merit goods through the market and the case for public collective provision. For the disadvantages of state provision, you could argue in terms of inflexibility and the costs of bureaucracy as well as discussing the question of consumer choice. It is worth noting that the state can provide a merit good such as education by subsidizing its private provision either as an alternative or as an addition to direct state provision.

Answer plan

1 Private market provision will under-provide a merit good such as education.
2 State provision is public collective provision. Schooling is compulsory but provided at zero price to ensure consumption.
3 Other advantages of state provision are (a) **distributional**: poor families benefit, and (b) **efficiency**: an aim is to make the best use of a national resource, the untapped ability of all the people.
4 Discuss the disadvantages: (a) possible restriction of consumer choice; (b) people who buy private education pay twice; (c) consumers may undervalue education because it is free; (d) bureaucratic costs.

Multiple Choice Questions

Questions 3, 4 and 5

(a) Both assertion and reason are true statements and the reason is a correct explanation of the assertion.
(b) Both assertion and reason are true statements but the reason is not a correct explanation of the assertion.
(c) The assertion is true but the reason is a false statement.
(d) The assertion is false but the reason is a true statement.

Assertion	*Reason*
Question 3 Services, such as defence, which are collectively provided and produced are called 'public goods'.	Because the provision of public goods for one person means that others in society benefit and are not impeded in their consumption.
Question 4 All the people who benefit from public goods are termed 'free-riders'.	Because free-riders receive a service without paying for it.
Question 5 Aircraft noise and other forms of pollution are called 'economic bads'.	Because they are free examples of externalities.

Understanding the Questions

Question 3 Alternative (a) is correct because public goods have the characteristics of non-excludability and non-rivalry as stated in the reason. Conversely, other people can be excluded from consuming a private good.
Question 4 Free-riders are correctly explained in the reason part of the question, but the assertion is false. Public goods can usually be provided to consumers who are not free-riders, but the temptation to become a free-rider or the costs of excluding free-riders are likely to cause the market to break down. It is also the case that consumers pay for the good through taxation when public goods are provided by the government. Therefore the consumers are not free-riders.
Question 5 Both the assertion and the reason are true statements, but the reason does not explain the assertion. Economic bads are so named because they are harmful and diminish economic welfare, rather than because they are externalities.

Question 6

Which of the following is an example of an external economy?
(a) A firm which obtains bulk supplies of raw materials at a discount.
(b) A firm which benefits from patents owned by an overseas subsidiary.
(c) An increase in production costs caused by traffic congestion.
(d) An increase in a farmer's crop yield which results from a new drainage scheme installed by a neighbouring farmer.

Understanding the Question

Alternative (a) is an example of an **internal** economy of scale, since the economy results from the bargaining power which results from the firm's size and market power. Alternative (b) is also wrong because the overseas subsiduary is a part of the firm. Traffic congestion causes an external diseconomy, leaving (d) as the correct answer.

Data Response Questions

Question 7 'The absurdity of the application to industry generally (including road haulage) of the principle that the "polluter must pay" can best be illustrated by referring to the pollution caused by railways, electricity generating stations and pylons, brickworks, coal-mines and other producers of goods and providers of services. It would not be sensible, in economic or environmental terms, to impose a pollution tax on rail fares and freight rates, on electricity bills, on bricks and on coal when such taxes, which would have to be paid by the ultimate consumers, would neither eradicate nor reduce pollution.

Affirming that taxation is not the way to reduce environmental hazards such as noise and excessive smoke, the Association considers that those hazards can only be reduced by regulation and by the strict enforcement of regulations. A quieter and cleaner technology in road haulage can best be achieved through modifications of, or developments in the design of, vehicles and their engines. The cost of such changes would be very high indeed...'
(Road Haulage Association's evidence to The Select Committee on Nationalized Industries, *H.M.S.O.*,1977.)

(a) Comment on the argument that a tax on pollution would simply be passed on to the consumer in the form of higher prices. Support your analysis with an appropriate diagram.
(b) What solutions would you advocate for the varied problems of pollution, and why?

(London: January 1980)

Understanding the Question

The first part of the question is a variation upon a standard examination theme: the ability of a firm to **shift the incidence** of a tax onto consumers. This aspect of the question turns up regularly in a variety of forms, including multiple choice questions. The tax shifts the firm's supply curve but the ability of the firm to raise price by the full amount of the tax depends upon elasticity of demand. Thus the impact of the tax will vary between different markets. The second part of the question requires a recognition that pollution is an externality generated, in this case, by firms in the course of production. A problem exists because of the divergence between private and social cost and benefit, and the inability of market forces to provide an incentive for the polluter to reduce the emission of pollution.

Answer plan

1 Explain how the pollution tax shifts the supply curve but that the eventual incidence of the tax depends upon elasticity of demand. It is irrelevant in this part of the question to discuss whether the tax **ought** to be imposed.
2 Briefly explain why pollution is a problem (the nature of economic bads and externalities).
3 Discuss the use of quantity controls (bans, maximum emission limits, etc.) and policies to influence price (taxation). Assess the advantages and disadvantages of each, noting that a combination of regulation and tax policy might be desirable.

8.6 FURTHER READING

Lipsey, R. G., *An Introduction to Positive Economics*, 5th edition (Weidenfeld & Nicolson, 1979) Chapter 31: Micro-economic Policy.

Lancaster, K., *Modern Economics, Principles and Policy*, 2nd edition (Rand McNally, 1979). Chapter 17: Failure of the Market.

9 Market Economies and Planned Economies

9.1 POINTS OF PERSPECTIVE

In the first eight units we have examined how the price mechanism is assumed to work, both in the 'ideal' circumstances of a perfect market, and in the more realistic conditions of monopoly, market imperfection and market failure. We are now in a position to draw together themes and strands of reasoning from earlier units, in order to make a comparison of **market economies** and **planned economies** as **economic systems**.

1 Ownership and economic systems

One way to define an economic system is in terms of **ownership** of the means of **production, distribution** and **exchange**. This approach is favoured by **Marxist economists**, who analyze the conflict between the **employed class** and the **class which owns the means of production**. Marxists are particularly interested in the dynamic change over time of society (and economic systems), in response to the apparent conflict between **economic classes**. Most Marxian economic analysis has centred on **capitalism** as an economic system. Capitalism is usually defined as a system in which the means of production are owned by private individuals who employ labour in order to produce output for private profit. Marxists believe that the supposed conflicts and contradictions of capitalism will eventually culminate in a final crisis out of which will develop **socialism**. In socialism the community as a whole, usually through the state, owns the means of production, distribution and exchange. Of course, it is not nearly as simple as this, and to many economists capitalism and socialism may have a number of different meanings.

2 Allocative mechanisms and economic systems

Market economies and **planned economies (command** or **collective economies)** are defined in terms of the **allocative mechanism** which is assumed to exist in the economic system. In a pure market economy all resources, goods and services other than free goods would be allocated through the market, whereas in a centrally planned economy a central authority would make all the allocative decisions. Both these extreme situations are obviously unrealistic. Where a very large proportion of economic activity takes place through the market, as for example in the Swiss economy, it is usual to refer to it as a market economy. Where, however, the bulk of economic activity is determined by a central planning authority, as in the Soviet Union, it is customary to refer to it as a planned or command economy even though some activities such as market-gardening may be outside the system.

3 Other possibilities

It is often wrongly stated that private ownership (or **'free enterprise'**) is a **necessary condition** for the existence of a market economy. While it is certainly usual for capitalism to exist within a largely market economy, it is by no means inevitable. One possibility is a system of **market socialism** in which communally owned co-operatives and collectives decide what to produce and sell through the market. This has been tried in Yugoslavia. Nationalized industries in Britain provide another example of socially owned enterprises operating in the market sector of an economy. Indeed, most of the economies of the advanced industrial nations outside the Communist block are referred to as **mixed economies**. This is a very broad label that covers a variety of possible systems. A mixed economy is sometimes defined in terms of ownership, as an economy containing large **private** and **public sectors**. It is equally possible to define a mixed economy in terms of allocative mechanisms; in this case, the co-existence of **market** and **non-market** sectors defines a mixed economy, each sector usually providing different categories of goods and services. However, some services such as health and education may be provided by both sectors.

9.2   Underlying concepts

1 The problem of scarcity revisited

The problem of what, how and for whom to produce in a situation where scarce resources have alternative uses was briefly mentioned in the introduction to Unit 1. Since a major part of the evaluation of market and planned economies must be in terms of how well they perform these allocative tasks, we shall restate the scarcity problem with the use of a **production possibility** diagram.

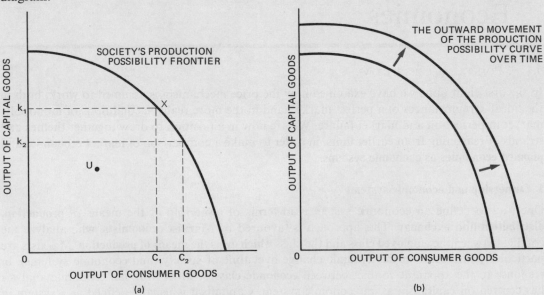

Fig 9.1 (a) The economic problem and society's production possibility curve
(b) economic growth causes the frontier to move outwards over time

The **production possibility frontier** drawn in Figure 9.1a shows what can be produced with the existing quantity of labour, capital, and land at a country's disposal, for a given level of technology or 'technical progress'. Although resources and capacity are limited, a choice of which type of good to produce exists. If we assume just two classes of goods, **capital** and **consumer** goods, the production possibility frontier represents the **technological choice** available to society between the two groups of goods. A point such as X on the frontier is associated with the output k_1 of capital goods and C_1 of consumer goods. The production possibility diagram also illustrates the following points of interest:

(i) If society is on its production possibility frontier, at a point such as X, more of one good can only be produced at the expense of some of the output of the other good. For instance, if the output of consumer goods is increased to C_2, the output of capital goods must fall by $k_1 - k_2$. The **opportunity cost** of the extra output of consumer goods is $k_1 - k_2$, the alternative output of capital goods which is given up.

(ii) If you refer back to Unit 3, you will see that the shape of the production possibility curve reflects the nature of **returns** to the resources as they are switched between the capital and consumer goods industries. Figure 9.1 shows **diminishing returns** in both industries: as more and more resources are transferred into the consumer goods industries, output rises by a smaller extra quantity for each unit of resource transferred.

(iii) All points on the production possibility frontier represent **full employment** of society's resources. A point such as U inside the frontier is associated with unemployment. Here it is no longer true that the opportunity cost of increasing the output of consumer goods is the sacrifice of some production of capital goods – production of both capital and consumer goods can be stepped up by utilizing unemployed resources.

(iv) An increase in the resources available to the society, or technical progress which improves the efficiency with which resources are used, can shift the production possibility curve outwards. This is illustrated in Figure 9.1b. Of course, the choice as to which original quantities of capital and consumer goods to produce may influence the outward movement of the frontier. **Capital goods** are goods which are used to produce other good and services, whilst **consumer goods** represent the final goods and services purchased by households. The output of capital goods has two purposes. Firstly it replaces the capital that is worn out in producing the current **flow** of capital and consumer goods (**depreciation investment** which maintains the society's capital **stock**). Secondly it may also add to the capital stock (**net investment**), thereby enabling a larger output to be produced in the future. In conditions of full employment it may be possible to increase the standard of living by producing more consumer goods at the expense of capital goods. However, in the long run the standard of living can best be increased by producing more capital goods now, thereby creating the growth in the economy's productive capacity which shifts the production possibility frontier outwards.

2 General Equilibrium in a perfectly competitive market economy

In Unit 1 we considered how the equilibrium price is determined within a single market, and in Unit 6 we investigated the equilibrium of a single firm within a perfectly competitive industry or market. For a **general equilibrium** to occur within a whole system of perfectly competitive inter-related markets, equilibrium prices and quantities must be simultaneously determined in each market. Such a general equilibrium would be both **productively** and **allocatively** efficient since it would be impossible either:

(i) to produce more of one particular good or service without diverting resources away from another, or

(ii) to make one consumer better off without making some other consumer or consumers worse off.

It is important to stress that these **'optimal properties'** of a perfectly competitive general equilibrium hold for a **given distribution of income**. There will be a different optimal general equilibrium for each and every alternative distribution of income! In these circumstances a strong normative case may exist for redistributing income in the interests of social fairness, for example, when 1% of the community is very rich and 99% are very poor.

9.3 ESSENTIAL KNOWLEDGE

1 The advantages of a market economy

A perfectly competitive market economy in general equilibrium would possess the following advantages:

(i) **Economic efficiency** (productive and allocative) would be achieved.

(ii) **Consumer sovereignty.** The goods and services produced would be determined by price signals which reflect consumer wants.

(iii) **Decentralized decision-making**. The optimal production and allocation of resources would be achieved without the need for an expensive bureaucracy. In a market economy the price system acts as a **social control mechanism**. This is often referred to as the **'invisible hand'** principle, describing the proposition that economic order rather than chaos results from the pursuit of individual self-interest in a market economy.

2 The disadvantages of a market economy

(i) Economic inefficiency. Productive and allocative efficiency will only be achieved if every market in the system is perfectly competitive and if trading takes place always at equilibrium prices in every market. Unless these almost impossible conditions are met, we cannot be sure that a perfectly competitive market system would be economically efficient.

Of course, the market economies of the real world are in no sense perfectly competitive. In a perfectly competitive system, price (and wage) flexibility would bring about **full employment** of all available resources in equilibrium. A criticism of the market economies in the actual world is the **persistence of unemployment** and the tendency for **business cycles** in the pattern of economic behaviour. Both these phenomena are indicators of inefficient utilization of resources.

(ii) Producer sovereignty. The existence of **increasing returns to scale** and **economies of scale** helps to explain why actual market economies are only distant approximations to the perfectly competitive 'ideal'. If markets are dominated by monopoly and imperfect competition, firms may decide what to produce, perhaps manipulating consumer wants through advertizing. In any case, price now functions as a misleading signal, contributing to resource misallocation.

3 The case for replacing the market

Supporters of the principle of a market economy argue that, however imperfectly the price mechanism works, it still results in sufficient efficiency and consumer sovereignty to justify the system. Nevertheless, many advocates of a **mixed economy** claim that in a number of specific instances the government planning mechanism should either **modify** or **replace** the market:

(i) The problem of income distribution. The best that can be claimed for a perfectly competitive market system is that it may be economically efficient **for a given initial income distribution**. It is completely 'value neutral' on the desirability or otherwise of the initial pattern of incomes. It is a function of government to use tax and public spending policies to achieve a 'satisfactory' distribution of income.

(ii) Goods which the market fails to provide. We examined in Unit 8 the nature of **public goods**, **merit goods** and **externalities**. In each case the market either completely fails to provide the goods in question, or provides the 'wrong' quantities. Governments usually plan the public collective provision of public goods such as national defence, and of merit goods such as education. Governments may also modify the market through regulation, taxation and subsidies, in order to encourage the consumption of market-provided merit goods, or to reduce the **divergency** between **private** and **social cost and benefit** in the case of externalities. You should refer back to Unit 8 for a detailed explanation of these examples of market failure.

4 Command Economies

A command economy, in which markets would be largely replaced by a command or planning mechanism, would of course be very different from the type of mixed economy we have just described. In theory at least, it is possible for a **centrally planned** command economy to achieve exactly the same distribution of resources as would occur in general equilibrium in a perfectly competitive market economy. As a result, there is no **theoretical** reason why a market economy must be more economically efficient than a command economy. Consider, however, the implications of the complete abolition of prices as sources of information. It has been calculated that in an economy such as the USA the central authority would have to issue over 200 billion orders in respect of a **single** commodity, allocating precise amounts of the good to each consumer. The costs of a completely centralized control system governing all production and consumption decisions would be immense! Such a command economy is as abstract and unreal an economic concept as the model of a perfectly competitive market economy.

The command economies of the real world, such as the Soviet economy, tend to be **command economies with some household choice**. The command system concentrates on the **production decision** of what to produce, rather than on the final allocation of goods and services to consumers. A **central plan** may allocate resources to particular industries and productive units which are required to meet the output targets of the master plan. In some circumstances, factory managers may be free to set final prices, though it is more usual for the central planners to decide the prices of important commodities such as bread and meat. Prices which are chosen by a central authority with the object of encouraging individual consumers to behave in a certain way are known as **shadow prices**.

Sometimes, shadow prices are deliberately set so as to ration final goods and services which are scarce in relation to an overwhelming unfulfilled consumer demand. In this respect, shadow prices imitate at least one of the functions of market prices. However, in a market economy the price would provide an incentive for producers to enter the industry. This incentive is lacking in a command economy, unless the planners respond to the signals of scarcity by diverting more resources into the particular industry.

9.4   LINKS WITH OTHER TOPICS

We have nearly completed our necessarily brief coverage of micro-economic theory. In Units 10 and 11 the emphasis is switched away from economic theory as we look at the way firms have grown in the British economy and how they raise finance. We then see in Units 12, 13 and 14 how government **micro-economic policy** attempts to make the British economy more competitive. In these units, the theory which we have developed in Units 1 to 9 will be used to **evaluate** the **aims** and **effectiveness** of government policies.

9.5   QUESTION PRACTICE

Essay Questions

Question 1 Examine some of the main objectives of private-sector firms producing goods or services, and discuss some of the difficulties which may arise for the firm and for society from the pursuit of these objectives. (25)   *(SEB: 1981)*

Understanding the Question This is a very wide-ranging question in which the candidate can hardly be expected to cover all the possibilities. However, good answers should cover three clearly defined aspects of the question.

1 **Alternative objectives** You should briefly introduce the **alternative theories of the firm** – **managerial** and **behavioural** which were mentioned in Unit 6.
2 **Problems facing firms seeking to maximize profit** At this level, short run profit maximisation, based on finding the output level where marginal cost equals marginal revenue, would form the core of the answer. This would open opportunities for candidates to show knowledge and understanding of the 'theory of the firm'. Special problems of different market situations could also be introduced, e.g. problems posed by the arrival of new competitors and the effects of this on the profits of existing firms.
3 **Social costs arising from the pursuit of profit** This issue encompasses such ideas as the concept of welfare maximisation; the problems of conflicting interests of entrepreneurs, consumers and the general public; distribution of income issues; externalities; and the manipulation of the consumer.
   The question is attempting to test one's understanding of the central issues of the behaviour of firms, and the candidate can create a good understanding of some of the key terms such as 'profit', 'marginal cost', 'marginal revenue'. Credit will come also from references to present-day issues affecting firms, for example the world recession, EEC regulations, etc.

Answer plan

1 Objectives may include: Profit maximisation, minimum profit level, increase in market-share, growth, prestige through quality products, avoidance of adverse publicity, desire for 'the quiet life', survival, power, satisficing, etc. Stress that few firms have a single objective.
2 Difficulties for the firm: Competition, finance, taxation, changing markets, changing technology, industrial relations, public relations, etc. Changes in demand and supply conditions and in government policy. World economic conditions.
3 Difficulties for the public: Prices, quality, choice, advertising pressures, the employment situation, wages, etc.

The good answer will not only develop some of the above, but by example, highlight both the conflict of interests between firms and society, and also the potential harmony of interest there.

Question 2

Compare and contrast the principal economic characteristics of a free market with those of a planned economy.

(London: June 1981)

Understanding the Question

The wording of the question allows a candidate some considerable scope in interpreting the concepts involved. For example, a free economy may mean a perfectly competitive market economy, but it can also include highly imperfect market economies in which economic agents are free to own private property, buy and sell labour services, etc., within the constraints of the imperfect market system. It would be as well to define what you mean by 'free' at the beginning of the essay. Good answers should suggest that the concept may mean different things to different economists. Similarly, a planned economy can refer to a completely centrally planned economy, a command economy with some household choice, or an economy in which planning is locally delegated.

It is essential to **compare the similarities** and to **contrast the differences** between examples of the two systems. Separated lists of the characteristics of each system are inadequate. You must stick to the **economic** characteristics, and avoid the temptation to discuss political systems and wider concepts of personal freedom. The best approach is to show how the market and the planning systems both attempt to solve the central economic problem of scarcity, but that the methods differ in each system. Although some of the characteristics of each economy may be considered as advantages or disadvantages, the question is not asking for a judgement on the superiority or otherwise of a market economy.

Answer plan

1 Briefly describe some of the meanings of free and planned economies.
2 Describe how free economies are characterized by private property and individual decentralized decision-making. This contrasts with the socialized ownership and centralized decision-making of planned economies. Compare the incentive motive in the two systems.
3 Firmly state that all economies are similar in having to deal with the problem of scarcity.
4 Contrast how the market mechanism and the decisions of a central authority deal with the problem.
5 A perfectly competitive market economy in a state of general equilibrium would display characteristics of consumer sovereignty and economic efficiency. In principle, economic efficiency but not consumer sovereignty could be achieved in a planned economy.
6 However, in real-world versions of both systems, inefficiencies are likely. Free economies will contain the problem of monopoly and producer power. In a planned economy, the decisions of the central authority may not accord with consumer preferences, and shortages will result.

Question 3 Describe the main features of a mixed economy and discuss its advantages and disadvantages.

(AEB: November 1981)

Understanding the Question This question contains two straightforward parts and your answer must show an even balance. It is advisable to define in clear terms what you understand by a mixed economy. As the unit explains, it can be defined in terms of ownership and in terms of methods of allocating resources. Also, mixed economies are characteristic of advanced economies in political democracies. Such economies contain sophisticated and varied agricultural, manufacturing and service sectors, each of which may display different problems. Some political and economic theorists believe that people 'vote' for a mixed economy through the political system as the most appropriate way of dealing with the diverse problems.

You can develop the advantages and disadvantages by introducing the concepts of private and public goods. In a mixed economy private goods are usually provided through the market and public goods through the planning mechanism. This has an advantage over a market economy in which public goods would be under-provided, and over a completely planned economy in which consumer choice would be restricted. Other advantages of a mixed economy might include the role of government in redistributing income in a socially desirable way and in regulating undesirable aspects of the behaviour of monopolies.

A mixed economy might possess disadvantages if the balance between private and public ownership, and market and planning decisions, is incorrect. For example, people criticize the mixed economy in Britain for containing either too much or too little nationalization! Others argue for the reduction of the National Health Service, or for its extension and the abolition of private medicine. The strength of these criticisms reflects personal judgement on the type of society we wish to live in.

A disadvantage of the mixed economy that is less dependent on personal value judgement relates to the 'trade-off' between short-term and long-term decision-making. In a mixed economy, citizens tend to 'vote' for short-term desired goals, associated with their immediate standard of living. Long-term benefits which might result from a higher growth rate may be sacrificed in favour of current consumption. Governments which tried to take a longer-term view and to introduce appropriate policies might be voted out of office.

Answer plan

1 Define a mixed economy in terms of (a) private and public ownership, (b) market and non-market provision of goods and services, and (c) the role of the government in reflecting the wishes of citizens as voters.
2 Explain the advantages of non-market provision of public goods and merit goods alongside market provision of private goods.
3 Public ownership of nationalized industries and public regulation, for example, of monopolies, may have the advantage of maximizing **social benefit** when a divergency occurs between private and social interest.
4 Discuss the disadvantages of a mixed economy, for example the inefficiences which may result from the reduction of market incentives, and the temptation for governments to take too short-term a view.

Multiple Choice Questions

Question 4 The statement 'There is no such thing as a free lunch' relates to the application of
(a) the concept of a merit good
(b) the working of the price mechanism
(c) the concept of opportunity cost
(d) the law of diminishing marginal utility

Understanding the Question This is a straightforward question on the concept of opportunity cost and the problem of choosing between the alternative uses of scarce resources. Free meals, for example for pensioners or school-children, can be examples of merit goods. Nevertheless, the provision of the free meals uses up scarce resources, and they have to be paid for by somebody. The correct answer is therefore **(c)**.

Question 5 Under the command economy system, the economic problem of deciding what goods shall be produced is decided mainly by
(a) advertizing
(b) profit levels
(c) government direction
(d) relative prices

Understanding the Question The decision will be based on the planning authority's perception of the wants of consumers, which may be judged subsiduary to other needs of the community or of the planners themselves.

Many command economies have concentrated on capital goods rather than on providing consumer goods. **(a)**, **(b)** and **(d)** are all features of a market economy, whereas **(c)** is characteristic of centralized decision-making.

Data Response Questions

Question 6 'The protagonists of the free market system explicitly state its advantages as freedom and efficiency.... They regard men and women as primarily motivated by individual economic self-interest. The laws of supply and demand are held to operate because individuals are so made that they seek to sell to the highest bidder and buy from the cheapest (supplier). It follows that a person's income or wealth reflects his economic worth. Thus, man is seen as economic man....'.

(Source: R. Holman, *Poverty: explanations of social deprivation*, Martin Robertson, 1978)

(a) In what sense does the behaviour of economic man lead to efficiency in the free market system?

(b) Discuss the assertion that an individual's productivity is a sound basis for determining the distribution of income.

(London: June 1980)

Understanding the Question Although this data response question resembles an essay question, you are expected to make use of the concepts included in the quoted passage. Answers which fail to refer to the 'data' will usually be penalized, perhaps heavily. You should be able to answer the first part of the question by drawing on the coverage of economic efficiency in Unit 6 and the application of the concept to a perfectly competitive market system explained in this unit. You can show that, subject to the strong assumption about perfect information, mobility of factors of production, no economies of scale and an absence of externalities, a state of allocative and productive efficiency can be brought about in perfect competition general equilibrium. However, perfect competition in all markets is a necessary condition for the achievement of economic efficiency, so the behaviour of economic man may not lead to efficiency in the markets of the real world. Indeed, it may lead to such inefficiencies as unemployment.

The **'determination'** of the distribution of income can have two quite distinct meanings, one **positive** and the other **normative**. In the perfectly competitive free market system which is implied in the passage, incomes are **determined** by the price system within the assumed mechanism of the market economy. Unit 15 explains how the wage in a particular industry is determined by the productivity of the marginal individual worker to be employed. This is simply a matter of logical deduction from the basic assumptions of perfect competition.

It is vital to distinguish between a government's **normative** view on how the distribution of income should be determined and the way in which a **positive economic theory**, such as the theory of perfect competition, determines wages and profits as a part of the mechanism of the theory. Governments make value judgements on the desirable distribution of income. A distribution of income based on individual productivity might be economically desirable, in providing incentives, and socially desirable if people believe they should be rewarded for individual effort.

However, governments might also decide that individual productivity is only one of a number of criteria to take into account when determining the distribution of income. It is highly unlikely in any case, in a market economy free from government interference, that individuals would be rewarded on the basis of labour productivity alone. Initial inheritances of capital and land would be significant. The existence of monopoly would reward the strong, who possess market power, at the expense of the weak. In these circumstances governments may decide to alter the distribution of income on some criterion of 'social fairness'. The old and sick, who have no factor services to sell, will deserve some sort of income. Public opinion surveys indicate strong support for the idea of determining wages using the criterion of the **social value** of a job in some system of **job evaluation**. On this basis nurses would be rewarded more highly than casino croupiers. In practice, however, it would be almost impossible to determine incomes in this way without the complete destruction of market incentives. Within mixed economies, governments have preferred to use **taxes and transfers** to **modify** the **market-determined** distribution of income, rather than to **completely replace** the market.

Answer plan

1 Briefly explain the meaning of economic efficiency.

2 Explain the meaning of the passage: men and women do not **consciously** attempt to achieve an economically efficient system. Within a perfectly competitive system, economic efficiency or the 'good of all' would result from the self-interest of individuals (Adam Smith's 'Invisible Hand').

3 Nevertheless, the free markets of the real world may fail to achieve a state of economic efficiency, and they produce inefficiencies of their own, such as unemployment.

4 Interpret the second part of the question in a normative sense. There may be a case for basing the distribution of income on individual productivity, but other criteria such as protecting the weak should also be taken into account.

9.6   FURTHER READING

Burningham, D., editor, *Understanding Economics, an Introduction for Students* (Macmillan, 1978).
Chapter 2: Economics Systems.

Livesey, F., *A Textbook of Economics* (Polytech Publishers Ltd., 1978).
Chapter 2: The Economic System: The Utilization of Resources.

10 The Size and Growth of Firms

10.1 Points of perspective

This unit describes important aspects of the structure of British industry, emphasizing in particular the manner in which the size of firms has changed. Together with Unit 11 on the finance of industry, the unit provides a link between the micro-economic theory of Units 1 to 9, and the evaluation of British micro-economic policy in Units 12, 13, and 14. In this unit we shall be concerned with business enterprises in the private sector of the economy; nationalized industries are the subject of Unit 14.

10.2 Underlying concepts

In micro-economic theory, understanding is facilitated by considering the behaviour of a **single firm** operating a **single manufacturing plant** to produce a **specific product** within a **well-defined industry**. Reality, however, is much more complicated. Though single-plant/single-product firms certainly exist, particularly in the **small business sector** of the economy, large firms tend to be much more diverse. J. K. Galbraith has divided the economy into two parts: the thousands of small and traditional businesses on the one hand, and the few hundred technically dynamic, massively capitalized and highly organized corporations on the other. Large businesses in this **corporate sector** of the economy commonly operate in a variety of different industries, producing many different products from a number of separated plants. The largest business corporations are **multinational companies**, such as BP or ICI, controlling subsidiary enterprises and plants throughout the world. Some companies, such as Shell, are also **transnationals**, with ownership and control located in more than one country.

1 Industrial structure in the United Kingdom

Published statistics of the output of different British industries are usually based on the **Standard Industrial Classification**. This contains over 20 major subdivisions, called **orders**, such as the food, drink and tobacco group, and the clothing and footwear group. Orders are further subdivided into nearly two hundred categories, called **Minimum List Headings**, which are the nearest approach in official statistics to what is normally meant by an 'industry'.

In comparison with similar industrial countries, the United Kingdom has a relatively small agricultural sector, reflecting the reliance on food imports. In 1978, agriculture accounted for about 3% of Gross National Product, while mining and quarrying contributed nearly 4%. The manufacturing sector is not particularly large in comparison with the relative share of manufacturing in countries such as Japan and West Germany. The share of manufacturing in Gross Domestic Product was 37% in 1955, falling to about 30% by 1978. This reflects the importance of financial service industries, largely located in the City of London, to the British economy. It may also reflect the fact that many services, including the gas and electricity utilities in the public sector, are in the **sheltered economy** rather than in the **competitive economy**. By the nature of the service they provide, they are sheltered from import competition. The service sector has not experienced the **de-industrialization** or **structural decline** in response to import penetration that has occurred in the manufacturing sector. Indeed, some economists, including R. Bacon and W. Eltis, have argued that the growth of employment in the service sector – particularly in the public services – has contributed to the decline of the manufacturing sector through the 'crowding out' effects of taxation.

2 Firms

A **firm** or **enterprise** is a unit of control and ownership. A common method of classifying firms is in terms of the legal status of the enterprise. On this basis the main types of business enterprise in the United Kingdom are **sole proprietors** or **traders, partnerships,** and **private** and **public joint stock companies**, though other types of enterprise such as co-operatives and building societies may be important in certain specialized areas of the economy. The concepts of **small businesses** and **large businesses** are less easy to define, since they do not refer to a precise legal status. Most small businesses are sole proprietors, partnerships and private companies, whereas the overwhelming majority of large businesses are public companies. There are about 400 000 private companies in the United Kingdom and 11 000 public companies. Nevertheless, some private companies such as the Littlewoods retailing group are sufficiently big to be regarded as large businesses, and a significant number of public companies are relatively quite small. When in 1971 the Bolton Committee reported on the role of small firms in the national economy, it found that there were 820 000 small firms responsible for 14% of GNP and 18% of the net output of the private sector. The inclusion of agriculture and the professions would have increased the 1971 total to 1 250 000 enterprises employing 29% of the working population. The government had recommended to the Bolton Committee that a 'small firm might be defined broadly as one with not more than 200 employees', but the Committee decided that this definition was unsuitable for most industries. It used other criteria such as turnover in distribution, and the number of vehicles in road haulage, to classify small businesses. Generally, the Bolton Committee decided to include three further criteria in addition to the employment criterion recommended by the government in its definition of the small firm. These were:

 (i) that it has a relatively small share of its market;
 (ii) that it is managed by its owners or part-owners in a personalized way;
(iii) that it is independent.

3 Plants

A **plant** or **establishment** is an individual productive unit within an enterprise, such as a factory, shop or farm. Many manufacturing processes require the separation of production into specific technical operations conducted in different buildings and workshops. The manufacture of most automobiles, for example, involves a large number of **vertically related** processes from the casting of engines and the pressing of car bodies to the final assembly of the completed vehicle. Many of these processes may be **internally integrated** within the various plants owned by an enterprise. Sometimes a firm may own several plants, which are vertically integrated, operating in different geographical locations. In other circumstances the separated tasks may be performed in different workshops within a single plant or large factory. In the case of a multi-product firm (a diversified firm operating in different industries), it is of course usual for different plants to produce the different products, except when products are **jointly supplied** from a common raw material and manufacturing process.

10.3 ESSENTIAL INFORMATION

1 The growing size of British firms

(i) The aggregate concentration ratio There is little doubt that British industry has become increasingly dominated by large firms. Nevertheless it is worth remembering that, in a world context, British firms are not usually very large, and where large British companies compete in world markets they may be substantially smaller than some of their competitors.

The growing importance of large firms in the economy as a whole is indicated by the aggregate concentration ratio which measures the share of the 100 largest firms in manufacturing output. These accounted for 16% of manufacturing output in 1909, 22% in 1940 and 41% in 1972. Since the Second World War, the changes in the aggregate concentration ratio indicate a substantial increase in the importance of large firms in the British economy. Evidence on concentration outside manufacturing industry is less satisfactory, though retailing in general, and grocery retailing in particular, have become increasingly concentrated in a few large firms. In 1972 the 100 largest manufacturing firms supplied two-thirds of the output of the food and motor vehicle industries, and half the output of the chemical industry. The importance of the 100 largest firms was least in timber and furniture, and in leather clothing and footwear, accounting for less than 10% of output.

The evidence also indicates that the growth in aggregate concentration has been much more rapid in Britain than in other countries, despite the relative smallness of even the largest British firms.

(ii) The market concentration ratio A common measure of concentration within a particular industry is the **five firm concentration ratio**. This ratio shows that, since 1968, the five largest firms have accounted for over 90% of domestic output in a quarter of the separate manufacturing groups or orders. Again, for many products, market concentration ratios are higher in the UK than in the USA, France and Germany. However, the concentration ratio can be a misleading indicator of monopoly power when there is substantial international trade and import penetration. Some economists believe that manufacturing industries in the United Kingdom are subject to much more competition than the concentration ratio suggests.

The fact that little of the growth in manufacturing concentration in the United Kingdom is explained by increasing plant size is of some significance. Between 1930 and 1968 the share of the

100 largest plants in manufacturing output remained the same at 10.8%. The explanation for increasing concentration must lie in **the increase in the average number of plants owned by the largest firms**. This suggests that an important cause of the increased size of firm is due to **take-overs** and **mergers** between existing firms, rather than a result of internal growth and the technical expansion of plants.

2 Economies of Scale

External economies There are two sets of circumstances in which external economies occur:

(i) External economies of scale These occur when an individual firm within an industry, irrespective of its size or scale, benefits from a change in the scale of the industry as a whole. For example, the expansion of a firm which supplies components, in response to the growth of the whole industry, may allow an individual firm to buy components at a lower average cost. Such economies, which are **external to individual firms**, are **internal to the industry**,

(ii) External benefits External economies of the first type are **received through the market**. This enables an individual firm to buy its inputs at a lower price than would otherwise be the case. In contrast, an external benefit is an **externality received outside** the market, for example when a farmer benefits from the drainage installed by his neighbour. You should refer back to Unit 8 for a more detailed explanation of externalities, including external costs as examples of **external diseconomies**.

Internal Economies of Scale It is useful to distinguish between **plant-level economies of scale, firm-level economies of scale**, and **learning or experience effects**, all of which can result in a larger size of firm having a greater opportunity to achieve lower unit production costs. An internal economy of scale occurs whenever an increase in the scale of the inputs, including factors of production which in the short run are fixed, results in a fall in the average cost of producing a unit of output. Internal economies of scale can only occur if the size of either the plant or firm is increased. In contrast, **learning effects** occur after a new technology has been adopted. A learning effect occurs when managers and workers learn from experience how to operate particular technologies more effectively. Although learning effects will usually be associated with a change in the scale of operations, this is not inevitable. Nevertheless the existence of learning effects suggests that the full benefit of economies of scale will not be experienced until some time after the change in scale has taken place.

(i) Plant-level economies of scale The main sources of economies of scale at the plant level are increased possibilities for the division of labour, better integration of technical processes within a particular plant, and better utilization of indivisible items of plant. Most of these advantages are **technical economies of scale**, though there may be some scope for **managerial economies** of scale at the plant level as a result of managerial division of labour. **Volume economies** are a further type of technical economy: as the volume of a plant such as a blast furnace increases, the input of energy required to produce a unit of output may diminish.

(ii) Firm-level economies of scale Presumably, firms will try to benefit as much as possible from the available plant-level economies of scale. They will also try to take advantage of economies associated with the growth of the firms which are independent of plant size, for example:

(a) risk-bearing economies: spreading risks over a number of products.

(b) capital-raising economies: large firms can often borrow from banks at a lower interest rate than small firms. The next unit explains how large firms have **access to the capital market**.

(c) bulk buying and bulk marketing economies: Large firms may be able to use their **market power** to buy supplies at lower prices and to market their products on better terms negotiated with retailers.

(d) economies in overheads: The costs of management and research and development can be distributed over a larger output.

(iii) The Importance of economies of scale Empirical evidence suggests that there are considerable economies of scale at the plant level in bulk chemicals and in assembly operations where mass production methods can be applied, *e.g.* motor vehicles and refrigerators. However, in some cases scale economies may be as easy to obtain in a number of closely associated plants, not necessarily owned by the same firm, as in a single plant. In many industries the penalty of operating below **Minimum Efficient Plant Size** is small. The fact that the increase in concentration in the UK since 1945 has been through an increase in the number of plants owned or controlled by firms, rather than through an increase in plant size, suggests that firms have believed that more scope exists for economies at the firm level than at the plant level. Nevertheless, recent studies have concluded that firms which have grown through merger have performed less well after the merger. This may indicate that **diseconomies of scale**, resulting at the firm level from merger and acquisition, have exceeded the hoped-for scale economies. One such diseconomy is **X-inefficiency**, which has been identified in American research into mergers. X-inefficiency results from a company's inability to successfully implement new ideas and methods, for example when middle management's goal of keeping things as they are conflicts with the aims of the directors or the top management of the company.

3 Vertical, Horizontal and Conglomerate Integration

There are various ways in which the activities of a firm can be integrated. At the plant level there is an obvious technical **internal integration** of processes, which are often carried out in separate workshops. This is an example of **vertical** integration. Vertical integration of processes is also a motive for a firm to grow by **internal growth,** *i.e.* to invest in new plant in order to extend its operations into producing its own raw materials, components, or market outlets.

Integration can also take place by **acquisition**. A firm may take over or merge with an existing independent firm in order to integrate the existing capacity of the other firm into its operations.

(i) Vertical Integration A firm can expand through vertical integration forwards or backwards. **Backwards integration** occurs when a firm buys into its **sources of supply**, for example when a car-assemblying firm buys a manufacturer of gearboxes. **Forwards integration** involves the buying up of **market outlets**. This type of integration would take place if a car-assembly firm acquires a chain of retail showrooms.

(ii) Horizontal Integration results when a firm takes over a similar firm at the **same stage of production** in the **same industry**. The merger between British Motor Holdings and Leyland Motors which created British Leyland in the late 1960s was largely horizontal.

(iii) Conglomerate Integration This is also known as **lateral** or **diversifying integration**. The defining characteristic of a lateral merger is the acquisition of a firm producing a different product in a separate industry. Large firms which have grown through lateral integration into highly diversified companies are known as **conglomerates**, for example Trafalgar House, whose interests range from construction to publishing.

(iv) Statistics on Mergers Many take-overs or mergers will contain elements of vertical, horizontal and conglomerate integration. Nevertheless, J. D. Gribbin and the Office of Fair Trading have compiled a classification of mergers in the United Kingdom:

	Percentages					
	1965		1970		1974	
Type	No.	Value	No.	Value	No.	Value
Horizontal	78	75	84	70	68	65
Vertical	12	13	1	–	5	2
Diversified	10	12	15	30	27	33
	—	—	—	—	—	—
	100	100	100	100	100	100

The data indicate that most mergers are horizontal, a growing minority are conglomerate, and that vertical motives have been insignificant. Recent evidence suggests that the conglomerate motive has continued to grow in significance.

(v) Motives, Advantages and Disadvantages

(a) The underlying motive for a merger of any type is a company's belief that it can profitably use the assets of the firm which is being acquired. We have already indicated that this belief may be misguided, since the results of many mergers have been disappointing.

(b) Economies of scale. This is an important motive in vertical and horizontal mergers. However, a proper **productive integration** of the **plant** of the merged companies must take place if the benefits are to be realized. Otherwise, diseconomies of scale may result and the merged firm may perform less well than the previously separate companies.

(c) Financial motives. Economies of scale at a plant level are not an important motive behind conglomerate mergers. Financial motives, including the hope of financial economies of scale, are often significant in lateral mergers.

(d) Monopoly power motives. Horizontal and vertical mergers may be planned in order to create a monopoly position in the market. The merged company may intend to use its market power to restrict output and raise price so as to increase its profits.

(e) **Other motives**. Vertical mergers sometimes try to achieve **security of supply** or **access to the market**. The **spreading of risks** and the **wish to diversify** into growing markets are frequently cited as motives behind conglomerate mergers. Many mergers in the 1960s and 1970s had an **asset-stripping** motive. Asset-stripping mergers can be horizontal, vertical or conglomerate. The asset-stripper takes over a company in order to close it down, usually sacking the labour force and selling off the company's assets which are redundant to his plans. The asset-stripper believes that he can profitably convert the **hidden assets** of his 'victim' to an alternative use. In many examples of asset-stripping, the land owned by the take-over victim was the most important hidden asset. Asset-stripping earned a bad reputation because it was often associated with closing down productive firms and converting the premises to property speculation. However, some economists view asset-stripping as merely a part of the process of rationalization which any economy must experience if it is to adapt to changing technology and demand.

10.4 Links with other topics

You should refer back to Unit 3 for a theoretical coverage of economies of scale, and to Unit 8 for examples of externalities which illustrate external economies and diseconomies. In the next unit, Unit 11, we examine the way firms finance growth in the British economy, and then in Unit 12 we introduce further aspects of economies of scale and merger activity, in the treatment of competition policy.

10.5 Question practice

Essay Questions

Question 1 In 1972 there were about 69 000 small manufacturing firms (with fewer than 200 employees) in Britain accounting for some 18% of net output, 22% of employment and 12% of investment. What do you think are the main reasons for the existence of so many small firms? What justification can you suggest for the tax and other concessions made to small firms in 1978?

(JMB: June 1979)

Understanding the Question Although the question refers to a specific date, the 1978 Budget, we shall refer to more recent government policy and other events, since this is a popular and recurring type of question which seeks an understanding of the small-firm sector. The data and classification are based on the Bolton Report which has been described in the unit. You need not waste any time describing or explaining the data, which simply identify the contribution of small firms to the economy for your benefit.

   The first part of the question requires a straightforward list of the reasons why small firms survive:

(i) **entrepreneurial choice**—the owners of small firms may prefer the intimate surroundings and personal contacts of the business environment.

(ii) **limited market size**—this applies particularly to the provision of services such as hairdressing in local geographical areas.

(iii) **the demand for a personal or specialized service**—again, hairdressing provides a good example.

(iv) **the existence of diseconomies of scale**—in these circumstances, cost advantages will create a competitive advantage for small firms.

(v) **the absence of economies of scale**—many industries display an absence of noticeable economies or diseconomies of scale, and there is likely to be a wide distribution of different-sized firms competing side by side in such an industry. In other industries there may be 'niches' in the market, or in the supply of specialist services to bigger firms, which can best be filled by small businesses.

(vi) **'sunrise' industries**—a 'sunrise' industry is a completely new industry based on a new technology or a new product, such as digital watches. To start with, demand is small, accounting for the fact that firms are small. Over time, however, the small firms may grow into large businesses or be taken over by large firms in other industries, as the market expands.

   In order to earn a good pass grade, you must tackle the second part of the question. This particular question assumes some knowledge of the previous year's budget. More generally, it may be useful for students to display knowledge of the report on *The Financing of Small Firms* published in 1979 by the Wilson Committee which had been set up to review the functioning of financial institutions in the United Kingdom. The report criticizes the clearing banks for their approach to small firms, arguing that they are excessively cautious in lending to customers who have no personal capital. The Wilson Committee favoured a state-backed guarantee scheme for bank loans, a system finally adopted in the 1981 Budget. The Committee also agreed that specific tax advantages should be given to small firms to stimulate the flow of equity investment into small business from external sources. Quite clearly, the proposals of the Wilson Committee, as well as the earlier Bolton Committee, have influenced government policy to small firms. For example, in 1980 the government gave an incentive of marginal tax relief on investments between £1000 and £10 000, as long as the funds were committed for five years and did not form more than 30% of the equity. Political factors have also been important in determining government policy. Conservative governments are particularly committed to supporting a thriving small business sector, though in practice the policies of both Conservative and Labour governments tend to have favoured larger firms. The recent emphasis on the plight of small businesses can be viewed as an attempt to restore the balance. Also, in recent years it has frequently been said that if each small business took on one extra worker, unemployment would be reduced by one million workers. Increasingly, the growth of small businesses in the service sector has been seen as one way of reducing the unemployment caused by the decline of larger businesses in the manufacturing sector.

Answer plan
1 Briefly comment on the contribution of small firms to the economy.
2 Explain why so many small firms exist, giving examples to support the reasons.
3 Explain the problems of small firms and the contribution they can make to the economy. Go on to explain that the tax changes are probably intended to reduce the problems and to increase the contribution. It is worth mentioning that many economists do not believe that the small-firm sector can make any significant contribution to overcome the more important problems of the British economy. These economists might regard aid to small firms as either misplaced or the result of political opportunism.

Question 2 (a) Why and how do firms pursue economies of scale? **(15)**
(b) What disadvantages to society may arise from the pursuit of economies of scale in production? **(10)**
(SEB 1981)

Understanding the Question Part (a) of the question receives the bulk of the available marks (60%), thus there is ample opportunity to provide a full annotated list of the 'how' after some explanation of the 'why'. Reasons why can be developed from the perspective of the objective of the firm e.g. the search for economies of scale is usually consistent with the profit maximizing motive. Alternatively the search for economies of scale may result from a growth maximizing objective.

How?–answers should be a straightforward list of the different types of economy of scale: technical, managerial etc.

Part (b) is an example of the **divergency between the private and social costs and benefits** arising from private decisions of firms and the possible conflict between the aims of private sector firms and the general welfare of society at large. Note that the question does not ask for the gains for society arising from the pursuit of scale.

Answer plan
1 Define economies of scale, taking care to distinguish economies of scale from increasing returns to scale and the short run principle of increasing returns.
2 Discuss why firms pursue economies of scale.
3 Discuss how they achieve the various types of economy of scale.
4 Disadvantages will occur if diseconomies rather than economies of scale arise.
5 Other disadvantages may result from divergencies between private and social cost and benefit.

Multiple Choice Questions

Question 3

Industry   *Number employed (thousands)*

	Year 1	Year 2	Year 3
Shipbuilding and marine engineering	243	211	205
Textiles	836	776	767
Vehicles	891	886	862

The conclusion that these industries are declining is valid if
(a) the industries have become more capital intensive
(b) output varies directly with the number employed
(c) the size of the working population has remained the same
(d) diseconomies of scale have been experienced.

Understanding the Question The correct answer to the question is **(b)**. Alternative **(a)** is completely incorrect since a growth in capital intensity could accompany a growth in output and a decline in the labour force. Alternatives **(c)** and **(d)** are simply irrelevant to the meaning of the question.

Question 4 Which of the following statements offers the best explanation of the existence of economies of scale?
(a) Demand for some products is greater than for others.
(b) Labour becomes more efficient when added to fixed capital.

(c) Large firms can obtain the benefits of monopoly.
(d) Some factors of production are not easily divisible.

Understanding the Question Demand must of course be sufficient to allow a firm to benefit from economies of scale, but demand does not explain such economies. Alternative (b) refers to the short-run laws of returns which should be carefully distinguished from long-run returns to scale and economies of scale. The benefits of monopoly are not directly related to economies of scale, though the market power which a large firm may possess can reduce the cost of inputs. The best answer is (d), which is based on the concept of **indivisibilities**.

Data Response Questions

Question 5 The following passage is adapted from a report in *The Guardian*, 23 October 1979.
'Audiotronics Ltd. is an electronics distributing group which sold off the famous but loss-making Lasky Hi-Fi retail chain to Ladbroke for over £3 million. (Ladbroke had no previous connections with Hi-Fi retailing.) Audiotronics can now look forward to a profitable future; it imports and distributes a range of industrial and consumer electronic goods. It can now expand overseas operations and expects to purchase another U.K. wholesale electronics distributor. The sale of the former Lasky retail chain has brought profits as former retail competitors are now willing to purchase supplies from Audiotronics Ltd.'

(a) Comment on the disadvantages of vertical integration.
(b) Why might a company be willing to buy a chain of loss-making shops?

(London: June 1981)

Understanding the Question In answering the first part of the question you must avoid the temptation merely to write a list of disadvantages, unrelated to the data in the passage. Vertical integration can pose problems of maintaining control between the various vertically related parts of a firm, creating a type of diseconomy. For example, Audiotronic may build up stocks of imported equipment which are greater than the amount Lasky's can sell. The passage indicates that other retail firms were unwilling to buy these stocks from Lasky's. In certain circumstances, monopoly might be a problem, if for example Audiotronics refused to supply competitors of Lasky's. It is worth pointing out that the passage does not indicate this disadvantage.

The takeover by Ladbrokes, a company in the leisure and gambling industry, is an example of lateral or conglomerate diversification. The general motive is that the owners or managers of Ladbrokes believe that they can make profitable use of the loss-making company's assets, either in their existing use, or by conversion to an alternative use. Since high street retail outlets have many possible uses, asset-stripping could be a motive. It is unlikely, however, that all the hi-fi shops would be converted to betting shops, which is Ladbroke's main line of business! It is more likely that the company wishes to diversify out of an area which may be experiencing restricted growth prospects.

Answer plan
1 Define vertical integration.
2 Explain the disadvantages, indicating which disadvantages are in evidence in the passage and which are not. Distinguish between disadvantages to the firm and to the community.
3 Explain that the Lasky's take-over is an example of a diversifying merger.
4 Suggest motives for such a take-over – spreading of interest, complementary activities, asset-stripping, etc.
5 Mention the fact that other firms may have vertical or horizontal motives for taking over a chain of retail shops.

10.6 FURTHER READING

Prest, A. R., and Coppock, D. J., editors, *The UK Economy, A Manual of Applied Economics*, 9th edition (Weidenfeld & Nicolson, 1982).
Chapter 4: Industry and Commerce.

Morris, D., editor, *The Economic System in the UK*, 2nd edition (Oxford University Press, 1979).
Chapter 3: The Behaviour of Firms.

A Review of Monopolies and Mergers Policy, A Consultative Document (HMSO Command 7198, 1978).

11 The Capital Market and the Stock Exchange

11.1 POINTS OF PERSPECTIVE

In Unit 10 we explained how firms grow through a process of either **internal** or **external** growth, or through a combination of both. We now examine how a firm might finance the process of growth, involving as it does the investment in new plant and productive capacity in the case of internal growth, and the acquisition of other firms by take-over or merger when external growth takes place.

11.2 UNDERLYING CONCEPTS

1 Saving and Investment

Although saving and investment have a similar meaning in everyday language, the economist uses each word in a distinct way. **Saving** is defined as **income which is not spent on consumption**, including funds that simply lie idle. In contrast, **investment** involves the **productive use of savings** in the purchase of capital goods, stocks, and raw materials. As a generalization, **households** make **savings decisions** and **firms** make **investment decisions**. Nevertheless, up to 70% of the investment carried out by British firms is financed by **internally generated funds**, when a firm provides its own savings out of revenue from the sale of its output.

Alternatively, firms may be able to obtain savings directly from households, for example by advertizing the sale of **shares**. It is more usual, however, for firms to gain access to the savings of households via **financial intermediaries** such as banks, insurance companies and pension funds, known generally as the **financial institutions**.

2 Alternative sources of finance

It is useful to distinguish between **internal** and **external** sources of finance, taking care not to confuse these terms with the concepts of internal and external growth which were mentioned earlier:

(i) Internal finance We have already defined internal finance as the savings which a firm generates internally out of revenue. These funds are sometimes known as **ploughed-back profits**. It is worth repeating that self-finance provides by far the most important source of funds for British industry.

(ii) External finance. Some 30% of the financial requirements of firms in the private sector of the economy are raised through borrowing, the sale of shares, and government grants or subsidy. The main forms of external finance are:

(a) Trade credit. This refers to the practice of delaying the payment of bills for as long as possible while trying to persuade customers to settle their debts as quickly as possible in order to improve cash flow. Trade credit is equivalent to an interest-free loan.

(b) Borrowing from banks. Bank loans account for approximately 10% of the funds which are available to firms from all sources in the United Kingdom. British banks have often been criticized for failing to provide long-term risk capital to British industry. But traditionally British banks have lent to finance investment in **working or circulating capital**, such as the building-up of stocks, in preference to **fixed investment** in new plant. We shall examine this criticism later in the unit, paying particular attention to the financial needs of small firms.

(c) Provision of finance by the government. This takes two main forms: firstly, the provision of loans to the private sector, and secondly, government grants and subsidies, for example in the form of regional aid and support policies to agriculture.

(d) Raising funds on the capital market. Students commonly confuse the **capital market** and the **Stock Exchange**, and exaggerate the importance of both markets as sources of finance for British industry. The capital market is not a single institution. It comprises all the institutions, including banks, insurance companies and pension funds, which are concerned with either the supply of or demand for long-term funds, or securities which are claims on existing capital. It is thus the market for **long-term loanable funds**, as distinct from the **money market** which is the market for short-term funds.

11.3 ESSENTIAL KNOWLEDGE

1 The Role of the Stock Exchange

'When the capital development of a country becomes a by-product of the activities of a casino, the job is likely to be ill done.'—J. M. Keynes, in the *General Theory.*

The Stock Exchange is often criticized as being a place of mere speculation, a casino where dealers are interested only in making immediate capital gains through buying securities at one price and selling at another. This criticism stems from the fact that the Stock Exchange is the **secondary** or 'second-hand' part of the capital market. The Stock Exchange is viewed as a casino by its critics because it has little direct role in the raising of long-term funds or risk capital for industry. Figure 11.1 illustrates why this is so. The actual raising of new capital takes place when public companies or the government decide to issue and sell new **marketable securities**. Companies may sell long-dated securities which guarantee a fixed rate of interest (**debentures or corporate bonds**) or they may sell a stake in the ownership of the company (**shares** or **equity**). New issues of shares can be sold when a company goes public for the first time, or when an existing public company decides to raise extra capital by a new equity issue, usually a **rights issue**. A rights issue gives existing shareholders the right to buy at a favourable price.

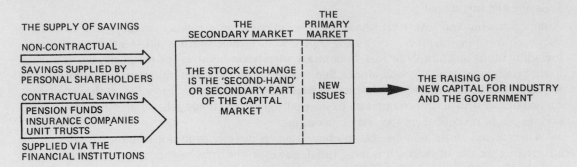

Fig 11.1 The stock exchange and the capital market

New issues are not sold on the Stock Exchange, though occasionally the new issues of small companies are **placed** through Stock Exchange firms. Instead, new issues are sold on the **primary part** of the capital market, usually through newspaper advertisements arranged by merchant banks, or through direct contact with existing shareholders when a rights issue is made. It is important to stress that the amount of new capital raised through new issues in any one year is only a small fraction of the total trading taking place in existing securities on the Stock Exchange. It follows that most share sales are second-hand deals in which one member of the general public or a financial institution sells an existing security to another person or institution. The person who buys the security prefers to hold an interest or dividend-earning financial asset instead of money, whereas the seller is switching out of securities in order to store his wealth in the more liquid form of money. Thus the majority of security sales reflect individual decisions, called **portfolio balance decisions**, to adjust the form in which personal wealth is held, rather than a decision to supply risk capital to industry.

Nevertheless, it is often argued that the Stock Exchange has important **indirect roles** in the provision of capital and the promotion of efficiency in British industry:

(**i**) When a private company decides to 'go public', its principle objective is to raise capital by securing access to the capital market. A Stock Exchange quotation, whereby the company's shares are *listed* and the market price *quoted* on the Stock Exchange, is certainly useful, and perhaps essential, if the general public are to be persuaded to buy the shares. New issues of shares would find fewer buyers if it was impossible to resell the securities on the Stock Exchange.

(**ii**) The Stock Exchange Council examines the financial structure and control of all quoted companies. There may be greater public confidence in companies if only the shares of 'reputable' companies are quoted.

(**iii**) The Stock Exchange has an important role in the restructuring of British industry in the face of changing technology and demand. Companies which fail to adapt will perform badly, and low profitability will cause share prices to fall. The quotation of a public company's shares on the Stock Exchange provides both an indicator of performance and a means through which the company can be taken over by new owners who believe they can use the company's assets more profitably. The threat of a future take-over can also provide an incentive for the existing managers to improve their performance.

2 The Government and the Capital Market

Only a small proportion of the securities traded on the capital market and the Stock Exchange represent either new or old capital raised by British industrial companies. A large proportion of securities are **overseas securities**. Others are **British Government Securities**, usually called **gilt-edged securities** or simply **gilts**. Gilts are similar to debentures although the government sells far more gilts than the private sector sells debentures. Thus gilts secure a fixed-term loan to the government, after which the gilts mature and the face value is paid back. In addition, the government guarantees to pay a fixed interest each year during the life of the security. What is not guaranteed is the day-to-day market price at which the security can be resold second-hand on the Stock Exchange, or indeed the price which the government can persuade the general public to pay when it sells the gilt as a new issue.

The total quantity of new gilts which the government sells each year is strongly dependent on the size of the **budget deficit** and the **Public Sector Borrowing Requirement** (PSBR). Generally speaking, the higher the level of public spending in relation to tax revenue, the larger the PSBR and the government's need to borrow on the capital market. A large issue of gilts tends to depress their price, thereby converting the guaranteed interest rate or yield into a higher effective or true interest rate. In this way, public spending may 'crowd out' the private sector in the capital market, since the sale of gilts eventually raises interest rates and the cost of borrowing by companies.

3 The Role of the Financial Institutions

It is widely believed that a large proportion of the shares in British companies are owned by small shareholders who are ordinary members of the general public. As the following table shows, this is no longer the case.

The ownership of company shares (percentages)

	1963	1973	1978
Persons and charities	61.3	46.4	40.3
Insurance companies	10.6	16.2	15.9
Pension funds	7.0	12.2	16.8
Investment trusts	6.7	6.5	10.0
Unit trusts	1.2	3.4	4.1
Banks	2.3	3.3	0.7
Industrial and commercial companies	4.8	4.3	3.0
Public sector	1.6	2.5	3.6
Overseas holders	4.4	5.2	5.6
	100	100	100

Source: *Report of the Royal Commission on the Distribution of Income and Wealth*, and the *New Statesman*.

These figures indicate that individuals now directly own well under half of all shares whereas financial institutions, including insurance companies, pension funds, and unit and investment trusts, own the greater proportion. Banks own relatively little equity, though they control a substantial amount through the management and advice given to pension funds and to ordinary shareholding customers of the banks. In fact, the degree of concentration of control over shares in the hands of the financial institutions is greater than the statistics of ownership suggest. The growing power of the financial institutions is an important cause of imperfection in the capital market. Nevertheless, it can be said in defence of the institutions that they represent the growth of the **indirect** ownership of industry by ordinary workers via their contributions to pension and insurance schemes. Yet while it is undoubtedly true that workers receive the benefits of ownership from the pensions and insurance endowments which are financed through company profits, it is much more debatable whether the growing indirect ownership of shares via the financial institutions gives workers any real control over industry.

4 The financing of small businesses

Access to the capital market tends to be restricted to public companies, especially those with a Stock Exchange quotation. Since most small businesses are sole traders, partnerships or private companies, they must rely on bank borrowing, rather than on the sale of securities on the capital market, as their principal source of external finance. Many owners of small businesses complain that banks treat them much less favourably than large companies when providing loans to finance investment. This view was supported in the report of the **Wilson Committee** on **The Financing of Small Firms**, published in 1979. Nevertheless, there are several reasons why investments by small firms are riskier than those undertaken by large companies:

(i) Large firms are likely to engage in a wider range of investments. If one investment fails, the likelihood that at least some of the other projects will succeed reduces the risk of bankruptcy. In any case, large firms usually have greater cash reserves to draw upon in just such a crisis.

(ii) Large public companies are less highly **geared**. A high gearing means that a large proportion of a company's assets are financed by borrowing rather than by shareholders' funds (accumulated profits and shares). Firms must usually pay a fixed rate of interest on their bank loans and debentures, even when no profits are being made. A high **gearing ratio** increases a firm's vulnerability to bankruptcy when business is bad. In contrast, a low-geared public company may survive a recession by suspending the payment of dividends to shareholders. Small businesses are usually highly geared, since they possess little or no equity capital. Banks may simply regard them as less attractive risks in comparison with lower-geared larger companies.

The Wilson Committee suggested a number of ways in which the financial position of small businesses could be assisted. The Committee favoured a **state-backed guarantee scheme for bank loans**, and the implementation of such a scheme was announced in the 1981 budget. The banks have in any case been introducing special advisory services for small firms and have advertized special **term loans** of between about one and seven years' duration, in an attempt to improve the facilities offered to small businesses. The banks have long claimed that the supply of finance is available and that the real problem lies in demand; businessmen do not wish to borrow at fixed interest rates for long periods in conditions of uncertainty about future profitability.

The Wilson Committee also advised the government to establish a **Small Firms Investment Company** (SFIC), and an **English Development Agency**, intended to be the beginning of a full-scale **Small Business Agency**. These bodies would function as intermediaries through which small businesses could raise equity capital. The Wilson Committee further proposed that 'over the counter' markets in unlisted shares be promoted, which would make it less expensive for small public companies to raise capital through share issue. In November 1980 an **unlisted securities** market was established by the Stock Exchange. However, the Wilson Committee's recommendations on the SFIC and the English Development Agency have not, as yet, been implemented, though the 1981 budget announced a **business start-up scheme**. This provides tax allowances for investment by individuals in new businesses.

11.4   LINKS WITH OTHER TOPICS

In this unit we have considered the financing of businesses in the private sector of the economy. We go on to examine government financial assistance to industry in Unit 13 and the financing of investment by nationalized industries in Unit 14. The financing of public investment in roads, schools and other forms of **social capital** is discussed in Unit 17 on public finance.

11.5   QUESTION PRACTICE

Essay Questions

Question 1 What factors are likely to be important in the determination of share prices and of movements in the Financial Times Ordinary Share Index? Why do you think that movements in the latter are regarded as significant?

(JMB: June 1979)

Understanding the Question This question requires analysis, using supply and demand techniques, rather than description. It does not require a detailed explanation of how the FT Index is constructed. Nevertheless, it is useful to show that the FT Index is a measure of the average market price of a sample of ordinary shares. The index is an arithmetic average (1935 = 100) for thirty 'blue chip' shares – the ordinary shares of leading British companies. It is one of the stock indices published daily in the *Financial Times*.

Some textbooks suggest that the stock market is an example of perfect competition. It is assumed that shareholders are 'price-takers' and that supply can be quickly varied. However, the growth of institutional investors and 'insider trading' have tended to undermine these assumptions.

Two main factors which influence the demand for shares are **speculation** and **expectation**. Both of these may in turn be influenced by historical prices, and public and private information. Speculators may hope to make short-term **capital gains** by buying shares before the price rises and by selling later at a higher price. Alternatively, shares may be sold before the price falls in the hope of re-purchasing at the bottom of the market. It is useful to distinguish between the speculator's hope of a capital gain and the desire of small shareholders, and perhaps the big institutions, to secure a regular income from dividends. On the supply side of the market, new share issues form only a very small part of the total of quoted, and mostly second-hand, securities. Nevertheless, a crop of new issues will tend to depress share prices, particularly if the market is already stagnant, by shifting the supply curve of securities rightwards. This is even more true when the government sells a large quantity of gilt-edged securities to finance the budget deficit. You can explain how share prices are depressed through the 'crowding out' effect.

You can answer the second part of the question by explaining how the movement of the index measures the **confidence** of the financial community. Confidence affects long-term economic decision-making, particularly investment decisions since share prices influence the cost of borrowing. The FT Index is an indicator of business optimism or pessimism about the future. Furthermore, it may indicate the faith, or lack of it, in current government policy and the government's ability to achieve certain economic targets. For instance, if the government fails to limit inflation, wealth held in the form of shares becomes worth less in real terms. This in turn may cause the selling of shares to increase and buyers to disappear, depressing prices and causing the real value of shares to be further reduced.

Attention is usually centred on short-term fluctuations in the FT Index, but it is worth noting that the index would have to be well above 1000 in the 1980s in order to maintain the real value of shares at their 1970 level. In fact, the FT Index has seldom been much above 500. This emphasizes the long-term relative fall in share prices and the falling value of British industry – the 'real economy' behind the veil of share prices.

Answer plan

1 Carefully distinguish between the FT Index and individual share prices.
2 Show the different factors, such as profits, plans, sales, government decisions, industrial problems and international developments which affect particular shares. Draw a diagram to show the application of supply and demand analysis.
3 Explain how the FT Index is a more general indicator of trends, but still subject to supply and demand. Distinguish between its short-term volatility and the long-run trend.

Question 2 Discuss the role of the Stock Exchange in the allocation of investment capital. How has the growth of larger institutional investors increased market imperfections?

(London: June 1980)

Understanding the Question You should treat the question as being made up of two equal parts – many students tend to write at length on *how* firms raise capital by obtaining a stock market quotation and the issue of shares, but this is largely irrelevant to the question. One approach to the first part of the question is to explain how new issues of shares raise only about 10% of the investment funds of the private sector, and how only public companies can use the Stock Exchange. Emphasize the fact that the role of the Exchange is indirect, since it is the second-hand part of the capital market. You will be expected to explain how the price of shares affects the cost of raising new funds on the capital market. It is useful to remember that the nationalized industries account for a large part of total industrial investment. Public corporations do not usually borrow directly on the capital market, though in the early 1980s the Conservative Government started to experiment with the issue of shares in nationalized industries. Indirectly, the capital market does provide investment finance to public corporations. The government **borrows** on the capital market through the sale of gilts, and then **lends** to nationalized industries from the National Loans Fund. It would be relevant at this point to introduce the 'crowding out' controversy which we explained in the unit and in the context of the previous question.

Financial institutions now own over half the securities which are quoted and traded on the Stock Exchange. Many of the pension funds are in fact managed by insurance companies and banks, which further increases the concentration of **control**, as distinct from **ownership**, of shares. The large institutions possess superior **market information** than is available to the small shareholder, and they can exercise **market power** through their buying and selling policies. Market imperfections may be accentuated by the institutions' habit of operating 'behind closed doors'. The institutions are reluctant to take an active role in the management of industry, despite the fact that they are the hidden controllers, and often the owners, of British industry. Critics assert that this inactive management role further increases the divorce between ownership and decision-making which is characteristic of large public companies.

Answer plan

1 Explain how the Stock Exchange has an indirect rather than a direct role in capital-raising.
2 The role is restricted to public companies in the private sector. Discuss the relative importance of debentures and shares, and the much greater significance of other forms of capital-raising which are unrelated to the Stock Exchange.
3 Nationalized industries' investment may depress share prices via effects on the interest rate, thereby 'crowding out' private sector investment.
4 Briefly describe the institutional investors.
5 Explain how market imperfections may result from differences in the quality of information possessed by large and small shareholders, and from the market power enjoyed by the big institutions.

Multiple Choice Questions

Question 3 A small public joint stock company declares a yearly dividend of 25p on each £1 share. Assuming that the stock market is a perfect market and that the market rate of interest is 10%, the market price of the company's shares should now be:
(a) £1.00
(b) £0.10
(c) £2.50
(d) The price will depend on how close the share is to maturity.

Understanding the Question The question is testing whether you can handle the simple formula required to calculate share prices or the rate of interest:

$$\frac{\text{dividend}}{\text{market price}} = \text{market rate of interest}$$

In this case we get:

$$\frac{25p}{250p} = 10\%$$

The question illustrates two important economic concepts, the **inverse** relationship between security prices and the rate of interest, and the distinction between, on the one hand, the nominal value of the share (£1) and the nominal yield (25%) and, on the other hand, the market price of the share (£2.50) and the effective yield (10%).

Question 4 Which of the following types of financial asset does not secure a loan?
(a) a gilt-edged security

(b) a debenture
(c) a National Savings Certificate
(d) an ordinary share

Understanding the Question Wealth assets can be divided into **physical assets** (or **non-financial assets**), such as property and consumer durables, and **financial assets**. Financial assets are often called securities, since they secure ownership of **loans** in the case of **(a)**, **(b)**, and **(c)**, or ownership of a part of the assets of a company in the case of shares. **(d)** is therefore the correct answer.

11.6   FURTHER READING

Livesey, F., *A Textbook of Economics* (Polytech Publishers Ltd., 1978)
Chapter 6: Investment.

Prest, A. R., and Coppock, D. J., *The UK Economy, a Manual of Applied Economics*, 9th edition (Weidenfeld & Nicolson, 1982).
Chapter 2: Monetary Credit and Fiscal Policies.

12 Competition Policy

12.1   POINTS OF PERSPECTIVE

Competition policy is a convenient term which covers government policy and legislation on monopolies, mergers, and restrictive trading practices. It is an important part of the government's industrial policy – the **micro-economic policy** which attempts to improve industrial performance by altering the **structure** or **supply side** of the economy. Underlying the policy is the presumption that competition promotes economic efficiency, and that the more competitive the economy, the better the performance in terms of living standards, the growth rate and the Balance of Payments that can be achieved.

We can use the problem of monopoly, and the related problems of mergers and restrictive practices, to introduce three different approaches to economic policy-making:

1 A non-interventionist approach

It is sometimes argued that the government should never intervene in the market economy. Instead it should leave the allocation of resources and production decisions entirely to market forces and the price mechanism. According to this view, government economic policy should be an 'anti-policy' or a policy of 'having no policy at all'. Thus it is not the function of government to break up monopoly if monopoly is the 'natural' product of free market forces.

2 An automatic rule approach

Some economists and politicians, who believe equally fervently in the virtues of private enterprise and free market forces, adopt a rather different attitude to economic problems. They take the view that only when the economy approximates fairly closely to the conditions of perfect competition can the desirable properties of economic efficiency, and consumer sovereignty and choice, be achieved. Monopoly *per se* must be regarded as bad. The adoption of an **automatic policy rule** to break up existing monopolies is suggested by this approach. Similar rules could ban mergers which would create new monopolies, and outlaw restrictive trading practices, whatever the circumstances that might be used to justify them. Automatic policy rules of this type are examples of **non-discretionary** economic policy, a concept which will prove highly useful when we examine **monetarism** and **Keynesianism**.

3 A pragmatic or discretionary approach

British monopoly policy adopts neither the laissez-faire approach nor the anti-discretionary policy stance which we have just described. Instead, it is firmly based on the essentially pragmatic view that each case of a monopoly or a trading practice that restricts competition must be judged on its merits. Supporters of British policy claim that this is its greatest virtue, but critics argue that the policy is so pragmatic or discretionary as to be much too weak, ineffective, and inconsistent. They would like to see legislation introduced on the American model to break up monopolies and prevent all mergers above a certain size. The evidence of recent cases in the American courts suggests, however, that US monopoly policy is becoming rather less automatic.

12.2 UNDERLYING CONCEPTS

1 The case against monopoly

The pragmatic approach of British policy is sometimes justified by the argument that there is an economic case both for and against monopoly. The theoretical arguments have been treated in greater depth in Unit 6, but we shall briefly summarize the main points:

(i) In economic theory it is assumed that firms pursue their self-interest, which is usually held to be profit-maximization. A public policy problem exists when a **divergency** arises between the **self-interest** of the firm and the **public interest** (or between the **private** and **social costs and benefits** resulting from the activities of the firm). Monopoly profit-maximization, contrary to perfect competition, restricts output and raises prices, resulting in **economic inefficiency** (the combination of **productive** and **allocative inefficiency**);

(ii) Monopolies may have less incentive to innovate;

(iii) Monopoly may restrict consumer choice;

(iv) Monopolies may use their market power to discriminate 'unfairly' between different groups of customers.

2 The case for monopoly

(i) The argument that monopolies restrict output and raise prices assumes that monopolies and competitive firms have similar cost curves. Monopoly may nevertheless be justified in industries which benefit from **economies of scale**. There is a case for a **natural monopoly**, or perhaps a **natural oligopoly**, when limited market size imposes a constraint which makes it impossible for more than a few firms to benefit from full economies of scale.

(ii) When British firms compete against very large foreign firms in world markets, a large British monopoly may be justified to **countervail** the market power of the foreign firm and to reduce import penetration.

(iii) There is a strong argument for monopoly in the case of the **utility industries**, such as the gas and electricity industries. Competition would lead to unnecessary and costly duplication of distribution networks. The public policy choice in the case of the utility industries is not so much between competition and monopoly, as a choice between **public monopoly** through **nationalization**, and **private monopoly subjected to severe public regulation**.

(iv) Whether innovation is likely to be increased or diminished by monopoly may depend upon the reason for the creation of the monopoly. It is useful to divide monopolies into:

(a) **Cartels**. A cartel is usually regarded as the worst form of monopoly, one that is likely to exhibit most of the disadvantages of monopoly with few, if any, of the benefits. A cartel is a **price ring** which is formed when separate firms make a restrictive agreement to charge the same price, and possibly to restrict output. A cartel acts as a monopoly in the marketing of goods, but the benefits of economies of scale are unlikely to occur, since the physical integration of the productive capacity of the members of the cartel does not take place. Consumer choice is restricted and cartels tend to keep inefficient firms in business while the more efficient firms make monopoly profits. In these circumstances it is quite likely that the incentive to innovate may indeed be lacking.

(b) **Fully-unified monopolies**. In contrast, a fully-unified monopoly may result from accident rather than design. A firm which grows and benefits from economies of scale may end up as a monopoly, the reward for successful competition! The monopoly position can be the result of the firm's success in innovating, introducing new products, and reducing costs. Even though a monopoly has been created, the firm may continue to behave well, continuing its innovating habits and using its monopoly profit to finance new developments.

12.3 ESSENTIAL KNOWLEDGE

1 Key dates in the history of British competition policy:

(i) **1948**: The establishment of the **Monopolies Commission** marked the beginning of monopoly policy in the UK.

(ii) **1956**: Restrictive trading practices were treated separately from the problem of monopoly, through the **Restrictive Practices Court (RPC)**.

(iii) 1965: The scope of the Monopolies Commission was widened. The Commission, now re-named as the **Monopolies and Mergers Commission (MMC)**, now investigates mergers as well as established monopolies.

(iv) 1973: The **1973 Fair Trading Act** provides the framework of the current competition policy. It established the **Office of Fair Trading (OFT)**, which completes the triumvirate of institutions which implement competition policy – the MMC, RPC and OFT.

(v) 1980: The 1980 Competition Act extended the role of the MMC to undertake **efficiency audits** of nationalized industries.

2 Competition policy in the 1980s

(i) Monopoly policy Since 1973 a **statutory monopoly** has existed if: either one firm has at least 25% of the market for the supply or acquisition of particular goods or services (a **scale monopoly**); or a number of firms, which together have a 25% market share, so conduct their affairs as to restrict competition (**a complex monopoly**). The decision on whether a monopoly operates or is likely to operate against the public interest is made by the MMC, an independent administrative tribunal composed of up to 26 part-time members and a full time Chairman, all appointed by the government. It is useful to identify three separate stages in the discretionary implementation of monopoly policy:

(a) Firms which fall within the statutory definition of a monopoly are not automatically investi-gated; nor can the MMC choose the firms or industries it wishes to investigate. Before 1973, an important criticism of British monopoly policy was that governments could exercise too much discretion in deciding whether or not to refer a statutory monopoly to the MMC for investigation. It was argued that many monopolies which should have been investigated were never referred. In response to this criticism, the 1973 Fair Trading Act empowered the **Director General of Fair Trading (DGFT)** to make references to the MMC. Almost all such references of statutory monopolies are now made by the DGFT.

(b) The members of the MMC who conduct a particular investigation are free to determine their own procedure of inquiry. The 1948 Act specified a number of factors which the MMC should take into account in interpreting the public interest, but many of the early reports of the MMC in the 1950s were inconsistent with each other. To overcome this problem, the 1973 Fair Trading Act laid down more precise guidelines for interpreting the public interest. In its early days the MMC employed no economists. It now possesses a full time research staff and consults with and seeks advice from the DGFT in deciding how to conduct its investigations and in interpreting the public interest. The MMC conducts its inquiries into monopolies within a time limit, usually of eighteen months to two years. There has been some criticism from industry about the length of time and cost to firms of monopoly investigations.

(c) The MMC does not possess any powers to implement or enforce its recommendations. Instead, it reports to the government, which may either implement some or all of the recommendations, shelve the report and do nothing, or take action which is completely contrary to the MMC's recommendations. For example, in 1981 the Minister for Prices allowed credit-card companies to insist that retail outlets charge the same price to both cash and credit-card customers, despite an MMC recommendation that this was against the public interest. Usually, however, the government complies with the spirit of the MMC's report. The government has quite wide powers to take action, including the power to make an **order** requiring that firms split up or sell off assets. In practice, these order-making powers are seldom if ever used. It is currently usual for the government to ask the DGFT to talk with the firms involved to persuade them to abandon any undesirable practices and to give undertakings about their future conduct.

(ii) Two recent trends in monopoly policy have been:
(a) **The increasing involvement of the DGFT**. We have already noted that the DGFT advises the MMC and makes almost all monopoly references. In addition he has taken on the continuous function of scanning or screening British industry for evidence of anti-competitive behaviour, for example by filtering evidence from consumer complaints. Monopoly policy has been criticized in the past for lacking consistency in the way references to the MMC are made. To meet this criticism, the DGFT has developed a systematic screening process of highly con-centrated sectors of industry using **market structure, conduct, and performance indicators**. **Concentration ratios**, if due allowance is made for imports, can provide evidence of changing **market structure**. The DGFT has used four **conduct indicators**: (i) consumer and trade complaints; (ii) evidence of parallel pricing (price discrimination) or price leadership; (iii) evidence of merger activity; and (iv) the ratio of advertizing expenditure to sales. The

four **performance indicators** adopted by the DGFT have been: (i) price movements; (ii) changes in profit margins; (iii) the ratio of capital employed to turnover; and (iv) the return on capital employed. Performance indicators such as these help to measure the extent to which economic efficiency, both productive and allocative, is being achieved.

(b) **The extension of monopoly policy to the nationalized industries.** Some of the largest and most powerful monopolies in the UK are nationalized industries, yet before 1973 monopoly policy was restricted to the private sector of the economy. Indeed, Labour governments in particular have often taken the view that the problem of monopoly results from private ownership and the pursuit of profit. A logical result of this view is that **public ownership**. or **nationalization**, provides an appropriate policy to deal with monopoly. Few people now accept that a change of ownership, to operate in the social or public interest, will by itself overcome the problem of monopoly. Indeed, it may merely change the nature of the problem. Nationalization may encourage inefficiency and resistance to change if workers and managers in the state monopolies believe that poor performance will never be 'disciplined' by bankruptcy or take-over. It is not surprising, therefore, that recent Conservative governments have extended monopoly legislation to the nationalized industries. The government can now refer a nationalized industry to the MMC for an **efficiency audit**. In one of the first of its reports since the 1980 Competition Act, the MMC recommended that the British Gas Corporation sell off retail showrooms to firms in the private sector in order to create more competition in the sale and and servicing of gas appliances.

(iii) Restrictive trading practice policy It is useful to distinguish between the trading restrictive practices independently undertaken by a single firm, and collective restrictive practices which involve either a written or implied agreement with other firms. There is no separate legislation dealing with the former type of restrictive practice, for example **parallel pricing** (price discrimination) and the refusal to supply a particular resale outlet. Instead, such practices will normally be considered as evidence of market conduct when the DGFT decides on monopoly references to the MMC. In its reports the MMC frequently recommends the dropping of such practices. In contrast, collective restrictive agreements and practices come within the terms of reference of the Restrictive Practices Court. It is often argued that British policy towards collective agreements, such as cartel agreements, is more effective than policy towards statutory monopoly. This is because the RPC is a **court** and not an **investigatory commission**. By law, a firm must register a restrictive agreement with the DGFT, who automatically notifies the RPC. The restrictive agreement is presumed to be illegal unless the firm can persuade the court that the practice is in the public interest. Eight 'gateways' have been permitted which allow a firm to argue that a restrictive agreement is in the public interest. For example, an agreement can be justified if its removal might cause a substantial reduction in exports.

(iv) Merger policy Some economists argue that the increasing effectiveness of restrictive practice legislation was a major cause of the take-over and merger booms which occurred in the 1960s and 1970s. Firms sought to circumvent the outlawing of restrictive agreements by internalizing the restrictive practice through merger! Nevertheless, it has generally been assumed in British policy that mergers are beneficial unless it can clearly be shown that the effects are likely to be adverse. This explains why so few mergers which qualify for investigation have actually been referred to the MMC. Currently, a merger is eligible for reference by the government if the merger creates a combined company with at least 25% of an industry, or if the assets of the company being acquired are valued at £15 million or more. Although he cannot make merger references to the MMC, the DGFT has important screening and advisory roles. He must keep himself informed of all eligible merger situations, by picking up information from the firms themselves and from the financial press.

Before advising the government on a merger reference, the DGFT first consults the **Mergers Panel**, a non-statutory inter-departmental committee of civil servants who represent all government departments which might have an interest in the case. The Mergers Panel also gives confidential guidance to firms contemplating a merger, indicating whether a reference to the MMC is likely. Thus, although there were only 43 merger references to the MMC between 1965 and 1978 (out of a total of more than 1500 eligible mergers), it has been argued that the policy is more effective than these statistics indicate. The possibility of a reference makes companies think carefully before going ahead with a merger. It usually takes over six months to investigate a merger reference. The time taken is a considerable disadvantage to the firms involved and may effectively prevent the merger, even though the MMC may eventually find the merger beneficial to the public interest.

Nevertheless, British merger policy is still criticized for being too weak and inconsistent. Critics have argued that the stance of the policy should be significantly changed to a presumption that mergers have **adverse** rather than **beneficial** effects. Added weight was given to this criticism in the 1970s, when a number of studies provided evidence on the disappointing results of mergers. The 1978 Green Paper which reviewed monopoly and merger policy accepted this criticism, but recommended that a **neutral** merger policy be adopted. It now seems that the DGFT and the MMC pay more attention to the likely anti-competitive effects of a merger than to the possible advantages of economies of scale.

12.4   LINKS WITH OTHER TOPICS

Examination questions frequently require an evaluation, in the light of economic theory, of either the aims or the effects of some aspect of competition policy. Although we have summarized some of the essential theoretical arguments in this unit, you should refer back to Units 6 and 7 for a more rigorous treatment of the required analysis.

In Units 13 and 14, we go on to consider other aspects of government micro-economic policy – the policy which aims to improve performance on the supply side of the economy. Unit 15 then considers the role of trade unions as monopoly suppliers of labour in the factor market.

12.5   QUESTION PRACTICE

Essay Questions
Question 1 Compare and contrast alternative methods of dealing with the problem of monopoly.

(London: June 1979)

Understanding the Question This is not a question on the history of British monopoly policy, though it is permissable to illustrate your arguments from British experience (or the experience of any other country). You must obey the instruction to compare and contrast different types of policy. Separate accounts can be heavily penalized by examiners when the question specifies a comparison. A **comparison** involves noting the **similarities** between different types of policy whereas a **contrast** notes **differences**. When answering this type of question, it is equally valid either to compare and contrast two or three alternative policies in some depth or to cover a longer list more briefly.

Not all the possible methods of dealing with monopoly have been used in the United Kingdom. We have stressed in the unit how British competition policy has favoured a pragmatic rather than a non-discretionary approach. You could structure your answer around this choice, or you might make use of a list of more specific policy measures:

1 The compulsory breaking up of monopolies and the banning of mergers.
2 A 'watchdog' or investigatory approach, watching out for monopoly abuse and investigating monopolies and mergers when abuse or inefficiency is suspected.
3 The use of price controls to restrict the monopolist's freedom in the market place.
4 Taxation of monopoly profits.
5 Socializing monopolies, by taking them into public ownership as nationalized industries.
6 Privatizing the public monopolies, by selling off nationalized industries to the private sector.
7 Exposing monopolies to greater competition:
  (i) Removing the legal monopoly status of, for example, the Post Office or commercial TV companies, thereby exposing them to greater domestic competition.
  (ii) The encouragement of import competition. This can be quite effective in reducing the market power of public and private monopolies in the **competitive economy**, but it is less effective in the case of monopolies, usually nationalized industries, in the **sheltered economy**.

Answer plan
1 Define a monopoly, distinguishing between pure monopoly and highly concentrated industries which qualify as statutory monopolies in the UK.
2 Discuss **briefly** the advantages and disadvantages of monopoly and state whether you consider it to be a problem.
3 Compare and contrast a discretionary monopoly policy with one based on enforcing an automatic anti-monopoly rule.
4 Compare and contrast specific anti-monopoly policy measures. Show how different policy measures may have similar aims but differ in the methods used to restrict monopoly abuse.

Question 2 'Since mergers lead to economies of scale they should be encouraged in order to improve our competitive position in world markets'. Discuss.

(SUJB: June 1980)

Understanding the Question You must avoid the temptation to write a detailed description of either economies of scale or the various motives for merger. However, it is well worth while to emphasize that the hope of achieving economies of scale is only one of many motives for merger. It is generally agreed that economies of scale are more likely in the case of horizontal and vertical mergers than when a conglomerate merger takes place. You could point out that, even when economies of scale provide a motive for merger, it does not automatically mean that the merged company will actually achieve the expected economies. The weight of empirical evidence published in recent years suggests that the results of mergers have often been disappointing. If economies of scale result from a merger, a firm should become more competitive in world markets because lower costs should lead to lower prices. You should point out that UK mergers are usually for domestic rather than international motives, and so the reason given in the question for encouraging mergers is not a strong one in practice. Many acquired companies have been asset-stripped or their products have not been developed. The potential to export may actually be reduced.

Answer plan

1 Distinguish between different types of merger such as **aggressive** and **defensive** mergers and **briefly** describe what is meant by economies of scale.
2 Discuss whether economies of scale are likely to result from different types of merger.
3 Explain how other advantages may result from merger besides economies of scale, *e.g.* countervailing market power. However, private and social advantage may not coincide. Briefly discuss disadvantages which may result from merger.
4 You can conclude that mergers should be encouraged if the estimated advantages exceed the disadvantages. This suggests that a pragmatic or discretionary policy is appropriate.

Multiple Choice Questions

Question 3 For the purposes of British monopoly policy, a statutory monopoly is defined as an industry in which
(a) there is only one firm
(b) one firm produces 33% of the industry output
(c) one firm produces 25% of the industry output
(d) the dominant firm has assets valued at £15 million or more

Understanding the Question This question tests factual recall and your knowledge of the qualifying condition for industries or firms to be referred to the MMC. Alternative (a) defines a pure monopoly rather than a statutory monopoly. Alternative (b) is the definition of a statutory monopoly which was applicable before 1973, whereas (d) introduces the distraction of the size of an acquired company if a merger is to be eligible for investigation. This leaves (c) as the correct answer.

Question 4 All except one of the following restrictive trading practices are generally illegal in the United Kingdom. The exception is:
(a) cartel agreements
(b) resale price maintenance
(c) patents
(d) refusal to supply retail outlets

Understanding the Question None of these restrictive practices or agreements are always illegal, since in some circumstances they may be judged to be in the public interest. Cartels are generally illegal, though the Building Societies Association provides an example of a lawful cartel. Resale price maintenance (RPM) was legal before 1964 but was outlawed by the 1964 Resale Prices Act; nevertheless, the Restrictive Practices Court judged that RPM was justified in the case of books and certain medicines and drugs. In 1981 the Monopolies Commission ruled in the case of Raleigh bicycles that refusal to supply is an unjustifiable restrictive practice. Patents are, of course, a legally enforced restriction. Thus (c) is the correct answer.

Data Response Questions

Question 5 Mr Justice Brennan, a US Supreme Court judge, said in the case of United States v Philadelphia National Bank (1963): 'We are clear that a merger, the effect of which "may be to substantially lessen competition", is not saved because on some ultimate reckoning of social, or economic, debits or credits it may be deemed beneficial . . . Congress determined to preserve our traditionally competitive economy. It therefore proscribed (forbade) anti-competitive mergers, the benign and the malignant alike.'.
In the light of this quotation, comment on British merger policy. *(London: January, 1981)*

Understanding the Question Although this is a data response question, in many ways it resembles a conventional essay question. However, it is essential to draw on and to interpret the key concepts in the quoted passage: social and economic credits and debits, and benign and malignant mergers. Your answer would be severely penalized if it merely described British policy without relating to these concepts. The question is testing whether you can **infer** from the passage that American policy is based on an automatic rule to prohibit all mergers which would create a monopoly.

Answer plan

1 Try to interpret the general meaning of the passage, taking care not just to paraphrase the quotation.
2 Explain how British merger policy is based on a completely different approach to that indicated in the passage. Relate the concepts of debits and credits, and benign and malignant mergers, to the pragmatic cost-benefit approach of British policy.
3 You may illustrate the working of British merger policy from relevant case studies if you wish, but this is not essential.
4 Likewise, you may wish to draw a conclusion about which approach to merger policy is preferable, but only do this if you can base your conclusion on evidence of the results of the policies in the two countries.

12.6 FURTHER READING
Livesey, F., *A Textbook of Economics* (Polytechnic Publishers Ltd., 1978). Chapter 18: Competition Policy

Prest, A. R., and Coppock, D. J. editors, *A Manual of Applied Economics*, 9th edition (Weidenfeld & Nicolson, 1982)
Chapter 4: Industry and Commerce.

Morris, D., editor, *The Economic System in the UK*, 2nd edition (Oxford University Press, 1979)
Chapter 16: Anti-Trust Policy

A Review of Monopolies and Mergers Policy, A Consultative Document (HMSO Command 7198, 1978)
Sparkes, J. R., and Pass, C. L., *Monopoly*, 2nd edition (Heinemann, 1980)

13 Industrial Location and Regional Policy

13.1 POINTS OF PERSPECTIVE

1 The Nature of the Regional Problem

There are several different regional problems in the United Kingdom. Regions such as the Scottish Highlands suffer from **remoteness**, often combined with a **lack of employment opportunities in manufacturing and service industries**. At the other extreme, problems of **congestion** caused by economic success have occurred, for example in south-east England. Most recently, the **decline of the inner city** has emerged as a serious problem, both in the older industrial regions and in London and the previously successful Midlands. Nevertheless, a striking feature of the British economy is a lack of the contrast between industrial and agrarian regions that exists in some other countries.

Until very recently, the dominant regional problem in the UK could be defined by a division of the country into two halves: a **'successful' half**, broadly the Midlands and the South-East; and an **'unsuccessful' half** in the north and west. Although mixed industrial-agricultural economies exist in both halves of Britain, the industrial base of the north and west is narrower and contains a larger proportion of older staple industries, usually in **structural decline**. Growth took place in both halves of Britain during the thirty years after the Second World War, but it was better sustained in the successful half of the country. A regional policy seemed necessary to prevent a further widening of the gap in living standards, wages and employment levels between the two halves of Britain.

2 Regional policy and the problem of de-industrialization

The importance attached by governments to regional policy has tended to vary according to whether the economy is in boom or recession. Regional policy was not very important during the period of relatively successful growth after the Second World War, but it re-emerged during the 1960s when the older industrial regions experienced an increase in unemployment. In recent years one might have expected a renewed emphasis on regional policy with the onset of much more serious recession. A possible reason why this has not occurred lies in the fact that the previously successful industries, such as the automobile industry, of the South-East and Midlands have also experienced structural decline.

De-industrialization has become a national and not just a regional problem. The onset of de-industrialization, or the structural decline of a large part of manufacturing industry, has undercut the assumption fundamental to regional policy – that national economic performance can be improved if part of the wealth created by growth in the South-East and Midlands is transferred to the problem regions. This is no longer possible when manufacturing industry in all regions suffers from structural decline. Since about 1975, therefore, British governments have switched the emphasis of policy away from specifically regional problems towards a more general **industrial policy**, aimed at halting and reversing industrial decline wherever it occurs. Regional policy is also less important to Conservative governments, which believe in a lower level of political interference in the market economy.

13.2 UNDERLYING CONCEPTS

1 Industrial location and the theory of the firm

As well as the problems of **what, how** and **for whom** to produce, firms must face the problem of

where to produce. It follows from the profit-maximizing assumption of the theory of the firm, that firms should choose the lowest-cost locations for their plants. In a perfectly competitive world, firms which failed to choose the least-cost locations would not survive, and market forces would achieve the most productively efficient location of industry. In practice, firms are seldom disciplined by such competitive forces in markets dominated by imperfect competition, monopoly profits and barriers to the entry of new firms. Sub-optimal location may reduce profits without producing a situation in which only the fittest survive. In any case, research indicates that firms are more interested in achieving a **satisfactory location**, chosen from just a few alternatives, than in risking the time and expense needed to obtain information about all possible locations.

2 Industrial Inertia

For various reasons, including technical progress and changing energy and transport requirements, the best or lowest-cost location may change with time. Industrial inertia occurs whenever a firm survives in a particular location after the best location has moved elsewhere. Again, the existence of monopoly profits may contribute to industrial inertia, which is especially likely when there is little difference in costs between alternative locations. Very often a build-up of **external economies** takes place in a region where an industry is established, which serves to counter some of the cost advantages of newer competing locations. The cost of writing off fixed investments may also encourage industrial inertia.

3 Footloose Industries

The absence of important differences in costs between alternative locations should encourage a 'footloose' industrial structure. This would have great significance for regional policy since it implies that only a small loss of efficiency results from the direction of footloose industries to the problem regions. It is not surprising, therefore, that the question whether production costs are influenced by location is of great importance in assessing the arguments for and against regional policy. Some industries are obviously tied by their nature to **specific locations**. The mining industry and other **extractive industries** provide many examples. **Bulk-reducing industries** such as metal-smelting and refining have traditionally been tied to the fairly specific location of either raw material or energy input, while brewing and other **bulk-adding industries** have often been located near to local markets. Over time, however, the transport and energy constraints, which previously determined a highly specific location, have lessened, and many industries are considerably more footloose than they used to be.

13.3 ESSENTIAL KNOWLEDGE

1 Different approaches to the regional problem

An obvious symptom of the regional problem in the United Kingdom has been the continuing **excess supply of labour** at existing wage-rates in certain parts of the country. This can also be represented as a **capital shortage**. In theory, such a **market disequilibrium** can be cured either by greater **capital mobility (taking work to the workers)**, or by greater **labour mobility (taking workers to the work**, assuming of course that the work exists elsewhere). A **market-orientated solution** to the regional problem would encourage the emergence of price and wage differentials between regions to provide incentives for both capital and labour mobility through the market.

The case for British regional policy has been based partly on the proposition that the operation of market forces has itself contributed to the regional problem. It has also been argued that it is socially unacceptable to create such conditions in which price differentials will be a sufficient incentive for factor mobility.

Regional policy can, in principle, try to improve either labour mobility, or capital mobility, or both. A successful improvement in labour mobility of the size sufficient to cure the regional problem would result in a great loss of population from the declining regions. Severe social costs might result. For this reason, employment policies have placed more emphasis on the improvement of **occupational** rather than **geographical mobility** of labour. Job-advertizing, government re-training schemes, and Industrial Relations and Employment legislation to reduce restrictive practices in the labour market have all been used in the attempt to improve occupational mobility of labour. However, the main thrust of regional policy in the UK under successive governments has been to encourage the mobility of capital into the regions with high unemployment, supplemented by policies to improve the occupational mobility of labour within regions.

2 The case for regional policy

(i) The social case. A recent examination question asked for a discussion of whether regional policy is **good social policy** but **bad economic policy**. The social case for regional policy is based on:

(a) The social undesirability of wide disparities in standards of living, employment and economic opportunities between different regions.

(b) The social undesirability of unemployment and the human disruption to families caused by the need to move out of a region in search of work.

(c) The social effects of distorted age-structures on populations in the different regions, particularly in declining areas with aging populations.

(ii) The economic case:

(a) By making better use of the nation's resources, including labour, regional policy may be able to increase the national growth-rate, thereby creating higher living standards and welfare levels in the future.

(b) A case for regional policy stems from the existence of **divergencies between private and social costs and benefits**. A firm is assumed to be motivated by private cost and benefit, but the private location of industry may generate **externalities** received as **social costs** by the community at large. The government's duty is to assess social costs resulting from congestion and inefficient use of social capital in different regions. If the external benefits of regional policy received by the community exceed the private costs to firms, then a net gain in welfare results from the policy. The actual financial subsidies paid by the government to firms in the operation of regional policy can be regarded as compensation for the additional private costs incurred, paid out of the welfare gain.

3 The case against regional policy

We have noted how the failure of the market is used as an underlying economic justification for regional policy. However, some economists argue that the market failure results from too much, rather than too little, government intervention. Regional policy may lead to the subsidy of inefficient businesses, and the encouragement, amongst both workers and businessmen, of a resistance to change. Economists who believe in the virtues of free market forces regard regional policy as just another example of a misguided extension of the economic role of the government and a waste of public money. The economists who adopt this point of view are often **monetarist** in their macro-approach to the economy. They have a view of the world in which market forces are orderly, efficient and stabilizing, and in which private businessmen, disciplined by possible bankruptcy or takeover, 'know better' than the civil servant who faces no such discipline. The **opportunity cost** of every £ spent on regional policy is measured by its sacrificed use elsewhere in the economy. According to this view, the £ would be better spent by a profit-motivated firm subject to a lower level of taxation.

4 The framework of regional policy

(i) The underlying strategy. Two distinct **strategies** have influenced the development of the current framework of regional aid:

(a) A relief of unemployment strategy. Regional policy was first introduced in the 1930s in response to the high levels of regional unemployment during the Great Depression. Financial assistance tended to be directed to areas or towns with the highest local unemployment. This strategy of concentrating regional aid on **unemployment 'blackspots'** was continued in the renewed emphasis on regional policy around 1960, once again in response to growing regional unemployment. A large number of small **Development Districts** were created, each located in a specific community suffering from high unemployment.

(b) A growth area strategy. The present-day geographical framework of regional aid dates from 1966 when the relief of unemployment strategy gave way to a **'growth area' strategy**. Development Districts were abolished, being replaced by fewer, but much larger, **Development Areas**. This reflected the view that single towns with high local unemployment levels were often in bad or high-cost locations for modern industry. Hence a policy which mainly directed financial assistance to unemployment blackspots was reinforcing an inefficient and uncompetitive location of industry. In contrast, much larger Development Areas might contain potential growth-points, perhaps in **'greenfield' locations** away from existing centres of population. A 'greenfield' location is a completely new location for industry, usually having the advantages of a land-extensive and easily accessible site. Growth-points in such locations, for example, Milford Haven in South Wales, could become centres of industrial regeneration within the larger Development Areas.

(ii) The present-day geographical framework. The present-day structure of regional policy results from the mix of the two strategies we have just described. The growth area strategy created the large Development Areas, but the government responded to growing unemployment in the late 1960s by returning to the relief of unemployment. **Special Development Areas** were established, usually within the larger Development Areas in localities of high unemployment. Shortly afterwards, regions just outside the Development Areas were given **Intermediate Area** status. The present-day framework of **assisted areas,** divisible into Special Development Areas, Development Areas, and Intermediate Areas, had been largely created by 1970, though various adjustments have since occurred. Broadly speaking, the pattern of regional assistance is similar in all the areas, but the amount of financial aid available to individual firms is greatest in Special Development Areas, and reduces in Development and Intermediate Areas.

(iii) Incentives and controls. In a pure market economy there would be no role for regional or industrial policy, except in the sense of 'laissez-faire'. At the other extreme, in a complete command economy, the regional direction of both capital and labour would be just one part of the wider planning mechanism. British regional policy illustrates an important function of government in a mixed economy: the **modification** rather than the **replacement** of market forces in the allocation of resources. During the Second World War the government adopted powers to direct capital and labour, and in peace-time governments have used their control over civil service offices to direct employment within the public sector in accordance with regional policy. For the most part, however, successive governments have relied on what might be described as a **'carrot and stick'** approach to regional policy-making.

The **Industrial Development Certificate (IDC)** is the principal 'stick' or control which has been used in British regional policy. A firm must apply for an IDC if it wishes to build a new factory above a certain minimum size outside a Development Area or Special Development Area. In theory, an IDC is difficult to obtain, except when a firm can make a strong economic case for locating a new plant outside an assisted area. In practice, the IDC policy has been of questionable effectiveness, partly because it has not always been stringently applied. Also, firms may evade the policy by locating elsewhere in the EEC or by moving into one of the large number of empty factories, the product of de-industrialization, which now exist in the South-East and Midlands.

The principal incentive or 'carrot' in regional policy is the availability of **financial aid** to firms moving into the assisted areas. **Employment aid**, or **manpower aid**, such as the **Regional Employment Premium** (REP) was available until 1975. However, it might be unwise to base hopes for a regeneration of regional economies on labour-intensive industries, which are usually in competition with similar industries in the lower wage conditions of developing countries. Under a manpower aid scheme firms are given a grant or subsidy for each worker employed. Manpower aid can prove cost-effective in reducing regional unemployment since **labour-intensive** firms are likely to be attracted to the assisted areas, but British firms might not survive such competition without continuous subsidy or protection. Recent thinking has therefore favoured **investment aid,** on the grounds that it is more likely to attract **capital-intensive** industry. This can be costly to the government in terms of the relatively few jobs immediately created. It may also attract the type of heavy industry which is particularly vulnerable to swings in demand. A problem associated with labour- and capital-intensive industry alike is the **branch factory problem**. Factories attracted to the assisted areas in the 1960s were often branch factories of large companies whose head offices were located elsewhere. This created an unbalanced employment structure, with a lack of higher management employment in the regions. The branch factories have been especially vulnerable to closure in the recession of the early 1980s.

The other main type of incentive used in regional policy relates to the provision of low-rent factories, good roads and other social capital by the state. These have the effect of providing **external economies** and an improved **regional infrastructure**, to counter the disadvantages which exist in the regions.

5 Recent policy measures

In 1975 the Labour government established the **Scottish and Welsh Development Agencies**, as regional counterparts to the National Enterprise Board in England. The Agencies have had an important function in providing public funds to businesses investing in Scotland and Wales. In particular, the managements of the Agencies possess considerable freedom to attract businesses, both home and overseas firms, by advertizing and other special promotional efforts. The Agencies have claimed considerable success in attracting **inward investment**, especially from the USA, though this might have served to exacerbate the branch factory problem.

However, the Scottish and Welsh Development Agencies were by no means the only government-backed agencies attempting to attract investment into particular localities. In conditions of growing unemployment in the early 1980s, local authorities both inside and outside the official assisted areas began to make use of a provision of the 1972 Local Government Act, under which they could spend the equivalent of a 2p rate on the promotion of industry. Together with the thirty or so government-backed agencies which include the development agencies and New Town Development Corporations, local authorities have been spending about £750 million a year, essentially in an attempt to attract new industry from one another.

In the early 1980s the Conservative Government has continued to fund the Scottish and Welsh Development Agencies, though on a reduced scale. This was in line with the policy changes announced in July 1979 to reduce regional aid, abandon office development permits and to ease the IDC system. The map of the assisted areas was substantially altered, reducing from 40% to 20% the proportion of population living within their confines.

6 The effectiveness of regional policy

Since it is difficult if not impossible to tell whether faster growth would have occurred without a regional policy, the policy must be judged by the test whether several decades of government interference have reduced regional differences in growth and unemployment. Various estimates have been made of the number of jobs created in the assisted areas, but it is less easy to know how many of these are completely 'new' jobs and how many would have been created in other parts of the country in the absence of a regional policy. Various measures of regional disparity indicate that the best that can be said of regional policy is that it has prevented regional inequalities from widening.

The relative ineffectiveness of regional aid may be explained in part by the low size of the **regional multiplier**. In Unit 22 we shall explain how the **government spending multiplier** measures the change in national income resulting from a change in public spending. The larger the multiplier, then the greater the effectiveness of fiscal policy and government spending in expanding output and employment. However, if the income generated is spent on imports, the **leakage of demand** reduces the size of the multiplier. In the context of regional policy, income generated by regional aid can be spent on goods and services produced in other parts of the UK as well as on imports, thereby reducing the size of the regional multiplier and the effectiveness of regional policy.

7 The EEC Regional Fund

Before the 1970s, regional assistance from the EEC was available from a number of funds such as the EEC Social Fund which financed training schemes for unemployed workers. The EEC had always intended to adopt a more unified regional policy, which was finally created with the establishment of the **EEC Regional Fund** in 1975. Financial assistance from the Fund is channelled through the UK government, essentially supplementing rather than replacing its own regional aid. Special Development Areas and Development Areas are classified as **European peripheral regions** which qualify for a higher level of EEC assistance than other parts of Britain, designated **central regions**. In general, EEC policy prefers selective rather than automatic regional aid, and investment in regional infrastructure rather than subsidies to operating costs. Regional Employment Premium was especially frowned upon before its abolition.

8 Postscript: de-industrialization and Industrial Policy

With the onset of structural decline in major sections of British manufacturing industry, the regional problem has spread in recent years to the rest of the United Kingdom. Structural decline has resulted from the inability of manufacturing firms to compete with foreign firms producing similar products at lower cost, and from changing demand. The 1974 Labour Government responded to the growing industrial problem by increasing the amount of government intervention in industry. Amongst the industrial policies either contemplated or adopted in the Labour Government's **Industrial Strategy** were: the creation of the National Enterprise Board (NEB) as a **state holding company; planning agreements;** the extension of **public ownership** and **nationalization**; and **indicative planning**. In the latter, the government indicates planning targets and it rewards with government business and patronage firms which adapt to government policy.

In contrast, the industrial policy of the Conservative Government elected in 1979 was based on a philosophy of disengagement and an attempt to create conditions in which market forces might work better. The functions of the NEB were first reduced, and then in 1981 merged into the British Technology Group. The Conservative Government has aimed to regenerate industry through greater tax incentives, particularly for small businesses, and the establishment of **Enterprise Zones**, which it has conceived of as areas of reduced 'red tape', in which newly established firms can benefit from tax advantages, minimal bureaucratic regulations and exemptions from local rates.

13.4 LINKS WITH OTHER TOPICS

In this second of three units in the general field of industrial policy, we have drawn on various important aspects of micro-economic theory, including the theory of the firm (Unit 6) and market and planned economies (Unit 9). We have referred to the influence of externalities in industrial location, and divergencies between private and social costs and benefits. You should refer back to Unit 8 for a more detailed treatment of these concepts. Finally, regional and other forms of financial assistance to industry figure significantly in the pattern of public spending and taxation, topics which are covered in Unit 17.

13.5 QUESTION PRACTICE

Essay Questions

Question 1 Explain why a government might want to increase the domestic mobility of the labour force and discuss how it might set about achieving this aim.

(AEB: November 1980)

Understanding the Question Full employment, economic growth, and some standard of fairness in the distribution of income and wealth are usually held to be principal aims of government policy. An improved mobility of labour should assist the task of achieving all these aims. In the first place, it will reduce **frictional unemployment**, defined as the unemployment resulting from the time-lags involved in the changing of jobs. Secondly, an increase in labour mobility will create the conditions for a better and more flexible use of the nation's resources. This should improve the prospects for economic growth. Lastly, the unemployed account for some of the poorest sections of society, and any policy which aims to reduce poverty must attempt to reduce unemployment.

In answering the second part of the question it would be advisable to distinguish between **geographical** and **occupational** causes of the immobility of labour. Improved **information**, for example through Job Centres, can reduce both types of immobility. The main cause of geographical immobility in the UK is probably the problem of housing; you could describe various policies the government might adopt to make it easier to move. Retraining schemes and the abolition of restrictive practices and discrimination in the labour market can be used to reduce the occupational immobility of labour.

Answer plan

1 Distinguish between geographical and occupational immobility of labour.
2 Explain how improved mobility assists in the achieving of the aims of reducing unemployment, securing economic growth and reducing poverty.
3 Nevertheless, too much geographical mobility of labour may produce distortions in the regional population structures. Governments are likely to encourage capital mobility as well as labour mobility.
4 Describe the policies which can be used to improve geographical and occupational mobility of labour.

Question 2 Consider the case for and against state intervention in the location of industry.

(WJEC: June 1980)

Understanding the Question Whereas the previous question asked for an explanation of government policy to improve labour mobility, this question relates to policy towards the mobility of capital. You must avoid the temptation to turn it into a factual question about British regional policy, though you may wish to illustrate your points from British experience.

Answer plan

1 Assume that firms choose locations to maximize their private advantage.
2 State intervention in the location of industry can be justified if the social costs to the community which result from a firm's private locational decision exceed the private advantage to the firm. The government is more likely to be able to take account of all the long-term benefits and externalities which state intervention may create.
3 Explain how it is easier to justify state intervention in the case of footloose industries; it is less easy to justify intervention when industries require a specific location.
4 Some economists argue that state intervention 'improves on the market', since locational decisions within the market may be based on inadequate or misleading information.
5 Others dispute this view. Opponents of state intervention argue that businessmen, subject to market disciplines, make better decisions than civil servants.
6 Decisions by the state may be influenced by political lobbying, the short-term need to win elections, and possibly even corruption.
7 The case for and against state intervention may also be judged by the evidence of the effectiveness, or lack of it, of regional policy in Britain.

Question 3 Briefly describe the chief characteristics of industrial policy in Britain in recent years. Discuss whether, in your opinion, experience supports the view that less direct government intervention is desirable or that more is required.

(JMB: June 1981)

Understanding the Question The phrase 'industrial policy' is capable of wide interpretation. It includes open and covert government initiatives. The direct intervention may be through nationalization or denationalization and the passing of new legislation, or the use of existing institutions such as the Monopolies and Mergers Commission or through tax changes introduced in the budget. Indirectly, changes in government administrative procedures may affect industry's costs and operation. Alternatively, direct industrial policy can be defined as a policy to replace the working of the market, for example through controls, while indirect policy operates through modifying rather than replacing market incentives.

You could also consider why governments have industrial policies and whether they are coherent strategies or ad hoc responses to crises. The 'recent years' aspect should be noted and taken as at least post-1945, and preferably post-1970. Then demonstrate the contrast between the industrial policies of successive governments. There is a political dimension too: Conservative governments tend to be less interventionist than Labour.

The second part of the question requires the application of evidence and argument in supporting a view. Different evaluations of the evidence are possible and acceptable. Clearly a consideration of government economic objectives is important, but you should concentrate on the micro-economic aims of stimulating efficiency rather than on macro-economic policy-making. In assessing the results of government intervention a realization of the constraints upon government, e.g. other economic aims and political motives, is important.

Answer plan

1 Explain what is meant by the term 'industrial policy' and why it is used.
2 Describe the principal direct and indirect elements in the policy.
3 State the case for or against less direct government intervention.
4 Support the case you have made with some empirical evidence and reasons.
5 In conclusion, explain the difficulties of evaluation and the complexities caused by other economic and political constraints.

Multiple Choice Questions

Question 4 All except one of the following policy measures have the direct aim of reducing the regional problem. The exception is:
(a) Advance factories
(b) Regional development grants
(c) Industrial Development Certificates
(d) Rate support grants

Understanding the Question This is a simple factual question which is testing knowledge of current government policies. Alternatives (a), (b), and (c) are directly related to regional policy; 'advance factory units' are built by the government for sale or lease to businesses at attractive rates, and regional development grants have been a form of financial assistance. In contrast, alternative (d) is a method by which central government finances local authority spending. Although the pattern of distribution of the rate support grant can influence the regional problem, this is not a direct objective of the system of grants.

Question 5 Which of the following would be unlikely to reduce regional unemployment?
(a) Information about employment vacancies in Job Centres.
(b) An increase in unemployment benefits as a ratio of average pay.
(c) A reduction in Corporation Tax paid by firms in assisted areas.
(d) The introduction of government-sponsored retraining schemes.

Understanding the Question Policies (a) and (d) are examples of standard government policies to improve labour mobility and reduce frictional unemployment. Policy (c) is also likely to reduce regional unemployment by making it more attractive for firms to locate in the problem regions, though unemployment elsewhere might rise. This leaves alternative (b) as the correct answer; the incentive to find a new job would be reduced, causing a lengthening in the 'search period' for a new job, and an increase in frictional unemployment.

Data Response Questions

Question 6

Comparison of Regional Disparity

Factor		North	Yorks and Humber-side	East Midlands	East Anglia	South East	South West	West Midlands	North West	Wales	Scotland	N. Ireland	National Average
Regional unemployment as a ratio of total unemployment	1965	1.73	0.73	0.60	0.86	0.60	1.07	0.60	1.06	1.73	2.00	4.07	1.0
	1973	1.77	1.05	0.82	0.73	0.59	0.95	0.77	1.32	1.36	1.68	2.41	1.0
Net migration: average annual change ('000s)	1951–61	− 5.7	− 7.5	+ 7.2	+ 3.8	+ 55.0	+ 12.3	+ 8.0	− 7.7	− 3.0	− 28.2	− 8.9	+ 25.3
	mid 1971 mid 1973	6.0	5.0	+ 14.6	+ 21.6	− 35.2	+ 38.0	− 4.1	16.1	+ 8.4	− 19.2	− 10.0	− 13.0
Gross domestic product current prices % of UK	1966	5.0	8.4	5.9	2.8	35.7	6.2	9.8	11.8	4.2	8.5	1.7	100.0
	1972	5.0	8.1	5.9	2.9	36.0	6.6	9.4	11.3	4.3	8.5	2.0	100.0
Average gross annual earnings (£'s) men 18–64	1967	1,158	1,159	1,171	1,128	1,355	1,155	1,252	1,219	1,189	1,163	1,057	1,249
	1972	1,905	1,903	1,906	1,811	2,204	1,877	2,002	1,993	1,968	1,930	–	2,039
women 18–59	1967	578	571	585	581	689	593	581	594	624	608	630	622
	1972	973	938	957	964	1,136	962	948	969	1,041	987	–	1,015

Source: *Midland Bank Review*

(a) Which four regions had the highest comparative rates of unemployment in 1965 and in 1973?   (3 marks)

(b) Was there any connection between unemployment and migration in these regions?   (3 marks)

(c) What economic reasoning can you offer to explain your finding in **(b)**?   (4 marks)

(d) 'A loss of population through migration should reduce the importance of a region as a generator of domestic product.'

　(i) Indicate whether this statement was true with reference to the North, the South East, Scotland and Northern Ireland.   (4 marks)

　(ii) How do you think it is possible to explain the performance of these four regions?   (4 marks)

(e) The 1972 figures for the gross annual earnings of men show only one figure, that for the South East, above the national average. Can one conclude that there must be an error in the average figure?   (2 marks)

(Cambridge: June 1980)

Understanding the Question The format of this question illustrates the **'incline of difficulty' approach** to data response questions, an approach adopted by some, but not all, of the examining boards. The question is set so as to start with the simple extraction of one or two facts or details from the statistical data, leaving the economic interpretation and analysis of the significance of the data to later parts of the question. You must take care when answering question **(a)** not to interpret the statistics as percentages. Regions with a ratio above 1.0 display a rate of unemployment higher than the national average, while figures below 1.0 indicate lower than average unemployment. The data refer to the eleven Planning Regions into which the country is divided, rather than to Development Areas as such.

The data show a clear correlation between high unemployment and outward migration in the regions with the highest unemployment rates, though the Welsh region experienced inward migration in 1973 despite the above average regional unemployment. Question **(c)** requires you to draw on the economic reasoning developed in the unit to explain why labour moves out of regions with high unemployment.

Again, the first part of question **(d)** is testing the simple skill of extracting information from the data. It is worth noting that the data only show whether a region's percentage contribution to domestic product has risen or fallen; no information is given on the absolute change in GDP between 1966 and 1972. The data indicate a slight reduction in regional disparity in these years. You can explain this in terms of market forces, or the success of regional policy if you wish.

Finally, the last part of the question is based on an understanding of statistical averages. It is certainly possible for only one region to display an annual earning figure above the national average or **mean**, if a large proportion of both the population and the high income earners live in that particular region.

13.6   FURTHER READING

Livesey, F., *A Textbook of Economics* (Polytech Publishers Ltd., 1978).
Chapter 16: Regional policy

Prest, A. R., and Coppock, D. J., editors, *The UK Economy, a Manual of Applied Economics*, 9th edition (Weidenfeld & Nicolson, 1982).
Chapter 4: Industry and Commerce.

Lee, D., *Regional Planning and Location of Industry*, 3rd edition (Heinemann, 1980).

14 Nationalized Industries

14.1   POINTS OF PERSPECTIVE

There is some dispute about the most appropriate way of defining a nationalized industry. An official definition, used in a report by the **National Economic Development Office** (NEDO) in 1976, includes only **public corporations** in the **market economy**. Public corporations such as the BBC are omitted on the grounds that they are in the non-market economy. Likewise, public services such as defence, roads, education, and the health service are excluded. However, for many purposes it is better to use a wider definition of a nationalized industry than that suggested by the NEDO. Although companies such as British Leyland are nominally in the private sector, they should be regarded as nationalized if the state possesses a sufficient shareholding to have gained control of the enterprise. In other countries, nationalized industries are often owned and controlled in this way through a **state holding company**. In the United Kingdom, the **National Enterprise Board** (NEB) operated as a state holding company in the late 1970s.

A distinction should also be made between **nationalized industries**, owned and controlled through **central government**, and **municipalized enterprises**, such as London Transport. These are business enterprises within the public sector of the economy, but they are not usually regarded as nationalized industries.

The **overall size** of the public sector is determined by the government. Generally, Labour governments have extended the size of the public sector through nationalization whereas Conservative governments have pursued a deliberate policy of **denationalization** or **privatization**. Such sales of parts of a nationalized industry to the private sector give a short-term boost to government revenues.

The **content** of the public sector varies between western mixed economies. In most countries, for instance, the railways are nationalized but the steel industry is not.

14.2   Underlying concepts

1 Private v public interest

It is usually assumed that firms in the private sector of the economy aim to maximize their **private** or **internal interest**, which is held to be the maximization of profits for the owners of the enterprise. Private sector firms need not, in principle, take into account any **external costs** generated which are harmful to the community. In contrast, nationalized industries are expected to operate in the **public** or **social interest**, though there are considerable problems in defining what this is. They must consider the **social costs and benefits** resulting from their private action. Indeed, industries have been nationalized because they are considered too important to the national interest to be left to what might be the narrower sectional interest of private ownership.

2 Public monopoly

Nationalization is also a means of dealing with the problem of monopoly. By restricting output or raising price in the pursuit of profits, private monopolies can create productive and allocative inefficiency, and the restriction of consumer choice. Public monopolies acting in the social interest may be less likely to abuse their position in this way. However, critics of nationalization argue that other forms of abuse emerge, related to the inefficiency which results from the belief by management and workers that the enterprise can never be made bankrupt. With this in mind, it is useful to divide the nationalized industries into those, such as electricity and gas, in the **sheltered economy**, and the others such as steel in the **competitive economy**. Public enterprises in the competitive economy may in effect be **price-takers** when exposed to a sufficient degree of import competition. In contrast, the **public utilities** in the sheltered economy are **natural monopolies**: they would be monopolies whatever the system of ownership. These industries provide services which by their nature cannot be exposed to import competition, or even to domestic competition without an unacceptable increase in plant duplication. However, the utilities such as electricity and gas may be in competition with each other and the coal industry in both household and industrial energy markets.

14.3   Essential knowledge

1 The history of nationalization

Table 14.1 summarizes the main periods of nationalization and denationalization in the United Kingdom. Although most nationalization has been undertaken by Labour governments, you should note that industries or firms have been nationalized by other governments for reasons which include natural monopoly, public safety and service, and the rescue of bankrupt firms or 'lame ducks'. Most nationalized industries in Britain are public corporations which have been established by statutory Acts of Parliament. It is useful to divide such **statutory nationalizations** into three categories:

(i) The compulsory purchase of assets owned by the private sector British Aerospace and British Shipbuilders were nationalized in this way in the 1970s.

(ii) The reorganization of enterprises already within the public sector Many Acts of nationalization in the 1960s were reorganizational. For example, the Post Office Act established the Post Office Corporation in 1969. The Post Office had previously been a part of the civil service.

(iii) The founding of completely new enterprises, for example the British National Oil Corporation (BNOC). Sometimes Acts of nationalization have been used to create a legal monopoly for a public corporation, by preventing competition from firms in the private sector. Much political debate has centred on whether public corporations such as the National Bus Company, and the postal and telecommunication corporations, should be exposed to competition through the removal of their legally protected monopoly, or simply be **denationalized** or **privatized**.

Table 14.1: The History of Nationalization in the UK

19th Century	The Post Office established as a civil service department.
Pre World War 1	1908: Port of London Authority, the first public corporation.
Inter-war	The early public corporations, the Central Electricity Board, the London Transport Passenger Board.
1945–1950 1st Main Period of Statutory Nationalization of the 'Commanding Heights' of the Economy	**1946:** National Coal Board **1946:** Airlines – BOAC and BEA **1947:** Central Electricity Generating Board and area distribution Boards **1947:** Transport – British Rail and British Road Services **1948:** Gas Council and area Boards **1949:** Iron and Steel
1951–1963 1st period of Denationalization	Denationalization of steel and most of BRS in the early 1950s – but Atomic Energy Authority established in 1954
1964–1969 2nd Main Period of Statutory Nationalization – Mostly Reorganization	**1965:** Reorganization of gas industry – British Gas Corporation **1965:** British Airports Authority **1967:** Renationalization of steel – British Steel Corporation **1968:** National Freight Corporation **1969:** Post Office Corporation
1970–1973 Denationalization Again	The Conservative Government sold or 'hived off' ancillary activities rather than denationalize complete industries. Nevertheless it also extended the nationalized sector by taking Rolls Royce into public ownership in 1971 and creating two new atomic energy corporations.
1974–1978 3rd Main Period of Nationalization	STATUTORY NATIONALIZATION British Aerospace British Shipbuilders British National Oil Corporation The Ports THROUGH THE NEB The largest company owned and controlled through the *State Holding Company* function of the NEB was British Leyland.
1979 Denationalization Again	**'Privatization'** – the sale of profitable public corporations, for example the National Freight Corporation. Plus the sale of shares or an equity stake. Plus encouragement of private competition.

2 Reasons for nationalization

There have been many different reasons for nationalization in the UK, and elsewhere, some of which we have briefly mentioned in preceding sections. You should note that what one person regards as a good reason for nationalization, such as the saving of jobs in the rescue of bankrupt companies, may be regarded by others as 'bad economics' – reasons may **explain** nationalization without necessarily **justifying** it. Reasons include:

(i) Natural monopolies Utility industries, such as gas and electricity, are likely to be monopolies whatever the ownership. Nationalization provides a means of controlling monopoly. The taking of the utilities into public ownership has been called 'gas and water socialism'.

(ii) Socialist planning of the economy A large part of nationalization in the UK has been undertaken by Labour governments in the belief that public ownership is essential for planning the economy and for achieving a more equal distribution of income and wealth.

(iii) Standards of public service It can be argued that the country's citizens are entitled to the same standard of essential services, wherever they live in the country.

(iv) The rescue of 'lame ducks' or 'hospital cases' Large companies in the private sector such as the Rolls Royce aircraft engine firm have been nationalized to save jobs which have been threatened by impending bankruptcy, or to prevent British technology from being bought up by foreign competitors.

(v) National prestige Many countries possess nationalized airlines in order to 'wave the flag'.

(vi) Fiscal reasons Governments may be tempted to nationalize the gambling, tobacco and alcoholic drink industries and to use their profits as a source of revenue. Nationalization also allows the government to directly regulate the production of **demerit goods** (for instance, tobacco in France and alcohol in Finland).

(vii) Defence and national security Atomic energy is state-controlled for reasons of public protection.

3 Problems and Policy

(i) The White Papers on Nationalized Industries The nationalization statutes which established the major public corporations in the 1940s required that the industries should pay their way 'taking one year with another'. The public corporations were expected to be profitable, yet at the same time to act in the public interest. This created a conflict between commercial objectives and the statutory duty to provide social, and often uneconomic, services, for example to citizens living in remote areas. Successive governments failed to provide more precise instructions on how to resolve this conflict until the publication of two **White Papers on Nationalized Industries in 1961 and 1967**. These, together with a **third White Paper in 1978**, have been described as **'attempts to compensate for the unhelpful generality of the nationalization statutes'**. The three White Papers provide the basis for understanding the pricing and investment policies of nationalized industries, and the relationship between government and the public corporations.

(ii) Pricing policy

(a) Marginal cost pricing The 1967 White Paper instructed the nationalized industries to adopt **marginal cost pricing policies**, by charging a price equal to the cost of producing the last unit of each good or service. At this stage you should refer back to the discussion of marginal cost pricing and the concept of **allocative efficiency** in Unit 6. Because nationalized industries are imperfectly competitive, price tends to be higher than the **short-run** marginal cost, indicating that output must be increased if allocative efficiency is to be improved. The adoption of marginal cost pricing should improve efficiency by shifting the system towards a closer approximation to perfect competition.

However, there are a number of serious difficulties, both in the theory and the application of marginal cost pricing. Theoretical difficulties include:

(1) Whether the price should be set equal to **short-run** or **long-run** marginal cost; and
(2) Marginal cost pricing will improve allocative efficiency if **all other prices** in the economy equal marginal cost. It is by no means certain that efficiency will be improved when other prices, for example in the private sector, do not equal their relevant marginal costs.

The practical problems include:

(a) It is unlikely that a large business will possess the necessary information to allow it to know the marginal cost of producing all its varied goods and services.
(b) When **externalities** occur, **social marginal cost** differs from **private marginal cost**. To maximize the social benefit, a nationalized industry should set price equal to the social marginal cost, but there can be great problems in putting money values to, and calculating, the social costs and benefits.
(c) Economies of scale cause falling long-run marginal costs, resulting in losses if price is set equal to **long-run** marginal cost. The use of taxation to finance the deficits of nationalized industries causes fresh allocative distortions and is likely to reduce industry morale.

(b) Political interference and pricing policy While there is some agreement that the prices of nationalized industries should be used to improve allocative efficiency, there is much less agreement on whether government should use pricing policy to achieve other micro-economic or macro-economic objectives. It is sometimes argued that price should be kept low so the poor may benefit. Others argue that there are much more cost-effective ways of helping low-income groups through specific cash grants. High-income groups may derive more benefit from artificially low prices than the poor for whom the prices are intended. Alternatively, public enterprise prices may be kept artificially low in a macro-economic attempt to reduce inflation. In the early 1970s a Conservative government used the prices of nationalized industries as a policy instrument in the fight against inflation. Huge losses resulted as costs continued to rise, and the new pricing and investment policies introduced by the 1967 White Paper were rendered ineffective. Morale and industrial relations also suffered.

(iii) Investment

(a) Investment appraisal A recent examination question asked whether nationalized industries and companies in the private sector base investment decisions on different considerations. If a nationalized industry acts commercially as a straightforward profit-maximizer, the considerations would be the same. But if a public enterprise is a **social benefit maximizer**, part of its investment will be in the provision of non-commercial, and perhaps uneconomic, services. The 1967 White Paper included an attempt to distinguish between the **economic** and the **social services** provided by the public corporations. It introduced the use of **investment appraisal techniques**, similar to those used in parts of the private sector. Commercial investment projects were required to pass a **Discounted Cash Flow test** (DCF). The test discount rate was chosen on the basis of private sector custom and practice. In the years after 1967, a number of difficulties arose with the use of DCF and the policy was modified in the 1978 White Paper. Industries are now given more freedom in deciding how to appraise individual investment projects, but total investment in each industry still has to pass a **Required Rate of Return test** (RRR). DCF and other aspects of investment appraisal are explained in rather greater detail in Unit 23.

The 1978 White Paper also set specific **financial targets** for each industry. The choice of target reflected the special circumstances of each industry. Certain industries, such as gas, were expected to achieve an average **return on net assets** of 9 per cent, whereas the loss-makers, for example British Shipbuilders, were allowed a maximum deficit on trading – £90m in 1980/81.

(b) Investment performance The public corporations account for about 20 per cent of fixed investment undertaken by British business enterprises, although they produce only 10 per cent of national output and employ 8 per cent of the labour force. Their capital requirements are proportionately large because of the nature and structure of many of the industries. The utility industries such as electricity and gas are highly **capital intensive**, and a reason for the nationalization of coal and rail stemmed from the difficulties experienced by their private owners in the raising of sufficient capital to modernize the industries.

However, critics of the nationalized industries argue that they make wasteful use of capital, by engaging in investment projects which the private sector would reject as not worth while. According to this view, the government cushions bad investment decisions by being prepared to write off loans, which are thereby effectively converted into subsidies. Critics also argue that investment by nationalized industries is a part of the **'crowding out'** process. Not only do nationalized industries obtain finance on favourable terms compared to the private sector, from the **National Loans Fund**, but indirectly these funds are obtained from taxation and government borrowing on the capital market. This raises both the level of taxation and the rate of interest which the private sector must pay.

Since 1979 the Conservative Government has imposed **external financing limits**, or 'off-stage targets', on the public funding of nationalized industries. The adoption of financial limits marks a departure from the 1978 White Paper – a departure in which the government appears to sacrifice the objectives of the nationalized industries to the aim of reducing the government's Public Sector Borrowing Requirement (PSBR). The Conservatives see external financing limits as imposing a form of market discipline on nationalized industries which, in their view, will harden the industries' approach to wage-bargaining. Their opponents claim that it will merely lead to the sacrifice and cancellation of worthwhile investment projects which, if undertaken by a private sector company, would almost certainly be financed from external sources.

(iv) Public accountability and relations with the government The relations between public corporations and successive governments have frequently been unsatisfactory. Each industry is run by a Corporate Board and a Chairman responsible to a government minister. The minister lays down the **long-term strategic objectives** of the industry, but he is supposed to leave short- and medium-term decision-making to the corporate board and the managers employed by the corporation. In practice there has been a lengthy history of behind-the-scenes 'arm-twisting', resulting from the attempt by ministers to use nationalized industries to achieve other government aims, such as 'buying British' or the saving of jobs. The chairmen of the corporations have frequently appealed both for government intervention to be more out in the open and for a clearer dividing line between the commercial and the social service obligations of the industries. In 1976 the NEDO Report (the McIntosh Report) highlighted the deterioration in relations between government and the corporate boards, but the suggestion of a new layer of 'Policy Councils' between the two was not well received. The 1978 White Paper responded to the NEDO Report with the proposal that the government should take on more power to direct the industry boards on specific decisions. Thereby, it is hoped, government interference can be brought out into the open.

For many years the nationalized industries were not directly accountable to MPs, who felt, perhaps naturally, that accountability to the government was an insufficient public accountability. Pressure from the back-benches led to the establishment in 1956 of the **Parliamentary Select Committee on Nationalized Industries**. The Committee has accomplished much valuable work in investigating the performance of nationalized industries and their relations with the government. Nevertheless, members of the Select Committee have claimed that the Committee has neither the powers nor the available time for a sufficient parliamentary accountability to be maintained. Since 1979, the responsibility for nationalized industries has been divided between several of the new Select Committees, according to which government department sponsors the industry.

The general public may be more concerned with the direct accountability of nationalized industry to consumers. Recent Conservative governments have extended the powers of the

Monopolies and Mergers Commission to undertake audits which investigate the efficiency and competitive practices of nationalized industries. The Director General of Fair Trading receives consumer complaints about the standard of service and conduct of the public corporations, and he can advise the government about policy.

14.4 LINKS WITH OTHER TOPICS

In this unit we have covered the major business enterprises in the public sector of the British economy. Unit 10 on the size and growth of firms, and Unit 12 on competition policy, are essentially complementary, respectively emphasizing business organization and conduct in the private sector. Important aspects of the theories of pricing and investment policy are developed in more detail in Units 6 and 23 respectively, while the financing of the nationalized industries touches upon the subject matter of Unit 11 (the capital market) and Units 17 and 18 on public finance and the PSBR.

14.5 QUESTION PRACTICE

Essay Questions

Question 1 Discuss the effects on the profitability of nationalized industries if they were to set their prices equal to marginal costs.

(London: June 1978)

Understanding the Question It would be difficult if not impossible to write a good answer to this question without the specific knowledge of **marginal cost pricing** which is summarized in the unit. In particular, it is important to distinguish between **short-run** and **long-run** marginal costs. To illustrate the short run, you should construct a diagram to show a profit-maximizing monopoly (for which P > MC) and compare the profits in this situation with the profits made at the output where P = MC on the same diagram. Your diagram will show that abnormal profits are still made, but the profit rectangle is smaller than at the profit-maximizing output.

However, if price is set equal to **long-run** marginal cost, the industry will make a loss if LRMC is below LRAC. This will be the case when economies of scale occur. Finally, it is irrelevant to this particular **set question** to discuss improvements in allocative efficiency which might result from the adoption of marginal cost pricing.

Answer plan

1 Explain marginal cost pricing, distinguishing between short-run and long-run, and private and social, marginal costs.
2 Assume that in the absence of a marginal cost pricing instruction, nationalized industries act as profit-maximizing monopolies.
3 Draw a diagram to show monopoly equilibrium. Compare the monopoly profits which would be made if output were fixed at a level where P = MC.
4 Introduce the long run and economies of scale. Conclude that the effect on profits will depend upon whether it is a short-run or a long-run marginal cost pricing rule and whether economies of scale occur.

Question 2 What are the main characteristics of the pricing and output policies of nationalized industries? Illustrate your answer by reference to specific examples.

(SUJB: June 1980)

Understanding the Question You should interpret the question as referring to present-day pricing and output policies. An answer which deals only with the nationalization statutes of forty years ago will not earn many marks. Nevertheless, it is perfectly admissable to explain present-day policies in terms of historical change. Good answers should display some knowledge of the latest White Paper, or at least the marginal cost pricing framework introduced by the 1967 White Paper. You might also introduce aspects of pricing policy which we have not described in the unit, for example **peak and off-peak pricing**, special prices for pensioners, etc.

Answer plan (Illustrate your answer with examples as you go along.)

1 Explain that the broad policy is laid down by the 1978 White Paper, but that earlier White Papers and the Nationalization Statutes are also relevant.
2 Distinguish between the part of output which is regarded as economic or commercial, and the part which is non-economic or social.
3 Explain that the concept of marginal cost pricing was introduced in the 1967 White Paper. The 1978 White Paper is more general, perhaps because of the realization of the difficulties involved in marginal cost pricing. It states that 'the Government believes that it is primarily for each nationalized industry to work out the details of its prices with regard to its markets and its over-all objectives, including its financial targets'.
4 The 1978 White Paper introduced the idea of **financial targets** for each industry, and a **corporate plan** for output and investment decision-making.
5 Explain how government interference has at times been the main influence on both pricing and output decisions.
6 Give examples of other aspects of pricing, *e.g,* off-peak prices, standing charges used by electricity and gas boards, etc.

Question 3 What are the arguments for and against the government selling off the profitable parts of publicly owned enterprises?

(O & CSEB: June 1980)

Understanding the Question Many candidates are tempted to write politically one-sided answers to this type of question. Such answers are inadvisable, whatever the merits of your personal views. You should attempt to distance yourself as a neutral observer. A sensible tactic is to separate your answer into a prediction of the likely consequences and then to discuss their advantages and disadvantages. You could perhaps pretend that you were a civil servant or economic consultant employed to advise the government, whichever party is in power.

Answer plan

1 Distinguish between the consequences of selling a complete industry, and those of selling just part of an industry, with an unprofitable rump left in the government's hands.
2ˊ Consider the consequences on
   (a) the part which is sold off: will it be run more efficiently, or be asset-stripped?
   (b) the morale of the work-force in a state-owned rump.
3 Discuss the short- and long-term effects on the PSBR and government finances. Opponents of privatization claim that it leads to a once-and-for-all reduction in the PSBR, with the long-term effect of increasing the PSBR as a result of loss of profits, the cost of financing a loss-making rump, etc. Supporters stress the long-term reduction in the PSBR as privatized industries are forced to seek funds from the market.
4 Will public monopoly be replaced by private monopoly, or will greater competition result?
5 Will standards of service vary in different parts of the country?
6 Discuss what you consider to be the advantages and disadvantages of the consequences you have listed.

Multiple Choice Questions

Question 4 The public sector of the economy comprises the economic activities of:
(a) nationalized industries and public authorities
(b) public utilities
(c) public corporations
(d) public companies

Understanding the Question Public utilities and public corporations are, of course, included in the public sector, but neither provides a definition of what constitutes the public sector of the economy. Alternative **(a)** is a much more comprehensive definition of the public sector, since it includes the activities of central and local government in the provision of non-marketed services and the ownership of municipal enterprises. Alternative **(d)** is a complete red herring; public companies are predominantly in the private sector.

Question 5 All except one of these guidelines influence the pricing and investment decisions of nationalized industries. The exception is:
(a) investment is based on the appraisal of alternative investment projects
(b) prices should reflect marginal costs when appropriate
(c) prices should be determined by government ministers
(d) prices should discourage cross-subsidization

Understanding the Question The correct answer is **(c)**, since the government lays down general policy rather than specific pricing decisions. The 1978 White Paper discouraged arbitrary **cross-subsidization** between different groups of consumers. Cross-subsidization should not be confused with monopoly price discrimination, though there are some similarities. Monopoly price discrimination refers to the charging of different prices to different consumers for the same product, in the pursuit of profit maximization. In contrast, cross-subsidization occurs when an enterprise uses the profits from the sale of one product to subsidize the provision of another product. Cheap fares for old age pensioners, and other off-peak fares do not necessarily involve cross-subsidization, since off-peak consumers may be buying a service which can be provided at a very low marginal cost.

Data Response Questions

Question 6 An official of the Smaller Businesses Association wrote to *The Times* in August 1976 in the following terms:
'Your headline ... prompts me to ask why businessmen are singled out as unfitted to benefit from reduced air fares. If airlines ran their businesses in a normal commercial manner it would be reasonable to grant small reductions in fares to passengers who booked to return or ... who booked well ahead. The enormous discounts now offered by airlines for "package" flights, however, could not be justified by any commercial organization. These are a straight subsidy from businessmen to holidaymakers ... only a government and its agencies would try to enforce a policy whereby those who had to travel abroad for the benefit of the country's commerce and industry had to give large financial assistance to those travelling purely for pleasure.'
Comment on the points made in this letter.

(London, June 1978)

Understanding the Question Although this question is not strictly about a nationalized industry, it develops some interesting aspects of pricing which relate to the concepts of marginal cost pricing, cross-subsidization, and off-peak fares. The writer of the letter is obviously asserting that airlines use business travellers to cross-subsidize holidaymakers. He recommends that the government, if not the airlines, should take account of the **externalities** that businessmen generate in terms of the national interest. But is it correct that cross-subsidization occurs? Scheduled airlines travel to a timetable and will usually fly even when an aircraft is nearly empty. Package flights are organized through the charter or hire of a complete aircraft, or by the sale of a block of seats on a scheduled flight to a travel company. The airline achieves economies of scale through the bulk sale of seats, and the fact that the sale is well in advance of the flight may reduce uncertainty and ensure that each ticket is sold. Indeed the travel company and not the airline may bear the risk of unsold seats. It follows that scheduled and package flights are different products which incur different costs.

Answer plan

1 Describe the assertions made in the letter.
2 Discuss whether cross-subsidization takes place.
3 Discuss whether the airlines are behaving, in this instance, as discriminating monopolists – are they charging different prices to different customers for the **same** product?

4 Conclude that scheduled and package flights are different products with different costs. Both are provided by airlines in the pursuit of profit. The letter shows a great deal of confusion.

14.6 FURTHER READING

Livesey, F., *A Textbook of Economics* (Polytech Publishers Ltd., 1978).
Chapter 19: Nationalization.

Morris, D., editor, *The Economic System in the UK,* 2nd edition (Oxford University Press, 1979).
Chapter 18: The Nationalized Industries.

Prest, A. R., and Coppock, D. J., *The UK Economy, a Manual of Applied Economics,* 9th edition (Weidenfeld & Nicolson, 1982).
Chapter 4: Industry and Commerce.

15 Trade Unions and Wages

15.1 POINTS OF PERSPECTIVE

In earlier units we examined the behaviour of firms and how prices are determined when firms sell their output in the **goods market** or **product market**. We generally assumed that the **prices of the inputs** necessary for production, or the **prices of factor services**, were given. We now reverse the assumption, and examine how the prices of **factors of production** are determined in the **factor market**, assuming that conditions and prices in the product market are generally given. We shall concentrate on the labour market and the determination of wages, applying our analysis where necessary to the other factors of production and their prices.

We shall follow the convention of dividing the factors of production into **land** and **labour**, which earn **rent** and **wages** respectively, and **capital**, which is further subdivided into **loan capital**, earning **interest**, and **entrepreneurship**, or **enterprise**, earning **profit**. This is strictly a theoretical division which conforms neither to official statistics nor to the everyday use of such words as rent and interest. For example, a businessman will think of rent as the payment he makes for the use of a building. However, from a theoretical point of view, part of the payment is the rent of land, but the rest is an interest payment on capital.

Table 15.1

The Functional Distribution of Income Distribution of total domestic income by percentage			*The Size Distribution of Income* Distribution of pre-tax income by percentage		
	1972	1978		1972/3	1977/8
Income from employment	67.6	67.9	Top 10% of population	26.9	26.1
Gross trading profits and surpluses of private and public enterprises, minus			Next 11–20% of population	15.8	16.3
			Next 21–50% of population	33.3	33.5
			Bottom 50% of population	24.0	24.1
stock appreciation	15.4	15.2			
Other income, including rent and income from self-employment	17.0	16.9			

The distribution of income between the factors of production is called the **functional distribution of income**. This should not be confused with the **size distribution of income**, which measures, for example, the proportion of total income received by the top ten per cent of income earners, compared with the bottom fifty per cent. Table 15.1 illustrates both distributions of income. Although the official statistics do not exactly match the theoretical distinctions between the factors of production, they do tend to show, albeit only slightly between 1972 and 1978, the increasing share of wages in national income. This has occurred at the expense of the share of profits, a fact of some importance in explaining the performance and difficulties of the British economy.

15.2 Underlying concepts

Distribution theory introduces no new methods of analysis and only a few new theoretical concepts. It is merely the **price theory** of the earlier units, but viewed from the 'other side'. As we shall see, it can be subjected to the same criticisms as other aspects of conventional price theory. In earlier units we examined the interaction of **households** and **firms** in the goods market, where households are the source of demand for goods and services supplied by firms. We now view households as the source of supply of factor services, which are demanded by firms in the pursuit of profit.

You should note:

(i) Wages and other factor prices are assumed to be determined by **supply** and **demand**.

(ii) The assumption of maximizing behaviour. The assumptions of **profit-maximizing behaviour** on the part of firms and **utility maximization** by households are as crucial to distribution theory as they are to the rest of price theory. Firms will only demand the services of factors of production if profits can be increased by their employment. Similarly, households will only supply more labour, or hire out the capital or land they may own, if it maximizes their **net advantage**. The concept of **net advantage** covers all the rewards, **monetary** and **non-monetary**, which a household gains from the sale of its factor services. For example, if a person enjoys his work, the net advantage obtained from employment will include the pleasure gained from the work itself, as well as the **utility of the wage** – or more strictly, the utilities obtained from the goods and services bought with the money wage.

(iii) The demand for factor services is a derived demand. The essential difference between consumer demand in the goods market, and a firm's demand for factor services, is that the latter is a **derived demand**: the services of labour or land are demanded only because they are necessary in the production of goods and services to sell for profit.

(iv) Entrepreneurial profit, and indeed the **entrepreneurial function**, is regarded as different from those of the other factors of production. The entrepreneurial function of **risk-taking** and the bearing of **uncertainty** is undertaken by the owners of a business, who bear the financial risks. However, the existence of such a separate entrepreneurial function in modern companies can be questioned. Very often all the important decisions are made by **management**, who are a part of the labour force. In so far as entrepreneurial profit exists, it is essentially a **residual**, the difference between the total revenue obtained from the sale of output in the product market, and the other factor rewards which constitute the firm's costs of production.

(v) Transfer earnings and economic rent. So far we have used the term **rent** in its everyday meaning as the price which must be paid to hire the services of land. To the economist, however, rent or **economic rent** has a rather different meaning. It is a more general meaning which applies to all the factors of production, yet it is more specific since it refers to only a part of the earnings of each factor. Figure 15.1 illustrates the demand and supply for a particular type of labour. L_1 represents a worker who is just prepared to supply labour if the wage is W_1, but who would withdraw from this particular labour market if the wage fell below W_1. We now assume that the firm pays the same wage to all the workers it employs. This is the equilibrium wage W_2, determined where the demand and supply curves intersect at A. Worker L_1 receives the wage of W_2 even though he would be prepared to work for the lower wage of W_1. The part of his wage above the supply curve at point B is economic rent, while the part below is transfer earnings. Transfer earnings represent the factor's **opportunity cost**, while economic rent is the difference between what the factor is actually paid and its opportunity cost. If the wage falls below W_1, worker L_1 will transfer out of this particular labour market, or at least decide to supply less labour. Taking all the workers together, their economic rent is shown by the shaded area above the supply curve, while their transfer earnings are shown by the area below. Worker L_2 is the marginal worker, who is only just prepared to supply labour at the wage of W_2. All his wage is transfer earnings.

The concept of economic rent is sometimes applied to entrepreneurial profit, as well as to the

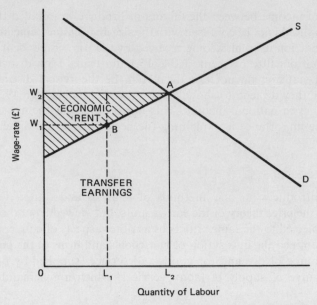

Fig 15.1 Economic rent and transfer earnings

earnings of the other factors of production. In this case, **normal profit** is regarded as a transfer earning, since the entrepreneur will leave the industry if normal profit is not earned. **Abnormal profit** which is earned over and above normal profit becomes the 'economic rent of enterprise'.

15.3 ESSENTIAL INFORMATION

1 The Supply of Labour

The aggregate supply of labour in the economy is ultimately constrained by the size of the total population. Nevertheless, for a given total population size, the aggregate supply can increase or decrease if, for example, married women decide to enter or leave the working population, which is determined by demographic factors and migration. However, for the purpose of this unit we are more interested in examining the supply of labour within a single labour market than with investigating the factors which cause the aggregate supply of labour to change.

Within a single labour market, the supply of labour is the sum of the supply curves of all the individual workers in the market. We assume, perhaps unrealistically, that each worker voluntarily chooses how much labour to supply at each wage-rate, and indeed whether to supply any labour at all. Essentially, a worker is **choosing between work and leisure**. However, it is impossible to be sure whether a worker will supply more or less labour as the wage-rate rises. Under most circumstances, the supply curve might be upward-sloping or 'normal', with more labour supplied at higher wages. The explanation for this lies in the assumption that both the **money wage** (or the goods which can be bought with the money wage) and **leisure** yield a **diminishing marginal utility**. When more labour is supplied at a particular wage-rate, the extra income which is earned will yield less and less additional utility. At the same time, each extra hour of leisure which is sacrificed results in an increasing utility loss. It follows that utility will be maximized when labour is supplied up to the point where **the marginal utility of the wage equals the marginal utility of the last unit of leisure sacrificed**. A higher wage would be needed to encourage a worker to voluntarily supply more labour beyond this point.

Under some circumstances, however, the supply curve of labour may be **backward-bending** or **perverse**, showing that as the wage rises, less labour is supplied. The backward-bending supply curve is explained by the assumption that workers aim to achieve a **target level of income** (sometimes called an **aspiration level**). This is a plausible behavioural assumption if the work is unpleasant. In the coal-mining industry, a wage rise may cause absenteeism if miners find that they can fulfil their aspirations by four days work instead of five!

A backward-bending supply curve has an important implication for tax policy. If the supply curve is upward-sloping, an increase in income tax results in less labour being supplied, because the tax is equivalent to a cut in wages. If, however, the supply curve is backward-bending, the rise in income tax will act as an incentive, since people will now have to work longer to fulfil their aspirations!

2 The Demand curve for Labour

We have already indicated that the demand curve for a factor of production is a **derived demand**. We assume that a firm will only voluntarily employ an extra worker if this increases total profit.

To find out whether profits will indeed increase, a firm must know (a) how much the worker adds to total output, and (b) the money value of the extra output when it is sold in the product market. The amount which is added to a firm's revenue by employing one more worker is called the **marginal revenue product** (MRP) of labour. The two elements which comprise the MRP of labour are represented in the equation:

$$\text{Marginal Revenue Product (MRP)} = \text{Marginal Physical Product (MPP)} \times \text{Marginal Revenue (MR)}$$

In Unit 3 we explained the 'Law' or principle of diminishing marginal returns, which states that a variable factor such as labour will **eventually** add less and less to total output as labour itself is added to other factors which are held fixed. In the context of distribution theory it is usual, if rather confusing, to refer to the **marginal physical product (MPP)** of labour. This is exactly the same as the marginal returns of labour. The falling MPP curve which is drawn in Figure 15.2a is explained by the principle of diminishing returns!

To find the money value of the MPP of labour, we multiply the MPP by the addition to total revenue resulting from the sale of the physical output in the goods market. In other words, we must multiply MPP by **marginal revenue**. In Figure 15.2 it is assumed that conditions of perfect competition exist in the goods market. In a perfectly competitive market, MR is identical to the good's price. Thus the MRP curve is derived by multiplying MPP by a constant price at each level of output. In these conditions, the slope and elasticity of the MRP curve are determined by MPP alone, though a change in the good's price will shift the position of the MRP curve. If the goods market is a monopoly or imperfectly competitive, MR will decrease with output. This causes the MRP curve to be steeper than when the goods market is perfectly competitive.

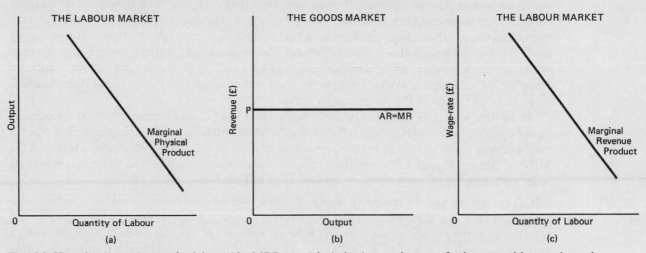

Fig 15.2 How the demand curve for labour (the MRP curve) is derived, assuming a perfectly competitive goods market

3 The equilibrium wage

In a particular labour market, the MRP curve of labour is the employer's demand curve for labour. An employer demands labour up to the point where MRP = the marginal cost of employing an extra worker. If the employer goes beyond this point and hires a worker who adds more to total costs than to total revenue, profits must fall. Conversely, if the firm decides to limit the size of the work-force at a point where the MRP of the last worker is greater than the MC of employing him, the firm is sacrificing potential profits. It follows that a **profit-maximizing firm** must demand labour up to the point where MRP = MC. However, the nature of the resulting equilibrium wage depends upon the assumptions made about the competitive state of the labour market. We shall explore some of the possibilities:

(i) A perfectly competitive labour market This is illustrated in Figure 15.3a. In these conditions, there are a large number of firms and a large number of workers, all acting independently in the market. An individual firm is a **price-taker**, in a position to employ as much labour as it wishes at the **ruling market wage**. The ruling wage is determined at the intersection of the supply and demand curves for labour in the labour market as a whole, but for an individual firm in the market the ruling wage is its supply curve. In Figure 15.3a, this is shown by the perfectly elastic supply curve SS. We assume that a firm can employ any quantity of labour it wishes at this wage. In these market conditions, employment is L_1. Each worker receives the equilibrium wage W_1, which is equal to the MRP of labour.

(ii) A monopsony buyer of labour Figure 15.3b illustrates a particular case when the equilibrium wage is not equal to the MRP of labour – though the size of the labour force is still determined

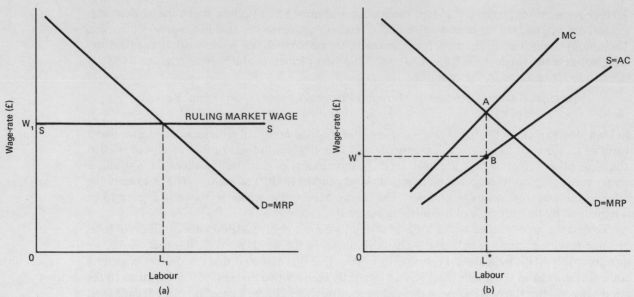

Fig 15.3 The equilibrium wage in different labour markets (a) a perfectly competitive labour market (b) a monopoly buyer of labour

where MRP = MC of labour. A single employer is a **monopsony** buyer in the labour market. Assuming an upward-sloping supply curve of labour, the intersection of the supply and demand curves no longer determines either the equilibrium wage or the size of employment. The supply curve S, or **average cost curve of labour**, shows the wage which must be paid to **all** workers at each size of employed labour force in order to persuade them to supply labour. However, the supply curve S is **not** the **marginal cost curve of labour!** The employer will have to pay a higher wage to attract an extra worker, and the higher wage must be paid to all the other employed workers. Thus the MC of an extra worker includes the total amount by which the wage bill rises. The MC curve of labour is **above** the AC or supply curve!

If the firm wishes to maximize profits, employment will be at L*, immediately below point A on the diagram where MRP = MC. However, the equilibrium wage W* is determined at point B on the supply curve of labour. In this type of labour market, the equilibrium wage is **less** than the MRP of labour. It is useful to note the similarity between this analysis and that for a **monopoly seller within the goods market**, which we explained in Unit 6.

(iii) Trade unions and the monopoly supply of labour We have so far assumed that perfect competition exists in the labour market and that workers always act **independently**. If the workers join together to form a trade union, they will now act **collectively** – an effective trade union being a monopoly supplier of labour. We shall examine some of the possible effects a trade union might have on wages in the context of one of the questions at the end of the unit. In some circumstances a union may only be able to raise wages at the expense of employment, whereas at other times it may be able to increase both wages and employment, for example by shifting the demand curve for labour rightwards. This can happen when a union encourages an employer to introduce new technology or methods of working which increase labour productivity, or if a general increase in wages resulting from union activity increases demand in the economy as a whole. Lastly, a union can sometimes exercise sufficient power, through the threat of strikes and the disruption of the continuous flow upon which modern industry is often dependent, to persuade a firm to sacrifice profit-maximization for the sake of securing at least some profit from uninterrupted production. In this situation, both the wage and the level of employment are determined at a point 'off' the employer's demand curve for labour. The union forces the firm to employ more workers than it would wish to at the wage-rate achieved by the union; hence the firm incurs extra avoidable costs and cannot be maximizing profits.

4 Explanations of different wage levels

Many economists argue that the real reason for the existence of different wage levels lies outside the explanation provided by distribution theory. For example, **social** and **political** factors must surely be highly relevant to any explanation of why female workers are paid less than men in many occupations which require similar skills. Nevertheless, the following reasons are suggested by conventional distribution theory to explain differences in wages:

(i) The separation of labour markets The economy comprises many separated labour markets rather than one large market. In each market, demand and supply conditions are different, resulting in different equilibrium wages. If perfect competition existed throughout the economy, differences in wages would create **incentives** for labour to move between markets and for entrepreneurs to substitute capital for labour. In this way, market forces would reduce wage variations between different industries and occupations. The continuing persistence of wage differences is explained by the forces which prevent labour mobility and factor substitution:

(a) It takes time for a worker to acquire the skills required in another occupation. Costs are also involved in acquiring the skill.
(b) Not all workers will possess the necessary aptitude or ability for a particular type of work.
(c) There are man-made barriers which prevent a worker from moving between labour markets, for example a union closed shop, or restrictions on entry to medical school.
(d) Technical considerations can make it impractical for a firm to employ more capital in place of labour.

(ii) Differences in the elasticities of supply and demand The elasticities of both the supply of and demand for labour are likely to differ between separated labour markets. If the demand for labour is relatively elastic, a rightward shift of the supply curve will have a greater effect on employment than on the wage level. In a similar way, the effect of a shift in demand will depend on the elasticity of the supply curve. A shift in either curve will have the greatest effect on the wage in a particular market when both the supply and demand curves are relatively inelastic. The **time period** in question is an important influence on both elasticities, with elasticities being higher in the long run than in the short run. It follows that a sudden change in the conditions of either supply or demand in a particular labour market will cause a larger change in the equilibrium wage in the short run than in the long run. In the long run, market forces serve to reduce wage differentials through the impact of labour mobility and factor substitution.

The supply of unskilled labour is generally more elastic than the supply of a particular type of skilled labour, since the training period of unskilled labour is usually very short. The existence of unemployed labour will also influence the elasticity of supply.

In general, the demand for labour will be relatively inelastic if:

(a) wage costs are only a small part of total production costs – this is sometimes known as the 'importance of being unimportant';
(b) the demand for the good produced by the firm is inelastic;
(c) it is difficult to substitute other factors of production for labour, or other types of labour for the particular type in question.

(iii) The relative importance of monetary and non-monetary rewards This varies between different occupations. A worker who enjoys his job may be prepared to accept a lower wage than a worker of similar skill and ability employed in an unpleasant occupation. Similarly, the existence of perks and fringe benefits in kind contribute to differences in money wages.

5 Criticisms of distribution theory

(i) The most important propositions of conventional distribution theory are that:
(a) in competitive markets, the equilibrium wage will equal the value of the marginal product of labour in each market, and
(b) the condition that the wage equals the marginal product of labour in each market is a necessary condition to achieve **allocative and productive efficiency** throughout the economy;
(c) the actual combination of labour and other factors of production employed will depend upon their relative prices. In competitive markets, where the price of each factor equals its marginal cost, a firm will employ factors until the

$$\frac{\text{MRP of labour}}{\text{wage}} = \frac{\text{MRP of land}}{\text{rent}} = \frac{\text{MRP of capital}}{\text{rate of interest}}$$

The most fundamental criticism of distribution theory is that it does not really explain anything at all. The theory is **circular**. The demand or MRP of a factor depends upon the value of what is produced; this in turn depends upon the effective demand of consumers exercised in the goods market; finally, the consumers' effective demand depends upon the distribution of income. Hence, the distribution of income is dependent upon the distribution of income! To give the theory some sense, an initial distribution of income must be assumed, and this initial distribution cannot of course be explained by the theory.

(ii) Even within its own terms, the theory can only explain the distribution of income within a small part of the total economy, assuming that conditions in the rest of the economy are held constant. In these conditions, a fall in the wage may cause an employer to demand more labour. However, if the wage level falls throughout the economy, the resulting decrease in aggregate demand can cause the demand curve for labour in each labour market to shift inwards. Unemployment may follow from the wage cut. This is the **Keynesian critique** of the micro-economic theory of distribution.

(iii) The theory assumes that the marginal productivity of labour can be separated from the marginal productivity of capital. However, in many technical processes capital and labour are **complementary** rather than substitutes. Output can only be raised by increasing both capital and labour in some fixed ratio. In these circumstances the marginal productivity of labour is impossible to isolate and identify.

(iv) The MRP theory of wage determination can only be used to explain the wages of workers employed in the market economy. It is impossible to place a market value on the labour productivity of the growing proportion of the British labour force employed in the **public services** provided by central and local government. The determination of public sector pay provides one example of the importance of **differentials, comparability** and **relativity** in wage-bargaining. It is by no means always clear, however, whether public sector pay is determined by comparability with the 'rate for the job' for similar employment in the private sector, or vice versa.

(v) Distribution theory is sometimes criticized for **unrealistically** ignoring the role of **collective bargaining** and other methods of pay determination in the British economy. In one sense the lack of realism is not very important. The theory states that a firm can only maximize profits if it employs labour up to the point where the MRP of labour equals the MC of labour. If this equality does not hold, the firm cannot be maximizing profits! In a perfectly competitive world it would be the forces of competition rather than the deliberate decisions of firms that would bring about the situation where MRP = MC. Firms which strayed away from profit-maximization would either be competed out of existence, or they would have to mend their ways. However, in a world in which firms may not be profit-maximizers, and in which markets are imperfectly competitive, there is no reason why the predictions of distribution theory should come true.

Nevertheless, distribution theory does tend to encourage the attitude that perfectly competitive markets are normal, that workers are paid what they **deserve** in terms of the value of what they produce, and that real-world bargaining patterns and institutions such as trade unions are distortions in otherwise perfect markets. While the markets for capital and land may be closer to the conditions of perfect competition, labour markets would probably be highly imperfect even without the existence of trade unions. Indeed, the principal argument used to justify trade unions is that, in their absence, market power would lie in the hands of employers. It is doubtful if labour markets ever existed in which all employers and all workers act as passive price-takers. More typically, market power would lie in the hands of the employers in a labour market in which a small number of employers bargained individually with a large number of workers unrepresented by a trade union. By bargaining collectively through a trade union, workers are seeking to create a market power to equal or exceed that possessed by the employer.

6 Methods of Wage Determination in the UK

In distribution theory it is generally assumed that wages are determined by individual negotiation between workers and employers and that market forces eventually bring about a ruling market wage. When trade unions are introduced into this analysis, it is assumed that firms decide how much labour to employ at a wage level determined by the union acting as a monopoly supplier of labour. The actual process of wage and salary determination in the UK is both more complicated and more varied.

(i) Collective bargaining In 1978 there were over 13 million trade union members in the UK, or about 54 per cent of the labour force, including the unemployed. The pay of most trade union members is determined by collective bargaining. The union represents its members' interests collectively by bargaining with employers to improve pay and other conditions of work. For further discussion of the nature of collective bargaining and its effectiveness, you should refer to the question practice at the end of this unit.

(ii) Individual negotiation generally takes place in non-unionized parts of the economy. Highly paid managers, executives and consultants who offer specialist professional services will normally negotiate on an individual basis. At the other extreme, unorganised low-paid workers such as fruit-pickers and other casual workers also negotiate individually. In these circumstances the employer usually has much more bargaining power than the individual worker. Consequently the wage may effectively be determined by the employer on a 'take it or leave it' basis.

(iii) State determination There are various ways in which the state intervenes to influence both market forces and the collective bargaining process:

(a) Protecting low-paid workers In low-paid industries such as catering, trade unions are difficult to organize and they tend to be ineffective. **Wages councils** have been established to determine minimum rates of pay. Wages councils represent a form of **minimum wage legislation**. In some countries, a minimum wage has been established by law, to cover all industries.

(b) Statutory incomes policies At various times since the Second World War, British governments have imposed a statutory incomes policy on the process of wage determination. An incomes policy usually lays down an **upper limit** to wage settlements. During a statutory incomes policy, 'free' collective bargaining is either **constrained** or perhaps even **suspended**. Trade unions have often been suspicious of incomes policies which they believe may undermine the bargaining function of a union. The government's main purpose in introducing an incomes policy has usually been to attack the **cost-push** causes of inflation which result in part from the nature of wage bargaining in the UK. Incomes policies have also been justified as a method of ensuring a **fairer distribution of income** than that resulting from the collective bargaining process.

(c) The state as an employer In most industries where the state or a public authority is the employer, unions are recognised and wages are determined by collective bargaining. However, there are exceptions, such as the armed forces and the police, where normal trade union activity is not allowed. Pay in the armed forces is effectively determined by the state.

(d) Arbitration and conciliation In the process of free collective bargaining, a trade union will often demand a pay rise which is greater than the increase the employer is initially prepared to pay. Bargaining is a process in which each side modifies its offer or claim until agreement is reached. The vast majority of agreements are reached without a breakdown in the bargaining process and without dispute. Occasionally, however, agreements cannot be reached and a dispute either occurs or is threatened. Many collective agreements contain negotiating procedures to be followed when the next round of bargaining takes place. The procedural arrangements commonly specify the stage in the breakdown of bargaining at which outside **arbitrators** or **conciliators** should be brought in to help both sides reach agreement. In 1975 the Employment Protection Act established the **Advisory Conciliation and Arbitration Service** (ACAS). If both sides in a dispute agree, ACAS may be called in to try to settle a dispute.

15.4 LINKS WITH OTHER TOPICS

In this unit we have considered the determination of wages and the level of employment from a micro-economic point of view, bringing to a close the section of the book devoted to micro-economics. In the second half of the book, we shall see how many of the special concerns of macro-economics, such as the level of employment and the causes of inflation, require an understanding of how individual labour markets work. In particular, the process of wage determination is a most important part of the theories of inflation (Unit 24). In Unit 25 we shall note the different views on the wage determination process which are held by Keynesians and monetarists.

15.5 QUESTION PRACTICE

Essay Questions

Question 1 'A trade union is able to obtain an increase in the *real* wages of its members only at the expense of reduced employment conditions for those members'. Discuss.

(London: June 1978)

Understanding the Question In the main body of the unit we restricted our analysis of trade unions in the context of distribution theory to the rather general statements that (i) unions can increase both wages and employment for their members if union activity results in the MRP curve shifting rightwards, and (ii) if the main result of union activity is to shift the supply curve of labour leftwards by restricting entry to the labour market, wage rises will normally be at the expense of employment. Figure 15.4a also illustrates a situation in which wages rise at the expense of employment. We assume rather unrealistically that the union can fix any wage-rate it chooses, and that employment is then determined by the amount of labour which employers will hire at this wage. If the wage is fixed at W_2, above the competitive wage determined by supply and demand at W_1, the line W_2AS becomes the supply curve of labour. Employers are faced with a perfectly elastic supply of labour at the union-determined wage, up to a supply of L_3. Beyond this point they will have to offer a higher wage in order to attract more labour. However, they will only willingly employ a labour force of L_2, thereby restricting employment below the competitive level of L_1. At the union-determined wage-rate, there is an excess supply of labour of L_3-L_2. This will create a pressure to undermine the union if unemployed workers are prepared to supply labour at a wage below W_2. Whether W_2 continues as the wage-rate will depend upon the union's power to resist wage-cutting

Figure 15.4b illustrates a market structure in which the introduction of a union can increase both the wage-rate and employment, without the need to shift the MRP curve rightwards! This is when a **monopsony buyer of labour** bargains with a trade union which is a **monopoly seller of labour**. We explained earlier, in the context of Figure 15.3b, how in the absence of a trade union the competitive supply of labour would result in an equilibrium wage rate at W^*, and an employment level at L^*. Suppose now that a trade union fixes the wage-rate at W_1. At this wage-rate the supply curve of labour is the line W_1XS, and the marginal cost curve of labour is W_1XZ MC. You should note that the MC of employing another worker is the same as the union-determined wage, as long as the labour force is below L_1. If a labour force above L_1 is to be employed, the wage must rise in

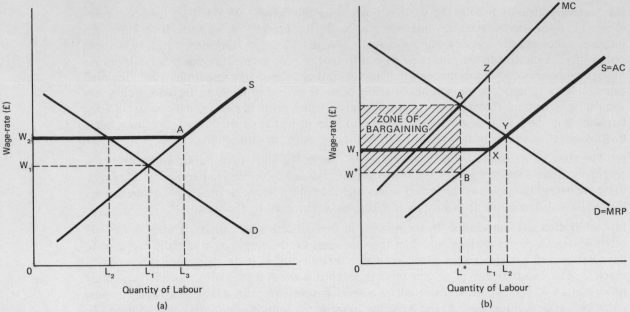

Fig 15.4 The effect of the introduction of a trade union into different labour markets (a) competitive demand for labour (b) monopoly demand for labour

order to persuade additional workers to supply their labour. Because all workers must be paid the higher wage, the MC of employing an extra worker is now above the supply curve. Between the horizontal section of the MC curve for levels of employment below L_1, and the 'competitive' section of the curve Z MC, is a vertical line or discontinuity, XZ. The equilibrium level of employment at the wage of W_1 is L_1. This is determined where the demand curve for labour (MRP) intersects the vertical section of the MC curve between X and Z. The union can increase both the wage-rate and the level of employment as compared with the situation without a union. Providing of course that the union possesses the required power, both the wage-rate and the level of employment can be increased up to an employment level of L_2 determined at point Y. Wages can be increased beyond Y up to a level fixed at A, but only at the expense of some of the extra employment which the union created.

Answer plan

1 Distinguish between an increase in the **money wage** and the **real wage**. If an increase in the money wage causes or is associated with an equal increase in prices, there is no increase in the real wage. In order to increase the real wage of its members, a union must secure a rise in the wage-rate which is greater than the rate of inflation.

2 In these circumstances, employment and the real wage may rise if the MRP curve shifts rightwards. Whether such a shift in the demand curve for labour is the result of the union's existence, or would have taken place anyway, is open to debate.

3 If the union raises the real wage by restricting entry to the labour market, thereby shifting the supply curve of labour leftwards, employment is likely to fall. However, the unemployed may not be members of the union!

4 Introduce and explain other market situations such as those we have explained in these notes.

Question 2

(a) What is collective bargaining?

(b) Assess the possible consequences of collective bargaining on (i) real wages and (ii) employment.

(Cambridge: November 1980)

Understanding the Question In 1968 the Royal Commission on Trade Unions and Employers' Associations (the Donovan Commission) defined a **trade union** as '**any combination of employees, the principal activity of which is the regulation of relations between employees and employers**'. The main function of both trade unions and employers' associations is to bargain collectively on behalf of their members to determine rates of pay and other conditions of employment, ranging from pensions, holidays and disputes procedures to conditions of work within a particular workshop or office. There are many different forms of collective bargaining, which reflect both the structure of industry and the haphazard way both unions and employers' associations have developed their present-day structure. In one industry, a single trade union representing all the employed workers may bargain with a single employer, or perhaps with all the employers together. In other industries, separate unions representing specific groups of skilled or unskilled workers may jointly bargain with the employer or employers, or they may bargain separately and in competition with each other. It is also useful to distinguish between **national collective bargaining** and various forms of **local collective bargaining** at the regional, plant or shop-floor level. **Basic wage-rates** are usually determined by national bargaining, while **local bonuses** and **piece-rates** are locally negotiated. During periods of incomes policy, there has been a tendency for more and more of total **earnings** to be locally negotiated, so that the basic wage forms a decreasing proportion of total earnings. This is known as **wage drift**. Wage drift occurs because locally negotiated rates of pay, which are often specific to a particular piece of work which is passing through a factory, provide a means of escaping from the effects of an incomes policy.

The second half of the question is perhaps more important than the first half, which is merely descriptive, and it must be answered at some length. We have covered the relevant theory in our notes on the previous question, to which you should now refer. It is worth pointing out that part of the real wage includes such things as pension rights. Unions can sometimes bargain successfully for increased pensions and a reduction in the working week, when incomes policies or market forces make it more difficult to increase the money wage of their members.

Answer plan

1 Define collective bargaining. Describe some of the various forms collective bargaining may take and show how it aims to improve other conditions of work besides pay.

2 Assume that collective bargaining allows a union to fix the wage-rate above the level that would be determined by supply and demand in the absence of a union. Examine some of the different effects on the equilibrium wage and employment in different market structures (see previous question). Distinguish between the real wage and the money wage.

Multiple Choice Questions

Question 3 An employer with a labour force of 10 men, each paid at the rate of £20 per day, raises the wage-rate by £1 per day to attract one more worker. If other costs remain constant, the marginal cost of employing the additional worker is

(a) £1.00

(b) £11.00

(c) £21.00

(d) £31.00

Understanding the Question Figures 15.3b and 15.4b are especially useful in understanding this question. If the wage-rate is increased to attract one more worker, the marginal cost of labour will include the increase in the wage paid to all the other workers as well as the wage paid to the new worker. MC = £10 + £21. (d) is therefore the correct answer.

Question 4 A pop-singer earns £10 000 a week. He would be prepared to remain in his present occupation even if his wage fell as low as £50 a week. £9950 therefore represents his

(a) transfer earnings

(b) opportunity cost

(c) economic rent

(d) quasi rent

Understanding the Question This is a straightforward question on the division of wages, and other factor incomes, between economic rent and transfer earnings. In this case, the singer's transfer earnings are £50 and the economic rent, which is the difference between what he actually earns and the minimum he would be prepared to accept, is £9950. Thus (c) is the correct answer. The concept of **quasi rent** in alternative (d) is closely related to economic rent. The short-run supply curve of a factor of production is likely to be less elastic than the long-run curve. This means that a factor which will eventually be transferred to an alternative use in the long run, in response to a fall in its factor price, may not be transferred in the short run. That part of its earnings which is economic rent in the short run, but transfer earnings in the long run, forms a **quasi rent**.

Data Response Questions

Question 5 How far can the marginal productivity theory of wages explain the following differences in earnings? What additional factors are relevant?

Occupation	Full-time Men aged 21 and over	Full-time Women aged 18 and over
Teacher in Further Education establishments	64.2	
Teacher in Secondary Education establishments	52.7	45.3
Shop-Assistants	35.0	18.6
Firemen	45.9	
Farm-workers	25.7	
Plumbers, pipe-fitters	38.4	
Repetitive assemblers (metal and electrical)	39.2	24.5
Face-trained coalminers	46.9	
Bus and Coach drivers	34.7	
Refuse-collectors, dustmen	31.8	
Registered and enrolled nurses, midwives		25.7
Secretaries and shorthand typists		28.9

Average Gross Weekly Earnings (£) (excluding overtime pay) April 1974

(SUJB: June 1976)

Understanding the Question Since overtime earnings are excluded, the statistics may not properly reflect the true differences in money earnings. For example, coalminers, bus-drivers and other **manual workers** often receive overtime payments, whereas **white-collar workers** such as schoolteachers and typists may not.

You should explain how marginal productivity theory may account for some of the differences, but how other factors are obviously important too. Indeed, it is difficult to use marginal productivity theory to explain the earnings of teachers, nurses and other workers who do not usually produce a good or service for sale in the market. Supply and demand may partially explain a teacher's earnings, but the demand is determined by social and political factors. Non-monetary rewards, the role of trade unions, and man-made and natural barriers to entry should all be brought into your answer. Should the productivity of a nurse be measured by the number of sick people treated, the number cured or by some other measure? Clearly any measure is going to be rather unsatisfactory.

The data clearly show that female workers are paid less than men, both in similar occupations and in 'traditional' female occupations. Part of the explanation for the lower pay of female teachers may lie in the fact that a higher proportion of male teachers are higher-qualified graduates further up a salary scale. Because of family commitments, many women are unable to develop their careers, even though teaching has for many years been an 'equal pay' career.

Answer plan
1 Briefly explain marginal productivity theory.
2 Some of the wage differences may be related to productivity, but perhaps not the significant ones. Explain the problems in measuring the productivity of the highest-paid group, college lecturers, or nurses.
3 Introduce the social and political factors, the role of unions, historical patterns and differentials, etc.
4 Lastly, examine why women are generally lower-paid than men.

15.6 FURTHER READING

Williamson, H., *The Trade Unions*, 5th edition (Heinemann, 1979).

Burningham, D., editor, *Understanding Economics, an Introduction for Students* (Macmillan, 1978).
Chapter 10: Factor Markets and the Distribution of Income

Lipsey, R. G., *An Introduction to Positive Economics*, 5th edition (Weidenfeld & Nicolson, 1979).
Chapter 27: Wages and collective bargaining.

16 Money

16.1 POINTS OF PERSPECTIVE

1 Money as a medium of exchange and unit of account
In a developed market economy, nearly all the exchanges involved in production and distribution require the use of money as a **medium of exchange**. In a very simple economy, exchange could be based on **barter**, but barter is inefficient and impractical in a more complex economic system. Successful barter requires a **'double coincidence of wants'**: if someone wishes to buy a typewriter, he must find another person who not only has a typewriter to sell, but who also wants the goods which the purchaser is selling. Time and energy will be wasted in searching the market to establish the double coincidence of wants. The existence of such **transactions and search costs** is likely to discourage specialization and large-scale production in an economy.

Besides functioning as a medium of exchange, money usually acts as a **unit of account**, allowing the prices of all goods to be compared. In modern economies the unit of account is almost always the medium of exchange, but there are exceptions – the prices of antiques or racehorses offered for sale at an auction are sometimes expressed in guineas, even though the guinea has long ceased to be a monetary unit.

2 Money as a store of value

Monetarists and **Keynesians** hold rather different views on the nature and functions of money. Monetarists have inherited what is sometimes known as the **classical tradition**, which separates the role in the economy of **'real'** and **'monetary'** forces. They believe that the **relative prices** of goods, which are determined in the real economy by the forces of supply and demand, are independent of money even though they are commonly expressed in monetary units of account. Money merely determines the **general price level**. For example, if the amount of money in the economy doubles, all prices double, but relative prices and equilibrium outputs in the economy remain the same.

Keynesians argue that this view of the role of money ignores the essential function of money as a **store of value**. For example, a person who sells his labour and receives money in exchange may decide to store the income he received in the form of idle money instead of using it to demand goods and services. This can result in a lack of demand for the output which is currently being produced, resulting in the breakdown of the **monetary linkage** between the **markets of the real**

economy. Thus, the function of money as a store of value is an important part of the Keynesian argument that unemployment can be caused by a lack of **effective aggregate demand** in an economy.

3 The historical development of money

(i) Commodity money In order to function as money, an asset must be an acceptable medium of exchange and a possible store of value. Early forms of money which replaced barter were **commodities**, such as beads, shells, cattle and slaves, usually with an **intrinsic value** of their own. Gradually the **precious metals**, gold and silver, replaced other forms of commodity money because they possessed to a greater degree the other desirable characteristics necessary for a commodity to function as money: relative **scarcity, portability, durability, divisibility,** and **uniformity.**

(ii) Representative money Nevertheless gold and silver are vulnerable to theft and difficult to store, and it became the custom for precious metals to be deposited with goldsmiths for safe-keeping. The goldsmiths developed into banks, and the gold receipts which they issued became bank-notes or paper money. The notes were acceptable as a means of payment since they could be exchanged for gold on demand. Although relatively worthless in itself, the money **represented** ownership of commodities with an intrinsic value.

(iii) Token money Banks discovered that they could increase their profits by issuing notes to a value greatly in excess of the gold deposits which they held. Imprudent banks would over-expand the note issue, and depositors suffered in the crashes which periodically occurred when banks could not meet demands by the public to convert notes into gold. As a direct result of these bank crashes, the 1844 Bank Charter Act largely removed from English and Welsh banks the right to issue their own notes, though some banks continued to issue notes on a limited scale until the last 'country' bank merged in 1921. This change in the law encouraged a new development in banking, the creation of **deposit money**. Instead of issuing its own notes when a customer requested a loan, a bank would make a **ledger or book-keeping entry** crediting the customer's account with a loan or bank deposit. Such a bank deposit is obviously a store of value. However, a bank deposit is also a medium of exchange if it is customarily accepted that payment can be made by shifting ownership of the deposit, for example through the medium of a cheque.

Bank deposits are of course **token money**. They are **customary money** rather than **legal tender**, and generally accepted as money because of people's confidence in the banks and the monetary system. Bank deposits make up by far the largest part of modern money, between two-thirds and 85 per cent of the money supply in 1978, depending on how money is defined. In contrast, **cash** (notes and coins, or the **currency**) is just the 'small change' of the system. Nowadays the state has a monopoly of the issue of cash, in England and Wales at least, and cash has gradually developed to become purely token money, just like a bank deposit. Unlike a bank deposit, however, cash is usually legal tender – 'fiat money' made legal by government decree – which must be accepted as a medium of exchange.

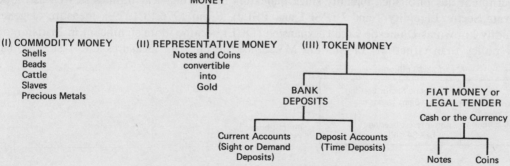

Fig 16.1 Historical and present-day forms of money

16.2 UNDERLYING CONCEPTS

1 Money, near money, and money substitutes

It is generally agreed that bank **current accounts (sight deposits** or **demand deposits)** function as money. They are both a store of value and a medium of exchange since cheques can be drawn on the deposit and are accepted in payment of a debt. Nowadays many people use credit cards as a medium of exchange. However, a credit card is not a store of value, and its use merely delays the settling of a debt through a cash transaction or the shifting of a bank deposit. A credit card is a **money substitute** rather than a form of money in its own right.

Whereas a money substitute is a medium of exchange but not a store of value, the reverse is true of **near money**. A number of financial assets such as building society deposits are currently regarded as near monies. A building society deposit is a substitute for a bank current account or a cash holding as a convenient form of storage for wealth or value, but it does not serve as medium of exchange unless cheques can be drawn on the deposit.

2 The problem of defining the money supply

Thirty years ago, neither economists nor politicians gave much attention to the precise definition of the money supply, since it was generally accepted that 'money did not matter' in the macro-economic management of the economy. As we shall see in later units, this is no longer the case. According to the monetarists, money does matter, and the **control of the money supply** is an important part of monetarist economic management in general, and monetary policy in particular. Even if it is accepted that monetarist theory is correct (we shall later see that Keynesians dispute this) **practical monetarism** may be impossible if the money supply is a 'will-o'-the wisp' which cannot by its nature be controlled. Suppose that the **monetary authorities** (the Bank of England and the Treasury) decide either to restrict the rate of growth of the money supply or to reduce the absolute size of the money stock. The more successful they appear to be in controlling whatever they define as the money supply, the more likely it is that **near monies**, outside the existing definition and system of control, will take on the function of money as a medium of exchange. In this sense, 'money is as money does'! Keynesians sometimes argue that the money supply is impossible to control, since it **passively** adapts to whatever level is required to finance the transactions which are desired at the existing price level. We shall examine the implications of this argument in the contexts of monetary policy in Unit 19 and inflation in Unit 24.

Whether or not this view on the impossibility of controlling the money supply is completely accepted, it does help to explain why policy-makers have commonly used more than one definition of the money supply. The 'narrow definition' favoured in Britain is **M1**, comprising cash and bank sight deposits. However, wealthy individuals and companies will normally hold interest-earning **deposit accounts** or **time deposits** alongside their current accounts or sight deposits. Should time deposits be defined as money? Unlike a sight deposit, the ownership of a time deposit cannot be shifted by cheque; hence a time deposit is not a medium of exchange. But to compete with the building societies, the banks have allowed deposit accounts to become increasingly more liquid. A customer may keep a very low balance in a current account, upon which cheques can be drawn; when a large payment is due to be made, part of the deposit account is simply shifted into the current account. Bank customers therefore treat their deposit accounts as money, a practice encouraged by the banks in order to attract funds away from building societies and National Saving Certificates. For this reason, time deposits are included in the 'wider definition' of the money supply, **Sterling M3**, which is illustrated along with M1 in Figure 16.2.

But why stop at the inclusion of time deposits? If building society deposits are as liquid as bank time deposits, they also should be included in a definition of the money supply. Indeed, other definitions of the money stock such as **M4**, **M5** and **M6** have been suggested, and the government has published **liquidity stock indicators** measuring near monies as well as money: **Private Sector Liquidity 1 and 2 (PSL1 and PSL2)**. From 1976 to 1979 a measure of general liquidity known as **Domestic Credit Expansion** (DCE) became more significant in British monetary policy than either M1 or Sterling M3. Since Sterling M3 measures UK residents' bank

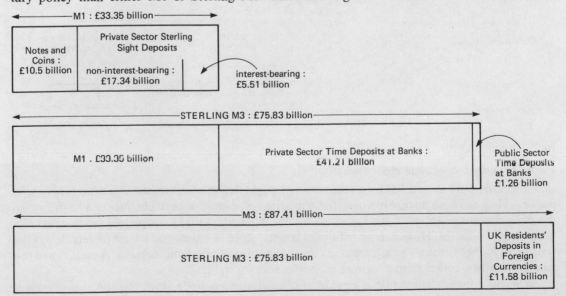

Fig 16.2 The UK money supply, end of third quarter 1981.
Source: *Bank of England Quarterly Bulletin*, December 1981

deposits (in addition to notes and coins in circulation) it represents the **liabilities side** of the banks' balance-sheets. In contrast, DCE is measured from the **assets side** and is a measure of the **credit or money generated in the domestic economy alone**. When the balance of payments is in deficit, Sterling M3 tends to fall because payments for the excess of imports involve a transfer from residents' bank deposits (within Sterling M3) to non-residents' bank deposits (outside Sterling M3). Alternatively, if the payments are made in foreign currency, UK residents' bank deposits are again reduced when they surrender sterling to buy foreign currency from the government. Broadly speaking, DCE can be conceived of as equal to Sterling M3 plus (or minus) the Balance of Payments deficit (or surplus). Since, in contrast to Sterling M3, the size of DCE is not influenced by whether the Balance of Payments is in surplus or deficit, it is considered by some to be a better measure of liquidity in the economy than Sterling M3, particularly when the Balance of Payments is in deficit.

In summary, the narrow definition of the money supply M1 concentrates on the medium of exchange function of money, whereas wider definitions, such as M3, include financial assets which are both temporary stores of value and are sufficiently liquid to be converted into a medium of exchange quickly and without capital loss.

16.3 ESSENTIAL KNOWLEDGE

1 The creation of bank deposits

Figure 16.2 shows clearly how bank deposits form the largest part of both M1 and M3. Bank deposits are the main form of money because banks possess the ability to create new deposits or **credit**. We shall delay until Unit 19 an explanation of how this is done in the complex conditions and institutional framework of the British monetary system. In this unit we restrict the analysis to a very simple model of credit creation in an economy in which there is just one **commercial bank** which has a monopoly of all bank dealings with the general public. For our purposes a bank is defined as an institution which:

(i) accepts **deposits** which can be transferred by cheque; and

(ii) makes **advances** (which can be either **overdrafts** or **term loans**).

We shall further assume that the commercial bank aims to maximize profits, but is required to hold a reserve of 10 per cent cash against its total deposit liabilities. The 10 per cent **cash ratio** may be a **reserve requirement** of the **central bank**, or it may be chosen for **reasons of prudence** by the bank itself.

Suppose that a member of the public now makes a new deposit of £1000 in cash. From the bank's point of view £1000 is both a **liability** and an **asset**, and will be recorded as such in the bank's balance sheet:

Liabilities	Assets
Deposit £1000	Cash £1000

As things stand, all the bank's deposit liabilities are backed with cash. If this remained the position, the 'bank' would simply be a safe-deposit institution. However, the bank can increase profits by crediting £9000 to the account of a customer who has requested a loan.

On the assets side of the balance sheet this will be shown as an **advance** of £9000 – whether the loan is an overdraft or a term loan granted for a definite period or term of years does not matter. Since the bank must honour any cheques which are drawn on the account up to the value of £9000, **deposit liabilities** have increased by exactly the same amount as **interest-earning assets**:

Liabilities	Assets
Deposits £10 000	Cash £1000
	Advances £9000

Both the customer who made the original deposit and the customer in receipt of the advance can draw cheques to a combined value of £10 000 on their deposits. The initial £1000 has expanded deposits, and hence the money supply, to £10 000. As we are assuming a monopoly bank, there is no danger of customers drawing cheques payable to customers of other banks. Nevertheless, there could be a **cash drain** from the bank, if customers decide always to keep some proportion of their money assets in the form of cash. A cash drain would limit the bank's ability to create deposits to a figure somewhat below that illustrated in our example.

Deposits will be expanded whether the bank expands advances or purchases interest-earning assets such as securities or bonds from the general public. Suppose the bank creates £6000 of advances and purchases £3000 of bonds. The bank pays for the bonds with a cheque for £3000 drawn on itself, thereby increasing total deposit liabilities to £10 000 when the payment is credited to the account of the person who sold the bonds. The spectrum of assets owned by the bank is different from the previous position, but the deposit liabilities, which represent the creation of money, are the same as in our last example:

Liabilities	Assets
Deposits £10 000	Cash £1000
	Bonds £3000
	Advances £6000

Of course, the assumption of a monopoly commercial bank is completely unrealistic, but it does illustrate the central principle of credit creation – that the banking system as a whole can create an expansion in bank deposits (and thus the money supply) which is a **multiple** of the **liquid reserves** held by the banks. Because, in our example, cash is the only liquid asset or reserve held to **fractionally back** the bank's deposit liabilities, the ability of the banks to expand deposits is dependent on the cash ratio. The **money multiplier** measures the maximum expansion of deposits (or 'low-powered' money) which is possible for a given increase in cash (or 'high-powered' money) deposited in the banking system. Assuming that there is no cash drain, for our model we can write:

$$\text{money multiplier} = \frac{1}{\text{cash ratio}}$$

In Unit 19 we shall see that the monetary authorities have usually required the British banks to keep some form of **liquid assets ratio** or **reserve ratio**, rather than the simple cash ratio of our model. It is useful, therefore, to write the money multiplier more generally as:

$$\text{money multiplier} = \frac{1}{\text{liquid assets ratio}}$$

When we assume a **multi-bank system**, similar to that in the UK, the general conclusions of our model still hold. If the increase of £1000 in cash deposits is spread over all the banks, deposits can expand to £10 000 providing that every bank is prepared to create deposits to the full extent the cash ratio allows. However, if only one bank is willing to expand deposits to the full, it will soon face demands for cash which it cannot meet. Customers will draw cheques on their deposits which will be paid into the accounts of the customers of the banks that have refused to expand credit. When the cheques are cleared, the bank must pay cash to the other banks, equal to the shift in deposits. To avoid this possibility, the bank will restrict the extent to which it is prepared to expand deposits. However, if all banks expand credit to the full, payments to customers of other banks will largely cancel out. The banking system as a whole can expand deposits to £10 000, though some banks may gain business at the expense of others.

2 The demand for money

So far we have assumed implicitly that banks will create new bank deposits, and hence increase the supply of money, to the fullest extent possible. In our model, the ability of the banks to create new deposits is constrained, firstly by the size of the **cash base** of the banking system, and secondly by the **prudential requirement** to maintain a cash ratio – in Unit 19 we shall extend the analysis to the situation where the monetary authorities decide the reserve ratio and then attempt to influence the reserve assets in the implementation of monetary policy.

However, we have begged the question of whether bank customers actually **demand** and take up all the new deposits or credit which the banks are prepared to create. The **actual money stock** in the economy will be determined by both the demand and the supply of money.

The nature of the demand for money is one of the most important areas of debate between Keynesian and monetarist economists, a debate which is significant both in terms of economic theory and practical policy-making. Unfortunately, in a book of this type we can do no more than scratch the surface of the issues involved. Keynesians and monetarists share common ground in believing that part of the demand for money results from **transactions** and **precautionary motives**:

(i) **The transactions demand for money** A certain amount of money is required as a medium of exchange so that people can undertake day-to-day purchases of goods and services. The transactions demand for money depends upon:

(a) **real income** – people with high incomes are likely to require larger transaction balances to finance their purchases for the simple reason that they usually plan to spend more than poorer people.

(b) **the price level** – a rise in the price level is likely to increase the transactions demand for money, since more money is needed to finance the same real expenditure.

(c) **institutional factors such as the length of time between pay days** – if a worker is paid a salary of £800 once every four weeks instead of £200 weekly, he is likely to keep a larger balance, on average, in his bank deposit or in cash in order to finance the expenditure planned over the month.

(ii) The precautionary demand for money A certain amount of money may be held to meet unforeseen emergencies, though it is more usual nowadays to hold such assets in building society deposits and other near monies. For most purposes the precautionary demand for money can be merged into the transactions demand, since it is also likely to be determined by real income, the price level and institutional factors.

(iii) The speculative demand for money The main area of controversy between Keynesians and monetarists on the nature of the demand for money centres on the speculative demand for money, which is the third reason for holding money balances. The transactions and precautionary demands for money are sometimes called the demand for **active balances**. Money is also held for **passive** reasons as an **idle balance** or store of wealth. Figure 16.3 illustrates some of the various asset forms in which an individual may decide to store his personal **portfolio** of wealth. Wealth may be stored in **physical assets**, for example consumer durables, which yield a stream of consumer services or utility to their owner. Some physical assets such as property, antiques and works of art may be especially attractive as a **hedge against inflation** (or the falling real value of money) if their prices are expected to rise. However, for our purposes we shall assume that an individual makes his portfolio decisions over a range of financial assets, represented for the sake of simplicity by money and bonds.

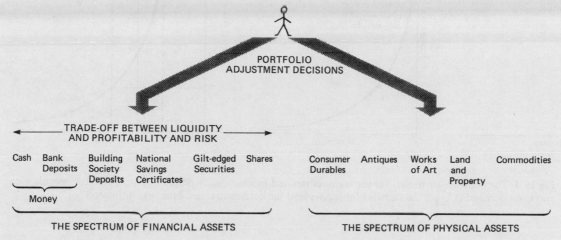

Fig 16.3 An example of some of the financial and physical assets in which an individual may decide to store his personal wealth

If people expected, with complete certainty, that the existing interest rate would persist for ever, it would be irrational to hold any passive money balances as a store of wealth, providing that the interest rate was above zero. In these circumstances money would be held for transactions and precautionary purposes only. The fact that some money balances are held as a passive store of wealth whatever the interest rate is explained by people's uncertainty about future interest rates. As we explained in Unit 11, the **rate of interest varies inversely with bond or security prices**. Some people may have no views on which way the interest rate will change, except that they expect it to change at some time in the future. If the interest rate rises, bond prices must fall, and owners of bonds will suffer **capital losses**. For such people, it will make sense to keep part of their store of wealth in passive money balances to counter the risk of capital losses if interest rates rise. The demand for money balances as a passive wealth asset is known as the **asset demand for money**.

Some people may go further, believing that they 'know better than the market'. They may speculate that the rate of interest will rise and bond prices will fall. In these circumstances they will deliberately sell bonds at their current prices and hold more money balances, in order to avoid the capital losses they expect. Conversely, if interest rates are expected to fall they will move out of money and purchase bonds at their currently low prices, in order to realize a capital gain in the future.

We can now draw the demand curve for money (the **liquidity preference curve**) by adding up the demand curves for active and idle balances. Since the demand curve for active balances, L_{T+P} in Figure 16.4a, is completely **interest inelastic**, the interest elasticity of the liquidity preference curve, L in Figure 16.4c, is determined from the demand curve for idle balances, L_S in Figure 16.4b. You should note: (i) that the demand for idle balances varies inversely with the rate of interest, and (ii) demand is **interest inelastic** at high interest rates, but that the **interest elasticity** increases as the interest rate falls. This conclusion, which is derived essentially from the assumption of speculative motives for holding money, has important implications for monetary policy, as we shall shortly see.

3 The rate of interest

The **rate of interest** can be defined as the **price of borrowed money** or the **opportunity cost of holding money**. As in any market, the equilibrium price is determined where intended demand equals intended supply. Thus the equilibrium interest rate is found where the demand for money equals the supply of money. Of course, it may well be that the supply of money is not independent of the demand, and that near monies take on the function of money in response to demand if the existing money stock is held down artificially. However, if we assume that the money supply can be independently determined and controlled by the monetary authorities, we now have a theory of interest determination in which the rate of interest is determined by market forces. If the money supply is fixed at Ms_1 in Figure 16.4c, the rate of interest is determined ar r_1. If the authorities now increase the money supply to Ms_2, the rate of interest falls to r_2. This then feeds through to the **real economy** since businessmen will be expected to invest more at lower rates of interest. In this way, **an increase in the money supply has an expansionary effect in the real economy**.

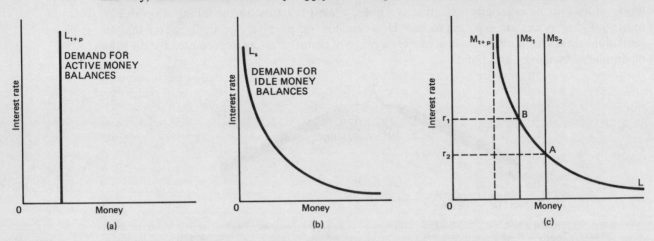

Fig 16.4 The demand for money (a) the transactions and precautionary demand (L_{T+P}) (b) the speculative and asset demand (L_S) (c) the demand for money and the determination of the rate of interest

4 A first look at the monetarist-Keynesian controversy

Keynesians argue that monetary policy is both **less effective** and **less predictable** than fiscal policy in its expansionary or contractionary effects on the economy. It is less effective because Keynesian theory suggests that businessmen's investment decisions are influenced more by the state of business confidence than by the rate of interest. It is less predictable for two reasons:

(i) Figure 16.4c indicates that the effects of an increase in the money supply on the rate of interest depend on the interest elasticity of the liquidity preference curve. There will be a greater effect on interest rates at high rather than at low interest rates.

(ii) The speculative motive for holding money balances causes the liquidity preference curve to be highly unstable, shifting erratically leftwards and rightwards. In these circumstances, the effects of a change in the money supply must be unpredictable.

These conclusions depend essentially on the assumption of a speculative demand for money balances. In rejecting these conclusions it is not surprising, therefore, that monetarists reject the significance of a speculative motive for holding money balances. According to the monetarists:

(a) The demand for money is a relatively **stable** function of a few variables such as real wealth, income, and the yield on various wealth assets. The relationship does not change much over time.

(b) Money is mainly demanded for **transactions purposes**.

(c) The demand for money is relatively **interest inelastic**.

Taken together, these conclusions mean that a change in the money supply will have a significant and predictable effect on money national income, supporting the monetarist argument that monetary policy has greater effects on the economy than does fiscal policy. Monetarists usually argue that an increase in money supply will lead, ceteris paribus, to a situation in which people possess larger money balances than they wish to hold for spending on existing planned transactions. There is some debate on the actual transmission mechanism by which money national income then expands. One possibility is that people reduce their money holdings towards the desired level by purchasing bonds. The price of bonds is bid up, causing the interest rate to fall, thereby stimulating business investment as we have described. Another possibility is that they will simply spend their excess money holdings.

16.4 LINKS WITH OTHER TOPICS

As yet we have hardly touched upon the various controversies between Keynesian and monetarist economists. In particular, we have not yet discussed whether the main effects of a monetary expansion will be on **real income or output** or on **prices.** This issue is discussed in Unit 24. In this unit we have introduced a simple model of credit creation and we have discussed in a general way whether the authorities can control the money supply. It is now generally agreed that the government's fiscal and monetary policies should not be treated as if they are independent of each other – public spending and its method of finance have significant effects on both the money supply and the government's freedom of choice in monetary policy. With this in mind, we shall examine the determinants of government revenues, expenditure and the PSBR, before we go on in Unit 19 to examine the detailed methods by which the authorities attempt to implement monetary policy.

16.5 QUESTION PRACTICE

Essay Questions

Question 1 What are the functions of money? Explain how the quantity of money is determined.

(AEB: June 1979)

Understanding the Question This is a deceptively simple question, which can be answered with varying degrees of sophistication. In order to secure a pass grade you must list and briefly explain the medium of exchange, unit of account and store of value functions of money. Some text-books mention a fourth function of money as a means of deferred payment. You should go on to show how the quantity of money is determined by market forces at the intersection of the supply and demand for money curves. It is probably better to adopt this approach than to assume that the quantity of money is simply determined by the banking system's ability to create new deposits. However, you should explain how the creation of credit helps to determine the supply of money. Similarly you should at least briefly describe the determinants of the demand for money.

Throughout the unit we have hinted that controversy rages at the highest academic level on exactly how the quantity of money is determined. Is the supply of money under the control of the monetary authorities? If this is the case, then the authorities could, in theory at least, determine the quantity of money, leaving the price of money or the interest rate to be determined by demand. Or is the supply of money itself dependent on demand, passively adapting to whatever level is demanded to finance desired transactions at the existing price level?

Answer plan

1 List and briefly describe the functions of money. Perhaps explain how monetarists and Keynesians give different emphasis to the medium of exchange and store of value functions.
2 Draw a diagram to show the supply of and demand for money. State that the usual assumption in such a diagram is that the money supply, which is under the control of the authorities, determines the quantity of money.
3 State that most of the supply of money is created by banks, but the monetary authorities may attempt to control the ability of banks to create new deposits.
4 The alternative view is that the demand for and supply of money are not independent of each other. The money supply adapts to whatever level is demanded.

Multiple Choice Questions

Question 2 The following table gives details of items comprising the money stock of the UK in 1979:

Notes and coins in circulation	£9701 m
Private sector sterling current accounts	£20 345 m
Private sector sterling deposit accounts	£27 376 m
Public sector sterling deposit accounts	£1255 m
UK residents' deposits in other currencies	£5306 m

In 1979 the money stock defined as Sterling M3 amounted to:

(a) £30 046 m
(b) £57 422 m
(c) £58 677 m
(d) £63 983 m

Understanding the Question Alternative (a) is M1, the sum of notes and coins in circulation and private sector sterling current accounts, the most liquid measure of money apart from actual cash. Alternative (b) is equivalent to M1 plus private sector sterling deposit accounts. However this does not equal Sterling M3 because it excludes public sector sterling deposits. Thus (c), which includes public sector deposits, is the correct answer. Alternative (d) is the wider measure of M3 which includes foreign currency deposits as well as holdings of sterling.

Questions 3 and 4

(a)	*(b)*	*(c)*	*(d)*
1, 2, 3 all correct	1, 2 only correct	2, 3 only correct	1 only correct

Question 3 There will be positive real interest rates if:

1 The Bank of England increases its lending rate.

2 Nominal interest rates rise above the rate of inflation.

3 The capital values of fixed interest securities are index-linked.

Understanding the Question The real rate of interest may be positive if the Bank of England raises its lending rate, but we cannot be certain without knowing the lending rate and the rate of inflation. The correct answer is (c). Alternative 2 is a necessary condition for real interest rates to be positive, while the linking of the capital value of a security to an index of the inflation rate, such as the Retail Price Index, ensures that the fixed interest rate is a real yield on the security – providing of course, that the index accurately measures the inflation rate.

Question 4 In Keynesian theory, which of the following are determinants of the demand for money?

1 The rate of interest.

2 The level of real income.

3 Expectations about the future level of security prices.

Understanding the Question The answer is (a) since, according to Keynesians, all three of the specified variables influence the demand to hold money balances. The demand for money depends upon expectations of future interest rates and security prices (the speculative demand for money) and upon the present interest rate (asset demand and liquidity preference). The level of real income is accepted by Keynesians as well as by monetarists as a determinant of the demand for money (transactions demand).

Data Response Questions

Question 5

'The money supply rose sharply last month taking the growth rate well above the government's target rate for the current year . . . the sterling money stock on the wider definition (M3) . . . rose by 2.3 per cent. The need to maintain control over the money supply is likely to reinforce the cautious advice on the size of the budget stimulus which is being received by the Chancellor . . . . Many Cabinet members are likely to favour as large as possible tax cuts . . .'   (Abstract from *The Financial Times*, 17 February 1978.)

(a) It may seem puzzling to the non-economist why there should be different definitions of the money supply. Explain to such a person, in non-technical terms, why different definitions are thought necessary.

(b) Specify M3 for the United Kingdom.

(c) Under what economic circumstances is the Cabinet likely to favour tax cuts?

(London: June 1979)

Understanding the Question We have already noted that it is only in recent years that economists have given much thought to a precise definition of the money supply. The earlier view, which was enshrined in the *1959 Radcliffe Report on the Working of the Monetary System,* was that the money supply passively adapts to demand. If an attempt is made to control tightly the money supply or its rate of growth, near monies will simply become money. The underlying reason why there are so many different definitions of the money supply relates to the emergence of modern **monetarism**, and the belief that the money supply is important either as a **policy instrument, intermediate objective**, or **economic indicator** in the management of the economy. (These concepts are explained and discussed in Unit 25.) Monetarists now usually admit that if monetary policy attempts to control a defined monetary stock, uncontrolled assets or near monies outside the defined stock are likely to increase in importance, certainly as stores of value and perhaps as mediums of exchange. For this reason, monetary control, as practised in the UK, has combined the setting of a target rate of growth for a chosen definition of the money supply, Sterling M3, together with a continuous monitoring of a range of credit and liquidity indicators such as M1, PSL1, etc. The rate of growth of Sterling M3 has been the intermediate policy objective of monetarist policy, whereas other measures of the monetary stock and the stock of liquid assets or near monies have functioned as supplementary indicators.

Answer plan

1 Explain how different definitions of the money supply might be used for different purposes. M1 is a measure of immediate means of payment; M3 a measure of general liquidity.

2 More than one measure of the money supply is necessary when monetary policy is aimed at controlling the money stock. Explain how near monies become money and how various definitions of the money stock have been used as control instruments or general liquidity indicators.

3 Specify M3, distinguishing between M3 and Sterling M3.

4 Different taxes may be cut to stimulate demand, to create incentives, to channel spending into desired directions and to influence saving versus consumption, to encourage investment, or simply for reasons of political opportunism to win elections. (You should refer to Units 17, 18, 22 and 25 which consider taxation and fiscal policy in greater detail.)

16.6 FURTHER READING

Burningham, D., editor, *Understanding Economics, an Introduction for Students* (Macmillan, 1978). Chapter 14: Money and Banking. Chapter 15: The Control of the Monetary System.

Lipsey, R. G., *An Introduction to Positive Economics* 5th edition (Weidenfeld & Nicolson, 1979). Chapter 39: The nature and history of money. Chapter 40: The banking system and the supply of money.

17 Taxation and Public Spending

17.1 POINTS OF PERSPECTIVE

This is the first of two units devoted to important aspects of **public finance**. This unit, which covers the **structure** of **taxation** and **public expenditure** in the United Kingdom, emphasizes the more **micro-economic elements** of public finance, leaving until Unit 18 a consideration of what happens in the economy as a whole when government expenditure exceeds revenue and a **budget deficit** occurs. The **macro-economic** and **monetary** implications of public finance are further developed in later units.

It is worth stressing at the outset that taxation and public spending are 'opposite sides of the **fiscal** coin'. Thus an argument for (or against) public spending is usually also an argument for (or against) taxation.

A large part of the **public sector** exists in the **non-market economy**, which means that the output of goods and services produced are not sold at a **market price**. There are of course important exceptions, particularly the activities of **nationalized industries**, which exist largely in the **market economy**. In some cases the distinction is rather unclear, when for example an art gallery is largely financed out of taxation even though a **token price** is charged for admission. We shall, however, follow the convention of excluding from our definition of public spending the direct spending by nationalized industries, since the expenditure is largely financed from the revenue raised by selling the industries' output in the market place. In this unit we restrict our analysis to the direct spending by **central** and **local government** and the taxation which largely finances this spending.

17.2 UNDERLYING CONCEPTS

1 Types of Taxation

A **tax**, which is a **compulsory levy** charged by a government or **public authority** to **pay for its expenditure**, can be classified in a number of ways:

(i) According to who levies the tax Most taxes are levied by **central** government in the UK, but the **local rate** is an example of a **local government** tax. A few taxes, such as the **water rate** and **airport taxes**, are levied by **non-governmental** public authorities.

(ii) According to what is taxed The major categories here are **taxes on income, expenditure and capital**, though other categories include **pay-roll** and **poll taxes**. **Personal income tax** is the most important tax on income in the UK, though employees' **National Insurance contributions** (NIC) and **corporation tax** (a tax on company income or profits) are other examples. The **Inland Revenue** is the department of the civil service mainly responsible for collecting taxes on income and capital, whereas the **Board of Customs and Excise** collects expenditure taxes. Expenditure taxes are usefully divided into **ad valorem** or **percentage taxes** such as **value-added tax** (VAT), and **specific taxes** (or **unit taxes**) which include the excise duties on tobacco, alcohol and petrol. A specific tax on, for example, wine is levied on the quantity of wine rather than on its price. Thus a bottle of expensive vintage champagne bears the same tax as a bottle of cheap table-wine. Similarly, a **user tax** such as a **television licence** or **motor vehicle tax** is levied irrespective of either the price or the current market value of the TV set or car.

Local rates, which are based on the capital value of property, and **capital transfer tax** (CTT), which is a **gifts tax**, are examples of taxes on capital. **Capital gains tax** is a tax on the income received when a capital asset is sold at a higher price than the price at which it was bought. No **wealth tax** (apart from CTT) exists as yet in the UK, though the proposal to introduce such a tax has prompted the appearance of examination questions on the subject. Finally, amongst other examples of taxes the **employers' National Insurance contribution** is a **pay-roll tax**, since the tax paid varies according to the number of workers employed; and a local **poll tax** or tax 'on being a human being' has been one of the alternatives considered to replace rates, in the reform of local government finance.

(iii) Direct and Indirect Taxation These concepts are often used interchangeably with taxes on income and expenditure, though it is not strictly true that a tax on spending *must* be an indirect tax. Income tax is a direct tax because the income receiver, who **benefits** from the income, is

directly liable in law to pay the tax (even though it is frequently collected through the PAYE scheme from the employer). In contrast, **most** taxes on spending are indirect taxes since the **seller** of the good, and not the purchaser who benefits from its consumption, is liable in law to pay the tax. Nevertheless, as we shall see later, the seller usually tries to **pass on the incidence** of the tax to the purchaser by raising the price of the good by the amount of the tax! There are, however, examples of **direct taxes on expenditure**, such as the **stamp duty** paid by the purchaser rather than by the seller of a house.

(iv) Progressive, Regressive and Proportionate Taxation In a progressive tax system a **progressively larger proportion** of income is paid in tax as income rises, while in a **regressive** system a **progressively smaller proportion** is paid. A tax is **proportionate** if exactly the same proportion of income is paid in tax at all levels of income.

You should note that in these definitions the word **progressive** is completely **'value neutral'**, implying nothing about how the revenue raised by the government is spent. Nevertheless, progressive taxation is likely to be used by the government to achieve the social aim of a 'fairer' distribution of income. However, progressive taxation cannot by itself redistribute income – a policy of **transfers** in the government's public spending programme is required for this. Progressive taxation used on its own will merely reduce **post-tax income differentials** compared with **pre-tax differentials**.

Progressive, regressive and proportionate taxes can also be defined in terms of the **marginal** and **average tax rates**. The **marginal tax rate** measures the proportion of the last pound paid in tax as income rises, whereas the **average tax rate** at any level of income is simply the total tax paid as a proportion of total income. In the case of a progressive income tax, the marginal rate of tax is higher than the average rate, except when no tax at all is paid on the first band of a person's income. If income tax is regressive, the marginal rate of tax is less than the average rate, while the two are equal in the case of a proportionate tax.

2 Types of Public Spending

We have already noted why we are excluding the direct spending by nationalized industries from our definition of public spending. Amongst the various divisions that can usefully be made between types of public spending are those between **central** and **local government spending**, and between **capital** and **current spending**. Capital spending involves **public** or **social investment** in a project (or **public work**) such as a new hospital, school or motorway. Current spending includes items such as the wage costs of staffing and the maintenance costs of running existing capital assets.

Perhaps the most important distinction to be made between types of public spending is between **real** and **transfer expenditure**:

(i) Real Expenditure Real expenditure occurs when the government directly provides goods and services which add to national output. All capital spending is real expenditure, as is the current expenditure on the wages and salaries of civil servants, local government officers, teachers, police, the armed forces and workers in the National Health Service. In contributing directly to output, real expenditure **uses up scarce resources**; indeed it is sometimes known as the **'direct command of resources'** by the government.

(ii) Transfer Expenditure Conversely, transfer expenditure merely redistributes income between different members of the community. Tax revenues are used to provide **income** via pensions, welfare benefits, grants and subsidies both to households in the personal sector and to firms within the corporate sector. The various forms of regional and industrial aid and assistance, including the transfers to nationalized industries, are an important part of total transfers. Transfers do not contribute directly to production although their administration uses up scarce resources, and indeed transfers to low-income groups usually encourage consumption since poorer people have high **marginal propensities to consume**. Massive transfers from central to local government also take place **within** the public sector. A large part of the spending of local authorities is financed in this way. **Interest payments** on past government borrowing (which we cover in more detail in the context of the PSBR and the **National Debt** in Unit 18) are a form of transfer from taxpayers to those people who have lent to the government. Strictly, however, the term **transfer payment** (which must not be confused with the **transfer earnings** of Unit 15) is restricted to payments which are not made in return for some productive service.

Statistics which show public spending as a percentage of either GDP or GNP are sometimes used to indicate the relative importance of real expenditure by the government. However, great care must be taken in using such statistics; the figures can be very misleading unless both transfers and the spending by nationalized industries have first been excluded.

17.3 ESSENTIAL INFORMATION

1 The Principles of Taxation

Adam Smith's four **principles** or **canons** of taxation are commonly used as the starting-point for analyzing and evaluating the operation of a tax system. Adam Smith suggested that taxation should be **equitable, economical, convenient** and **certain**, and to these we may also add the canons of **efficiency** and **flexibility**:

(i) Equity A tax should be based on the taxpayer's **ability to pay**. This principle is sometimes used to justify **progressive taxation**, since the rich have a greater ability to pay than the poor. A tax system should be **fair**, but there are likely to be different and possibly conflicting interpretations of what is fair or equitable.

(ii) Economy Collection of a tax should be easily and cheaply administered so that the yield is maximized relative to the cost of collection.

(iii) Convenience The method of payment should be convenient to the taxpayer.

(iv) Certainty The taxpayer should know what, when, where and how to pay, in such a manner that **tax evasion** is difficult. (**Tax evasion** is the **illegal** failure to pay a lawful tax, whereas **tax avoidance** involves the arrangement of personal or business affairs **within the law** to minimize tax liability.)

(v) Efficiency A tax should achieve its intended aim without side-effects. If for example the raising of the top rate of income tax, in order to raise revenue, results in increased disincentives to work, then the tax is inefficient. Since it is usually impossible to avoid all the undesirable side-effects of a tax, the tax system should attempt to minimize them.

(vi) Flexibility If the tax system is used as a means of economic management then, in order to meet new circumstances, certain taxes may need to be easily altered.

2 The Aims of Taxation

The **aims** of taxation should not be confused with the **principles** or **canons** of taxation, although an aim may well be to arrange the tax system as much as possible in accordance with the principles of taxation. It is useful to distinguish between a number of aims or objectives of taxation and to note how the importance attached to some of the objectives has varied according to the changing fashions in economic thought:

(i) Revenue Raising One of the oldest and most obvious aims of taxation is to raise revenue so as to pay for government expenditure. Before the **Keynesian 'revolution'** of the 1930s most economists believed that revenue-raising was by far the most important objective of taxation. Indeed many went further and argued that the levels of both public spending and taxation should be as low as possible, with the government restricting its activities to the provision of goods and services that could not be provided adequately and privately through the market. According to this **pre-Keynesian** or **neo-classical** view, recently revived in modern **monetarism**, a government should engage in the **financial orthodoxy** or **'sound finance'** of **balancing its budget**.

(ii) The Correction of Market 'Failures' In the traditional view we have just described, the primary purpose of government intervention in the economy is to correct or to reduce the various **market failures** which we first introduced in Unit 8. A government may be justified in using taxation to:

(a) Tax monopoly profits, both to deter monopoly and to remove the 'windfall gain' accruing to a monopolist as a result of barriers to entry and inelastic supply.

(b) Finance the collective provision of public goods and merit goods. The market might **fail to provide public goods** such as roads and defence, while education, health care and other **merit goods** might be **underconsumed** at market prices.

(c) Discourage the consumption of demerit goods. Demerit goods such as tobacco might be **overconsumed** at market prices. Note that a conflict may arise between the revenue-raising aim of taxation and this aim of reducing the consumption of demerit goods.

(d) Alter the distribution of income. The government may decide that the distribution of income resulting from unregulated market forces is undesirable. Taxation and transfers can be used to modify the distribution of income resulting from market forces.

(iii) Keynesian Economic Management While **Keynesians** certainly accept that taxation should be used to achieve such objectives as the provision of public goods, and the switching of expenditure away from demerit goods, they go much further by arguing that taxation should also be used to correct what they regard as the **greatest market failure of all**: the tendency for unregulated market forces to produce **unemployment** and **unacceptable fluctuations** in economic activity. In subsequent units we shall explain how Keynesians have advocated the use of taxation, public spending and the **budget deficit** as **policy instruments** in a **discretionary fiscal policy** aimed at controlling the level of **effective aggregate demand** in the economy to achieve the objectives of full employment and stable economic growth, without an excessive inflationary cost. We shall also show how monetarists reject the use of the **demand management techniques** involved in a discretionary fiscal policy, supporting instead the older view that the government should balance its budget and restrict the role of public finance to the correction of more conventional market failures at the micro-economic level.

3 The Meaning of Fiscal Policy

Fiscal policy has various meanings. It is sometimes used as a rather general term referring to any aspect of a government's policy towards the level and structure of taxation and public spending. During the Keynesian era, fiscal policy took on the narrower and more specific meaning we introduced in the previous paragraph involving the use of taxation and public expenditure in the **macro-economic management of demand**. Such a **discretionary fiscal policy** can be contrasted with the **fiscal stance** currently advocated by monetarists based on an automatic **fiscal rule** to balance the budget or to reduce public spending as a percentage of gross domestic product (GDP). Increasingly, attention is also devoted by both Keynesians and monetarists to the **micro-economic** objectives and effects of fiscal policy on the **supply-side** of the economy, examining such areas as the role and effectiveness of government grants, subsidies and tax allowances in **regional and industrial policy**, and the general question whether public spending financed by taxation or borrowing displaces or 'crowds out' private spending.

4 Taxation and the Level and Pattern of Expenditure

Indirect taxes such as VAT will affect **consumer preferences** and **spending patterns** by causing **relative price changes**. The total level of expenditure can be reduced by levying higher taxes, assuming there is no dis-saving and that the tax revenue is not spent by the government. Some taxes are also considered as **automatic stabilizers** which reduce the amplitude of fluctuations in the business cycle. For instance, when there is full employment, inflationary pressures may be caused by money incomes rising faster than production. A progressive income tax can then drain off some potential consumption into taxation. Conversely, in a recession, transfers such as unemployment pay will tend to boost consumption while the government's tax revenue will fall at a faster rate than national income.

5 The Incidence of Taxation

The **formal incidence** of a tax refers to which particular tax-payer is directly liable to pay the tax to the government. In the case of indirect taxes upon expenditure such as VAT, the question arises whether the seller of the good who bears the formal incidence can **shift the incidence** or

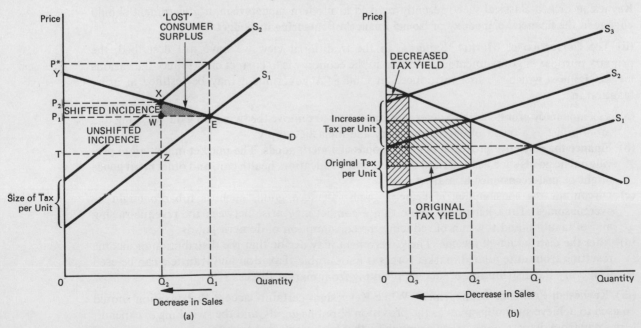

Fig 17.1 Elasticity and taxation (a) the ability of a supplier to shift the incidence of an expenditure tax depends upon elasticity of demand (b) an example of a tax increase producing a fall in the government's tax revenue when demand and supply are both relatively elastic

burden of the tax onto the purchaser by raising the price by the full amount of the tax. A firm's ability to shift the incidence of a tax depends upon price elasticity of demand. Figure 17.1a illustrates the situation where demand is relatively elastic and only a small proportion of the tax can be successfully shifted.

The imposition of a tax raises a supplier's costs; thus at each price the firm is prepared to supply less. If the tax is a specific or unit tax charged at the same rate irrespective of the good's price, the supply curve will shift **upwards**, from S_1 to S_2, the **vertical distance** between the two curves showing the tax per unit. If all the tax is to be successfully shifted, the price must rise to P^*. **This will only happen if demand is completely inelastic**. In any other circumstance, **some** consumers will reduce their purchases as the price rises. However, many consumers will still want the good and so the price is bid up from P_1 to P_2. The size of the government's tax revenue is determined by the amount bought and sold at the new equilibrium (Q_2) multiplied by the tax per unit. This is shown by the rectangle $TZXP_2$. You should now note that the part of the tax rectangle *above* the initial equilibrium price, P_1, represents the successfully shifted incidence of the tax, whereas the part of the tax rectangle *below* P_1 cannot be shifted and must be borne by the supplier. When demand is relatively elastic, only the smaller proportion of the tax can successfully be shifted.

We leave as an exercise for the reader the tasks of drawing appropriate diagrams to show what happens when demand is inelastic and to show the converse effects resulting from the imposition of a **unit subsidy** paid to the supplier.

6 The Tax Yield

If the principal aim of a tax is to raise revenue, the government will wish to maximize the tax's **yield**. In the case of taxes upon expenditure the government needs to consider the price **elasticities of both demand and supply** of the goods upon which taxes are levied. When a tax is first introduced, it will produce a positive yield providing that at least some of the good is bought and sold after the imposition of the tax. However, the quantity bought and sold will usually fall after the imposition of a tax, so the government may not receive the revenue it was expecting. If the size of the tax is increased, the absolute size of the government's revenue may rise, fall, or indeed stay the same, depending on the elasticities of supply and demand. Figure 17.1b illustrates the effects of an increase in taxation when demand and supply are both relatively elastic. In this case the tax yield falls. Although the government receives a larger tax revenue from each unit bought and sold at the new equilibrium, the loss in revenue resulting from the fall in sales more than offsets the revenue gain. When demand and supply are relatively inelastic, however, government revenue will increase.

Some important public policy implications result from this analysis. If the government wishes to **maximize revenue** it should tax as many goods and services as possible. Not only will this **widen the tax base**, but it will also reduce the elasticity of demand for the bundle of goods and services being taxed, taken as a whole. If only one good is taxed, demand is likely to be relatively elastic since untaxed goods are likely to contain some fairly close substitutes! Conversely, if the government aims to use taxation to **switch expenditure**, for example away from a **demerit good** such as tobacco, it should tax specific types of goods rather than wide categories. On this basis it could introduce different rates of taxation, for example taxing high tar and low tar cigarettes at different rates in order to switch expenditure away from the more harmful good. In a similar way, it can use **tariffs** or **import duties** to switch expenditure towards home-produced goods. In this way there may be a significant 'trade-off' between the **revenue-raising** and the **expenditure-switching** aims of taxation.

7 Taxation and Consumer Surplus

In Unit 2 we introduced the concept of consumer surplus as the **utility obtained by consumers from the goods and services they purchase, which is valued over and above the price paid**. Essentially, consumer surplus is a measure of **welfare**; the more consumer surplus a person obtains, the greater his personal welfare. At the initial price of P_1 in Figure 17.1a, consumer surplus is shown by the triangle P_1EY. The imposition of a tax reduces consumer surplus to the smaller triangle P_2XY. The question now arises as to what happens to the consumer surplus no longer received by the purchasers of the good or service. The answer is that the part shown by the rectangle P_1WXP_2 has been **transferred to the government** in the form of **tax revenue**, but the part represented by the small triangle WEX is **completely 'lost'**. On the basis of this analysis, economists have argued in favour of reducing taxes to as low a level as possible; the lower the rate of taxation, the smaller the loss of consumer surplus.

However, the conclusion is not as clear-cut as is suggested by this analysis. Low-income groups are likely to obtain a greater utility from an extra pound of income (or from the goods and services an extra pound can purchase) than high-income groups. Correspondingly, the welfare loss experienced by a rich person who loses a pound in taxation is likely to be smaller than the welfare gain accruing to a poor person receiving the same pound in the form of a transfer payment. This argument can justify progressive taxation and the redistribution of income through transfer payments. (The effect of taxation upon consumer surplus is very similar to what happens when the **formation of a monopoly** raises the price of a good. Part of the consumer surplus is transferred to the monopolist as a **monopoly profit**, but part is 'lost' to everyone.)

8 Other Aspects of Taxes on Income and Expenditure

(i) Taxation and Incentives It is often argued that a progressive income tax damages the economy through its effects on personal incentives. After all, the most obvious way legally to avoid an income tax is to work fewer hours, or even to stop working altogether. It is argued that expenditure taxes are preferable to income tax because they have no effect on the **choice between work and leisure**. Instead expenditure taxes affect the choice between **saving** and **spending**, and they also switch expenditure into the consumption of untaxed goods and services.

Nevertheless, economic theory **does not prove** that an increase in income tax **inevitably** must have a disincentive effect upon personal effort. If the supply curve of labour is upward-sloping, a disincentive effect will result, since a tax increase is equivalent to a wage cut and less labour is supplied as wages fall. But in circumstances where workers aspire to a 'target' disposable income, when the supply curve of labour is perverse or backward-bending, a tax rise will mean that people have to work longer to achieve their desired target income. The tax is an incentive to effort!

(ii) Fiscal Drag and Fiscal Boost **Fiscal drag** occurs in a progressive income tax structure when the government fails to raise **tax thresholds** or personal tax allowances at the same rate as inflation. Suppose that prices and all **money incomes** double. In the absence of taxation **real incomes** will remain the same. However, **real disposable incomes** will fall if inflation drags low-paid workers, who previously paid no tax, across the tax threshold to pay tax for the first time. In a similar way, higher-paid workers may be dragged deeper into the tax net, possibly into higher tax bands where they will pay tax at steeper marginal rates. In these circumstances the government's total revenue from income tax will rise faster than the rate of inflation, even though the tax structure has not been changed.

Conversely, in times of inflation **fiscal boost** is likely to reduce the **real value** of specific expenditure taxes (but not of *ad valorem* taxes such as VAT). Unless the government adjusts the rate of specific taxes to keep pace with inflation, their **nominal value** will stay more or less the same, but their real value will be eroded.

The simultaneous occurrence of fiscal drag and fiscal boost (such as occurred in the period of rapid inflation in the UK in the 1970s) shifts the structure of taxation away from taxes on expenditure and towards taxes on income. This can be avoided either by replacing progressive income tax with a proportionate tax, and specific expenditure duties with *ad valorem* taxation, or by **indexing** personal tax allowances, income tax bands, and the rates at which specific duties are levied.

(iii) The Poverty Trap The vulnerability of the tax structure in the UK to the process of fiscal drag is closely related to the emergence of a phenomenon known as the **poverty trap**. The poverty trap occurs because the **tax threshold at which income tax is paid** overlaps with the **threshold at which means-tested welfare benefits cease to be paid**. If a low-paid worker is caught within this zone of overlap, he not only pays tax and National Insurance contributions on an extra pound earned, but he also loses part or all of his right to claim benefits. The resulting 'marginal tax rate' may be very high indeed, sometimes over 100 per cent.

The existence of the poverty trap supports the argument that the major disincentives to personal effort resulting from the structure of taxation and welfare benefits in the UK are experienced by low-paid rather than by highly paid workers. Not only is the 'effective marginal tax rate' paid by the lower income groups frequently higher than the top rate of 60 per cent paid by the well-off; poorly paid workers are likely to experience less job satisfaction and to have less scope for perks and fringe benefits. Indeed the low-paid may be tempted to escape from the poverty trap either by **avoiding** tax through not working at all and living off benefits, or by **evading** tax through working in the **untaxed 'hidden economy'** or **Black Economy**.

The poverty trap is undoubtedly made worse by fiscal drag drawing low-paid workers into the tax net. Amongst the policies which could eliminate or reduce the effects of the poverty trap are the **raising of tax thresholds** and the replacement of **means-tested benefits** either by untaxed benefits granted as of right (such as **child benefit**) or by benefits subject to tax **'clawback'**. In the latter case, the government grants a benefit as of right and without a means test, but 'claws back' a fraction of the benefits through the income tax system from recipients who are above the tax threshold. Alternatively, the introduction of a **negative income tax** (NIT) has been suggested to merge the existing income tax and benefits structures. In a NIT scheme there would be a **single tax threshold**, above which people would pay (**positive**) income tax, and **below which** they would receive payments from the Inland Revenue (negative income tax) in lieu of welfare benefits. Amongst possible disadvantages of a NIT scheme are its tendency to reinforce the means-testing principle (though some may consider this an advantage), and the argument that civil servants in the Inland Revenue Department are not the most appropriate 'experts' to assess welfare needs.

9 How Progressive is the British Tax System?

The existence of the poverty trap and the process of fiscal drag have tended to reduce the advantages to the low-paid accruing from the progressive structure of British taxation. In any case the British income tax structure is probably much less progressive than is commonly supposed. Employees' National Insurance contributions are generally a regressive tax falling most heavily as a proportion of income on low-paid and middle income groups, while the degree of progression in the upper reaches of the income tax structure is greatly reduced by the possibilities of legal tax avoidance open to the better-off. On the expenditure side, some excise duties such as tobacco duty are probably regressive whereas others, including petrol duty, are progressive. Value-added tax is probably slightly progressive since some necessities are excluded from the tax, but this may be countered by the fact that the low-paid spend a larger fraction of their income than the well-off, their savings being correspondingly lower. Moreover, the introduction of VAT in 1972 was a **regressive change** to the tax structure since VAT replaced **purchase tax**, which had been a distinctly progressive tax levied on a narrower base composed largely of luxuries.

10 A Summary of the Advantages and Disadvantages of Different Types of Taxation

TAXES ON INCOME	TAXES ON CAPITAL	TAXES ON EXPENDITURE
Advantages:	*Advantages:*	*Advantages:*
(i) progressive/equitable	(i) equitable	(i) certain
(ii) certain	(ii) efficient	(ii) convenient
(iii) convenient		(iii) flexible
(iv) efficient		(iv) stabilizing (except specific duties)
(v) stabilizing		(v) no disincentive effects
(vi) high yield		
Disadvantages:	*Disadvantages:*	*Disadvantages:*
(i) disincentive effects	(i) administrative costs	(i) regressive
(ii) reduces savings	(ii) reduces savings and limits investment funds	(ii) inflationary
(iii) evasion and avoidance	(iii) evasion and avoidance	(iii) misallocation of resources
	(iv) low yield	

11 The Relative Importance of the Different Types of Taxation in the UK

The table which follows shows the approximate importance of the major categories of taxation in the United Kingdom. Local rates are classified in the miscellaneous section, though sometimes they are treated as a tax on capital, and sometimes as an expenditure tax.

Income	%	Capital	%	Expenditure	%	Miscellaneous	%
Income Tax	32	Capital Transfer Tax	2	Value-Added Tax	14	Rates	10
Corporation Tax	5	Capital Gains Tax		Excise and Customs		Others (including	
National Insurance				Duties	13	oil taxes)	5
Contribution	19						
Totals	56		2		27		15

Approximately 36% of local government expenditure is financed from the local rate. The largest part (48%) is financed by government transfers, and 16% is financed from the revenue received from the sale of local government services.

12 The Control of Public Expenditure

Textbooks sometimes portray the level and pattern of public spending as a tractable policy instrument capable of being 'fine-tuned' or easily adjusted in the macro-economic implementation of fiscal policy and the management of the economy. In practice, however, the control of public expenditure presents a number of formidable difficulties:

(i) Much expenditure is on necessary services such as education, the police and health care which are difficult to cut.

(ii) Control of public expenditure is made more difficult in a democracy by the popularity of state spending and the unpopularity of cuts.

(iii) As we have already explained, many types of expenditure change autonomously for reasons outside the government's direct control, and sometimes these changes occur automatically in the upswings and downswings of the business cycle.

(iv) Central government may have little direct control over local government. It can attempt to impose limits (and to place **external financing limits** upon nationalized industries), but in practice these limits may often be exceeded.

13 Cash Limits

Each year the British government publishes a **White Paper** outlining its planned expenditure and use of resources over a medium-term period of about five years. Before the 1980s the public expenditure White Paper was published a month or two before the government's **Budget** at the beginning of each new financial year. Traditionally, the **Chancellor of the Exchequer** (the government's **Finance Minister**) has undertaken two main tasks on Budget Day. He introduces the government's **Finance Bill** (later to become a **Finance Act**) in which tax proposals are put into effect, and secondly he publishes a **Financial Statement** or 'red book' containing the Treasury's review of the economy over the past year and its forecasts for the next year. It should be obvious that the Chancellor's freedom of manoeuvre on the **revenue side** in the Finance Bill is ultimately constrained by the plans announced on the **spending side** in the White Paper on public expenditure. It makes sense therefore, at least from the government's point of view, to publish the public spending White Paper and details of the Finance Bill at the same time on Budget Day, and this indeed has been the practice since the early 1980s.

Before 1976 the annual survey on public spending contained in the White Paper was conducted in **constant prices**, or in **'volume'** terms. This approach meant that expenditure estimates were based on **physical inputs** such as people, buildings and equipment needed. This emphasis on the use of **real resources** reflected the Keynesian approach to demand management in the economy.

However, the pricing of the inputs included in the White Paper was based on out-of-date figures, causing a serious problem in the 1970s when in a period of increasing inflation government expenditure rose rapidly and actual spending exceeded the budgetary projection. If the prices paid by a department rose, more cash was made available to enable the volume of the programme to be maintained. This caused budget deficits and increased the PSBR, as explained in Unit 18. To prevent this happening, the government introduced **cash limits** for the first time in 1976. These were grafted onto the volume system of planning, requiring volume plans to be revised each year at the expected prices of the year subject to the cash limit. In 1981 the government decided to plan all public expenditure from the outset in cash rather than volume terms. By 1981 cash limits were covering about 60% of total public expenditure. If inflation is faster than the government anticipates or allows for, and the volume of spending cannot be maintained within the cash limit, then the volume must now be reduced and factor inputs dispensed with. As a result, **'finance now determines spending'** rather than spending determining finance.

The 40% of public expenditure not covered by cash limits is largely influenced by demand. Social security and unemployment benefits are significantly influenced by economic activity. Thus in a depressed economy the government's ability to control public spending is weakened, at a time when, according to monetarist theory, the credibility of the government's economic policies depends most on the need to show a clear control of the level of public spending.

17.4 LINKS WITH OTHER TOPICS

This unit is closely linked with Unit 18 because the levels of taxation and public spending largely determine the PSBR. This in turn influences the **money supply** and **monetary policy** as explained in Unit 19. We then go on in Units 21, 22, 24 and 25 to develop the roles of taxation and public spending as **fiscal policy** instruments in the Keynesian theory of aggregate demand management, comparing the **discretionary** fiscal policy of the Keynesians with the older **balanced budget tradition** revived by the monetarists.

17.5 QUESTION PRACTICE

Essay Questions

Question 1 'The rating system is an inefficient and inequitable form of taxation'. Discuss. *(AEB: June, 1982)*

Understanding the Question The **local rate** is the principal tax directly levied by local government, but it covers only the smaller part of local authority expenditure, being supplemented by transfers from central government and by borrowing. The rate is commonly classified as a **direct tax on capital** (the capital value of property), calculated on the notional or imputed market rent paid by a hypothetical tenant. However, in the National Income Accounts the local rate is treated as an **indirect tax upon expenditure**.

We have already explained how **efficiency** and **equity** are two **principles** of taxation; a tax is **inefficient** if it results in unintended side-effects and **inequitable** if it falls unfairly on those without the ability to pay. The principal arguments against the local rate relate mainly to the question of the tax's supposed inequity rather than its inefficiency. The local rate **can** be progressive since high-income earners who tend to live in larger properties in more desirable locations pay higher rates than the lower-income occupiers of less desirable housing.

Nevertheless, the local rate can be seriously regressive in particular instances. In the first place, the rate is regressive when an elderly single person and a large family including several income-earners live in identical houses; the rate is a much larger fraction of the income of the single occupant. The existence of rate rebates payable to the poor gives one indication of the unfairness of the rating system.

The rate can also be regressive because of the geographical division between local authority areas. The tax actually paid by a rate-payer depends upon two factors: the rateable value of the property, and the percentage of the rateable value levied by the local authority. In 'prosperous' areas occupied by the well-off, rateable values tend to be high. Nevertheless, in such regions there may be fewer 'social problems' requiring expenditure by the local authority. It may well be that the percentage rate levied is much higher in poorer areas, falling more heavily upon the generally less well-off income groups who live under those rating authorities. As a result, the total tax paid may be a larger proportion of the income of the lower-income groups living in the poorer rating areas, and in some cases the absolute burden may even be higher. (The political complexion of the local authority and the nature of transfers from central government may also have an important influence, and it is also worth noting that this problem would not necessarily be overcome if another type of local taxation, for example a local sales tax or income tax, was merely substituted for the local rate.)

Another inequitable aspect of the local rate derives from the fact that rate-payers form only a fraction of the electorate who vote in local elections. Many of the beneficiaries of local public spending are not themselves rate-payers, but they may effectively vote for increased expenditure by the local authority, knowing that they will not have to pay the tax to finance the expenditure. It is also the case that a substantial part of the local rate is paid by businesses which do not possess the vote, except in the sense that a business owner can vote in the local authority area where he or she is a local resident. It is often argued that a local income tax, sales tax or poll tax would be more equitable since a much larger proportion of the people who benefit from local expenditure would also be tax-payers.

In 1981 the Conservative Government published a Green Paper inviting discussion on these three options to reform the system of local government finances, together with the option of reforming domestic rates. It also rejected other possibilities such as local duties on petrol, alcohol and tobacco, a local vehicle excise duty, and a local payroll tax. The Green Paper assessed each potential local tax against seven criteria:
 (i) Is it practicable?
 (ii) Is it fair?
 (iii) Does it make councillors who take decisions on local expenditure properly accountable to the local tax-payers?
 (iv) Are the administrative costs acceptable?
 (v) Are the implications for the rest of the tax system acceptable?
 (vi) Does it encourage proper financial control?
 (vii) Is it suitable for all tiers of local government?

The Green Paper did not set out firm proposals but sought to identify the range of realistic alternatives to the local rate, so that a process of discussion and consultation could then take place.

The local rate results in various inefficiencies, though once again some at least of the inefficiencies may be common to all forms of local taxation. Such inefficiencies could only be removed by some system of transfers, possibly via central government, from rich to less properous local authority areas. In the absence or inadequacy of such transfers, people and businesses may move from high-rated to low-rated areas, thereby narrowing the tax base in the high-rated areas. Such an area may find itself responsible for an increasing proportion of poor families whose social problems require local public expenditure. A cumulative vicious circle of high rates, local 'emigration' and even higher rates may then set in. The local rate may also create a disincentive to improve property. Although this is probably not a very great problem, it would be removed if the rate was replaced by another form of local taxation.

Answer plan

1 Briefly describe the rating system.
2 Define the meaning of 'efficiency' and 'equity' as principles of taxation.
3 Discuss how the rate is inequitable and the extent to which the inequity is common to all forms of local taxation.
4 Similarly discuss the inefficiencies caused by the local rate.

Question 2 What are the major determinants of the pattern of government expenditure? Illustrate your answer by reference to recent changes in expenditure.

(London: January, 1978)

Understanding the Question It is important to note that the question asks for a discussion of the **pattern** rather than the overall **level** of public expenditure, though the two concepts are closely related. A factor which is responsible for changing the pattern will probably also change the level, and vice versa. We have already noted that public spending is the 'other side of the fiscal coin' to taxation and other forms of revenue raising; therefore you can discuss the determinants of public spending in much the same way as we have already discussed the determinants of taxation. There are various useful ways of discussing the pattern of expenditure, distinguishing between:

(i) **central** and **local government** spending;

(ii) **capital** and **current** expenditure;

(iii) the broad categories of **real expenditure** on production, **transfers** and **interest payments** ;

(iv) expenditure resulting from deliberate government (**discretionary**) decisions and expenditure that changes **autonomously** for reasons outside the government's control.

You could usefully illustrate these distinctions by introducing an example of public spending such as unemployment pay which is a transfer made by central government as a part of current spending. At the same time spending on unemployment benefits is largely outside the direct control of the government, since it tends to rise and fall with the downswings and upswings of the business cycle which determine how many workers are unemployed. Nevertheless, the government can determine who qualifies for unemployment benefit and the rates at which it is paid.

In answering this type of question, students often adopt a very superficial 'shopping list' approach, simply listing types of public expenditure on such worthy services as health care, education, roads and police, and stating that they are provided because they are 'necessary' and a 'good thing'. Such an approach contains no serious economic analysis and earns few marks. The question demands a deeper treatment of why public expenditure and not private provision through the market is considered more suitable for the provision of **public goods, merit goods** and perhaps the subsidization of **external benefits**. You could then go on to discuss how some public spending, such as grants, subsidies, and other transfers, are used to **modify** the distribution of income resulting from market forces, while other elements of public spending **replace** the market, providing goods and services completely outside the market. In the final analysis, political choice and constraints imposed by availability of resources decide how much should be provided in each of these categories.

Answer plan

1 Distinguish between important broad categories of public spending: central and local, capital and current, discretionary and non-discretionary.

2 Explain how the pattern of public spending is the result partly of current government decisions, partly of inherited decisions and partly of autonomous changes taking place in the economy. Illustrate your argument with an example such as unemployment pay, and show recent changes.

3 Government decisions to alter the pattern of spending will depend on the political and economic objectives of the government. Introduce recent examples.

4 Introduce the concepts of real expenditure, transfers and interest payments, and go on to show how a large part of public expenditure attempts either to modify or to replace the working of the market. Transfers modify income distribution, whereas public spending on roads and other public goods occurs because the services would not otherwise be provided.

Multiple Choice Questions

Question 3 For which of the following taxes would the amount paid in tax become a larger proportion of taxpayers' income in a period of inflation, if tax rates and allowances, and the quantities of goods bought and their relative prices, remained unchanged, but incomes kept pace with inflation?

(a) Value-added tax

(b) Specific tax on alcohol

(c) Motor vehicle tax

(d) Progressive income tax

Understanding the Question This question is based on the concepts of **fiscal drag** and **fiscal boost**. Fiscal boost refers to the tendency for the real value of **specific taxes** on spending to fall during a period of inflation unless tax rates are adjusted to keep pace with rising prices. The specific tax on alcohol and the specific motor vehicle tax will therefore tend to fall as a proportion of income as taxpayers' income rises. In contrast, an **ad valorem** tax on expenditure, such as VAT, will keep pace with inflation, but it will not rise as a proportion of income unless conditions specified in the question are relaxed. However, in a period of inflation a larger proportion of taxpayers' income will be drawn across the tax threshold and into the tax net, and some people on low incomes who previously paid no tax will begin to pay tax for the first time. This is known as fiscal drag. The answer is therefore **(d)**.

Question 4 A transfer payment is recognised by the fact that

(a) No goods or services are produced in exchange

(b) The distribution of income is made more equal

(c) National Income is reduced

(d) People receive incomes from the state

Understanding the Question The correct answer is **(a)** since a transfer payment involves the redistribution of income from taxpayers to people who do not produce any productive service in return for the income received. Taxation is a transfer payment to the government, whereas pensions, unemployment and other benefits are transfers from the government. A large proportion of transfers do indeed reduce income inequality, but it is perfectly possible for transfer payments to be made to the better-off sections of the community. As a further example, significant transfers are made from wages to profits in the form of various government subsidies and grants to industry. Transfer payments have no *direct* effect on National Income, though indirectly they may either increase or reduce income and output, depending on their effect on demand, production and incentives. Lastly, transfers are only one form of income from the state; people who work for or sell goods to the government and holders of the National Debt also receive incomes from the state.

Data Response Questions

Question 5

Shares of UK central government revenue raised by taxes on expenditure

Base of tax	Commodity	Percentage of central government revenue 1965	1976
Unit	Beer	3.3	1.8
	Wines and spirits	2.8	2.6
	Tobacco	9.9	4.2
	Oil	7.6	4.6
	Total of above	23.6	13.2
Ad valorem	Purchase tax	6.3	—
	Value-added tax	—	9.4
	Car tax	—	0.5
	Total of above	6.3	9.9
	Total Customs & Excise*	33.6	25.4

*Totals exceed detail because some minor items are omitted.

(Source: C. V. Brown and P. M. Jackson, *Public Sector Economics*, Martin Robertson, 1978.)

(a) Explain the meaning of 'unit' and *'ad valorem'* taxes.

(b) Comment on the above figures and on their implications for public policy.

(London: January, 1981)

Understanding the Question **(a)** In the case of a **unit tax** or **specific tax**, a fixed amount of tax is charged on each item sold. For instance, the excise duty on a bottle of Scotch whisky was £4.08 in 1981, whether the bottle was sold for £6 or £7. In contrast, **ad valorem** taxes are usually charged as a percentage of the price of a good or service.

(b) In answering the second part of the question, you need to consider the data by rows and by columns and to note that the figures are in **percentages**. The final row of data indicates that taxes on expenditure fell as a proportion of central government revenue between 1965 and 1976. This could be explained by **discretionary government decisions** to increase income tax while at the same time reducing taxes on expenditure, but this is not the most likely explanation. Instead, the data are much better interpreted in terms of **fiscal drag** and **fiscal boost**, respectively affecting the revenue from taxes on income and expenditure.

You can explain in some detail the evidence of fiscal boost discernible in the changing structure of expenditure taxes illustrated in the data. All the unit taxes have fallen in relative importance, while the *ad valorem* taxes have increased their relative share of tax revenue, though this is partly explained by the widening of the *ad valorem* tax base which occurred when value-added tax replaced purchase tax. Purchase tax was imposed largely on luxuries, excluding necessities and services, whereas value-added tax includes a range of necessities (though not food, home energy bills and public transport) and most services.

When expressed in percentage terms, many unit taxes are imposed at very high rates, often above 100%. If a specific tax is increased in real terms, the effect on government revenue may depend strongly on the elasticity of demand for the good in question. Tobacco companies and whisky distillers have frequently argued that an increase in taxation on cigarettes or spirits is counter-productive in revenue terms since the resulting fall in sales may wipe out the prospective revenue gain from the tax increase. This conclusion is consistent with, but not proved by, the data.

Answer plan

1 Briefly explain unit and *ad valorem* taxes, introducing examples of each.

2 Explain how no conclusions can be drawn on the absolute changes in any of the taxes, and that any conclusions must be tentative because of the rather long gap between the two years illustrated.

3 Explain how and why the data illustrate a trend during these years away from taxes on spending towards taxes on income. Clearly explain the concepts of fiscal drag and fiscal boost.

4 Illustrate further aspects of fiscal boost from the data on unit and *ad valorem* taxes.

5 Show how elasticities of demand and the introduction of VAT may also have affected the structure of taxes on expenditure.

6 Discuss various public policy implications:

(a) The effects on incentives resulting from the shift towards income taxes.

(b) Taxation may have been successful in reducing consumption of **demerit goods** such as tobacco and alcohol.

(c) The raising of **income tax thresholds** and **rates of specific taxation** in line with the rate of inflation would be needed to prevent further fiscal drag and boost. They would have to be raised by more than the rate of inflation to shift the structure of taxation back towards the balance existent in 1965. Discuss how **indexation** of income tax thresholds and rates of specific taxation might then be used to prevent further fiscal drag and fiscal boost.

17.6 FURTHER READING

Marshall, B. V., *Comprehensive Economics*, 2nd edition (Longmans, 1975).
Chapter 7: Public Finance.

Morris, D., editor, *The Economic System in the UK,* 2nd edition (Oxford University Press, 1979).
Chapter 11: Public Finance.

18 The Public Sector Borrowing Requirement

18.1 POINTS OF PERSPECTIVE

1 Definitions

The public sector borrowing requirement (PSBR) is the difference each year between the income and expenditure of the whole of the public sector, a difference which has to be met from borrowing. It is made up of three components, the borrowing of central government (CGBR), local authorities (LABR), and public corporations (PCBR), or:

$$PSBR \equiv CGBR + LABR + PCBR$$

In using this identity, care must be taken to avoid double-counting, which can arise because a large part of the borrowing by local authorities and nationalized industries is from central government. In 1979/80, for example, total central government borrowing was £8228 million. However, only £4260 million of this was spent by the central government (*the CGBR on 'own account'*); the rest was a **transfer loan** to the other parts of the public sector. Thus in 1979/80:

$$\frac{PSBR}{£9964m} \equiv \frac{CGBR \text{ on own account}}{£4260m} + \frac{LABR}{£2943m} + \frac{PCBR}{£2761m}$$

Alternatively, the components of the PSBR in 1979/80 can be shown as:

$$\frac{PSBR}{£9964m} \equiv \frac{CGBR}{£8228m} + \frac{LA \text{ contribution}}{£2126m} + \frac{PC \text{ contribution}}{(-£390m)}$$

The statistics for 1979/80 show that nearly half the borrowing undertaken by central government was transferred to local authorities and public corporations. Local government supplemented its borrowing from the central government by borrowing on its own account, for example through the sale of local authority bonds. In contrast, nationalized industries repaid £390m of their outstanding debt in 1979/80, receiving at the same time direct lending of £3151m from the central government.

2 The importance of the PSBR

(i) Keynesian deficit financing The PSBR is a closely related concept to the **budget deficit**, the difference between central government expenditure and income, which equals the CGBR. Both the budget deficit and the PSBR tend to move in the same direction because central government borrowing dominates the PSBR. Until fairly recently a large PSBR was not regarded as a problem in itself, or a cause of other problems. Indeed, Keynesian economists for long took the view that the budget deficit, and hence the PSBR, should be deliberately used as a policy instrument to control and influence the level of aggregate demand in the economy. Broadly speaking, the Keynesian view has been that when **households save too much** and **firms invest too little**, unemployment will be caused by a **lack of effective aggregate money demand** (AMD) in the economy. In these circumstances the public sector should borrow the savings of households in order to inject demand back into the economy through public spending. For much of the post-war era such deliberate **deficit financing** occupied a central place in the **discretionary fiscal policy** used by Keynesians to 'fine-tune' the level of aggregate demand in the economy.

(ii) The PSBR and monetarism In recent years the use of discretionary fiscal policy, and hence of the budget deficit as a policy instrument to manage demand, has come under attack from the monetarists. We shall explain, both later in the unit and in Units 19 and 24, how monetarists regard the level of public spending and its method of finance through the PSBR as the underlying cause of inflation, through an excessive rate of growth in the money supply. They also claim that it leads to the 'crowding out' of private sector consumption and investment. It is not surprising therefore, since monetarists believe that the size and growth of the PSBR give rise to undesirable phenomena, that a reduction in the PSBR is an important monetarist objective – not the **ultimate objective** of monetarist policy, but an **immediate objective** which must be achieved in order to create the conditions in which other, more long-term objectives can be attained. Thus the PSBR, which was an almost unmentioned concept as little as 10 or 15 years ago, is now in the forefront of economic debate, conflict, and policy-making. Whereas Keynesians have emphasized the role of the budget deficit in the economy as a **fiscal policy instrument**, largely independent of any monetary effects, the monetarists place their emphasis on the **monetary effects** of the method of financing the deficit.

18.2 UNDERLYING CONCEPTS

1 The PSBR and the National Debt

The National Debt is the **stock** of all the historically accumulated borrowing which the **central government** has not yet paid back. In contrast, the PSBR (and the CGBR) are the differences between the two very large **flows** of public income (mostly tax revenue) and public expenditure. You should note that the total outstanding public sector debt is larger than the National Debt, which only records the central government debt. Each year the absolute size of the National Debt will increase by the size of the CGBR or budget deficit – the flow of new central government borrowing adds to the stock of outstanding debt. Conversely, if a **budget surplus** occurs, a small part of the National Debt can be paid off.

2 Front-end loading

Both government spending and the collection of tax revenue are uneven processes. Much government expenditure takes place at the beginning of the financial year, for example contributions to the EEC, whereas a lot of its receipts are acquired towards the end. Thus the government is usually heavily in deficit in the first quarter of the year, and public borrowing is loaded onto the front end of the financial year, rather than spread evenly throughout.

3 Discretionary and automatic changes in the budget deficit

A **discretionary change** introduced by the government in either the structure of taxation, tax rates, or in some aspect of public expenditure, will obviously influence the size of the budget deficit, and hence the PSBR. However, changes take place in the economy which are not directly the result of discretionary government decisions. Changes which tend to occur automatically as a part of the **business cycle** can have a considerable and perhaps dominant impact on the budget deficit and PSBR. A down-turn in economic activity will normally cause tax revenue to fall and expenditure on unemployment pay and social benefits to rise. Thus, the budget deficit and PSBR tend to increase automatically in a recession and to decrease in a period of economic recovery. In this way, progressive taxation, unemployment pay and social benefits act as **automatic stabilizers**, reducing the fluctuations in the business cycle.

It is over-simple, however, to completely separate the discretionary and automatic components of the budget deficit. Governments have reacted to the fall in tax revenues during a recession by increasing taxation in order to recover the lost revenue. Keynesians have argued that this deepens the recession and causes a further widening of the budget deficit. (This is an example of the national income multiplier which we explain in Unit 22.) Although the second stage in the increase in the budget deficit appears to be 'not the fault of the government', Keynesian analysis would trace its cause to the government decision to raise taxes in an attempt to close or reduce the earlier budget deficit. Thus government policy based on achieving a PSBR target may have the **perverse** effect of destabilizing rather than stabilizing the economy. Some commentators believe that a better indicator of the stance of government policy than the actual PSBR is the PSBR calculated on the basis of what tax receipts and expenditure would be if there were full employment: the PSBR (FE), an economic indicator used in the USA.

Current discretionary decisions made by the government may also commit future governments to levels of spending which are not easy to change. The decision to increase **capital spending**, for example on motorways or hospital construction, involves not only the public spending over the years it takes to complete the capital project, but requires also continuing levels of **current spending** on staffing, maintenance and other running costs over the life expectancy of the project. Such levels of current spending are very difficult to reduce in real terms unless the projects are closed down or 'moth-balled'.

18.3 ESSENTIAL INFORMATION

1 Financing the PSBR

PSBR financing can be looked at in two ways:

(i) By the type of liability used to raise funds The largest part of the PSBR is financed by the sale of long-term government securities (gilts), though if the government is unable to sell new issues of gilts at acceptable prices and interest rates, Treasury Bills are sold. Until recently National Savings accounted for a declining proportion of total government borrowing, but in the early 1980s aggressive attempts were made to sell more attractive forms of National Saving securities. The introduction of index-linked National Savings had the effect of attracting personal savings away from the building societies and the banks.

(ii) By the economic sector which provides the funds The **non-bank private sector** accounts for three-quarters of the funds provided. Part of this is provided by households (the **personal sector**), largely through National Savings. However, **financial institutions or intermediaries** such as Pension Funds and Insurance Companies account for the bulk of the funds provided by the non-bank private sector, though indirectly the funds they provide represent the **contractual savings** of households. The institutions are the principal purchasers of long-dated gilt-edged securities. The **banking sector** provides the bulk of the remaining funds, purchasing Treasury Bills or the **residual government debt**, therefore financing the part of the PSBR which the government cannot finance through the non-bank sector. The **overseas sector** is a very small contributor. Its importance varies with the exchange rate and with changes in official reserves.

2 Effects of the PSBR

(i) The traditional Keynesian view of the PSBR Until recently the Keynesians paid very little attention to the effects of the PSBR on the economy. Instead, the Keynesian emphasis was placed on the **direct fiscal effects** of the budget deficit and increased government expenditure on aggregate demand, and then on the levels of output and employment in the economy. We shall explain in Units 21 and 22 how and why the Keynesians believed that an increased budget deficit could increase output and employment via the national income multiplier. Keynesians either ignored or played down the importance of the **indirect monetary effects** which result from the method of financing the deficit. The PSBR itself was viewed as a marginal influence on the 'real' economy. Keynesians believed that the principal monetary effect of a rising PSBR occurs through increased interest rates which result from the increased need of the government to sell securities. But, as we explain in Unit 23, the Keynesians also believe that interest rate changes have a rather weak effect on private sector investment and the level of economic activity.

(ii) Monetarism and the indirect monetary effects of the PSBR In complete contrast to the Keynesians, monetarists place great emphasis on the indirect monetary effects of the PSBR and dispute the strength of the direct fiscal stimulus to output and employment of a budget deficit. According to the monetarists, the monetary effects of an increase in the PSBR include:

(a) The 'crowding out' of private sector investment as a result of increased interest rates caused by the growth in the PSBR. The crowding-out theory helps to explain why monetarists believe that fiscal policy is ineffective in stimulating output and employment; in the extreme case of crowding out, an extra £ of public expenditure simply displaces a £ of private sector spending.

(b) An expansion of the money supply. Again, an 'extreme' monetarist view asserts a 'one-for-one' relationship between the PSBR and the money supply: for every £ increase in the PSBR there is a £ increase in the money supply. However, the impact of an increase in the PSBR on the money supply varies with the way in which the borrowing is financed:

(i) If debt is sold to the non-bank private sector, the effect on the money supply is generally neutral. The increase in bank deposits which results from the injection of government spending into the economy is countered by a fall in bank deposits as a result of the purchase of government securities by the general public.

(ii) However, if the government sells to the banking sector, the money supply can expand. If the government is unable to finance the budget deficit at acceptable interest rates by selling debt to the non-bank public, it will have to sell Treasury Bills as *residual debt* to the banking system. In Unit 19 we shall explain how Treasury Bills are a highly liquid asset in the balance sheets of the commercial banks, and how a multiple expansion of bank deposits, and hence of the money supply, usually takes place when the government borrows from the banking sector.

(iii) The 'New Cambridge School' and the PSBR   In the late 1960s a crisis occurred in Keynesian economics, which continued to develop in the 1970s. A consequence of the failure of traditional Keynesian demand management policies to secure continuing full employment, economic growth and price stability, was the emergence of a breakaway 'New School' of Keynesian economists, the **Cambridge Economic Policy Group** (CEPG). Traditionally, Cambridge has been the academic centre of Keynesianism. The older-generation Keynesians at Cambridge University are sometimes known as the 'Old School' Keynesians. There are a number of well-publicized differences which separate the 'Old' and 'New' School Keynesians. Paradoxically, the New School shares with the monetarists a belief in the virtues of **medium-term economic policy** and a distrust of short-term demand management via the traditional Old School instrument of discretionary fiscal policy. However, unlike the monetarists, the New School retains the essentially Keynesian belief in the need for extended government intervention in the economy, particularly through **incomes policy** and **import controls**.

An important element of the New School model of 'how the economy works' is the **net aquisition of financial assets (NAFA)** of each of the three broad sectors in the economy, the **private sector, the public sector, and the overseas sector**. Any net accumulation of **financial assets** by one sector must be exactly balanced by an increase in the **financial liabilities** of one or both of the other sectors. In a two-sector economy comprising just the private and public sectors, the private sector surplus (or net saving) must exactly equal the public sector deficit. The principle holds true with the inclusion of a third sector, the overseas sector, and can be expressed as an **identity in which the net acquisition of financial assets by each sector must sum to zero**:

$$\text{Private Sector NAFA} + \text{Public Sector NAFA} + \text{Overseas Sector NAFA} \equiv 0$$

Thus a public sector deficit (or PSBR) must mean that the other two sectors are net accumulators of financial assets or claims against the public sector. It also follows that, unless there is an increase in the net saving or surplus of the private sector (households and firms), an increase in the public sector deficit must lead to the overseas sector accumulating financial claims against the UK, *i.e.* the **financial surplus** of the overseas sector is the **UK's balance of payments deficit**. According to the NAFA identity, the main effect of an increase in the PSBR will be to increase the balance of payments deficit, providing that the net saving of the private sector is relatively stable. This was the reasoning suggested by the CEPG to explain the simultaneous increases in the PSBR and the balance of payments deficit which occurred in the early 1970s. However, it should be noted that empirical evidence from more recent years does not support the CEPG's rather mechanical theory that the main effect of the PSBR is on the balance of payments.

3 The PSBR and economic policy

The growing importance of the PSBR as an economic policy variable has essentially been a part of the emergence in the 1970s and 1980s of monetarist economic policies. The PSBR first became prominent in official policy when the Labour government signed a 'Letter of Intent' to the International Monetary Fund in 1976. The IMF insisted on the adoption by the UK government of a monetarist economic policy as the condition for the granting of an IMF loan to tide the country over the 1976 sterling crisis. Consequently, the signing of the Letter of Intent, in which for the first time the British government announced a PSBR target, marks the transition from **Keynesian short-term demand management** to **monetarist medium-term policy in the UK.** In the monetarist strategy, targets for several years ahead are announced for variables such as the PSBR and the money supply. Monetarists then implement policies aimed at achieving the targets, at the same time hoping that the announcement of the targets will alter peoples' economic behaviour by influencing **expectations**. The monetarists argue that people will begin to behave in ways which make the attainment of the announced targets easier, for example by reducing wage claims, once they believe that the government is both firmly committed to its targets and prepared to take whatever action is necessary to achieve the targets.

However, an important problem which strikes at the heart of this monetarist philosophy results from the fact that the key variables for which targets are announced, the PSBR and the money supply, are by their nature highly unpredictable. The 'announcement effect' on expectations may 'backfire' if the government is singularly unsuccessful in achieving its openly declared targets! In general, British governments have been rather more successful in achieving the PSBR target than the money supply target. In the late 1970s, following the Letter of Intent, the size of the PSBR was within the forecast target. However, this has not been the case in the early 1980s. As a part of its **Medium Term Financial Strategy** (MTFS), the Conservative Government announced a target of reducing the PSBR from 5 per cent of gross domestic product in 1979, to $1\frac{1}{2}$ per cent in 1983/84. It seems most unlikely that this target will be achieved, largely because of the increase in the size of the budget deficit in a time of recession.

In summary, the PSBR has been variously interpreted as a **policy instrument**, an **intermediate objective**, and an **economic indicator** in the pursuit of monetarist economic policies. We have described its role as an **intermediate policy objective** in the preceding paragraphs. Alternatively, the PSBR can be regarded as a policy instrument in its own right, in attaining the money supply objective. In this light the PSBR is the intermediary between fiscal and monetary policy. Finally, some monetarists argue that since the PSBR (and the money supply) are notoriously difficult to forecast and control with any degree of accuracy, they are best used as general economic indicators rather than as either policy instruments or objectives in their own right.

18.4   LINKS WITH OTHER TOPICS

Because of the central importance of the PSBR in the economy, many of these links have inevitably been demonstrated in the earlier sections of the unit. The PSBR is intertwined with fiscal policy (discussed in Units 17 and 22) and monetary policy (Unit 19); it is also central to many of the issues between Keynesians and monetarists (Unit 25). The size of the PSBR and its method of financing have direct implications for inflation and unemployment (Unit 24), and interest rates and investment (Unit 23).

18.5   QUESTION PRACTICE

Essay Questions

Question 1 State what is meant by Public Sector Borrowing Requirement and discuss the problems that may follow from its growth.   *(AEB: June 1980)*

Understanding the Question You must explain that the PSBR is the difference between public sector income and expenditure each year and that it varies throughout the year. The three main components are central government, local government and public corporations borrowing.

The problems that growth in the PSBR may create depend on how fast it grows, its size, how the borrowed money is spent and how the finance is raised. The growth of the PSBR means that more borrowing is needed to finance government expenditure in one year than in the previous year. This increases the National Debt and may lead to a drain on national resources as explained in this unit. However, if the rate of growth of PSBR is slower than inflation, then in **real** terms the PSBR falls. Also, the PSBR, although increasing, may be a falling percentage of GDP.

An increase in the PSBR represents an injection of demand into the economy which may create employment. How the borrowed money is used is a crucial element. If the funds are for transfer payments, then consumption is fuelled, living standards are perhaps maintained in the short run at least, but inflation may also result. Increased consumption may in some circumstances encourage growth, through its effects on private sector business confidence, though according to the monetarists public spending will merely 'crowd out' the private sector. However, if public investment is increased, the conditions for long-term economic growth may be improved.

The extra spending through borrowing can be financed in different ways. The selling of government stock to the private non-bank sector of the economy is a transfer of funds between sectors and broadly neutral. However, a good answer requires some examination of the problem caused by the selling of (short-term) stock to the banking sector. This raises a bank's liquid assets and enables multiple credit creation, thus expanding the money supply and, in the view of the monetarists, causing worsening inflation.

Furthermore, if the PSBR attracts funds which might otherwise have financed private sector investment, then growth potential is reduced. Alternatively, borrowing from abroad raises National Income but drains the balance of payments in the long term, when interest payments are made. A growing PSBR may also necessitate raised interest rates to make the stock attractive to buyers, but this may have disadvantages for investment and company liquidity.

Answer plan

1 Define and explain the PSBR.
2 Explain how government discretionary decisions and automatic changes taking place in the economy can both cause growth in the PSBR.
3 Describe why the PSBR was not regarded as a problem in the Keynesian era.
4 Consider the major macro-economic problems which can result from growth in the PSBR, such as (a) effects on the money supply and inflation, (b) crowding out, and (c) National Debt management.

Question 2 Explain fully what you understand by the National Debt and distinguish the main forms of debt issued by central government. Critically assess the view that the size of the National Debt is unimportant.

(AEB: November 1981)

Understanding the Question The first sentence of the question is straightforward and requires simple recall of facts and ideas. The National Debt is the total **stock** of outstanding borrowing which the **central government** has not yet paid back. It can be considered in terms of **marketability, liquidity** and **source** *i.e.* from whom the government has borrowed. Most of the National Debt is **marketable**, comprising Treasury Bills and gilts. Gilts are examples of long-term securities or stock which promise to pay the purchaser a specified rate of interest for a certain length of time, and then repay the original nominal sum. Gilts and Treasury Bills can be resold before they mature, on the capital market and money market respectively. However, National Savings Certificates, premium bonds and certain other paper assets are **not marketable** and can only be redeemed, or cashed in, by the original buyer or his agent selling them back to the government.

The **liquidity** of the National Debt is also significant, varying from three months for Treasury Bills to twenty years or more in the case of gilts. In the past, 'undated' stock, such as Consols and the famous 1939 War Loans, were issued with no redemption date, thus leaving repayment at the option of the government. The government may decide to issue more long-dated stock and fewer 'shorts'. This is known as **funding**. We shall explain in the next unit how funding has been used as a technique of monetary control, because fewer shorts, such as Treasury Bills, mean fewer liquid assets in the banking system and less potential for the multiple creation of bank deposits.

The National Debt can also be categorized by **source**. The main holders are **Internal**, public and private financial institutions and individuals. The Bank of England, commercial banks, insurance companies, pension funds, building societies, public companies and trust funds all hold government debt. The **external** debt is that part of the National Debt which has been sold overseas. External holdings may be either in sterling or in other currencies.

The second part of the question seeks a careful consideration of the economic importance of the National Debt. It needs to be related to other factors, such as Gross Domestic Product (GDP), growth, national resources, inflation and the PSBR (and CGBR).

In the UK, National Debt is a declining percentage of GDP and national income. This could be explained by economic growth, if the economy grows in real terms faster than the National Debt. However, the main explanation lies in inflation. If the rate of inflation is greater than the rate at which the CGBR adds to the National Debt, the money value of the debt as a proportion of money GDP will usually fall. Similarly, if the rate of inflation is greater than the nominal interest rate the government pays to debt-holders, the government gains and debt-holders lose. In these circumstances the real burden of the debt on tax-payers is falling. However, debt-holders may begin to realize that they have been suffering from 'money illusion' in lending to the government at negative real rates of interest. When this happens, the government may experience considerable difficulty in persuading the general public to buy new debt, at least at current interest rates.

The larger the National Debt, the greater the money cost of debt **servicing**. The cost of servicing depends on the average liquidity of the debt, its total size, and the rate of interest offered when the debt was first issued. This servicing has to be met out of current income and borrowing. The greater the cost of servicing, then the greater the level of taxation and the PSBR. Current income which could be used for other purposes finances debt interest incurred by earlier generations. Effectively, this is a transfer from tax-payers to holders of the debt, rather than a burden on the community as a whole. It can also be argued that the debt is not a burden if the current generation is still benefiting from capital investment projects, for example roads or schools, which the debt financed. However, a large part of the National Debt is **deadweight** debt incurred by past governments to pay for war-time expenditure. Since the deadweight debt does not cover any real asset, interest payments on the debt are a burden on the country's citizens.

If the holders of the debt are external, however, then interest payments are a drain on national resources. In Britain's case the external burden is small, but a less developed country, without either large domestic savings or a developed banking sector, could be heavily reliant on outside lenders. Much of current income might be needed to pay interest on foreign borrowing, resources would flow out of the economy, and development could be impeded.

Answer plan

1 Define the National Debt.

2 Distinguish between the main forms of debt on the basis of marketability, liquidity, and source.

3 The importance of the National Debt depends in part upon whether it is regarded as a burden. Discuss the circumstances in which it may and may not be a burden. Take care to distinguish between the absolute size and the relative size of the debt, its money value and its real value.

Multiple Choice Questions

Question 3 The idea that interest payments on the National Debt constitute a future claim on the country's resources is true if

(a) the debt is partly or wholly incurred abroad.

(b) there is unemployment in the economy.

(c) the debt is long-term rather than short-term.

(d) interest rates are rising.

Understanding the Question (a) is the correct answer because part of government income which could be used in domestic production or consumption is spent on debt servicing and represents a drain from the domestic flow of income. Interest payments to people living within the country are a claim on the government, but they are merely a transfer as far as the country's resources are concerned. Although rising interest rates may affect future borrowing, the interest rate on the existing debt was fixed when the stocks were issued. (c) is incorrect because the maturity/liquidity profile of the debt affects the frequency of redemption, not the obligation. Alternative (b) is simply irrelevant, although the need to finance unemployment pay may be a cause of an increasing National Debt.

Data Response Questions

Question 4

Percentage of total government expenditure financed by:

	1970	1975
Taxes on income	33.9	29.9
Taxes on capital	3.1	1.5
Taxes on expenditure	38.5	26.0
National Insurance contributions, etc.	12.1	12.6
Gross trading surplus of public corporations	7.3	5.4
Rent, interest and dividends, etc.	7.0	5.7
Other	− 1.9	− 0.5
Public sector borrowing requirement	0.0	19.4
	100	100

(Source: *Lloyds Bank Review*, October 1976)

What factors do you think have accounted for the changes in the relative importance of the various sources of government finance between 1970 and 1975? Comment on the economic implications of these changes.

(London: January 1979)

Understanding the Question The question falls into three parts: describing the changes, giving reasons for the changes, and discussing their possible economic consequences. Although each item can be examined separately, in this type of question it is useful to identify the major changes and trends. It is also important to show the examiner that you understand what can and cannot be **directly inferred** from the data. We do not know the absolute figures involved, only the percentages, indicating a PSBR which was zero in 1970, growing to nearly 20 per cent of total expenditure in 1975. Clearly with percentage data, if one item grows in relative importance, the others taken together must fall; but we do not know from the data whether, for example, income tax revenue declined or increased in absolute terms. It is always a good idea to show clearly when you are introducing assumptions, economic theories and factual information from 'outside the data' to help in its interpretation. Thus if you know that the 1970s were years of inflation, you might reasonably state that the absolute totals of both expenditure and revenue would have increased. You could then introduce various concepts we have explained in Unit 17 and in this unit, such as the impact of discretionary tax changes, fiscal drag, fiscal boost and the effects of autonomous changes in the economy, amongst the possible explanatory factors. Clearly, however, you must suggest reasons for the growth in the PSBR as this is by far the most significant change. 1970 is actually a rather unrepresentative year, being about the only year since the 1940s when a government has balanced its budget. You could usefully discuss whether the increase in the PSBR was a deliberate act of government policy to stimulate the economy in a Keynesian sense, or whether it took place for reasons outside the government's control.

If you decide to examine the changes in each item of revenue in detail, you could suggest reasons, such as the impact of government price controls, to explain the decline in the relative importance of the trading surpluses (or profits) of nationalized industries. Public corporations hand over any temporary trading surpluses they enjoy to the government, thereby reducing the CGBR.

The economic implications of a large increase in the PSBR have been explained in this unit. You could also examine the implications of the shift in the structure of taxation towards direct taxation (on income) and away from indirect taxation (on expenditure). This could make the tax system more progressive, with implications for income distribution, and it could also have effects on incentives and tax evasion.

Answer Plan
1 Describe the main changes such as the growing importance of the PSBR and the changing structure of taxation. Note that the fact that the data are in percentage form limits the definite conclusions which can be drawn from the data.
2 Introduce general reasons to explain the most important changes, autonomous and discretionary changes, *e.g.* fiscal drag and fiscal boost, discretionary tax changes, etc.
3 Discuss the implications of a growing PSBR and a shift in the structure of taxation.

18.6 FURTHER READING

Livesey, F., *A Textbook of Economics* (Polytech Publishers Ltd., 1978).
Chapter 13: The Interaction between Fiscal and Monetary Policy.

Prest, A. R., and Coppock, D. J., editors, *The UK Economy, a Manual of Applied Economics,* 9th edition (Weidenfeld & Nicolson, 1982).
Chapter 2: Monetary Credit and Fiscal Policies.

19 Monetary Policy

19.1 POINTS OF PERSPECTIVE

Monetary policy refers to any deliberate action by the **monetary authorities** (the **Bank of England** and **the Treasury**) to influence the **quantity of money** in the economy or the **cost of money**, *i.e.* the **rate of interest**. The traditional approach to monetary policy adopted by many textbooks is rather artificial, implying that over the years British monetary policy has been largely concerned with controlling the supply of money with a view to controlling the level of aggregate demand in the economy. Textbooks often describe monetary policy in a simple mechanical way, emphasizing how the authorities attempt to control the banking system's ability to create new deposits or credit by influencing the size of a **reserve or liquid assets ratio**. In fact, the objectives and methods of implementation of monetary policy have changed very significantly in recent years, as has its importance relative to other policies such as **fiscal** and **incomes policies**. We shall spend some time, therefore, describing the background to monetary policy in the UK before we deal with the more precise detail of how the policy is currently implemented.

19.2 UNDERLYING CONCEPTS

1 Instruments and Objectives

At the risk of gross oversimplification, it is useful to conceive of economic policy as a problem of assigning particular **policy instruments** to particular **objectives**. Post-war British governments have faced the same broad range of objectives, namely:
  (i) to create and maintain **full employment**;
  (ii) to achieve **economic growth** and improved living standards;
  (iii) to achieve a fair or **acceptable distribution of income**, both between regions and different income groups in society;
  (iv) to **control or limit inflation**, or to achieve some measure of price stability;
  (v) to attain a **satisfactory balance of payments**, usually defined as the avoidance of an external deficit which might create an exchange rate crisis. The order in which we have listed these objectives is by no means accidental. There is general agreement that objectives (i) to (iii) are the **ultimate objectives** of economic policy – though there is considerable disagreement both on the nature of full employment and social fairness, and on how to attain them. In contrast, objectives (iv) and (v) are **intermediate objectives**, or possibly **constraints** in the sense that an unsatisfactory performance in terms of controlling inflation or the balance of payments can prevent the attainment of one or other of the ultimate policy objectives.

2 Keynesian monetary policy

For most of the post-war period, until about 1970, British monetary policy under both Conservaative and Labour governments could be described as **Keynesian**. Keynesian monetary policy displayed the following characteristics:
(i) Monetary policy was regarded as independent of fiscal policy, which was the principal Keynesian policy instrument used to **manage demand** in the pursuit of full employment and stable growth. In general, Keynesians have believed that fiscal policy is more effective than monetary policy in influencing the level of **aggregate money demand** in the economy, while monetarists adopt the reverse view.
(ii) Nevertheless, the Keynesians did use monetary policy on occasions as a **supplementary policy** to 'back up' or reinforce fiscal policy in the task of demand management.
(iii) More usually, however, monetary policy was assigned other objectives, particularly **National Debt management**. Being the largest borrower in the economy, the government stands to benefit from low interest rates. For much of the Keynesian period, the overriding aim of monetary policy was to procure **orderly financial markets** in which the government could sell new securities (gilts and Treasury Bills) at favourable prices, thereby easing the problems of financing the National Debt and the PSBR. Since Keynesians have believed, until recently at least, that the money supply is both impossible and unnecessary to control, they gave little attention to this aspect of monetary policy. (As we explain in Unit 24, Keynesians do not locate the cause of inflation in an excess supply of money.) Instead, Keynesian monetary policy usually allowed the

money supply to adapt passively to whatever level was consistent with the government's interest rate target. However, some attempt was made to influence consumer demand (and thus indirectly the supply of money) in the course of demand management via the **structure of interest rates** and **controls on bank lending**.

(iv) Occasionally, the interest rate target of Keynesian monetary policy was switched away from the 'normal' objective of **low and stable interest rates** and **National Debt management** to a **'crisis'** **objective** of **high interest rates** to **protect the exchange rate**. During most of the period we are discussing, the British balance of payments was in persistent deficit. **Capital outflows** occurred, which meant that the authorities had to sell **reserves** and buy pounds in order to maintain the **fixed exchange rate**. In the resulting sterling crisis, monetary policy and high interest rates were usually used to support the exchange rate and stem the capital outflow. This aspect of monetary policy became much less significant in the 1970s when the authorities allowed the pound to *float*. Nevertheless, there is evidence in the early 1980s that monetary policy is once again being used to support and maintain an 'unofficial' exchange rate target.

3 Monetary policy under the monetarists

The 1970s were a decade of transition in which monetary policy changed in a rather haphazard way from the Keynesian policy we have just described to a policy displaying the following monetarist characteristics:

(i) An important monetarist objective is the **control of inflation**. As we shall explain in Unit 24, monetarists believe that inflation is caused by an excess supply of money. The **immediate objective** of economic policy must therefore be to **control the rate of growth of the money supply** in order to reduce the rate of inflation. By 1980, under a firmly monetarist Conservative government, attempted control of the rate of growth of the money supply had replaced the other aims of monetary policy.

(ii) We have already noted that monetarists believe that monetary policy can have a greater expansionary or contractionary effect on aggregate money demand and the level of money national income than fiscal policy. Sometimes textbooks imply that monetarists wish, therefore, to use monetary policy in place of fiscal policy in order to manage the level of demand in the economy. In Unit 25 we shall explain why this view of monetarism is essentially misconceived. Under monetarism, monetary policy is a **medium-term policy** for influencing and stabilizing the general economic environment, rather than a tool of **short-term** or **discretionary** demand management. The framework of monetary policy in the early 1980s has been the **Medium Term Financial Strategy** adopted by the Conservative Government in its 1980 budget. The MTFS has incorporated the monetarist view that the **firm announcement** of a money supply target for several years ahead would itself bring down the rate of inflation, through its effect on **expectations**.

Nevertheless, for the reasons we suggested in Unit 16, the government has found that a **money supply target** is almost impossible to achieve, and according to the monetarists' own philosophy, a failure to achieve an announced target may influence expectations adversely! Consequently, since 1979 the Conservative Government gradually moved away from the announcement of a **single** money supply target, Sterling M3. Instead the government adopted a more flexible approach, monitoring a broad range of monetary indicators, Sterling M3, M1 and PSL2. Some commentators believe that because of the difficulties involved in 'hitting' **any** money supply target, monetary policy should aim to achieve either an **exchange rate target** or a **money GDP target**.

(iii) Monetarists place great emphasis on the **interdependence** of fiscal and monetary policy, arguing that the ability to control the money supply depends upon the fiscal policy adopted by the government. In general, monetarists believe that increased levels of government spending financed by increased borrowing from the banks are mainly responsible for excessive monetary growth, and hence ultimately for inflation. Accordingly, lower levels of public spending and a smaller PSBR are regarded as a necessary condition for controlling the money supply and reducing the rate of inflation. (If, however, the PSBR is financed through the non-bank sector, there is no reason why the money supply should expand.)

4 The money supply and the rate of interest

We explained in Unit 16 how the rate of interest is the price of money. Simple supply and demand analysis indicates that if the supply of any commodity is restricted relative to demand at the existing price, then price will rise. This suggests that monetary policy cannot hope to achieve simultaneously the twin objectives of restraining the growth of the money supply and low interest rates. In the next sections we shall describe the very important changes in the implementation of monetary policy which occurred in the 1970s and in 1980 and 1981. During this period, in the transition from Keynesianism to monetarism, it was often unclear whether the objective of monetary policy was the control of the money supply or the traditional Keynesian target of interest rate stability. However, by the end of the decade a Conservative government, under strong monetarist influence, was committed to the money supply target and the acceptance that interest rates would have to be both higher and more volatile than they had been in the past.

19.3 ESSENTIAL KNOWLEDGE

1 The banking system in the UK

In Unit 16 we defined a bank as an institution which accepts deposits that can be transferred by cheque and which makes loans and advances. Until the **1979 Banking Act** there were no legal restrictions to prevent any institution calling itself a 'bank'. Officially, however, the **UK banking sector** comprised all the **listed banks** which recognized the **uniform reserve ratio**, together with the **Banking Department** of the **Bank of England** (the *central bank*) and the **discount market institutions**. In order to regularize the situation, the 1979 Banking Act introduced restrictions on authorized banks by establishing a two-tier system of **'recognized banks'** and **'licensed deposit-taking institutions'**. It is now an offence to take deposits unless authorized to do so by the Bank of England. The authorized listed banks are divided into three main groups, the **British banks, overseas banks and consortium banks.** In recent years there has been a rapid growth in the operations in the UK of overseas and consortium banks, and also the more specialized British banks. In response to this growth, the controls which formerly applied only to the clearing banks have been extended to all listed banks. A consortium bank is a bank which is owned by a group of other banks, including at least one overseas bank, but no one bank owns more than 50 per cent of the share capital.

For our purposes we shall concentrate attention on the clearing banks, the institutions in the Discount Market, and the Bank of England:

(i) The clearing banks All the banks which we have mentioned, with the exception of the Bank of England, are **commercial banks** in the sense that the ultimate objective of their owners is to make a profit. The clearing banks, and in particular the **London clearing banks**, are by far the most important of the commercial banks, both in terms of the volume of their deposits and in the fact that the **current accounts** or **sight deposits**, which they accept and create, function as a most important part of the supply of money. The clearing banks are also known as **primary banks** and **retail banks**, since most of their deposit business is with the firms and members of the general public.

(ii) The banks and the Discount Market In Unit 16 we used a simple model of the banking system to explain the principle of credit or deposit creation. We assumed in this simple model that banks possess just three assets: cash, bonds and advances. Before we explain the role of the Discount Market and its important relationships with the clearing banks on the one hand, and the Bank of England on the other, we shall firstly introduce a rather more detailed version of the assets side of the balance-sheet of a clearing bank:

Table 19.1 The asset structure of a UK clearing bank

1 Notes and coin	Cash ratio	Liquid assets
2 Balances at the Bank of England		
3 Money at call		
4 Treasury Bills and other bills		
5 British government stocks of 1 year or less to maturity		
6 Special deposits		Illiquid assets
7 Advances		
8 Investments		

In arranging the structure of its assets, a bank faces a **'trade-off'** between **liquidity** and **profitability**. Since the illiquid assets in the balance-sheet are the most profitable of a bank's assets, it will expand deposits by as much as possible through the purchase of bonds or securities (investments) or through the creation of advances. However, in the event of a loss of deposits to other banks or a cash drain to the general public, the bank must be able to convert some at least of its interest-earning assets into cash. (It is important to note that balances at the Bank of England are equivalent to cash.) Banks come to possess highly liquid interest-earning assets, **money at call, Treasury Bills** and **commercial bills** as a direct result of their special relationship with the **discount houses** and brokers of the **London Discount Market** or **money market**. The money market is a market in short-term money or funds, as distinct from the long-term market, the **capital market**. Firms in the private sector may decide to raise funds in the money market by the sale of **commercial bills** (or **bills of exchange**) for the purpose, for example, of financing trade or a temporary cash-flow problem. In a similar way the government can obtain temporary funds through the sale of Treasury Bills, which the Bank of England sells on behalf of the government. A commercial bill becomes a marketable security when it is endorsed or accepted, usually by a merchant bank in its function as an **accepting house**. Specialized financial institutions known as **discount houses** then purchase the accepted bills of exchange and Treasury Bills. Instead of receiving a formal rate of interest, the discount house earns a **discount rate**, which is the difference between the **discount price** paid for the bill on the day of issue and the face value received when the bill matures three months or ninety-one days later.

In practice, many bills are resold by the discount houses to the banks before they mature, thereby accounting for item 4 in Table 19.1. Item 5, **government stocks with one year or less to maturity**, is essentially similar. From a bank's point of view, short-dated government securities, including Treasury Bills, are highly liquid. If the banks are ever in a situation in which they need to restore their cash ratio, the banks can either encash their securities as they mature or sell them to the general public at only a small capital loss.

Money at call, which is item 3 on the balance sheet, also results from the relationship between the banks and the discount houses. Each week the discount houses may purchase new issues of bills to the value of many millions of pounds. Money at call, which comprises overnight and very short loans or advances that the clearing banks can quickly recall from the discount houses, is a very cheap source of finance which enables the discount houses to conduct their discounting business at a profit.

(iii) The Bank of England Although the 'narrow function' of the money market is as a source of short-term money for the private sector and the government, its wider function, with which we are much more interested, is to act as a 'buffer' between the Bank of England and the clearing banks: a buffer through which the Bank of England implements monetary policy. And just as we make a distinction between the narrow and wider functions of the money market, so it is useful to separate the wider function of the Bank of England, the **implementation of monetary policy**, from the narrower functions which we shall first consider:

(a) The 'narrow' functions of the Bank of England.
The Bank of England is the country's *central bank*. It is organized in two departments, the *Issue Department* responsible for note issue, and the *Banking Department*, which conducts the banking business which we shall now describe. The Bank of England is:

  (*i*) **The government's bank**, keeping the government's principal bank accounts, receiving tax and other revenue, and paying for goods and services bought by the government. The Bank **manages the National Debt** on behalf of the government, selling new issues and redeeming maturing Treasury Bills and gilts. The Bank also manages and holds Britain's gold and foreign currency reserves, implementing the government's exchange rate policy and any exchange control regulations which are in force.

 (*ii*) **The bankers' bank** The commercial banks hold deposits at the Bank of England (item 2 in Table 19.1), which enable the settlement of debts between the banks.

(*iii*) **General banking supervisor** The Bank of England decides who can operate as a bank and the ways in which banks must operate in order to protect depositors. Recent banking legislation has expanded this function.

 (*iv*) **The 'lender of last resort'** Traditionally, the Bank of England has been prepared to supply cash to the banking system in order to maintain confidence and to prevent bank failures.

  (*v*) **Banker to other countries** The Bank acts as banker to other countries that wish to hold their foreign currency reserves in sterling on deposit in London.

(b) The 'wider' function of the Bank of England: the implementation of monetary policy.
Together with the Treasury, the Bank of England controls the banking system and implements the country's monetary policy. Earlier in the unit we discussed the changes which have taken place in the broad objectives of monetary policy; we shall now examine the more detailed changes which have occurred in the Bank of England's **techniques of monetary control**.

2 The techniques of monetary control

Important changes have taken place in the techniques of monetary control at roughly ten year intervals since 1951:

  (i) 1951 – The **28 per cent liquid assets ratio** replaced the 8 per cent **cash ratio**.
 (ii) 1960 – **Special deposits** were introduced.
(iii) 1971 – **Competition and Credit Control**: the **12½ per cent reserve asset ratio** replaced the liquid assets ratio.
 (iv) 1981 – A **modified cash ratio system (monetary base system)** replaced the reserve asset ratio.

(i) The cash ratio and the liquid assets ratio In Unit 16 we described a model of the banking system in which, prudently, the banks chose to keep 10 per cent of their assets in the form of cash. In a situation in which their only assets were cash, advances and bonds, the banks could then expand total deposits to ten times their cash holdings. It follows from this analysis that if the authorities can reduce the cash or **'high-powered' money** held by the banks, total deposits, which are largely the **'low-powered' money** which banks have created, will fall by £10 for every £1 of cash removed.

Before 1951, British monetary policy did indeed operate around the fulcrum of an 8 per cent cash ratio, but not in the simple mechanical way we have just described. We have already explained how until very recently the authorities were unwilling to accept the high and volatile interest rates which control of the cash ratio or **monetary base** implies. In fact, the authorities were always prepared to supply cash as the lender of last resort to the banking system in order to maintain orderly financial markets and interest rates. The techniques of monetary control which were available to the authorities were rendered largely ineffective by this readiness to supply cash.

Traditionally, the main technique of control has been through **open market operations** – the buying and selling of government securities on the open market. In theory, a sale of government securities (gilts) to the general public should lead to a multiple contraction of credit and deposits proceeding through the following stages:

(a) The public buy gilts by drawing cheques on their deposits in the clearing banks.
(b) The cheques are paid into the government's account at the Bank of England. The balance-sheets of the clearing banks will now show an equal fall in customers' deposits, on the liabilities side, and balances at the Bank of England on the assets side.
(c) The cash ratio thus falls, followed by a multiple contraction of deposits and credit when the banks reduce their rate of deposit creation in order to restore their cash ratios. In practice however, the banks could always restore the cash ratio by recalling money at call, thereby passing the cash squeeze on to the discount houses, who would be in the classic, exposed position of 'borrowing short and lending long'. At this stage the cash squeeze initiated by the Bank of England would be rendered ineffective by the Bank's own actions! The discount houses would obtain the cash to repay money at call by borrowing from the Bank of England (or by selling bills to the Bank) at the Bank of England's lending rate or discount rate.

Thus, under the cash ratio system, the authorities would always replace the cash which the Bank had initially squeezed. Such open-market operations were normally accompanied by a change in the Bank of England's lending rate (known as **Bank Rate** before 1972, and as **Minimum Lending Rate** until its abolition in 1981). Since a rise in Bank Rate would tend to increase money market discount rates and other short-term interest rates, the authorities could achieve some reduction in the demand for credit. However, the ability of the clearing banks to maintain their advances was not seriously restricted since the banks could restore their cash ratios by the running down of other liquid assets.

In an attempt to make the existing technique of monetary control, open-market operations, more effective, a required liquid assets ratio was introduced in 1951. It was believed that a liquid assets ratio could be more effective as a means of control than a simple cash ratio in a situation in which the authorities are always prepared to supply cash to the banking system. The banks would still continue to restore their cash ratios by the running down of other liquid assets when the authorities used open-market operations to squeeze cash. However, when liquid assets fell below the required percentage of total assets, the banks would now have to contract deposits in order to restore the required liquid assets ratio.

We have just described, in the preceding paragraphs, the 'textbook' model of deposit control via the technique of open-market operations and control of the liquid assets ratio. However, it is doubtful whether the authorities have ever used open-market operations with much success, at least in the manner just described. More often, the sale of government securities has been dictated, not by the attempted **discretionary control of deposit creation**, but by the authorities' need to finance the PSBR and to sell new debt to renew the National Debt as it matures. As a rule, the general public will only be prepared to purchase large quantities of government debt if security prices fall and interest rates rise – precisely the opposite of what the government had in mind in terms of achieving orderly financial markets and stable interest rates. Traditionally, therefore, the authorities have been prepared to supply cash to the banking system to allow the banks to purchase the **residual debt** which the authorities cannot sell to the general public, except at the cost of higher interest rates. Thus open-market operations have seldom, if ever, significantly restricted the process of deposit creation, since the authorities have not been prepared to accept the consequences on interest rates and National Debt management which would follow.

(ii) Special deposits In 1960 the authorities introduced **special deposits** as a new policy instrument capable of influencing the banking system's ability to create new deposits or credit. A call by the Bank of England for special deposits is equivalent to an increase in the required reserve asset ratio, since a part of a bank's reserve assets, its balances at the Bank of England, becomes frozen in an illiquid deposit at the central bank. As in the case of open-market operations, a call for special deposits will, in principle, be followed by a multiple contraction of credit when the banks take action to restore their ratios. However, calls for special deposits have never had much effect on total bank lending, partly because the banks have usually possessed a 'spare cushion' of liquid assets, over and above the minimum required ratio, which they have been able to run down in response to a call for special deposits. The spare cushion has itself been created by the sale, which we mentioned in the previous paragraph, of the **residual National Debt**, mostly Treasury Bills, to the banking system.

As a result of the ineffectiveness of open-market operations and special deposits as techniques of monetary control, the authorities introduced **qualitative and quantitative controls** on bank lending in the 1960s. Qualitative controls are **directional controls** instructing, or more usually **'persuading'**, the banks to lend only to certain types of customer, for example, exporters. (**Hire-purchase controls**, which are a particular type of directional control, had in fact been used for most of the post-war period.) Quantitative controls effectively imposed a maximum ceiling on the amounts which banks could lend.

(iii) Competition and Credit Control The imposition of a growing number of controls on the clearing banks had the effect of (a) discouraging competition between the clearers for new business, and (b) encouraging the emergence of **'fringe'** or **secondary banks** which were able to cream business away from the clearing banks, since these new banks were not subject to the rigid system of control. The problem with all kinds of direct control is that they lead to such **'disintermediation'**. Clearly, the authorities could take one of two possible courses of action: either they could abolish the existing structure of controls, or they could extend the controls to all banking institutions. In a sense, they tried to do both in the new system of control introduced in 1971 in the document **Competition and Credit Control**. Qualitative and quantitative controls were abandoned, but the new system of control was extended to all the listed banks. Essentially, the authorities decided to rely on the traditional techniques of open-market operations and the call for special deposits in a shift of emphasis 'towards the broader monetary aggregates (including) the money supply'.

The introduction of CCC thus represented the first move towards the monetarist policy which gradually developed over the next decade. Specifically, the 28 per cent liquid assets ratio was replaced by a new fulcrum of monetary control, a $12\frac{1}{2}$ per cent reserve asset ratio. All banks were required to keep specified reserve assets equal to $12\frac{1}{2}$ per cent of their eligible deposit liabilities. Eligible liabilities largely comprise customers' deposits placed in the banks in sterling rather than in foreign currencies. Cash in the form of till-money was excluded from the reserve asset ratio on the grounds that the banks would wish in any case to maintain cash ratios as a part of normal prudent banking practice. Instead, the specified assets in the $12\frac{1}{2}$ per cent ratio included those assets, such as balances at the Bank of England, Treasury Bills and short-dated government stock, which the authorities believed could quickly be influenced through a combination of open-market operations, special deposits and funding. (*Funding* of the National Debt occurs when the authorities sell relatively illiquid long-dated government securities to replace short-dated debt in the form of maturing Treasury Bills.)

(iv) The abolition of the reserve assets ratio and MLR in 1981 As we have noted, the new system of monetary control introduced in CCC represented the beginning of the transition to the monetarist system of control established in August 1981. The system of control introduced by CCC reflected a preference for indirect rather than direct government control, and a belief in the virtues of market forces and the price mechanism. Hence, it was entirely consistent with the spirit of CCC that **Bank Rate**, a policy instrument used by the authorities to **determine** short-term interest rates, was replaced in 1972 by **Minimum Lending Rate** (MLR), a market-**determined** lending rate. Nevertheless the market-determined nature of MLR was suspended on more than one occasion during the 1970s, so that MLR came more and more to resemble Bank Rate, which it had replaced.

The framework of control introduced by CCC did not function at all smoothly during the 1970s, however. The removal of controls on bank lending was accompanied by a greatly increased PSBR and a massive expansion of bank lending which financed property speculation and consumption rather than manufacturing investment. As a result, controls were reintroduced during the course of the 1970s – the **Supplementary Special Deposits** (SSD) scheme – and the determination of MLR by market forces was suspended.

However, the election in 1979 of a Conservative government committed to monetarist economic policies led firstly to the publication in 1980 of a Green Paper on Monetary Control, and then to the introduction in 1981 of significant changes in the system of control. It must be stressed that the new system may undergo further experimental change, or, alternatively, a new government could completely reject the monetarist thinking which underlies the recent changes.

The changes introduced in 1981 reflect a paradox which is evident in monetarism that (a) control of the rate of growth of the money supply is central to monetarist strategy, yet (b) monetarists reject the use of direct controls to achieve their aims. Monetarists believe that qualitative and quantitative controls distort the working of market forces, leading to inefficiency and a lack of competition. Essentially, therefore, monetarists wish to use the indirect methods of monetary control, open-market operations and special deposits policy, to limit the ability of the banks to create new deposits or credit. The major changes introduced in August 1981 were:

(a) **The reserve asset ratio was abolished**, being replaced by the requirement that banks hold cash balances at the Bank of England in special non-operational, non-interest-bearing accounts to an amount of not more than $\frac{1}{2}$ per cent of eligible liabilities.

(b) **The suspension of MLR** Instead of announcing a lending rate, the Bank of England indicated its intention to keep short-term interest rates within an undisclosed band, designed to influence the rate of growth of the money supply.

These changes represent a move towards a **monetary base control system**, in which monetary policy operates on the **cash base** of the monetary system. One of the problems with the old system of control was the inclusion in the reserve asset ratio of liquid assets which the banking system itself could effectively 'manufacture' – commercial bills and certificates of deposit. The essential feature of a monetary base control system is that cash, which is literally the monetary base of the banking system, becomes once again the fulcrum of control. Since cash is a liability of the government and the Bank of England, the monetary authorities should be able, at least in principle, to control the supply of cash to the banking system. However, in contrast to the old 8 per cent cash ratio system, a monetary base control system requires the authorities either (i) to abandon the tradition of supplying cash to the banking system via the money market and the lender of last resort function, or (ii) to supply cash, but only at a price or rate of interest designed to secure the authorities' money supply targets.

Table 19.2 illustrates the changes which have occurred in the assets structure of the London clearing banks since the introduction of the new system of monetary control in 1981.

Table 19.2
Assets of the London clearing banks, 21 October, 1981

		£ million	Per cent of eligible liabilities
Liquid assets	Notes and coin	911	
	Balances at Bank of England	155	
	Money at call	2133	
	Treasury Bills	229	
	Other bills	1025	
	British government stock of 1 year or less to maturity	313	
		Total 4766	12.81
	Cash ratio and special deposits	167	0.45
	Other market loans	7592	20.41
	Advances	33 737	90.71
	British government stock over 1 year	2049	5.49
	Other investments	1983	5.33
	Foreign currency assets	19 484	52.39
	Miscellaneous assets	8227	22.12

Source: *Bank of England Quarterly Bulletin*

The liquid assets structure of the balance-sheet reflects the fact that, for reasons of prudence, the banks still wish to hold till-money (cash), ordinary working balances at the Bank of England, and other forms of liquid asset. The most significant change in the balance-sheet is the item **cash ratio and special deposits** at 0.45 per cent of eligible liabilities. Since there were no calls for special deposits in 1981, this figure represents the compulsory cash balances of up to $\frac{1}{2}$ per cent of eligible liabilities which the new policy required the banks to hold at the Bank of England.

19.4 LINKS WITH OTHER TOPICS

In this unit we have developed the simple theory of deposit and credit creation explained in Unit 16. On several occasions we have referred to the links between monetary policy and fiscal policy and the PSBR (Units 17 and 18). In the next units we largely ignore the roles of money and monetary policy in the economy, as we construct and explain an essentially Keynesian national income/expenditure model of the economy. However, the debate and controversy about the importance and roles of money and monetary policy are reintroduced in Unit 24 on inflation and Unit 25 on the Keynesian/monetarist conflict.

19.5 QUESTION PRACTICE

Essay Questions

Question 1 What is the main function of commercial banks? Why might they need to be supervised and, if necessary, controlled?

(O & CSEB: June 1981)

Understanding the Question The main **objective** of a commercial bank is to make a profit for its owners, which it accomplishes by its main **function** of **accepting deposits from** and **creating deposits for** members of the general public and other customers. Much of a bank's profit results from the differential in interest rates between deposits and advances. Certain types of commercial banks, such as the merchant banks, may have other important functions, for example accepting commercial bills, but the acceptance and creation of deposits is certainly the main function of the clearing banks.

In developing the second part of the question, you could firstly stress that supervision and control may be necessary to protect the general public from the loss of their deposits when imprudent banks crash. However, the main reason for recent and present-day supervision and control results from the importance of bank lending and deposits to the money supply and the general state of liquidity in the economy. Keynesians might wish to influence bank lending and interest rates in order to manage the level of demand or to ease the management of the national debt, whereas monetarists generally reject a discretionary use of monetary policy in demand management. Monetarists are primarily concerned with the authorities' ability to influence the supply of money and thereby limit inflation. They prefer to influence bank lending through a reduction in the PSBR and by creating a scarcity of liquid assets in the banking system, rather than through a system of controls imposed on the banks.

Answer plan

1 Explain that there are various types of commercial bank, but that the clearing banks are the most important.
2 Describe the function of accepting and creating deposits.
3 Briefly describe less important functions such as buying and selling foreign currency, advice to customers, executor business, etc.
4 Some form of control is necessary to protect the public from bank crashes.
5 The main reason for control stems from the importance of bank deposits as money. Keynesians may wish to control bank lending to help achieve a discretionary monetary policy aim. Monetarists dislike controls which prevent competition, preferring to influence bank lending through controlling the supply of monetary base assets.
6 Perhaps explain how banks have evaded or subverted controls such as the 'corset' (SSD scheme), for example through disintermediation. This suggests that controls should be relaxed, or, alternatively, made more comprehensive.

Question 2 Explain why, in practice, the growth of the deposits of the commercial banking system in any period is often related to the budget deficit (or surplus). In what circumstances would there be no relationship between these two magnitudes?

(WJEC: June 1979)

Understanding the Question The question is aimed at a consideration of the monetarist view that the growth of government borrowing, which results from the level of government spending and the size of the budget deficit, leads to an expansion of the money supply. Indeed, an 'extreme' monetarist view is that a 'one-for-one' relationship exists between the PSBR and the monetary base of the banking system. Whether government borrowing has an **expansionary, neutral,** or **contractionary** effect on bank deposits, and hence on the money supply, will depend, however, on (i) **whether the government spends the borrowed funds**, and (ii) the **method of borrowing.** Some of the possibilities are:

(a) The government increases the level of public spending, which it finances by borrowing.
 (i) If the government borrows by selling securities to the general public, the effects on the money supply will generally be **neutral**. A **contractionary effect** on bank deposits results from the 'open-market' sale of securities, but this is cancelled out by the **expansionary effect** on bank deposits which results from the increase in public spending.
 (ii) If the government borrows from the banks, or alternatively from the Bank of England (which effectively prints more notes), bank deposits will now *expand*. The amount borrowed from the banks will create new deposits when spent by the people who have benefited from the increase in public spending.
 (iii) If the government borrows by selling Treasury bills to the banks, more liquid assets will be acquired by the banks, which under the old reserve asset ratio would allow the banks to expand deposits. Under the system in operation since 1981, the banks can still expand deposits as long as they maintain the required reserve cash balances at the Bank of England.

(b) If the government sells securities to the general public, but does not spend the funds it receives, bank deposits will probably contract. This situation would amount to the 'open-market operations' technique of monetary control which we have described in the unit.

Even if the authorities reduce the PSBR, or borrow in ways which are neutral or contractionary in their effects on the money supply, other factors may influence the growth of bank lending. The quantity of bank lending may be affected by the demand for money as well as by the ability of the banks to create new deposits. For example, at exactly the time in 1979/81 when the authorities were attempting to restrict the rate of monetary growth, indirectly their policies had the 'perverse' effect of expanding the monetary stock. There was an increase in 'distress lending' by the banks to firms experiencing severe cash-flow problems in the squeeze between the high interest rates and depressed sales to which the restrictionist monetary policy had itself contributed.

External borrowing and the balance of payments position can also distort the relationship between bank lending and the PSBR. For instance, if the government borrows overseas and redeems debt internally, then the budget may be neutral, but deposits can increase through the net inflow of funds into the economy. In a similar way, a balance of payments surplus will generate an inflow of funds and expand bank deposits, irrespective of the PSBR position.

Answer plan

1 Define a budget deficit, and relate the concept to the PSBR.
2 Explain how the method of borrowing undertaken to finance the deficit may have expansionary or neutral effects on bank deposits and the money supply.
3 In conditions of a budget surplus, government borrowing from the general public will usually have a contractionary effect on bank deposits, since the funds received by the government may not be spent.

Multiple Choice Questions

Question 3 The revision of the system of monetary control in 1980 and 1981 included all but one of the following measures. The exception was

(a) Increasing the number of banks under government control
(b) Abolishing Minimum Lending Rate
(c) Introducing a ½ per cent ratio for cash balances at the Bank of England
(d) Replacing Sterling M3 as a monetary target

Understanding the Question Under the 1979 Banking Act the government officially differentiated between institutions allowed to call themselves **'banks'** and others known as **'licensed deposit-takers'**. This extended the number of banks to 96. MLR was abolished in 1981, giving freer rein to market forces in the setting of interest rates. At the same time, the required reserve asset ratio was abolished and replaced by the new requirement that all 96 banks should keep ½ per cent of their assets as a ratio of eligible liabilities in balances at the Bank of England. Thus, (a), (b) and (c) were all implemented, leaving (d) as the answer to the question. Sterling M3 remained as the government's stated monetary target, despite its volatility and inaccuracy as a measure of the money supply.

Data Response Questions

Question 4

Banks' Eligible Liabilities, Reserve Assets and Reserve Ratios

Banks	Eligible Liabilities £m			Reserve Asset Ratios %		
	1973	1977	1978	1973	1977	1978
Total	26 819	37 692	43 404	14.2	14.5	13.5
London Clearing	15 543	20 953	24 981		13.5	13.1
Scottish Clearing	1439	2266	2641		13.8	13.3
Northern Ireland	373	719	848		14.8	14.6
Accepting Houses	1269	1846	1852		15.8	14.4
Other Banks	3627	6049	6141		16.0	13.6
American	1852	3507	3751		15.6	13.5
Japanese	855	224	276		16.0	14.3
Other Overseas		1985	2716		16.9	15.8
Consortium Banks	–	142	200		30.0	26.8

Constitution of Reserve Assets £m			
Total	3764	5472	5870
Balances with Bank of England	282	278	390
Money at Call			
– Discount Market	2520	2236	3248
– Other		241	234
Treasury Bills	67	1259	630
Other Bills			
– Local Authority	38	105	96
– Commercial	422	678	774
British Government			
Stocks up to 1 yr.	412	676	499
Stocks over 1 yr.	207	18	456

(a) Explain in a sentence each of the following terms: (i) Eligible liabilities; (ii) Reserve Asset Ratio; (iii) Consortium banks; (iv) Accepting houses; (v) Clearing banks. (5)

(b) Which types of bank listed had the highest growth rate of eligible liabilities 1973–78? Offer possible reasons. (6)

(c) How does the Reserve Asset Ratio of the banks listed compare with the required ratio? List the types of banks with ratios below that required. (2)

(d) Explain briefly (i) 'Money at Call'; 'Commercial Bills'. (2,2)
What changes have occurred in the structure of Reserve Assets during this period? Briefly offer some possible explanations for these changes. (6)

(e) Why does the table distinghish between British Government Stock up to 12 months and that over? (2)

(O & CSEB: June 1979)

Understanding the Question The data in this question refer to the system of monetary control in operation in the UK between the introduction of **Competition and Credit Control** in 1971 and the new system (which may not yet have fully evolved) introduced in August 1981. Current examination questions will be based on the present structure of reserve assets which we have described in the unit and listed in Table 19.2. Nevertheless, we shall use this question to explain certain aspects of the policy which operated between 1971 and 1981. For most of the period, all types of banks were required to maintain a uniform Reserve Asset Ratio of $12\frac{1}{2}$ per cent. The data clearly show that all the banks met the required ratio in the three years illustrated. By imposing a required Reserve Asset Ratio, which included balances at the Bank of England, Treasure Bills and short-dated government stock, the authorities hoped to be able to use open-market operations and calls for special deposits to influence the credit-creating ability of the banks. Since controls had been extended to all the listed banks, it was no longer the case that uncontrolled fringe banks experienced the fastest rates of growth. Instead, the eligible liabilities of overseas banks grew fastest, partly as a result of the attraction of London as a centre of the Euro-banking business. The data also indicate that considerable changes occurred in both the total of reserve assets and in their proportionate importance. Possible explanations include:

(a) Just like any firm (or household), banks make portfolio adjustment decisions, rearranging the liquidity/profitability structure of the assets they possess, including the liquid assets they are required to hold. In a sense, the liquid assets become illiquid as soon as banks are required to hold them. In these circumstances banks may decide to hold the required assets in the most profitable form possible.

(b) The authorities' objective in requiring banks to maintain a reserve asset ratio was to include within the ratio those assets which the Bank of England hoped to influence through Open Market Operations and the call for Special Deposits. It may well be that certain liquid assets, such as Treasury Bills, became less important in the ratio precisely because the authorities had restricted their supply.

19.6   FURTHER READING

Morris, D., editor, *The Economic System in the UK*, 2nd edition (Oxford University Press, 1979).
Chapter 12: Monetary Policy.

Prest, A. R., and Coppock, D. J., editors, *The UK Economy, a Manual of Applied Economics*, 9th edition (Weidenfeld & Nicolson, 1982).
Chapter 2: Monetary, Credit and Fiscal Policies.

20 National Income Accounting

20.1   POINTS OF PERSPECTIVE

The macro-economics which we know today originates in the publication in 1936 of *The General Theory of Employment, Interest and Money* by J. M. Keynes. In the pre-war years Keynes's predecessors, the **neo-classical school of economists**, who then dominated economic thought in western economies, concentrated their attention on how individual markets function and on how relative prices are determined in those markets. Before Keynes, economics usually meant micro-economics! When attention was turned to the determination of the general level of employment in the economy, it was believed that the economy automatically tended towards a **full-employment equilibrium**, provided only that market forces in the individual markets which made up the economy were allowed to work.

However, in the United Kingdom of the 1920s and '30s it occurred to some economists, and in particular to Keynes, that the economy had settled into an **underemployment equilibrium**, in which mass unemployment could persist from year to year. Keynes formed the opinion that the existing body of economic thought failed to provide an adequate explanation of the persistence of mass unemployment. The growth of modern macro-economic theory was a direct result of the need felt by Keynes and his followers to construct what they thought was a better and more general theory capable both of explaining the inter-war depression and of suggesting how full employment could once again be achieved. In the next three units we shall introduce and explain the essential elements of Keynes's theories of income, output, and expenditure, which provide the theoretical framework for understanding the modern macro-economics with which the name of Keynes is so closely associated.

Keynes was just as interested in practical policy as in abstract theory, and indeed the logic of his theory suggested that governments could achieve and maintain full employment by intervening in the economy and **managing the level of demand**. Such policies would require accurate information on what was being produced and on the composition and level of income and expenditure. During Keynes's lifetime there was a distinct lack of such information. The growth, in the post-war era, of **a system of National Income Accounts** developed directly out of the need to have comprehensive and up-to-date statistics on national income, output and expenditure if government was to successfully intervene in the economy. The principal function of the National Income Accounts has always been to provide the basic data for economic policy-making, particularly at the macro-economic level, and for economic forecasting.

20.2 UNDERLYING CONCEPTS

1 Accounting Identities

Many of the problems experienced by students in the understanding of macro-economic theory stem from an initial failure to recognize and understand the meaning of an **accounting identity**. The most basic of all the identities used in the system of national income accounts is:

$$\text{National Income} \equiv \text{National Product} \equiv \text{National Expenditure}$$

or in economics shorthand (in which it is convenient to use the letter Y for income):

$$\text{(i)} \quad NY \equiv NP \equiv NE$$

We shall keep to the mathematical convention of using the $\equiv$ sign to indicate an identity, in which the **left-hand side** of the $\equiv$ sign **always equals the right-hand side**. By definition, the two sides of an identity expression **must** be equal! It is also useful to note that all the identities used in the system of national accounts are **ex post identities**, measuring what has **actually** happened in the economy, rather than what people wish or intend to happen.

2 The circular flow of income

The identity $NY \equiv NP \equiv NE$ tells us that **actual incomes received** in the economy are equal to both **actual expenditure** and the **actual output** produced in the economy. The identity holds because all three are measures of the same thing, the **flow of new wealth** or **income** produced in an economy in a specific time period, usually a year, This can most easily be explained by assuming a highly simplified economy in which all income is spent on consumption and where there is no government sector or foreign trade.

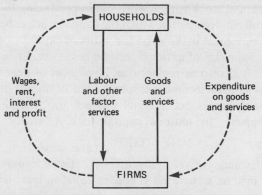

Fig 20.1 The circular flow of income

Figure 20.1 illustrates the **circular flow of income** in such a **two-sector closed economy** comprising households (the **personal sector**) and firms (**the corporate sector**), and two flows, the **'real'** **flow** of goods and services shown by the continuous line, and the **money flow** of income and expenditure represented by the broken line.

In such an economy it is obvious that if all income is spent on consumption, total expenditure must equal total output, since the value of total output is itself equal to the wages, rent and other factor rewards which go to make up income.

It is less obvious that the identity still holds when we relax the simplifying assumptions, for example by assuming that households now **save** part of their income in idle money balances. In this situation, consumption expenditure will indeed be less than national output, part of which will accumulate as **unsold stocks**. However, as a further part of the system of accounting identities, investment is defined not only as **planned** or **intended investment** on new machinery or raw materials but also as **actual** or **ex post** investment, which includes unsold stocks or **unintended inventory accumulation!** In these circumstances, national expenditure (actual consumption + actual investment) will still equal national output or product!

3 Capital, wealth and income

In Figure 20.2, national income is represented as the continuous **flow** of new wealth produced from the **national capital stock**. It is essential to distinguish **capital** and **wealth**, which are **stock concepts**, from income, which is a flow, measured for a particular period of time. The **national wealth** comprises all those assets which have value, whereas the **national capital stock** is that part of the national wealth which is capable of productive use. It follows that all capital is wealth, but not all wealth is necessarily capital. The national capital stock, which includes **social capital** such as roads and schools as well as **private capital** in the form of machines, raw material stocks and factories, is a measure of the physical wealth assets which are capable of producing more wealth. (The value of labour skills possessed by the population is sometimes defined as **human capital**. While such human capital is undoubtedly a national resource, it is not included in the definition of the national capital stock.)

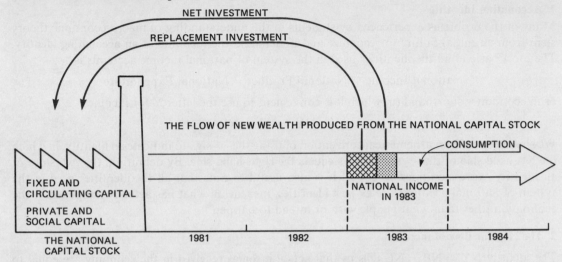

Fig 20.2 National income as an economic flow

We can use Figure 20.2 to illustrate some very important economic relations:

(i) The size of national income or output which can be produced in a particular year is ultimately limited by the size of the national capital stock.

(ii) Part of the national capital stock will be worn out in producing this year's national income. Assuming conditions of full employment in which the capital stock is being used to capacity, part of this year's national income must make good the national capital stock if the economy is to be capable of producing the same size of national income next year. Investment which makes good the national capital stock is known as **replacement investment** or **depreciation investment**. **Gross national product** and **gross national income** measure the size of output or income produced before allowing for depreciation, whereas **net national product** and **income** measure the goods and services available after replacing the national capital stock. As an accounting identity:

$$\text{(ii)} \qquad \text{NNP} \equiv \text{GNP} - \text{I}_{\text{REPLACEMENT}}$$

A similar distinction can be made between **gross** and **net national income**. However, in the presentation of official national income statistics it is conventional to treat national income as already being net of depreciation or capital consumption. Hence, in the official statistics, identity (ii) can be rewritten as:

$$\text{(iia)} \qquad \text{NY} \equiv \text{GNP} - \text{I}_{\text{REPLACEMENT}}$$

Official statistics also measure **money national income**, which should not be confused with **real national income**, the flow of real goods and services produced. Money national income is simply real national income valued at current prices.

(iii) If **economic growth** is to occur, real national income or output must increase over time. Of course, if there is already spare capacity, including unemployed labour, in the economy, some growth in output can take place without the need to increase the size of the national capital stock. But once full capacity is reached, economic growth requires that extra investment, known as **net investment** be undertaken, over and above the depreciation investment which merely replaces the existing national capital stock. Total investment in the economy may be expressed as:

$$\text{(iii)} \qquad \text{I}_{\text{GROSS}} \equiv \text{I}_{\text{REPLACEMENT}} + \text{I}_{\text{NET}}$$

(iv) Finally, we can use Figure 20.2 to illustrate the **'trade-off'** between current and future consumption and standards of living. The higher the rate of net investment, the smaller is the current output available for consumption purposes. However, the diagram implies that the higher the rate of net investment out of current national income or output, the higher the growth rate and hence the greater the future ability to produce goods and services for consumption. Thus higher living standards in the future require the sacrifice of consumption now! According to this rather simple analysis, it would seem that all a society has to do is to decide how much of current income should be consumed, and how much should be saved and made available for investment. Unfortunately, even if people could agree on this decision, the problem of procuring economic growth is not as simple as this. For example, a reduction in current consumption might make existing investments unprofitable. It may well be that a high rate of private sector investment is linked to the level of business confidence associated with a buoyant consumer market. We shall examine some of these problems in the subsequent units.

20.3 ESSENTIAL KNOWLEDGE

1 The three ways of measuring national income

The circular flow of income depicted in Figure 20.1 is a very great simplification of reality. We have already introduced some complications into the circular flow, which represent **injections** and **withdrawals** from the flow of income: households save part of their incomes, and firms retain profits in order to finance investment, and they may also hold stocks of unsold goods. We reserve until Unit 21 an analysis of how saving and investment, together with other important injections and withdrawals resulting from foreign trade and government intervention in the economy, affect the level of income or output.

Nevertheless, it remains true that even with the introduction of the government and foreign trade sectors into our model, the identity which states that income, output, and expenditure totals are equal, still holds. Any one of these **national income aggregates** can be used to measure the economy's flow of output.

(i) The income method We have already explained why, conceptually, national income must equal national output, since all payments for goods and services produced are also incomes. Income in this sense is a payment for productive services rendered, whether by labour or the services of land and capital. **Transfer payments**, such as pensions, welfare benefits and unemployment pay, must be excluded from the estimate of national income, since they are simply transferred from one group of people to another without the recipients adding to production. If such transfers were wrongly included in national income, the error of **double-counting** would occur.

Nevertheless, the national income statistics include arbitrary judgements on what is and is not 'productive work'. Thus an **imputed rent** is estimated for the values of the services received by owner-occupiers from the houses they live in, equal to the rent which would be paid if they were tenants of the same properties. But the housekeeping allowance paid by a husband to his wife is excluded, implying that housework is unproductive! It follows that if a man marries his housekeeper, or if he decides to paint his own house where previously he employed a decorator, the estimates of national income will fall!

The gap between the GDP total obtained by the income and expenditure methods is often used to approximate the size of the so called **'Black Economy'** – this refers to unrecorded income where a good or service is provided and the cash payment is not declared officially. Various estimates of the black economy have been made, the highest suggesting that it is $7\frac{1}{2}$ per cent of GDP. Most commentators feel that it is on the increase because of higher VAT (15 per cent since 1979) and increased unemployment. This increase in undeclared income is one possible explanation why consumption has been maintained despite falling output and depression in the UK economy since 1979. Thus the 'real' economy may not have declined as much as official figures indicate.

An estimate of British national income in 1980, based on the measurement of factor incomes, is shown in Table 20.1, taken from the 1981 National Income and Expenditure 'Blue Book'.

Table 20.1 illustrates the important distinction between **national** and **domestic** income (and product). **Total domestic income**, which is shown in row 8, is obtained from the addition of the various factor incomes in rows 1–7. Total domestic income is converted into **Gross Domestic Product** in row 11 by subtracting **stock appreciation**, which results from inflation and is not a reward to a factor of production, and a **residual error** (row 10). The decision where in the national accounts to include a residual error is essentially arbitrary. Although, conceptually, national income must equal national product and expenditure, the national income statistics are only **estimates** of what has happened in the economy. Mistakes in data collection inevitably occur, so a residual error or 'mistakes item' must be included in two of the tables to ensure their equality with the third table. Thus **Gross Domestic Product (GDP) at factor cost** in row 11 is a measure of the incomes received by factors of production through employment in the UK

Table 20.1

Factor Incomes 1980	£m
1 Income from employment	137 083
2 Income from self-employment	18 394
3 Gross trading profits of companies	24 979
4 Gross trading surpluses of trading corporations	6 015
5 Gross trading surpluses of general public enterprises	170
6 Rent	13 231
7 Imputed charge for consumption of non-traded capital	2 138
8 Total domestic income	202 010
9 *less* Stock appreciation	− 6 477
10 Residual error	− 2 045
11 Gross Domestic Product at factor cost	193 488
12 Net property income from abroad	− 38
13 Gross National Product	193 450
14 *less* Capital consumption	− 27 045
15 National Income ≡ Net National Product	166 405

economy. GDP is not the same as **Gross National Product (GNP)** because part of the domestically generated incomes may flow overseas to foreign owners of companies operating in the UK. Similarly, citizens living in the UK may receive incomes in the form of dividends and other profits remitted on assets they own abroad. GDP (in row 11) is converted into GNP (in row 13) by adding the **Net Property Income from Abroad** which results from such dividend flows. You will notice that the estimate for net property income from abroad in 1980 is negative. If this figure is correct (National Income estimates are continuously revised in the months and years following first publication) it shows that dividends and profits flowing out of Britain now exceed those remitted to the UK.

Finally, the estimate for National Income (or Net National Product) in row 15 is obtained by deducting capital consumption or depreciation from Gross National Product.

(ii) The output method of calculating national income involves adding up the money values of all goods and services produced in the economy. As with the income method there is a danger of double-counting. Only the **money values of final goods and services** sold to consumers must be totalled, or alternatively the **'value added'** by each industry, including the producers of raw materials and capital (or intermediate) goods. A distinction must also be made between Gross National Product (and Gross Domestic Product) at **market prices**, and GNP (and GDP) at **factor cost**. Market prices, or the prices consumers pay for final goods and services, are inflated by the effect of **indirect taxes**, but deflated by government **subsidies** paid to firms. National income aggregates at market prices must be converted to factor cost by **subtracting indirect taxes** and **adding subsidies**. The distinction between GNP at market prices and at factor cost, and other important national income aggregates, are summarized in Figure 20.3.

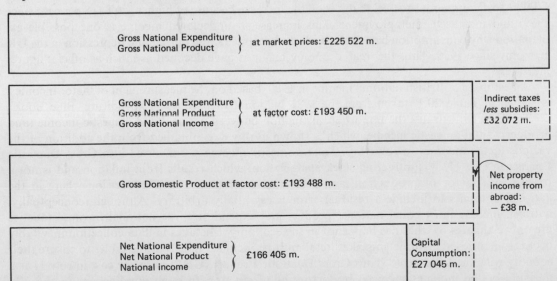

Fig 20.3 The national income aggregates in 1980

One of the most significant problems in the estimation of national product results from the fact that a large part of national output is not sold at a market price. In the case of public services, such as education, health care, police and administration, the **value of inputs**, including wages, is used as the measure for the value of output. In the case of production which takes place in the **'non-monetized' economy**, such as 'do-it-yourself' home improvement and housekeeping, either an **imputed value** must be estimated or, as we have seen, a decision is taken not to include such estimates in the measurement of national income. In developed industrial countries this may not be a serious problem; but quite obviously it would be rather absurd to omit an estimate of the non-monetized flow of output in a developing economy with a proportionately large subsistence agricultural sector.

Table 20.2 illustrates the calculation of GDP at factor cost by totalling the value added by groups of industries and services. You will notice that stock appreciation has already been deducted from the figures, but that the residual error is again deducted to convert the value of total domestic output in row 15 to GDP at factor cost in row 18. As before, GDP could be converted into GNP by adding the net property income from abroad.

Table 20.2

Gross domestic product by industry, 1980	£m
1 Agriculture, forestry and fishing	4 296
2 Petroleum and natural gas	7 649
3 Other mining and quarrying	3 222
4 Manufacturing	48 060
5 Construction	13 025
6 Gas, electricity and water	5 803
7 Transport	10 084
8 Communication	5 326
9 Distributive trades	19 328
10 Insurance, banking, finance and business services	18 288
11 Ownership of dwellings	11 996
12 Professional and scientific services	25 467
13 Miscellaneous services	18 734
14 Public administration and defence	13 987
15 Total domestic output	205 265
16 Adjustment for financial services	− 9 732
17 Residual error	− 2 045
18 Gross Domestic Product at factor cost	193 488

(iii) The expenditure method Table 20.3 shows how GNP (and GDP) at market prices and factor cost are estimated by measuring expenditure on the outputs produced in the economy. The main components of domestic expenditure are shown in rows 1–4, which add up in row 5 to total domestic expenditure at market prices. To convert this figure to Gross Domestic Product at factor cost (row 12), not only must indirect taxes be deducted and subsidies added, but a deduction must be made for domestic expenditure on imports (row 8). Similarly, the value of exports (row 6) must be added, since it represents expenditure on a part of British domestic output. You will notice the absence of a residual error item in Table 20.3, implying that estimates of expenditure are judged to be more accurate than the other two methods of measuring national income.

2 The use and misuse of national income statistics

Since national income statistics are the main source of data on what has happened and is happening in the economy, they are frequently used as **indicators of economic growth, economic and social welfare**, and for **purposes of comparison with other countries**. We have already mentioned some of the various problems in the construction and use of national income statistics, particularly the distinction between **money** and **real** national income, and the problem of imputing or excluding the value of activity in the non-monetized sector of the economy. We shall now summarize the most important problems which arise in the use of national income statistics.

(i) Comparisons over time

(a) Money national income is a misleading indicator of economic growth. For the growth rate to be calculated, money national income for each year, expressed in **current prices** of that year,

Table 20.3

Expenditure 1980	£m
1 Consumers' expenditure	135 403
2 General government final consumption	48 337
3 Gross domestic fixed capital consumption	40 050
4 Value of physical increase in stocks and work in progress	− 3 596
5 Total domestic expenditure at market prices	220 194
6 Exports of goods and services	63 198
7 Total final expenditure	283 392
8 *less* Imports of goods and services	− 57 832
9 Gross Domestic Product at market prices	225 560
10 *less* Taxes on expenditure	37 287
11 Subsidies	5 215
12 Gross Domestic Product at factor cost	193 488
13 Net property income from abroad	− 38
14 Gross National Product at factor cost	193 450
15 *less* Capital consumption	− 27 045
16 National Income, Net National Product	166 405

must be **deflated** to show real income in the **constant prices** of a single year. An index number, such as the Retail Price Index, used to deflate GNP to constant prices is known as a **GNP deflator**.

(b) Population usually grows over time, so real GNP per head of population (per capita) is a better indicator of living standards than the aggregate real GNP figure.

(c) The quality of goods and services available is likely to change over time, presenting a particularly difficult problem in the use of GNP statistics.

(d) More generally, the GNP figures cannot measure changes in intangibles, which affect the quality of life and the general level of welfare in society. **Externalities**, including both external benefits and costs, usually escape measurement in national income statistics, as do such intangibles as the value people place on leisure time and living close to work. When externalities are measured, what is in effect a welfare loss may appear as a welfare gain! For example, if motorists spend more time each day sitting in congested traffic, they will regard this as a welfare loss. However, as far as the national income statistics are concerned it will appear as extra consumption expenditure on the outputs of the vehicle and petroleum industries.

(ii) Comparisons between countries
(a) We have already mentioned how comparisons of GNP per head between countries are misleading if the relative importance of the non-monetized economy is greatly different.

(b) Further problems occur in the comparison of real income per head if different commodities are consumed. For example, expenditure on fuel, energy and building materials is likely to be greater in a country with a cold climate than in a warmer climate.

(c) A reliable comparison of real GNP per capita requires the accurate deflation of money GNP figures to constant prices in each country. There are considerable differences in statistical method and sophistication between countries, in the construction of both national income accounts and price indices. In addition, artificially managed exchange rates may distort comparison of internal price levels within countries, and even if exchange rates reflect the prices of goods which are traded internationally, they will not reflect the prices of goods and services which do not enter into international trade.

20.4 LINKS WITH OTHER TOPICS
Throughout this unit we have stressed that the system of national income accounts measures what has **actually happened** in the economy. We now go on in the next three units to introduce an essentially Keynesian national income/expenditure model of an economy, in which we are interested in whether **planned** or **intended** expenditure in the economy is consistent with the national output which is actually being produced. In particular, we shall examine what is likely to happen in the economy if planned expenditure either exceeds or falls short of actual output.

20.5 QUESTION PRACTICE
Essay Questions

Question 1 In each of the following cases, explain the distinction between the two concepts used in national income accounting in the United Kingdom:
   (i) Gross domestic product at factor cost; gross domestic product at market prices

(ii) Gross domestic product at factor cost; gross national product at factor cost

(iii) Gross national product at factor cost; national income

(iv) Total domestic expenditure at market prices; gross domestic product at market prices

(v) National income at current prices; national income at constant prices

(WJEC: June 1979)

Understanding the Question We shall use this question to revise the most important national income accounting identities, which could also be tested in a multiple choice or data response question

(i) GDP at market prices $\equiv$ GDP at factor cost + indirect taxes − subsidies

(ii) GNP at factor cost $\equiv$ GDP at factor cost + net property income from abroad

(iii) National income $\equiv$ GNP at factor cost − depreciation

(iv) GDP at market prices $\equiv$ TDE at market prices + exports − imports

(v) National income at current prices: each year's national income is measured at that year's price level. National income at constant prices: each year's national income is deflated to the constant prices of a single year, by means of a price index (national income deflator).

Data Response Questions

Question 2 Study the table below and answer the questions which follow:

UK national income and expenditure

National income	1960	1965	1970	1975	1976
Income from employment	15 174	21 292	30 425	68 255	77 751
Income from self-employment	2 008	2 510	3 774	8 913	10 228
Gross trading profits of companies	3 730	4 741	5 669	9 961	12 666
Gross trading surplus of public corporations	534	988	1 447	2 898	4 022
Gross trading surplus of other public enterprises	189	112	151	143	121
Rent of land and buildings	1 263	1 896	3 276	7 183	8 345
Domestic income and depreciation (including stock depreciation)	22 898	31 539	44 742	97 353	113 133
less Stock appreciation	− 122	− 318	− 1 162	− 5 203	− 6 565
Residual error	− 129	—	− 91	970	1 199
Gross domestic product at factor cost	22 647	31 221	43 489	93 120	107 767
Net property income from abroad	233	435	556	920	1 086
Gross national product	22 880	31 656	44 045	94 040	108 853
less Depreciation (capital consumption)	− 2 050	− 2 869	− 4 445	− 10 907	− 13 350
National income	20 830	28 787	39 600	83 133	95 503
Taxes on expenditure	3 378	4 959	8 412	14 154	16 587
less Subsidies	− 493	− 571	− 879	− 3 980	− 3 443
National income at market prices	23 715	33 175	47 133	93 307	108 647
National expenditure					
Consumers' expenditure	16 933	22 845	31 644	63 333	73 128
Public authorities' current expenditure	4 244	6 041	9 095	22 847	26 359
Gross domestic fixed capital formation	4 190	6 504	9 453	20 509	23 048
Value of physical increase in stocks and work in progress	562	496	442	− 1 300	28
Exports of goods and services	5 152	6 592	11 275	26 752	34 652
Total final expenditure at market prices	31 081	42 478	61 909	132 141	157 215
less Imports of goods and services	− 5 549	− 6 869	− 10 887	− 28 847	− 36 304

Source – *Economist Diary*

(a) (i) What types of expenditure are included in public authorities' current expenditure? (2 marks)

(ii) How has it grown in relation to total final expenditure at market prices? (2 marks)

(iii) What is the significance of public authorities' current expenditure for the economy? (2 marks)

(b) Comment on the changes in the relative shares of income from employment, gross trading profits of companies, and rent of land and buildings between the year 1960 and the year 1976. (4 marks)

(c) Why should the value of physical increase in stocks and work in progress be subject to so much irregularity? (4 marks)

(d) For 1976 the table shows that total final expenditure at market prices exceeds national income at market prices. Use the data in the table to effect a reconciliation between these two figures. (6 marks)

(Cambridge: June 1981)

Understanding the Question This is a question which makes use of data from all three methods of calculating national income, and tests a number of skills. Question (*a*) (i) is a simple question on the meaning of a single item in the system of accounts. Public authorities' current expenditure, which *does not* include transfers, comprises all public sector spending on, for example, wages, road and hospital maintenance, heating and lighting, etc. (Public sector capital spending is not separately listed, being included in gross domestic fixed capital formation.) Question (*a*) (ii) requires the simple detection of the rising trend of current public expenditure from roughly an eighth to about a sixth of total expenditure. Question (*a*) (iii) is very open-ended, and indeed it would be quite possible to answer this question at length; however, you should be warned against this by the fact that the question only carries two marks. Many factors could be significant. It is worth noting that current spending is mostly on wages. If wage costs become a larger part of both production costs and national income, the same level of public services will become more expensive to provide. This is consistent with the data in question (*b*), which show that 'income from employment' and 'rents' increase their shares of national income at the expense of company profits. Current spending by the authorities has an important effect on the living standards of the majority of the population: services such as education and health-care contribute to the **social wage**, increasing the general quality of life in the community.

In answering question (*c*), it is worth noting that the 'value of physical increase in stocks and work in progress' in fact contains two rather different items. Work in progress includes expenditure on capital projects, such as the building of power-stations, which take several years to build. Expenditure on such projects is unlikely to be highly variable from year to year, though in recent years there have been significant cuts in capital projects. In contrast, the value of physical increase in stocks relates to the stocking of raw materials or, when the figure is low, the de-stocking of previously accumulated raw materials. Decisions to stock and de-stock are strongly influenced both by current prices and interest rates, and by expectations of the future interest rate, inflation rate and state of demand. Hence the value of the increase in stocks in any year tends to be highly volatile.

Question (*d*) carries a high number of marks for a question which is essentially testing knowledge of accounting identities. If you refer back to Table 20.3, you will see that:

Total final expenditure − imports ≡ GDP at market prices
and GDP at market prices + net property income from abroad ≡ GNP at market prices

Finally, you must indicate that when depreciation or capital consumption is subtracted from GNP at market prices, the figure for national income at market prices is arrived at.

Question 3 You are given the following information on the economy:

	£ million
Consumers' expenditure	60 200
Gross trading profits of companies	11 300
Gross domestic fixed capital formation	25 100
Public authorities' current expenditure on goods and services	21 250
Exports of goods and services	26 100
Value of physical increase in stocks and work in progress	− 1 200
Taxes on expenditure	12 050
Imports of goods and services	28 300
Net property income from abroad	+ 950
Subsidies	2 500
Capital consumption	9 300

(*a*) Calculate
    (i) Gross domestic product at market price. [4]
    (ii) Gross domestic product at factor cost. [2]
    (iii) Gross national product. [2]
    (iv) National income. [2]
(*b*) Do you consider that the national accounts give an accurate measure of the level of economic activity of a country? [10]

(SUJB: June 1977)

Understanding the Question We shall leave the calculations in question (*a*) as a test of your understanding of the tables we have introduced in the unit. In undertaking calculations of this type, you must clearly show **all** your workings so that you can stand a chance of earning at least some marks in the event of an arithmetical slip.

Question (*b*) can be answered with a discussion of the use and misuse of national income statistics, incorporating the arguments we have introduced in the unit on the non-monetized sector of the economy, the Black Economy and the problem of measuring externalities and intangibles.

Multiple Choice Questions

Question 4 From the following information, calculate the Gross National Income of a country:

	£m
Wages	10 000
Salaries	6000
Government Pensions	2000
Unemployment pay and other social benefits	1000
Profits	1000
Rent and Interest	1000

The Gross National Income is:

		£m
A	18 000
B	20 000
C	22 000
D	23 000

Understanding the Question The question is testing your understanding of the fact that transfer incomes (pensions, unemployment pay and social benefits) are not included in national income, since they do not result from production. Double-counting would occur if they were included. The correct answer is therefore (A).

Question 5 The following information shows the changes experienced by an economy:

	Size of population	National Income	Price Index
Year 1	100m	200 bn	100
Year 2	110m	240 bn	120

Which of the following would be true?
A Real national income has risen
B Real national income has fallen
C Real national income per head has remained constant
D Real national income per head has fallen

Understanding the Question Since money national income and prices have both risen by 20 per cent, real national income has remained constant. However, population has risen by 10 per cent, so real national income per head has fallen. The answer is therefore (D).

20.6 FURTHER READING

Burningham, D., editor, *Understanding Economics, an Introduction for Students* (Macmillan, 1978). Chapter 11: The National Income.

Stanlake, G. F., *Macro-economics, an Introduction*, 2nd edition (Longmans, 1979). Chapter 2: The Meaning and Measurement of National Income.

21 Equilibrium National Income

21.1 POINTS OF PERSPECTIVE

In Unit 20 we briefly mentioned the fundamental difference between the **neo-classical** (or **pre-Keynesian**) view of 'how the economy works', and the view of Keynes himself. According to the older view, the operation of the price mechanism in each of the individual markets which make up the economic system automatically tends towards a situation in which there is full employment of all resources, including labour, in the economy – in other words towards a **full employment equilibrium**. We shall see in Unit 25 how modern **monetarists** adopt essentially the same view of the **stabilizing** nature of market forces (and the **destabilizing** effects of government intervention).

In contrast, the Keynesians believe that the price system contains no self-regulating mechanism to automatically produce full employment, and that government intervention can be a stabilizing force in the economy. Left to itself, a market economy may tend towards an equilibrium in which there is either **mass unemployment** resulting from **deficient demand**, or **demand-pull inflation** in conditions of **'over-full' employment** and **excess demand**. In this unit we develop and explain an elementary **national income and expenditure** model of the economy and illustrate these Keynesian propositions.

21.2 UNDERLYING CONCEPTS

1 The interrelationships between markets

A market economy is of course an interrelated system of markets. At the macro-economic level we usually consider such markets in highly aggregated form, dividing the economy into three great markets: the **goods market** (or product market) in which **output** is produced, the **labour market** (which is a part of the wider factor market) and the **money markets**. In this unit we concentrate attention on the interrelationships between the goods market and the labour-market – the markets of the **'real' economy**. At the outset we must stress, as a word of warning, that more advanced analysis than that considered in this unit investigates the simultaneous interrelationships between all three sets of markets in which the role of the money markets is particularly important. In this unit we largely ignore the role of money in the economy, though in Unit 23 on investment we shall consider the effects of money and the rate of interest on the level of output in the goods market.

2 Equilibrium national income

In Unit 1 we introduced the concept of equilibrium in the context of a single market within an economy. We defined equilibrium as a **state of rest**, or a condition in which the **plans** of all the economic agents in the **economic model** are **fulfilled** and **consistent with each other**. We shall continue to use this concept of equilibrium in examining the conditions necessary to achieve an **equilibrium level of national income or output** within the goods market of an economy. Nevertheless, equilibrium is essentially a state towards which the economy is heading; the equilibrium will not necessarily be reached. It is more realistic to think of the economy as being in a state of **disequilibrium**, tending, in the absence of outside disturbances or 'shocks', towards the equilibrium level of national income. Essentially, national income and output will be in equilibrium when the **planned** or **intended aggregate money demand (AMD)** of all the economic agents in the economy in the current period equals the output (or income) produced in the previous period.

21.3 ESSENTIAL INFORMATION

1 A two-sector model of the economy

For the time being we shall construct a two-sector model of the goods market in the economy by pretending that there is no foreign trade and no government sector. We are assuming a **closed** economy in which **households** (or the personal sector) exercise **consumption demand** for final goods and services, and **firms** (or the **corporate sector**) demand **investment goods**. In this highly simplified economy, AMD is represented by the identity:

$$\text{(i) } AMD = C + I$$

This identity is essentially different from all the identities introduced in Unit 20. It is an **ex ante** identity defining **planned** or **intended** demand in the economy in terms of the consumption and investment intentions of households and firms. In contrast, the national expenditure identity in the economy is an **ex post** identity, measuring what has actually been spent on consumption and investment:

$$\text{(ii) } E \equiv C + I$$

We must now introduce theories to explain how and why households and firms make consumption and investment decisions. For the sake of simplicity we shall delay the discussion of theories of investment until Unit 23, for the time being assuming that the level of investment in the economy is given outside our model, at a level $\bar{I}$. We must, however, introduce a theory to explain how consumption decisions are made by households. Such a **behavioural theory**, which explains how consumption plans are formed, is called a **consumption function**.

2 The consumption function

(i) The pre-Keynesian consumption function In Unit 2 we constructed a micro-economic theory of demand for one particular good or service, where households or consumers choose between a large number of available goods and services. We saw that an important variable influencing the demand for a specific good or service is its price relative to the prices of all other goods and services. The micro-economic theory of demand can be expressed as the functional relationship:

$$Q_D = f(P), \text{ ceteris paribus}$$

When in contrast we construct a macro-economic consumption function we take the relative prices of goods as given, and concentrate attention instead on how household decisions are made to divide expenditure between **consumption** on all goods and services, and **saving**. The choice between consumption and saving is expressed by the identity:

$$\text{(iii) } Y \equiv C + S$$

Ex ante, the identity states that, at each level of income, planned consumption and saving must add up to equal the level of income. By rewriting the identity, we can define **planned savings** as being simply that part of income which households do not intend to spend on consumption:

$$\text{(iv)} \quad S \equiv Y - C$$

In the pre-Keynesian era, the predominant view was that the **rate of interest** was the main variable influencing the division of income between C and S. The pre-Keynesian savings and consumption functions can be written as:

$$\text{(v)} \quad S = f(r)$$
$$\text{and (vi)} \quad C = f(r)$$

The lower the rate of interest, the greater the consumption and the lower the saving at each level of income. Saving is a **positive function** and consumption a **negative function** of the rate of interest.

(ii) The Keynesian consumption function Keynes accepted that the rate of interest was a variable which influenced consumption decisions, but he believed that the **level of income** was a much more important influence. In general terms, we can write the Keynesian consumption function as:

$$\text{(vii)} \quad C = f(Y)$$

and, from identity (iii), the Keynesian saving function is:

$$\text{(viii)} \quad S = f(Y)$$

The essential features of the Keynesian consumption and savings functions are expressed in Keynes's own words in the *General Theory*:

'The fundamental psychological law, upon which we are entitled to depend with great confidence ..., is that men are disposed, as a rule and on average, to increase their consumption as their income increases, but not by as much as the increase in their income.'

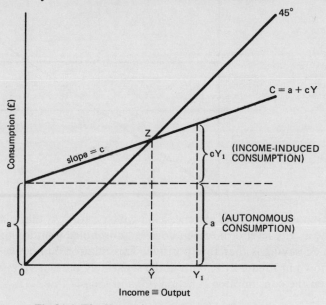

Fig 21.1 The Keynesian consumption function

Figure 21.1, which illustrates the Keynesian consumption function, also introduces the importance of the '45° line' in national income and expenditure models of the economy. Providing that the axes of the diagram are measuring in the same scale, a line drawn at 45° to origin locates all points at which output or income on the horizontal axis equals expenditure measured on the vertical axis.

Figure 21.1 also shows that planned consumption (C) is made of two elements:

(a) autonomous consumption This is the part of consumption which does not vary with the level of income. In Figure 21.1, autonomous consumption is equal to the vertical distance (a) at all levels of income.

(b) Income-induced consumption Because the consumption function in Figure 21.1 is drawn as a straight line (a **linear** consumption function) it can be expressed as the equation:

$$\text{(ix)} \quad C = a + cY$$

At any level of income, cY measures **income-induced** consumption, since an increase in income of $\triangle Y$ *induces* an increase in planned consumption equal to c $\triangle Y$. The greater the value of (c), the **steeper** will be the **slope** of the consumption function and the larger the increase in consumption resulting from an increase in income. In fact (c) is the measure of the **marginal propensity to consume**, a concept to which we shall shortly return.

In Figure 21.1, the consumption function crosses the 45° line at point Z, indicating that at the level of income $\hat{Y}$ households plan to consume all their income. At any level of income below $\hat{Y}$,

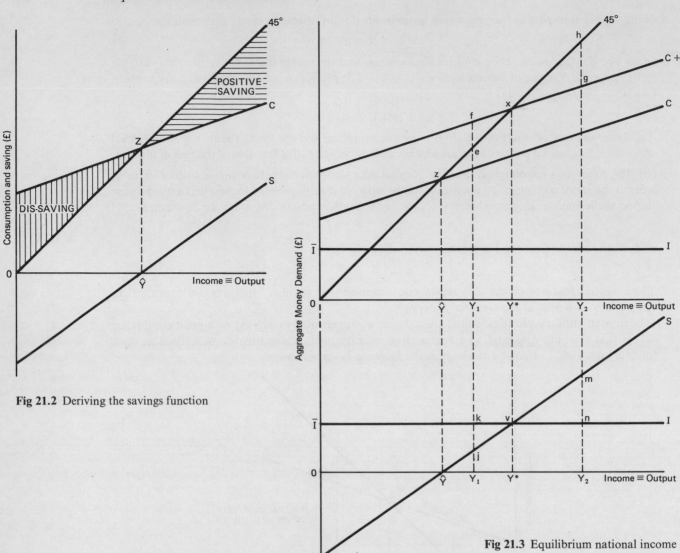

Fig 21.2 Deriving the savings function

Fig 21.3 Equilibrium national income

planned consumption is greater than income, from which it follows that planned saving must be negative! Similarly, at any level of income above Ŷ households plan to consume less than their income, and planned saving is therefore positive. This relationship between consumption and saving is clearly shown in Figure 21.2, both in the separately plotted savings function (S) and in the shading between the consumption function (C) and the 45° line.

3 The propensities to consume and save

In order properly to understand the Keynesian consumption and saving functions, it is necessary to introduce and define the propensities to consume and save:

(i) The average propensity to consume (APC) is the proportion of income which households plan to consume. (Formally, $APC \equiv \frac{C}{Y}$.) If income is £10 and households plan to consume £8, the APC is 0.8. When the APC is 0.8, the **average propensity to save** (APS) must be 0.2, since the APC and APS always add up to unity. In Figure 21.1, the APC falls as income rises, though total consumption of course rises. APC is greater than unity at all levels of income below Ŷ, equals unity at Ŷ, and falls below unity at levels of income above Ŷ. Conversely, the APS rises from negative to positive values as income rises, equalling zero at Ŷ.

(ii) The marginal propensity to consume (MPC) is the proportion of the **last** unit of income which households intend to consume. Formally, $MPC \equiv \frac{\triangle C}{\triangle Y}$ and $MPS \equiv \frac{\triangle S}{\triangle Y}$

Again, the MPC and the **marginal propensity to save** (MPS) must total unity. As we have already indicated, the **slope** (c) of the consumption function in Figure 21.1 is the marginal propensity to consume. In this diagram, the MPC is assumed to be constant at all levels of income. Since, however, the MPC is likely to decrease as income rises (though remaining between unity and zero), it would be more realistic to draw a consumption function whose slope diminishes at higher levels of income.

(iii) The relationship between the average and marginal propensity to consume Returning to our previous example in which household income is £10, planned consumption £8, and the APC 0.8, we shall now assume that if income increases by £1 to £11, planned consumption will rise by just 60 pence. The MPC is 0.6 and MPC < APC. The APC must now fall as income increases, in this case from 0.8 when income is £10 to 0.78 when income is £11. Since APC falls as income rises, it follows that the MPC must be less than the APC.

4 Equilibrium national income revisited

We can now represent our simple two-sector model of the economy in just three equations:

(ix) $C = a + cY$: The consumption function
(x) $I = \bar{I}$: Autonomous investment
(xi) $Y = C + I$: The equilibrium condition for the whole model

It is vital to avoid confusing the equilibrium condition $Y = C + I$ with accounting identities such as $Y \equiv C + S$, $E \equiv C + I$, and $AMD \equiv C + I$. At first sight they appear very similar, but the meanings are completely different! The accounting identities hold true at **all** levels of income, but, as we shall see, this is not the case with the equilibrium condition.

We can illustrate the concept of equilibrium national income in one of two ways, using either the upper or the lower panel of Figure 21.3. For the time being we shall refer only to the upper panel. The crucial difference between Figure 21.3 and our earlier diagrams is the inclusion of autonomous investment, $I = \bar{I}$, in the diagram. (Remember, we are treating investment as a constant, the value of which is determined outside our model.) Using the identity $AMD \equiv C + I$, we simply add autonomous investment (I) to consumption function (C) to obtain the AMD function (labelled $C + I$).

Let us now suppose that the level of income or output actually produced in the economy is Y_1. Making use of the property of the 45° line, we can also show this level of income or output by the vertical line Y_1e. At this level of income or output, aggregate demand, shown by the line Y_1f, is greater than the output available.

Thus, at income Y_1, $Y < C + I$. This is a **disequilibrium condition**, since the planned demand of the households and firms is greater than the output produced.

In a similar way we can show that a level of income such as Y_2 is also a disequilibrium level of income, since at income Y_2, $Y > C + I$, which again is a disequilibrium condition. At Y_2, actual output Y_2h exceeds aggregate demand Y_2g by the amount gh.

At Y_1, firms can only meet the planned demand in the immediate period by **destocking**, whereas at Y_2 they will experience **unintended stock accumulation**. Because, in each situation, demand differs from the output firms have actually produced, we now assume that firms react by changing the output they plan to produce in the next period. More precisely, we assume that firms react to destocking by increasing output to meet demand, and they react to unintended stock accumulation by reducing output. (For the time being we are also assuming that spare capacity exists so that firms can increase output, and that prices remain constant.)

If, when $Y < C + I$, firms increase output
and, when $Y > C + I$, firms decrease output,
it follows that only when $Y = C + I$ will output remain unchanged.

In Figure 21.3, national income is in equilibrium at Y^*, the only level of income where $Y = C + I$. Only at this level of income are the plans of the households and firms fulfilled and consistent with each other. At any other level of income or output, unintended destocking or stock accumulation creates an incentive for firms to change the level of output.

Figure 21.3 is an example of a **'Keynesian cross' diagram** in which equilibrium is determined at point x where the AMD or aggregate demand function crosses the 45° line. Sometimes the 45° line is represented as the **aggregate supply function** in the model, which means that the equilibrium condition can also be stated as:

aggregate demand = aggregate supply

Be sure to avoid confusing point x on the AMD function with point z on the consumption function. The equilibrium level of income is determined at x, whereas z merely determines the single level of income at which APC = 1!

5 Saving and Investment

The lower panel of Figure 21.3 illustrates an alternative way of stating the equilibrium condition of national income. You will notice that the equilibrium level of income Y^* is located where the savings function (S) crosses the investment function (I). Thus the equilibrium condition can be written as:

Planned Saving = Planned Investment

or (xii) $S = I$

It is important to stress that this statement of the equilibrium condition is merely an alternative to $Y = C + I$, adding nothing new to the model. This is shown when we derive equation (xii) by **substituting** the ex ante accounting identity (iii) into the equilibrium condition (xi):

substituting (iii) $Y \equiv C + S$
into   (xi) $Y = C + I$
we get $C + S = C + I$
or   (xii) $S = I$

Nevertheless this method of expressing the equilibrium condition possesses the advantage of showing that income is in equilibrium when **injections** of demand into the circular flow of income equal **leakages** or **withdrawals** of demand. In a simple two-sector model of the economy, saving is the only leakage and investment is the only injection. More generally we can write the equilibrium condition as:

Planned Leakages = Planned Injections

It is vital to avoid confusing the equilibrium condition $S = I$ with the **ex post identity** which states that **actual saving** will always equal **actual investment** whatever the level of income. Consider once again the level of income Y_2, but this time in the lower panel of Figure 21.3. Planned saving exceeds planned investment by the amount nm. You should notice that nm equals gh in the upper panel, which we earlier defined as **unintended stock accumulation** at this level of income. Actual investment at any level of income is defined by the identity:

(xiii) $I_{\text{ACTUAL}} \equiv I_{\text{PLANNED}} + I_{\text{UNPLANNED}}$

and unplanned investment occurs precisely when firms 'invest' in unsold stocks of finished goods. We can now explain why actual investment equals actual saving at the level of income Y_2, even though planned saving is greater than planned investment. In the first place, households are able to fulfil their savings plans, so actual saving equals planned saving. However, this creates the situation in which firms accumulate unsold stocks (resulting in unplanned investment) exactly equal to the excess of saving over planned investment! It follows from the way we have defined actual investment that actual savings and investment are equal. We shall leave it as an exercise for the reader to work out why the identity still holds at the income level Y_1 where destocking occurs and unplanned investment is negative.

6 The equilibrium condition in a four-sector economy

We shall complete the unit by extending our model in a very simple way to include a **government sector** and an **overseas** or **foreign trade sector**. Government spending (G) and overseas demand for the country's exports (X) represent additional injections of demand into the circular flow of income, whereas taxation (T) and import demand (M) are leakages. The AMD identity now becomes:

(xiv) $AMD \equiv C + I + G - T + X - M$

In order to keep the model as simple as possible, we shall treat the values of G, T, X and M as being **autonomously** determined outside the model, just as we have already treated I in this way. This is a highly artificial assumption since we might expect some at least of these components of aggregate demand to be related to the level of income. However, we shall delay relaxing this assumption until we examine the **multiplier theory** in Unit 22. We are also rather artificially assuming that households plan consumption decisions out of **pre-tax income** and that the level of taxation, T, is not determined by the level of income. In Unit 22 we see how the model changes when we assume that consumption decisions are made out of **post-tax disposable income**.

Since we are making the assumption that all the components of aggregate demand, with the exception of consumption, are autonomously determined outside the model, the AMD function drawn in Figure 21.4a has the **slope** of the consumption function (the MPC), and its position is determined by adding the values of I, G and X to, and subtracting the values of T and M from, the consumption function. The equilibrium condition for the model now becomes:

(xv) $Y = C + I + G - T + X - M$

or alternatively:

(xvi) $S + T + M = I + G + X$
    (leakages)   (injections)

As in the two-sector model of the economy, the equilibrium level of national income is depicted in Figure 21.4a and b at Y^*, where the AMD function crosses the 45° line.

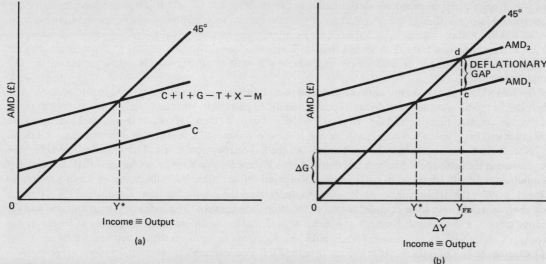

Fig 21.4 (a) Equilibrium national income in a four-sector economy
(b) Equilibrium national income and full employment equilibrium

7 Equilibrium National Income and Full Employment Equilibrium

Suppose that the equilibrium level of income Y* is insufficient to fully employ the available labour force in the economy. We can represent the size of national income or output which will employ all the labour force at Y_{FE} in Figure 21.4b. The existing level of aggregate demand represented by AMD_1 brings about an equilibrium level of national income at Y* rather than at Y_{FE}. In Keynesian terms, unemployment is caused by **deficient demand** in the economy. If any of the components of aggregate demand such as C, I, G or X autonomously increase, the **deflationary gap** between AMD_1 and AMD_2 might be closed, bringing about an equilibrium level of income at the full employment level.

Keynes, writing in the depression economy of the inter-war years, believed that the deficient demand was either caused in the first place, or certainly reinforced, by a **collapse** of private sector consumption and investment demand. (The tendency of households to save too much is called the **'paradox of thrift'**. According to the Keynesian view, saving, which is an individual virtue, becomes a vice in the economy as a whole if unemployment is caused by too little consumption. We shall examine Keynes's theory of deficient investment demand, the **marginal efficiency of capital** theory, in Unit 23.)

If Keynes was correct, it would be unwise to rely on an autonomous recovery in consumption and investment to close the deflationary gap and bring about full employment. Instead the government could deliberately use the **policy instruments** at its disposal, government spending (G) and taxation (T), to inject demand into the economy through a **budget deficit**. Essentially, the government **borrows** the excess savings of the private sector, which are injected back into the circular flow of income in public spending. This is the theoretical basis of **Keynesian demand management** or **discretionary fiscal policy**, used by the Keynesians to control the level of aggregate demand in the economy to a level consistent with achieving equilibrium national income at full employment.

21.4 LINKS WITH OTHER TOPICS

In the next three units we develop further important aspects of the Keynesian income/expenditure model of the economy. Unit 22 introduces the **multiplier theory** and investigates in more detail the relationship between a change in any of the components of aggregate demand and the resulting change in the equilibrium level of national income. This is followed in Unit 23 by the introduction of theories of investment into the model. Unit 24 extends the analysis to conditions of **excess demand** in the economy, **inflationary gaps** and the Keynesian **demand-pull** theory of inflation.

21.5 QUESTION PRACTICE

Essay Questions

Question 1 Distinguish the equilibrium level of National Income from the full employment level of National Income. Why may they differ?

(London: January, 1981)

Understanding the Question To answer the question you must firstly show an understanding of the meaning of the equilibrium level of national income. You can use any of the methods of writing the equilibrium condition, but it is probably best in this particular question to use $Y = C + I + G - T$. It is not necessary to introduce exports and imports, though the introduction of the government sector allows you to show how government policy can bring about equilibrium at the full employment level, assuming that the initial equilibrium was not at the full employment level. You should draw a 'Keynesian cross' diagram similar to those in the unit, to illustrate the deflationary or inflationary gap which will exist if equilibrium is below or above the full employment level.

To earn a high grade you must answer the second part of the question at some length, suggesting reasons why there can be too little or too much demand in the economy. In particular, you can explain how Keynes's theories of the consumption function and the marginal efficiency of capital (Unit 23) suggest that households may save too much and firms invest too little in a depressed economy, which settles into an underemployed equilibrium.

Not all economists agree that the equilibrium and the full employment levels of national income differ. We have noted in the introduction to both this unit and Unit 20 how the pre-Keynesians believed that the economy is automatically self-adjusting to a full employment equilibrium. After the publication of Keynes's *General Theory* in 1936, the debate continued. Properly to understand the debate between 'Keynes and the Classics', our analysis would have to be extended to the interrelationships between the goods and labour markets and the money market. For example, Keynes's opponents argued that in conditions of excess supply of labour prices would fall along with money wages. There would be a reduction in the transactions demand for money (Unit 16), causing the equilibrium rate of interest in turn to fall. If businessmen's investment decisions are responsive to the rate of interest, aggregate demand in the economy may now increase to close the deflationary gap. Thus market forces cure unemployment, and according to this view of 'how the economy works' Keynes's unemployment equilibrium is a special case in which wages and prices are inflexible downwards.

Answer plan

1 Explain the meaning of the equilibrium level of National Income, clearly stating the equilibrium conditions, and showing how the level of income or output will change towards the equilibrium if the condition is not met.
2 Draw a 'Keynesian cross' diagram to show equilibrium national income above or below the full employment level of income. Draw an aggregate demand function consistent with equilibrium at the full employment level, and indicate the inflationary or deflationary gap.
3 Explain the possible causes of excess or deficient demand in the economy.
4 Possibly discuss the fact that not all economists believe that the two concepts are different.

Question 2 If savings are always identical with investment in a closed economy, how can we refer to saving and investment having different values?

(SUJB: June 1979)

Understanding the Question The question is testing your understanding of the difference between **planned (intended** or **ex ante)** and **actual (realized** or **ex post)** saving and investment. You must show how and why actual investment always equals actual saving, whatever the level of income or output, but that in the absence of a government sector in a closed economy, planned investment will only equal planned saving at the equilibrium level of income. Explain how firms and households plan investment and saving decisions for essentially different reasons, and that in the Keynesian model it is the level of income or output which changes until the decisions are consistent with each other. You might also mention the classical loanable funds theory in which the rate of interest rises or falls until the supply of savings equals the demand for investment funds (see Unit 23).

Answer plan

1 Define savings and investment.
2 Distinguish between ex ante and ex post savings and investment.
3 Draw a diagram to show the savings and investment functions.
4 Explain how planned savings and investment decisions are made for different reasons and will not usually be equal.
5 Explain why actual or realized investment and savings are always equal – distinguish between planned and unplanned investment and their relation to actual investment.
6 In the Keynesian model of the economy, output or income rises or falls until planned saving equals planned investment: this is the equilibrium condition in the model.
7 Perhaps introduce the role of the rate of interest as an alternative explanation of how planned saving equates with planned investment.

Multiple Choice Questions

Questions 3, 4 and 5

Assertion		Reason
3 The marginal propensity to consume usually increases with income.	because	People usually consume more as their incomes rise.
4 An increased budget surplus (given constant government expenditure) will have a deflationary effect.	because	Given constant government expenditure, an increased budget surplus will reduce aggregate demand.
5 Other things being equal, an increase in the propensity to import will reduce the level of national income.	because	Imports represent a leakage from the circular flow of income.

(a) Both the assertion and the reason are true statements and the reason is a correct explanation of the assertion.
(b) Both the assertion and the reason are true statements but the reason is not a correct explanation of the assertion.
(c) The assertion is true but the reason is a false statement.
(d) The assertion is false but the reason is a true statement.

Understanding the Questions The answer to question 4 is **(d)**. This question tests your understanding of the relationship between total and marginal consumption. According to Keynes's theory of aggregate consumption, total planned consumption increases with income, but less than proportionately. Therefore the marginal propensity to consume decreases as income rises.

The correct answer to both question 5 and question 6 is **(a)**. An increased budget surplus represents a leakage of demand from the circular flow of income, causing the AMD curve to shift downwards. A similar effect occurs in the case of question 6, but with one notable difference. The **slope** of the AMD curve reflects the marginal propensities to consume, import (and tax) in the economy – although in the diagrams in the unit we dealt only with the marginal propensity to consume. Therefore an increase in the marginal propensity to import will reduce the slope of the AMD curve, shifting the curve downwards at all positive levels of income.

Data Response Questions

Question 6 Consider a closed economy, where investment expenditure is £310 million, government expenditure is £200 million, income tax is set at 30 per cent and consumption expenditure is 70 per cent of disposable income (i.e. income after deduction of tax).

(*a*) Calculate:
  (i) the equilibrium level of national income;
  (ii) the government budget surplus or deficit at the equilibrium level of income.

(*b*) The Chancellor of the Exchequer now halves the rate of income tax. Assuming nothing else alters, calculate

  (i) the new equilibrium level of national income;
  (ii) the new budget surplus or deficit at the new equilibrium level of income.

(SUJB: June 1980)

Understanding the Question (a) (i) You should start off your answer by clearly stating the equilibrium condition specified in the model indicated by the question:

$$Y = c(Y - T) + I + G$$
$$\text{or} \quad Y = c(Y - tY) + I + G$$

where c is the marginal propensity to consume and t is the marginal rate of taxation. The next stage is to substitute into the equilibrium condition the information presented in the question:

$$Y = 0.7(Y - 0.3Y) + £310m + £200m$$
$$\text{or} \quad Y = 0.7(0.7Y) + £310m + £200m$$
$$\text{or} \quad Y = 0.49Y + £310m + £200m$$

We can now gather all the Y terms on the left-hand side of the equilibrium condition:

$$Y - 0.49Y = £310m + £200m$$
$$\text{or} \quad 0.51Y = £510m$$

Finally, you should solve this equation to find the equilibrium value of Y. The answer turns out to be a neat round number. It is important to show all the stages of your working: in this type of question, most of the marks are awarded for economic understanding rather than for exactness of calculation.

(a) (ii) The budget deficit (or surplus) is shown by the identity:

$$\text{Budget deficit} \equiv G - T$$
$$\text{or} \quad \text{Budget deficit} \equiv G - tY$$

To calculate the answer (which turns out to be a budget surplus), simply substitute the values of G and t, and the equilibrium value of Y from your previous answer, into the identity.

(b) Simply repeat your calculations. You will note, however, that the calculations no longer produce a round number, and that the budget is now in deficit.

21.6 FURTHER READING

Stanlake, G. F., *Macro-economics: an Introduction*, 2nd edition (Longmans, 1979)
Chapter 4: Output, Demand and Equilibrium
Chapter 5: Consumption
Chapter 7: The Determination of Equilibrium
Chapter 8: Output and Employment

Lipsey, R. G., *An Introduction to Positive Economics*, 5th edition (Weidenfeld & Nicolson, 1979)
Chapter 32: The Circular Flow of Income and the Concept of National Income
Chapter 33: The Determination of National Income
Chapter 35: The Consumption Function
Chapter 38: Government and the Circular Flow of Income

22 The Multiplier

22.1 POINTS OF PERSPECTIVE

In this unit we develop an important aspect of the Keynesian national income/expenditure model of the economy which we introduced in Units 20 and 21. In Unit 21 we explained that when aggregate money demand (AMD) is greater (or less) than the income or output produced in the previous period, national income will rise (or fall) until an equilibrium is reached when AMD equals the available output. We now introduce the **multiplier theory** and investigate in more detail the process by which income or output changes when an autonomous change occurs in any of the components of aggregate demand.

The concept of the multiplier was first developed in 1931 by R. F. Kahn, who at the time was a colleague and former pupil of Keynes at Cambridge. The early theory was essentially an **employment multiplier**, which modelled how a change in public investment, for example in road-building, might cause a subsequent multiple expansion of employment. Keynes first made use of Kahn's employment multiplier in 1933 when he discussed the effects of an increase in government spending of £500, a sum assumed to be just sufficient to employ one man for one year in the construction of public works. Keynes wrote: 'If the new expenditure is additional and not merely in substitution for other expenditure, the increase of employment does not stop there. The additional wages and other incomes paid out are spent on additional purchases, which in turn lead to further employment... the newly employed who supply the increased purchases of those employed on the new capital works will, in their turn, spend more, thus adding to the employment of others; and so on.'

By the time of the publication in 1936 of Keynes's famous *General Theory*, the multiplier had become a vital part of Keynes's explanation of how an economy can settle into an **underemployment equilibrium**. In the *General Theory*, Keynes focused attention on the **investment multiplier**, explaining how a collapse in investment and business confidence can cause a multiple contraction of output. From this, it was only a short step to suggest how the **government spending multiplier** might be used to reverse the process. Analytically, in terms of the Keynesian expenditure/income model of the goods market in the economy, an increase in public spending which is unaccompanied by an increase in taxation has an identical expansionary effect to an autonomous increase in investment. Indeed, nowadays the concept of the **National Income multiplier** is used as a generic term to include the multiplier effects which result from a change in **any** of the components of demand. Thus the **autonomous consumption multiplier**, the **investment multiplier**, the **government spending multiplier**, and various forms of **tax** and **foreign trade multipliers** are all examples of specific National Income multipliers. At a local level, the **regional multiplier**, which we briefly mentioned in Unit 13, is sometimes identified. A regional multiplier indicates by how much regional income or output will increase when additional demand is injected into the regional economy. However, the **money multiplier** discussed in Units 16 and 19 should not be classified amongst the Keynesian or National Income multipliers, though its existence serves to illustrate that multiplier effects occur whenever a change in one variable cause **multiple and successive** stages of change in another variable. Indeed, if fiscal and monetary policy are interdependent, an increase in government spending can result in simultaneous fiscal and monetary multiplier effects.

22.2 UNDERLYING CONCEPTS

1 The dynamic multiplier

It is often forgotten that the multiplier process is essentially a dynamic process which takes place over a considerable period of time. In order to illustrate this, we shall continue to adopt for the time being the assumptions of Unit 21: namely that the values of all the components of aggregate demand, with the exception of consumption, are determined autonomously. Only the consumption decisions of households are related to level of income through the marginal propensity to consume (MPC). We shall assume that the MPC is 0.8 at all levels of income, which of course means that the marginal propensity to save (MPS) must be 0.2. Saving is the only income-related **leakage** of demand in the economy. Whenever income increases by £10, consumption spending increases by £8, and £2 is saved. Finally, we shall assume that prices remain constant in the economy and that a margin of spare capacity and unemployed labour exists which the government wishes to reduce.

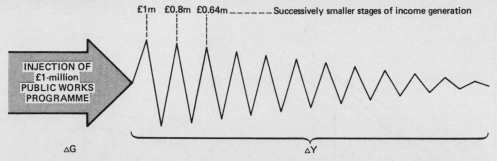

Fig 22.1 The multiplier process when the marginal propensity to consume is 0.8

Suppose that the government now increases public spending by £1 million, but keeps taxation at its existing level. The government could, for example, decide to increase **transfer incomes** such as pensions, welfare benefits and unemployment pay, or even aid to industry. Alternatively, the government might invest in **public works** or **social capital**, for example in road construction. Figure 22.1 illustrates that the increase in public spending represents an initial increase in incomes for the factors of production who are now employed in the construction scheme. At the second stage, demand for goods and services produced largely by the private sector will increase when the households employed in the public works spend 0.8 of their increase in income on consumption, in total £800 000. Further stages of income generation then occur, with each succeeding stage being smaller than the previous one. In our particular model, each successive stage is exactly 0.8 of the previous stage because the MPC is 0.8 at all levels of income and saving is the only income-induced leakage. Assuming that nothing else changes in the time it takes for the process to work through, the eventual increase in income resulting from the initial injection is the sum of all the stages of income generation.

$$\text{The value of the government spending multiplier} = \frac{\text{change in income}}{\text{change in government spending}}$$

$$\text{or } k = \frac{\triangle Y}{\triangle G}$$

where k is the symbol for the government spending multiplier. Providing that saving is the only leakage of demand, the value of k depends upon the marginal propensity to consume. In fact, the formula for the multiplier in this model is

$$k = \frac{1}{1-c} \text{ where c is the MPC}$$

$$\text{or } k = \frac{1}{s} \text{ where s is the MPS}$$

The larger the MPC (and the smaller the MPS), the larger is the value of the multiplier. In our model, the value of the multiplier is 5 (i.e. $\frac{1}{1-0.8}$), indicating that the initial increase in public spending will subsequently increase income by £5 million in total.

We have stressed the dynamic nature of the multiplier process in order to emphasize that the economy is likely to be in a permanent state of **disequilibrium**. It is wrong and artificial to imply that the multiplier is an instantaneous process, involving a move from one equilibrium level of national income to another. Not only does the process take time; it is also very likely that the economy will experience the 'outside shock' of an autonomous change in one or other of the components of aggregate demand while the multiplier process is working through. It is useful to think of the economy as **tending** towards an equilibrium as the multiplier process works through, yet unlikely to reach a state of equilibrium because of the renewed impact of 'outside shocks'.

2 The comparative static multiplier

Figure 22.2 illustrates the multiplier concept in terms of the change in the level of AMD necessary to change the equilibrium level of national income from one **static equilibrium** to another. Since saving is the only income-induced leakage of demand from the economy, the slope of the AMD function depends on the value of the MPC. An initial equilibrium level of income, Y_1, is determined by the level of aggregate demand AMD_1. When the MPC is 0.6, as in Figure 22.2a, an injection of government spending shown by $\triangle G$ increases the equilibrium level of income to Y_2. The change in income from one equilibrium level to another, $\triangle Y$, is two and a half times the change in government spending. However, a comparison of the equilibria indicates nothing about the length of the time path from one equilibrium to the other. The slope of the AMD function is less, and the MPC is smaller in Figure 22.2b. Thus the multiplier is also smaller, equal to 1.25 when the MPC is 0.2.

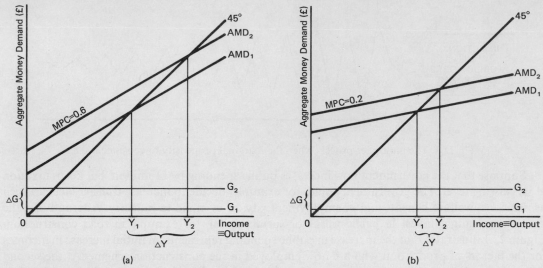

Fig 22.2 How the size of the multiplier is determined by the marginal propensity to consume (a) MPC = 0.6 (b) MPC = 0.2

22.3 ESSENTIAL INFORMATION

1 The simple multiplier

Our purpose is to show that there is **no unique formulation** for the multiplier; as we change the assumptions of our model, treating taxation and import demand as income-related, we shall arrive at different formulas for the relevant multiplier. Firstly, however, we shall restate the elementary multiplier in a model of the economy in which all the components of aggregate demand except consumption are **autonomously** determined outside the model.

Equation (i) is a behavioural equation showing the consumption function, and equations (ii) to (vi) depict the other components of aggregate demand, which are autonomous:

$$\text{(i) } C = a + cY, \text{ where c is the MPC.}$$
$$\text{(ii) } I = \bar{I} \qquad : \text{investment}$$
$$\text{(iii) } G = \bar{G} \qquad : \text{government spending}$$
$$\text{(iv) } T = \bar{T} \qquad : \text{taxation}$$
$$\text{(v) } X = \bar{X} \qquad : \text{exports}$$
$$\text{(vi) } M = \bar{M} \qquad : \text{imports}$$

The equilibrium condition for the model is:

$$\text{(vii) } Y = C + I + G - T + X - M$$
$$\text{or (viii) } Y = a + cY + \bar{I} + \bar{G} - \bar{T} + \bar{X} - \bar{M}$$

Since saving is the only income-induced leakage of demand, the simple multiplier in this model is $\frac{1}{1-c}$ or $\frac{1}{s}$, where s is the marginal propensity to save. If for example private investment changes by $\triangle I$, or government spending changes by $\triangle G$, then the resulting change in the level of income, $\triangle Y$, is represented by

$$\text{(ix) } \triangle Y = \frac{1}{1-c} (\triangle I) \text{ in the case of the change in investment;}$$

and by (x) $\triangle Y = \frac{1}{1-c} (\triangle G)$ when government spending changes. The formulas of the investment and government spending multipliers are identical.

2 The tax multiplier

If we assume that households make consumption decisions out of **post-tax disposable income** rather than out of pre-tax income, a different formula emerges for the **tax multiplier**. We can now write the equilibrium condition as:

$$\text{(xi) } Y = a + c(Y - \bar{T}) + \bar{I} + \bar{G} + \bar{X} - \bar{M}$$
$$\text{or (xii) } Y = a + cY - c\bar{T} + \bar{I} + \bar{G} + \bar{X} - \bar{M}$$

Following an autonomous change in taxation equal to $\triangle T$, the change in income, $\triangle Y$, is represented by:

(xiii) $\triangle Y = \dfrac{1}{1-c} \triangle(-cT)$

or (xiv) $\triangle Y = \dfrac{-c}{1-c}(\triangle T)$

where $\dfrac{-c}{1-c}$ is the tax multiplier.

This expression tells us two important things about the tax multiplier. In the first place, it is **negative**, which means that an autonomous **increase** in taxation results in a **fall** in the equilibrium level of income, the size of the fall being a multiple of the absolute change in taxation. Secondly, since the value of c (the MPC) is less than unity, the value of the tax multiplier in this model is **always** less than the value of the government spending multiplier $\dfrac{1}{1-c}$. For example, if the MPC is 0.8, the government spending multiplier $\dfrac{1}{1-c}$ will be 5, and the tax multiplier $\dfrac{-c}{1-c}$ will be 4. As an exercise, you might calculate the size of the two multipliers for other values of the MPC. Whatever the chosen value of the MPC, you will find that the absolute size of the government spending multiplier (forgetting the plus and minus signs) is always equal to the tax multiplier plus one! Thus a given increase in tax revenue has a smaller multiplier effect than a similar change in government spending. The explanation for this lies in the fact that disposable income falls by an amount equal to the size of the tax increase, but since part of disposable income is saved, spending does not fall by the full amount of the increase in taxation. In the initial stage of the multiplier effect, the change in spending is $-c\triangle T$ rather than $-\triangle T$. Summing all the successive stages of the multiplier process, the total change in spending and income equals $\dfrac{-c}{1-c}(\triangle T)$ rather than $\dfrac{-1}{1-c}(\triangle T)$.

3 The Balanced Budget multiplier

Now let us suppose that the government decides to increase public spending and taxation by equal amounts, so that $\triangle G = \triangle T$. The combined multiplier effects of $\triangle G$ and $\triangle T$ are shown by:

(xv) $\triangle Y = \dfrac{1}{1-c}(\triangle G) + \dfrac{-c}{1-c}(\triangle T)$

Since $\triangle G = \triangle T$, we can rewrite this as:

(xvi) $\triangle Y = (\dfrac{1}{1-c} + \dfrac{-c}{1-c})\triangle G$

or (xvii) $\triangle Y = (\dfrac{1-c}{1-c})\triangle G$

The expression $\dfrac{1-c}{1-c}$ is the **balanced budget multiplier**, which must be 1. This means that an increase in public spending financed by an equal increase in taxation has an expansionary effect on the level of income exactly equal to the size of the injection of public spending. (If you find the algebra difficult, you can note from the previous section that when, for example, the MPC is 0.8, the government spending multiplier is 5, and the tax multiplier is -4. The balanced budget multiplier is simply the addition of the two multipliers; in this case $5 + (-4) = 1$!)

4 Taxation and Import leakages

Up to this point in the analysis we have treated taxation and import demand in a highly artificial way. We have assumed that they are unrelated to the level of income, being determined instead **exogenously** outside our model. This is unrealistic, since a part at least of both taxation and import demand are likely to be dependent on the level of income. For the sake of simplicity, we shall now assume that **all** of taxation and import demand are **income-induced**, being determined **endogenously** within our model in the following ways:

(xviii) $T = tY$, where t is the marginal rate of taxation

and (xix) $M = mY$, where m is the marginal propensity to import.

We can write the equilibrium condition for the new version of our model as:

(xx) $Y = a + cY + \bar{I} + \bar{G} - tY + \bar{X} - mY$

In this particular model the multiplier is:

$$k = \dfrac{1}{1-c+t+m}$$

or $k = \dfrac{1}{s+t+m}$

The three income-induced leakages of demand in the model all affect the value of the multiplier. The greater the propensity to import, and the higher the rate of taxation, the smaller will be the multiplier effect resulting from a change in any of the autonomous components of demand. There is no such thing as a *unique* formulation of the multiplier, relevant to all the possible models we could specify. In general terms, however, the government spending or investment multiplier will be:

$$k = \frac{1}{\text{marginal change in income-induced leakages}}$$

5 The multiplier and economic policy

(i) Keynesian demand management In earlier units we briefly explained how Keynesians have advocated the use of **discretionary fiscal policy** to control or influence the level of **aggregate demand** in the economy. The greater the size of the government spending multiplier, the smaller the increase in public spending which is needed to bring about a desired increase in money national income. Similarly, the larger the tax multiplier, the smaller the tax cut which would be necessary. If the multipliers are large, and if most of the increase in money national income is in real output rather than in the price level, **fiscal policy** will be an effective way of controlling the economy.

But, as we have explained, the marginal propensity to import and high marginal tax rates reduce the size of the multiplier. The British economy is relatively small, compared for example with the USA, and open to trade. In recent years the propensity to import has noticeably increased. It is very doubtful whether the government spending multiplier is much higher than 1, and indeed, as we shall shortly explain, it may be less than 1.

(ii) Monetarism and 'crowding out' We have also indicated that the multiplier effect resulting from an increase in government spending will be greatest when taxation remains unchanged. According to this logic a government should deliberately increase the size of the budget deficit if it wishes to maximize the expansionary effects of an increase in public spending. However, our analysis has ignored the **monetary effects** of the widening budget deficit. It is precisely upon these **monetary effects of fiscal policy** that monetarists concentrate attention, arguing:

(a) That increased borrowing to finance the budget deficit causes interest rates to rise. Higher interest rates reduce private investment, thereby countering the expansionary effects of the increase in public spending. The net size of the multiplier may even be zero if the increase in public spending 'crowds out' and displaces an equal amount of private spending. Indeed 'extreme' monetarists have gone further, arguing that fiscal multipliers can be negative in the long run if 'productive' private investment is crowded out by 'unproductive' public spending. It is worth noting that the 'crowding out' view of 'modern' monetarists is by no means new – it is essentially a revival of the old 'Treasury view' against which Keynes personally argued in the early 1930s.

(b) In so far as a multiplier results from an increase in public spending financed by a budget deficit, the main effect may be on prices rather than on real income or output. Monetarists argue that expansionary fiscal policy will increase the rate of inflation if the budget deficit and PSBR are financed by methods which increase the money supply. Keynesians agree that fiscal stimulation can lead to inflation rather than an expansion of real output if the economy is at or near full capacity and full employment. The area of dispute between Keynesians and monetarists is whether the government spending multiplier will expand real output or prices when there is a considerable margin of spare capacity in the economy.

(iii) Fiscal policy multipliers We have already noted that the taxation multiplier is likely to be smaller than the government spending multiplier. However, there may also be variations in the nature of the multiplier depending on whether an increase in public spending is channelled into **public works** or **transfer incomes** and on whether changes in taxation involve **direct** or **indirect** taxation. In times of mass unemployment and gravely deficient demand, public works may be an effective fiscal policy instrument since:
(a) they can be directed to regions of especially high local unemployment;
(b) by providing lasting **social capital**, they can improve a region's economic infrastructure and create an environment attractive to private investment;
(c) the government is seen to be 'doing something about unemployment' – public works are likely to employ large numbers of manual workers;
(d) public works are not 'import intensive'; a large fraction of the initial injection of income is spent on the outputs of domestic industry, thereby increasing the size of the multiplier.

However, public works are not a very suitable policy instrument for the discretionary management of demand at or near the full employment level. Public works are slow to start, difficult to stop, and altogether difficult to 'fine-tune'. **Discretionary tax changes** may be more appropriate for controlling demand, except perhaps in conditions of very high unemployment. The multiplier effect of a tax change occurs through its impact on private sector consumption and investment. However, the size of the effect will be reduced if the propensity to import is high. As an alternative to both public works and tax cuts, a government can expand demand by increasing public spending in the form of **transfer incomes** paid to lower income groups, or even by re-distributing the existing level of public spending through greater transfers. The **transfer income multiplier** tends to be larger than other fiscal multipliers because the poor have higher propensities to consume and lower propensities to import than the better-off. Nevertheless, it is not usually practicable to raise and lower the level of welfare benefits and unemployment pay as a part of discretionary demand management. Instead, transfer incomes such as supplementary benefit, which form a state 'safety net' for the poor, act as an **automatic stabilizer** dampening or reducing the multiplier effects which result when 'outside shocks' hit the economy. As incomes fall, the increase in the total volume of transfer incomes paid to the unemployed and the poor reduces the total contraction in income and demand. Similarly, the **'means-tested'** nature of many transfer incomes and the progressive nature of income tax create an automatic stabilizer which reduces the multiple expansion that follows an injection of demand into the economy. As the economy approaches full employment, fewer people qualify for transfer incomes and the proportion of income paid in taxation increases. The volume of public spending falls while that of taxation rises.

22.4 Links with other topics

The multiplier theory is very closely related to the concept of equilibrium national income examined in Unit 21. In particular, you should refer to the discussion of **deflationary gaps** (in Unit 21) and **inflationary gaps** (Unit 24), which illustrate how the size of the multiplier determines the level of government spending needed to achieve equilibrium national income at the full employment level, without inflation. In Unit 23 we now go on to contrast the **accelerator principle** with the multiplier, showing how the two concepts can be brought together in **dynamic Keynesian models of economic growth** and of the **business cycle**. In Unit 25 we reintroduce the contrast between the Keynesian and monetarist views on the size and effectiveness of the government spending multiplier.

22.5 Question practice

Essay Questions

Question 1 Explain carefully what is meant by the multiplier. Show how the multiplier concept can be extended from a closed economy with no government sector to an open economy with a government sector.

(AEB: June 1981)

Understanding the Question We have described in the unit how the nature of the multiplier is largely dependent on the number of income-induced leakages of demand from the economy. If saving is the only leakage, the investment multiplier is $\frac{1}{s}$, but if marginal rates of taxation and a marginal propensity to import are introduced into the model of the economy, the multiplier becomes $\frac{1}{s+t+m}$. Alternatively, as we shall show in more detail in Question 5, the multiplier is $\frac{1}{s+ct+m}$ if consumption decisions are made out of **post-tax disposable income** rather than out of pre-tax income. More generally, the multiplier is $\frac{1}{\text{marginal change in income-induced leakages}}$. Since total leakages are likely to be greater in an open economy with a government sector than in a closed economy with no government, the multiplier is likely to be smaller than in the simple model of a two-sector economy.

Answer plan

1 Define the national income multiplier as the convergent expansion or contraction of income or output which occurs as the economy adjusts to a change in **any** of the autonomous components of demand or expenditure.
2 Show how the size of the multiplier in a closed economy with no government sector depends on the size of the MPC (or MPS).
3 Explain how more generally the size of the multiplier is determined by all the income-induced leakages of demand. The introduction of income-induced taxation and import demand reduces the size of the multiplier.

Multiple Choice Questions

Questions 2 and 3 Questions 2 and 3 refer to the following data.

Income (Y)	Consumption (C)	Saving (S)
0	150	− 150
100	220	− 120
200	290	− 90
300	360	− 60
400	430	− 30
500	500	0
600	570	30
700	640	60
800	710	90
900	780	120
1000	850	150

Question 2 Which of the following formulas represents the consumption schedule in the table above?

(a) $150 + 0.3Y$
(b) $150 + 0.7Y$
(c) $150 + 0.8Y$
(d) $- 150 + 0.3Y$

Question 3 In this example, the investment multiplier is:

(a) 0.7
(b) 3.33
(c) 1.43
(d) 0.3

Understanding the Questions Question 2 puts into numerical form the Keynesian consumption function of Units 21 and 22: $C = a + cY$. Autonomous consumption, which is unrelated to the level of income, is measured by a, whereas income-induced consumption is represented by cY. The marginal propensity to consume is c. According to the consumption schedule in the question, autonomous consumption is 150. (Thus alternative (d) must be wrong.) The schedule also indicates that the proportion of the additional income at each stage which is spent on consumption is 0.7. Thus the correct expression for the consumption function is $150 + 0.7Y$ (alternative (b)). The value of the MPC (0.7) can then be used to calculate the size of the investment multiplier.

By applying the multiplier formula $k = \dfrac{1}{1-c}$, we get: $\dfrac{1}{1-0.7}$ or $\dfrac{1}{0.3}$, which equals 3.33: alternative (b) in Question 3.

Data Response Questions

Question 4 In an economy the following values occur:

Consumption	$= 0.8Y$ Disposable
Net Investment	$= 260$
Government spending	$= 400$
Exports	$= 300$
Imports	$= 0.2Y$
Income Tax	$= 0.5\ Y$ (there are no indirect taxes)
$Y = $ National Income.	

(a) At what level of National Income will equilibrium occur?   [4]

(b) Because of unemployment the government wishes to increase total spending by 600. By how much must it increase its own spending to achieve this?   [4]

(c) What will this do
  (i) to the budgetary position;   [3]
  (ii) to the Balance of Payments?   [3]

(d) Explain, with aid of a diagram, the meaning of the term *deflationary gap*.   [6]

(SUJB: June 1981)

Understanding the Question

(a) The equilibrium condition for this particular model is.

$$Y = 0.8(Y - 0.5Y) + 260 + 400 + 300 - 0.2Y$$

where the marginal propensity to consume out of disposable income is 0.8, the marginal rate of income tax is 0.5, and the marginal propensity to import is 0.2. Solving the equation gives the equilibrium level of national income at 1200.

(b) We can calculate the change in government spending which will increase total income, output and expenditure by exactly 600 if we know the size of the multiplier. We have not explained in the main body of the unit precisely how the multiplier formula is derived from the equilibrium condition for national income, except to say that

$$k = \frac{1}{\text{marginal change in income-induced leakages}}$$

We shall now take the opportunity provided by this question to show in detail how the multiplier formula is derived in any particular national income model.

Representing the marginal propensity to consume out of disposable income as c, the marginal rate of income tax as t, and the marginal propensity to import as m, we can rewrite the equilibrium condition in general form as:

(i) $Y = c(Y - tY) + I + G + X - mY$

or (ii) $Y = cY - ctY + I + G + X - mY$

If we collect all the Y terms on the left-hand side of the equation, we get:

(iii) $Y - cY + ctY + mY = I + G + X$

or (iv) $Y(1 - c + ct + m) = I + G + X$

Dividing both sides of the equation by the expression in brackets, we get:

(v) $Y = \dfrac{1}{1 - c + ct + m}(I + G + X)$

The expression $\dfrac{1}{1 - c + ct + m}$ is the multiplier in this particular model.

Since c is the marginal propensity to consume, the multiplier can also be expressed as: $\dfrac{1}{s + ct + m}$, where s is the marginal propensity to save. This is the multiplier formula for an economy in which decisions to consume and save are made out of *post-tax disposable income*. If, in contrast, consumption and savings decisions were made out of *pre-tax* income, the multiplier would be $\dfrac{1}{s + t + m}$. (We introduced this multiplier earlier in the unit.) Since the MPC (c) is less than one, the value of ct must be less than the value of t. Hence the multiplier is larger when consumption decisions are made out of post-tax income because the leakages of demand are smaller.

Solving the expression $\dfrac{1}{s + ct + m}$, the value of the multiplier is 1.25. Therefore:

$\Delta Y = \dfrac{1}{s + ct + m}(\Delta G)$

or $600 = 1.25\,(\Delta G)$

or $\Delta G = \dfrac{600}{1.25}$

$\Delta G = 480$

Alternatively, you can obtain the correct answer by substituting the value of the new equilibrium level of national income (1800) into the equilibrium condition and solve the equation to find the level of government spending at the new equilibrium:

$1800 = 0.8(1800 - 0.5(1800)) + 260 + G + 300 - 0.2(1800)$

or $G = 1800 - 0.8(1800 - 0.5(1800)) - 260 - 300 + 0.2(1800)$

When G is calculated in this way, you must of course remember to subtract the original level of government spending (400) from the new level determined by the solution of this equation.

(c) Calculate the size of taxation and the level of imports at the original equilibrium level of income (1200) and work out whether the budget and the Balance of Payments are respectively in surplus or in deficit. Repeat the exercise at the new equilibrium level of Y(1800) and note the changes in both balances.

(d) Draw a 45° line diagram similar to Figure 21.4b in Unit 21, clearly labelling the deflationary gap and explaining its meaning.

Question 5 Recorded below are some figures for a hypothetical economy

		Weeks			
	1	2	3	4	n
1 Output (= income)	100	90	82	75.6	50
2 Investment	10	10	10	10	10
3 Consumption goods produced (= consumption goods demanded in previous week)	90	80	72	65.6	40
4 Planned (ex-ante) savings (= 20% of row 1)	20	18	16.4	15.1	10
5 Consumption goods demanded (= 80% of row 1)	80	72	65.6	65.5	40
6 Excess supply (= row 3 minus row 5)	10	8	6.4	5.1	 0
7 Planned savings minus planned investment (= row 4 minus row 2)	10	8	6.4	5.1	 0

(Source: W. Beckerman, *An Introduction to National Income Analysis*, Weidenfeld & Nicolson, 1968.)

(*a*) Specify and briefly explain the process which is at work over time in the case of the above economy.

(*b*) The last column on the right shows the values of the variables for a National Income equilibrium.

  (i) What assumptions are necessary for this equilibrium to be reached?

  (ii) When will the equilibrium be reached?

(London: June 1981)

Understanding the Question

(a) The data in the question illustrate how the **national income multiplier** or **investment multiplier** (the process to be specified) is a dynamic process through successively smaller stages of income and expenditure expansion, or in this case contraction.

Explain how in the first week planned saving exceeds planned investment, causing a leakage of demand or expenditure from the economy. In week 2, income equals the value of output sold in week 1. The marginal propensities to consume and save out of income are indicated as 0.8 and 0.2 respectively at all levels of income. Therefore, in week 2 planned saving continues to exceed planned investment, but by less than in week 1. The multiple contraction of income, output and expenditure continues until, in week n, planned saving equals planned investment (and planned consumption and investment equal the output available).

(b) (i) The model assumes that saving is the only leakage of demand in the economy. This particular equilibrium would not be reached if the marginal change in income-induced leakages was greater than the marginal propensity to save, or indeed if the MPS varied with the level of income. It is also assumed that investment is the only autonomous component of demand, and that the level of autonomous investment remains unchanged as the multiplier process works through between weeks 1 and n.

(ii) You are not expected to state the answer to the question in terms of a precise number of weeks. In fact, in the dynamic multiplier process there are an infinite number of successive stages of income and expenditure generation (or contraction), each stage being smaller than the previous stage. The size of each successive stage tends towards zero as n becomes larger and larger. In the question, week n is therefore the time period when any further contractions of income are so small that we can ignore them, when income and expenditure have converged approximately to the equilibrium value of 50 at which planned saving equals planned investment.

22.6 FURTHER READING

Stanlake, G. F., *Macro-Economics, an Introduction,* 2nd edition (Longmans, 1979).
Chapter 7: The Determination of Equilibrium
Chapter 8: Output and Employment

Livesey, F., *A Textbook of Economics* (Polytech Publishers, 1978).
Chapter 8: Total Expenditure Revisited.

23 Investment

23.1 POINTS OF PERSPECTIVE

In developing the simple Keynesian model of Units 21 and 22, we assumed that the level of **planned** or **intended investment demand** in the economy is **autonomous** or independent of the level of income or output currently being produced. Since this is obviously a gross oversimplification, we shall devote most of this unit to an explanation and brief comparison of a number of **theories of investment**. Economists generally agree that investment decisions are made by businessmen for a variety of different reasons. Consequently there is no 'correct' investment theory; instead, each theory may explain a different and relevant aspect of how investment decisions are made. However, our general conclusion will be that a large part of investment is indeed autonomous of the level of income, being determined by factors such as the cost of borrowing (the **rate of interest**), **expectations** about future profitability, the **relative prices** of capital and labour, and the nature of **technical progress**. Nevertheless, a certain part of investment may indeed be related to the level of income, and more particularly to the **rate of change of income**, via the **acceleration principle**.

23.2 UNDERLYING CONCEPTS

1 The different types of investment

We have explained in Unit 11 how economists distinguish between saving and investment. Investment involves the demand for, and expenditure on, **capital goods** capable of producing more income and wealth in the future. **Domestic investment** includes the purchase of new capital equipment and buildings – the **fixed capital formation** of Unit 20 – and also the accumulation in the form of **stockbuilding** of increased stocks of raw materials, work-in-progress and finished goods. Whilst the purchase of **financial claims** such as shares or debentures are not in themselves regarded as a part of domestic investment, the acquisition of paper claims on other countries is an important part of **overseas investment**, additional to the direct purchase of physical assets overseas. To the extent that they are not offset by counter-claims held by foreigners, increased holdings of foreign currencies and of foreign customers' trade debts to British exporters represent a net increase in the nation's total assets.

A large part of the investment which adds to the nation's capital stock is **public** or **social investment** in such assets as roads, hospitals and schools. **House-building** can also be an important part of investment. If expenditure on new dwellings is included in investment, why not include the purchase of other **consumer durables** such as televisions and cars? Logically, there is no reason why they should be excluded, since they can be regarded as capital assets yielding a service to their owners. The exclusion of consumer durables is therefore an important omission from the official estimates of investment.

2 Investment and simple Keynesian model

In the context of our simple Keynesian income/expenditure model of the economy, 'I' represents the **ex ante net investment demand** of the **private sector**. It is worth noting that:

(i) Total or **gross investment** is much larger than **net investment** since it includes **capital consumption** or **depreciation**. Indeed over half of the gross investment in the UK economy is **replacement investment** which makes good capital consumption. Net investment adds to the nation's capital stock, thereby enabling economic growth to occur by creating the potential to produce a bigger output in future years.

(ii) The investment function I shows the **planned** or **intended** investment decisions at each level of income of all the private sector business enterprises in the economy. However, ex ante or planned investment will not always equal **ex post** or **realized** investment. Unit 21 explained how **unintended stock accumulation** (or **unplanned investment**) occurs when the actual output produced in the economy is greater than intended expenditure or AMD. Ex ante investment only equals ex post investment at the equilibrium level of national income or output!

(iii) The investment function is usually taken to include only the intended net investment of the private sector. However, a large part of total investment, both gross and net, is **public investment** undertaken by the government and other public authorities such as nationalized industries. In 1977 central and local government accounted for 18 per cent of gross investment in the UK economy, with nationalized industries responsible for another 18 per cent. An increase in public investment, for example in public works such as road construction, is usually represented by a change in government spending, G, in the Keynesian model, though investment by nationalized industries can be included along with private investment in the investment function I. However, the statistics indicate that total fixed investment in the economy is strongly influenced by government policy and factors which influence the housing market. The kind of investment decision upon which we shall now concentrate attention – that of a private sector firm considering whether to purchase extra plant or machinery – is not nearly so typical as it is often considered to be.

23.3 Essential knowledge

1 The Micro-economic theory of investment

(i) Distribution theory revisited Just as the **aggregate consumption function of** Unit 21 is built up from the micro-economic theory of how individual **utility-maximizing** households choose to divide their income between consumption and saving, so the **investment function** is similarly obtained by aggregating all the individual investment decisions of **profit-maximizing** business enterprises. We start from where we left off in Unit 15 (on **distribution theory**) by stating that, in perfectly competitive markets, a profit-maximizing businessman or decision-maker will employ each factor of production, including capital, up to the point where the **value of its marginal product** equals the **marginal cost of employing** the last unit of the factor. According to this theory the demand for capital, and hence for investment, depends on the **marginal productivity** of capital and the rate of interest. Other things being equal, the lower the rate of interest, the greater both the demand for capital and the level of investment. The declining marginal productivity of capital means that extra capital is not worth employing unless the rate of interest falls.

If technology allows a firm to substitute one factor of production for another, then **changes in the relative prices** of factors of production will influence how a firm produces its desired level of output. For example, a rise in the price of labour relative to the rate of interest will create an incentive for firms to employ more capital-intensive methods of production, thereby increasing the demand for capital and the level of investment.

It is likely, however, that the ability of a firm to switch between the employment of capital and labour is limited, at least in the short run. We may be justified in assuming the existence of a technologically determined **capital output ratio** which indicates the amount of capital needed to increase output by one unit. If, for example, the capital output ratio is 3, then when a firm's existing capital is fully utilized, an investment of £3 is required in order to increase output by £1 in each future year (assuming constant prices).

(ii) Discounting the future Nevertheless, a businessman's demand for capital goods is rather different from his demand for labour. It is insufficient to state that a profit-maximizing firm will invest up to the point where the **current** marginal product of capital equals the rate of interest. We must modify the businessman's **decision rule** to take account of the fact that most of the returns on a new investment are **future returns**, which are produced over the **useful economic life** of the investment. In general terms, we can state that a profit-maximizing businessman will invest in a new capital asset if:

$$\left. \begin{array}{l} \text{the rate of return per cent per period} \\ \text{he \textbf{expects} over the life of the capital} \\ \text{assets} \end{array} \right\} > \left\{ \begin{array}{l} \text{the rate of interest per cent} \\ \text{per period that must be paid} \\ \text{for borrowed funds to finance} \\ \text{the investment} \end{array} \right.$$

Although our businessman may know the current cost of the investment and the rate of interest, he cannot know with complete certainty either the length of the asset's useful economic life or the details of the net returns or **income stream** which will be produced in each year of that life. Instead, he must **forecast** them, knowing that an asset's useful economic life may be much shorter than its **technical life**. The development of new technology or changes in input prices may render a machine **productively inefficient** long before it actually wears out. Likewise, an estimate of a machine's future net return or income stream is fraught with uncertainty: not only must the **physical product** or output of the machine be calculated for **each** year of its expected life, so also must the prices at which the output is sold, and the amounts and prices of other inputs such as raw materials and labour.

Assuming that estimates have been made of all these variables, and that the net returns have been calculated for each year of the asset's expected life, we can restate the firm's investment decision rule as:

$$\left. \begin{array}{l} \text{invest in all projects for which the \textbf{discounted}} \\ \text{\textbf{present value} of the stream of prospective} \\ \text{returns} \end{array} \right\} > \left\{ \begin{array}{l} \text{the known cost of} \\ \text{the capital asset} \end{array} \right.$$

This is the basis of the **Discounted Cash Flow** (DCF) technique of investment appraisal (which we first introduced in Unit 14 in the context of nationalized industries' investment decisions). If a firm is to maximize the profits resulting from an investment, the year in which the profits or net returns are received is crucial, since £1000 received this year is worth more than the same amount received next year (again assuming constant prices). Income received this year can be reinvested (or lent at the current rate of interest) so as to be worth more by next year. Any money received next year must be equal to that received this year plus the rate of interest if the incomes received in each of the two years are to be of equal value. It follows that **income received earlier in the life of an investment is worth more than similar income received later.**

The DCF method of investment appraisal 'picks up' information about both the *shape* of a project's expected income stream (or cash flow), and the rate of interest. Estimates of profits in each of the years of the expected life of an investment project are expressed in terms of their value in the year of the investment – known as the **present value** (PV). The businessman or decision-maker chooses an appropriate **rate of discount** which reflects the rate of interest that would be paid to borrow the funds which finance the cost of the project. If the PV of the expected future income stream is greater than the cost of the investment, the firm can expect to 'do better' by investing in its own capital project rather than by lending out the equivalent funds to earn the going rate of interest. Quite clearly, the higher the rate of interest, the higher the appropriate **test discount rate**. An investment project judged as just worthwhile when tested against an 8 per cent discount rate would fail a 10 per cent test.

Regardless of the complexities introduced by the DCF principle and the problems of anticipating the future, the general conclusion reached is the same as that suggested by simple marginal productivity theory: that a firm's demand for investment funds is **inversely related** to the rate of interest. At higher rates of interest, fewer projects are worthwhile to a profit-maximizing firm. However, as we shall shortly see, the introduction of the **role of uncertainty about the future** into the determination of investment decisions takes on a special significance in the Keynesian macro-economic theory of investment.

2 The Loanable Funds theory

The pre-Keynesian theory of the determination of the **aggregate level of investment** in the economy is based in part on the marginal productivity theory of individual investment decisions which we described earlier in this unit. This is represented by the investment function I in Figure 23.1, which is drawn as a downward-sloping curve showing that the demand for investment funds (or loanable funds as they were known in this theory) is greater at lower rates of interest. We introduced the other part of the loanable funds theory in Unit 21 in describing the 'classical' theory of savings as a function of the rate of interest. The curve, S in Figure 23.1, shows that the supply of loanable funds or savings is greater at higher rates of interest. Thus in the loanable funds theory, the aggregate levels of both investment and saving are determined by the rate of interest. As in any market, the market price (the rate of interest) tends to rise or fall to bring about an equilibrium which clears the market. In Figure 23.1, planned investment equals planned saving at the equilibrium interest rate, r*.

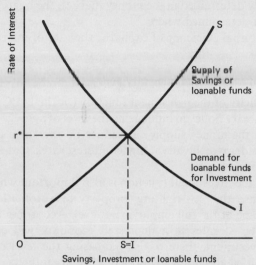

Fig 23.1 The 'Classical' loanable funds theory

3 The Keynesian Marginal Efficiency of Capital theory

The 'classical' loanable funds theory has largely been discredited and replaced by Keynes's own theory of investment, the Marginal Efficiency of Capital (MEC) theory (also known as the marginal efficiency of investment theory). We saw in Unit 21 how Keynes rejected the 'classical' view that the **aggregate** level of savings is largely determined by the rate of interest. (Note, however, that the rate of interest may still be important in **directing** savings between competing financial intermediaries such as banks and building societies, even though in the Keynesian theory it is the level of income that determines aggregate saving.) The rejection of the 'classical' savings function is insufficient in itself to destroy the loanable funds theory, since it merely leads to the conclusion that the savings function is vertical or **'interest-inelastic'**. Of much more significance in our present context is the Keynesian view that the rate of interest is determined in the money market (see Unit 16), being taken as given or **exogenous** by businessmen contemplating investment decisions.

It is worth noting, however, that there is one part of the loanable funds theory that Keynes did not completely reject: the **investment function** which is **inversely related to the rate of interest**. But while the pre-Keynesian investment function was stated in terms of the **current** marginal productivity of capital, Keynes incorporated into the theory the view we have already explained, that businessmen base investment decisions on their **expectations** of the future income stream resulting from each investment. Since the marginal efficiency of capital, which is the Keynesian investment function, is very closely related to the discounted cash flow technique of investment appraisal, we shall compare the two:

(a) A second look at DCF Suppose that a businessman is contemplating investing in a machine costing £1000, with an expected life of three years and no scrap value or disposal costs at the end of this life. Using the DCF method of investment appraisal, he can write the present value of the stream of prospective returns over the three years as:

$$\text{(i)} \quad PV = \frac{Q_1}{1 + r} + \frac{Q_2}{(1 + r)^2} + \frac{Q_3}{(1 + r)^3}$$

where $Q_1 \ldots Q_3$ are the returns expected in each year and r is the *known* rate of interest or discount.

As we previously explained, the investment is worthwhile if the PV exceeds the initial cost of the investment.

(b) MEC Alternatively we can rewrite formula **(i)** so as to calculate directly the rate of return which the businessman expects to obtain by purchasing the asset. We simply replace the *unknown* PV of formula **(i)** by the **known** cost of the asset, £1000. The **unknown** is now the rate of return which we shall call i:

$$\textbf{(ii)} \quad \frac{\text{asset's cost}}{(\pounds 1000)} = \frac{Q_1}{1+i} + \frac{Q_2}{(1+i)^2} + \frac{Q_3}{(1+i)^3}$$

Solving formula **(ii)** for i, we obtain the rate of return which makes the present value of the expected income stream exactly equal its initial cost. The rate of return, i, is the **marginal efficiency of the capital asset,** also known as the **internal rate of return**.

If the MEC is calculated for each and every possible capital project available to all the business enterprises in the economy, we can rank the projects in descending order. With the rate of interest, r, assumed to be exogenously determined in the money market, the aggregate level of investment in the economy is now itself determined where:

the marginal efficiency of capital = the rate of interest

or   i = r

4 The Marginal Efficiency of Capital and monetary policy

The greater the **interest elasticity** of the investment function (or the MEC curve), then the greater also the effectiveness of monetary policy in influencing the level of aggregate demand. By reducing interest rates, an increase in the money supply can induce businessmen to engage in investment projects they would not consider worthwhile at higher interest rates. Conversely, a decrease in the money supply will reduce investment.

The interest elasticity of the investment function is also important when considering whether the economic system contains the 'self-righting' property to automatically achieve an equilibrium level of national income at the full employment level. According to the 'classical' or pre-Keynesian view, falling interest rates in a depressed economy will create the incentive for businessmen to increase investment, thereby also increasing the level of aggregate demand in the economy. This effect will be greatest if investment is highly interest elastic.

5 The importance of expectations and uncertainty

Keynes doubted the interest elasticity of investment and he also believed that there was a lower limit (called the Liquidity Trap) below which the interest rate would not fall even in a depressed economy. However, even if the rate of interest is able to fall to a very low level and investment in its turn is responsive to the rate of interest, the MEC theory provided Keynes with a further very powerful explanation of why investment could collapse in a depressed economy. The **position** of the MEC curve depends on the state of **businessmen's expectations** about the future – or their **'animal spirits'**, in Keynes's colourful language. In a severe depression, business confidence is likely to be very low, causing a collapse of investment. The investment function or MEC curve shifts inwards, resulting in a situation in which little investment takes place even at very low interest rates. Indeed, given Keynes's belief that the consumption function is essentially stable, he needed a theory of an unstable investment function in order to explain how, in conditions of unregulated market forces, a collapse of investment could deepen a depression.

6 The Acceleration Principle

Thus, in the Keynesian view, expectations and the state of business confidence are more important determinants of investment than the rate of interest, and the level of investment is determined largely autonomously of the current level of income. Nevertheless, a part at least of net investment may be related to the **rate of change** of income or output, via the **acceleration principle**.

We have already mentioned in an earlier section how two motives exist for firms to invest in more capital equipment: firstly, when wages rise relative to the cost of capital, and secondly, when technology changes in such a way as to require larger quantities of capital than before – resulting in a larger **capital output ratio**. Assuming now that both the relative prices of capital and labour and the capital output ratio are fixed, a third motive for investment exists when firms believe that aggregate demand is increasing or will soon do so. In order to produce the extra output which they will now be able to sell, firms will need to invest in additional fixed capital, providing of course that an increase in sales is consistent with profit maximization. This is the basis of the **accelerator theory of investment**, in which it is assumed that firms try to keep to an optimal relationship between the amount of capital they possess and the volume of output. We can illustrate the acceleration principle by means of a numercial example:

Table 23.1 The Acceleration Principle

			Yearly Sales	*Existing Capital*	*Desired Capital*	*Replacement Capital*	*Net Investment*	*Gross Investment*
1st Period Steady Sales	year	1	£2000	£8000	£8000	£800	0	£800
	year	2	2000	8000	8000	800	0	800
2nd Period Rising Sales	year	3	2200	8000	8800	800	800	1600
	year	4	2400	8800	9600	800	800	1600
	year	5	2800	9600	11200	800	1600	2400
3rd Period Levelling off	year	6	3000	11200	12000	800	800	1600
	year	7	3000	12000	12000	800	0	800
4th Period Falling Sales	year	8	2800	12000	11200	0	0	0
5th Period Levelling Off	year	9	2700	11200	10800	400	0	400
	year	10	2700	10800	10800	800	0	800

We shall suppose that a firm initially sells an output of £2000 and that, because demand is unchanged, the output is stable from year to year. We shall further assume:

(a) a fixed capital output ratio of 4:1, which means that £4 of capital is required to produce £1 of output per year;

(b) the firm's capital has a life of ten years, after which it needs replacing;

(c) initially the firm possesses £8000 of capital which is exactly enough to produce its yearly output; and

(d) the initial capital has been built up evenly over the years, so that 10 per cent of it needs replacing each year.

In the first Period of Table 23.1 the demand for the firm's output remains stable. The firm has no need for additional capital so **net investment** is zero. **Gross investment** is solely replacement investment or depreciation of £800.

In Period 2, however, demand for the firm's output starts to grow. In year 3 when sales increase by £200, the firm needs additional capital of £800. A 10 per cent increase in demand or sales has had an **accelerated** effect upon investment: gross investment has increased by 100 per cent! In year 4 when sales increase by the same **absolute amount** of £200, investment remains constant, but in year 5 there is once again an accelerated effect on investment when the rate of growth of sales again increases.

In the third Period **the rate of growth** of sales **slows down** in year 6 and levels off completely in year 7. Note that investment declines in year 6 even though sales are still growing. Investment can decline without an actual decline in sales; all that is required is for the growth rate of sales or demand to slow down! In year 7 there is no need for any additional capital so net investment again is zero and gross investment equals replacement investment.

In the fourth Period, when the level of sales absolutely declines, the firm will actually need less capital. Consequently part of the capital which is wearing out need not be replaced and gross investment falls to zero in year 8.

Finally, in Period 5, we see a symmetrical effect to that observed in Period 3: in year 9 when sales continue to fall but the **rate of decline** in sales **slows down**, gross investment begins to recover. The firm must replace part at least of the capital which is wearing out if it is to meet demand, while in year 10 when capital is once again just sufficient to meet demand, replacement investment is back at its initial level of £800.

Thus the acceleration principle provides a second explanation (the first being the role of expectations and the state of business confidence) for the observed great instability of investment. In our numerical example, net investment depends upon the **change in consumption** (and indirectly, via the propensity to consume, upon the **change in income**), but investment fluctuates by a much greater percentage than consumption. The five Periods of our example broadly represent phases in the upswing and downswing of the **business cycle**. Consumption rises in the upswing of the cycle, but it must grow steadily if investment is to remain constant. However, it may be impossible to sustain a rapid growth of sales, and once the rate of growth declines, investment will begin to fall. In this way, the growth of consumption demand in the upswing of the business cycle creates the conditions for a subsequent collapse in investment and the beginning of the downswing.

7 Criticisms of the Accelerator Theory

(i) It is too mechanical It assumes that all firms react to increases in demand in the same way. Some firms may wait to see if the higher level of demand is maintained, whilst others may order more machinery and plant than is immediately required.

(ii) If firms already possess excess capacity left over from a previous boom in demand, they can simply utilize their spare capacity to increase output without the need to invest in any additional fixed capital.

(iii) An increase in demand may occur at a time when the capital goods industries are themselves at full capacity and unable to meet a higher level of investment demand. In these circumstances, a rise in the relative price of capital goods may encourage firms to economize on capital and to employ more labour, and it may also lead to technical innovation which reduces the capital output ratio.

23.4 LINKS WITH OTHER TOPICS

Our emphasis in this unit has been on explaining investment as one of the components of aggregate demand in the simple Keynesian model of the economy (Units 21 and 22). Essentially we have concentrated on investment as **expenditure** on new goods. However, there is another side to investment in its later effects on the **supply** of output, and as the **engine of economic growth**.

In Unit 10 on the size and growth of firms and Unit 11 on the Capital Market we examined how firms **finance** investment. Unit 14 considered the investment policies and problems of nationalized industries, while much of the basic theory of investment stems from the principle of diminishing marginal productivity, which is discussed in Unit 15.

23.5 QUESTION PRACTICE

Essay Questions
Question 1
(i) How may a firm compare alternative investment projects with different capital costs, different income streams over different economic lives?
(ii) How would a rise in the rate of interest affect firms' decisions to invest?

(SUJB: June, 1979)

Understanding the Question We have explained in the unit how a **profit-maximizing** firm can use the **Discounted Cash Flow** (DCF) technique of investment appraisal to compare the **present value** (PV) of the future income stream expected over the economic life of each project. **Any** investment will be worthwhile at the chosen test discount rate if the PV of the expected income stream is greater than the project's capital cost. The advantages of DCF are that not only does it take account of differences in the rate of interest; it also creates a basis for preferring projects which are expected to earn most of their income early in their economic life.

However, it is wrong to think of all firms as using the DCF rule to choose between competing investment projects. In the first place, firms may have other goals besides profit maximization. If, for example, firms are **innovation maximizers**, content with a **satisfactory level of profits**, the DCF technique may not appropriately describe their investment behaviour. Secondly, the DCF technique is costly in terms of the managerial and administrative time needed to compute the calculations. The greater the uncertainty about the future, the less useful it is. In the 1970s, when a rapid and increasingly erratic inflation rate added to other causes of business uncertainty, many firms which had enthusiastically adopted DCF in the 1960s discarded it in favour of more traditional 'rules of thumb' or entrepreneurial 'hunches'. Alternatively, they may use a simpler method of investment appraisal, the **payback method**, which also takes into account the shape of the future income streams. According to the payback method, firms should invest in all projects that are expected to pay for themselves within a certain period of time.

Nevertheless, even if firms do not formally use the DCF method, it has an important theoretical significance. Firms which stray too far from the investment path indicated by DCF will also stray away from the profit-maximizing path. If markets are sufficiently competitive, such firms will either be competed out of existence or they will be vulnerable to take-over. Conversely, firms investing in the way indicated by DCF will survive.

Answer plan
1 Explain that the assumption of profit-maximizing behaviour is important.
2 Describe how a profit-maximizing firm using DCF takes account of the capital cost, income stream and length of economic life of competing investment projects.
3 The higher the rate of interest, then the higher the relevant test discount rate. At higher test discount rates less investment is worthwhile.

4 However, if firms are not profit maximizers, or the greater the degree of uncertainty about the future, the less likely it will be that firms will use DCF.

Question 2 What are the main categories of investment in the United Kingdom economy? To what extent would you expect a change in interest rates to affect the level of investment?

(AEB: June 1981)

Understanding the Question The first part of the question requires a description of the types of investment explained at the beginning of the unit. You can distinguish between **planned** and **unplanned** investment, and between **gross** and **net** investment, but the main **categories** of investment can be divided in a number of ways. You can distinguish between:

  (i) investment by the private sector, central and local government, and by nationalized industries;
 (ii) investment in the primary, secondary and tertiary sectors of the economy, further subdivided into industry groups;
(iii) domestic and overseas investment.

The National Income Accounts distinguish between:

  (a) **gross domestic fixed capital formation**, subdivided into the categories of investment in vehicles, ships and aircraft; plant and machinery; dwellings and other construction; and
  (b) **capital formation in stocks and work-in-progress.**

In our analysis in the unit we have argued that the rate of interest is *one* of the variables, but not the most important variable in influencing the level of investment. Other things being equal, we may expect less of all the categories of investment, except possibly the acquisition of overseas assets, at higher rather than lower rates of interest. Nevertheless, other things are unlikely to remain equal, and changes in **expectations** and **levels of demand** may account for the observed fact that the level of investment has generally risen when interest rates have been rising and fallen when interest rates have also fallen. It is also worth noting that the **interest-elasticity** may vary between the different categories of investment listed in the answer to the first part of the question.

Answer plan
1 Define investment.
2 Explain that there are different ways of categorizing investment. Briefly compare the different methods, concentrating on the main categories identified in the system of National Accounts.
3 Explain **how** investment is inversely related to the rate of interest.
4 **Briefly** mention that marginal productivity theory suggests *why* they are inversely related.
5 Nevertheless, other variables such as expectations (in the MEC theory) and changes in the level of demand (the acceleration principle) may be more important than the rate of interest in determining the level of investment.

Question 3 Discuss the interrelationships between income, consumption and investment and show how a change in each of them might affect the other two.

(London: June 1979)

Understanding the Question This question provides an opportunity to revise some of the most important relationships in the simple Keynesian model of Units 21 and 22, and also to indicate briefly how the introduction of the acceleration principle can extend the model:

(i) A revision of earlier concepts
  (a) We saw in our discussion of the Keynesian consumption function in Unit 21 that we may write the consumption function as

$$C = a + cY$$

An increase in autonomous consumption (a) will have a **multiplier effect** on the equilibrium level of income.

  (b) However, a part of consumption is directly related to the level of income via the **marginal propensity to consume** (c). Thus an autonomous increase in consumption results in an increase in income (via the multiplier), which in turn causes an increase in income-related consumption (via the MPC).

  (c) An autonomous increase in investment will also have a multiplier effect upon income, which again induces a change in consumption.

(ii) Multiplier/accelerator interrelationships In the simple Keynesian model of the economy in Units 21 and 22 we **compared static equilibria**, noting the **multiplier effects** in the move from one equilibrium level of income to another. We ignored the possibility of subsequent **accelerator effects** resulting from the changes in income induced by the multiplier. When the acceleration principle is incorporated, the Keynesian model is converted from a simple comparision of equilibrium levels of income into a **dynamic model** of the economy showing how income, expenditure, and output continuously change through time. If k represents the multiplier, and v the capital output ratio (or accelerator), we can portray the dynamic movement of the economy through time as:

$$\triangle I \rightarrow k \rightarrow \triangle Y \rightarrow v \rightarrow \triangle I \rightarrow k \rightarrow \triangle Y \ldots\ldots \text{etc}$$
multiplier　accelerator　multiplier
　effect　　　effect　　　effect

Depending on the values of the multiplier, k, and the accelerator, v, such dynamic Keynesian models of the economy can be used to model **economic growth**, and the cyclical fluctuations around the growth path – the **business cycle**.

Answer plan

1 Briefly explain the multiplier and show how income changes in response to an autonomous change in either C or I.
2 Show how the level of C will then change via the MPC.
3 Introduce the accelerator effect on I resulting from the changes in Y and C.
4 Suggest that a continuing interaction between the multiplier and the accelerator can take place.

Question 4 Define technical progress and outline the forms it can take. Analyze the possible economic effects of rapid technological change upon the British economy.

(*JMB: June 1980*)

Understanding the Question There is no unique definition of technical progress. It can refer to the invention or development of new types of consumer goods, or to improvements in capital goods and methods of production, and also improvements in the quality of labour. In general it refers to the ability to increase outputs from inputs, or to maintain output with fewer inputs, thereby usually increasing the **productivity** of both labour and capital. Amongst the factors which influence the rate of technical progress are (i) the development of pure science, (ii) the ability of firms to apply the **inventions** of pure science as **innovations** in the process of production, (iii) the need in competitive markets to keep up with the 'best practices' of rival firms, including foreign competitors, and (iv) changes in the relative prices of labour and capital which may cause existing techniques of production to become uneconomic. A rising relative real cost of labour has meant that technical progress often involves the substitution of capital inputs for labour, for example in automation.

The economic effects can be considered in terms of different time periods and the bestowal of benefits and disadvantages. In the short run, rapid technical progress may lead to **technological** and **structural unemployment** (explained in Unit 24), but in the long run living standards may rise and extra employment may be created, particularly in the service sector. Of great importance is the question whether British firms can benefit from the rapid technical progress, or whether the main beneficiaries will be our overseas competitors. In the former case technical progress could promote an export-led boom created by an increased international competitiveness, whereas in the latter case British manufacturing would become less competitive, reinforcing structural unemployment and economic decline.

Answer plan

1 Define technical progress, giving different interpretations of its meaning. Distinguish between **invention** in pure science and **innovation** in the application of scientific developments to production.
2 Explain how technical progress usually means employing more capital-intensive methods of production.
3 Discuss possible effects upon employment and international competitiveness; perhaps introduce the **'virtuous circle'** argument that technical progress increases competitiveness, thereby increasing profitability and financing further technical innovation.

Multiple Choice Questions

Question 5 The cash flows shown in the table below are generated from four investment projects (A, B, C or D) available to a firm. Assuming that any funds generated can be reinvested at the current rate of interest, which is the most profitable project for the firm?

	Cash Flow (£)			
	Project A	Project B	Project C	Project D
year 1	0	20	5	80
year 2	0	20	20	15
year 3	5	20	50	5
year 4	15	20	20	0
year 5	80	20	5	0

Understanding the Question This question is based on the discounted cash flow technique of investment appraisal. All the projects earn a similar total income of £100, but each has a different shape of income stream. Project D is the most attractive to the firm since all its income is received early in the five-year period. Thus the £80 received in year 1 can be reinvested over years 2 to 5.

Question 6

year	No. of units demanded	No. of machines purchased
1	900	30
2	1800	30
3	2700	30
4	2790	33
5	2970	36
6	2970	?

The table shows how the level of investment undertaken by a small textile firm beginning production in year 1 is determined by the level of demand. Machines need replacing after three years. How many machines will be purchased in year 6?

(a) None
(b) 30
(c) 33
(d) 36

Understanding the Question This question is testing your knowledge of the acceleration principle and the relation between net and replacement investment. Since 30 machines are needed to produce 900 units of output in year 1, the capital output ratio is 30:1. In years 2 and 3 demand increases by 900 units each year, so a constant net investment of 30 machines is required. In these years, gross investment equals net investment since no replacement investment is needed. In year 4, when the rate of increase in demand is less than in years 1 to 3, less net investment is needed, but the machines purchased in year 1 have now worn out and must be replaced. Thus in years 4 and 5 gross investment equals replacement investment of 30 machines plus some net investment. However, in year 6 there is no need for any net investment since the level of demand is unchanged. Gross investment equals the investment in 30 machines to replace those bought in year 3 (Alternative (b)).

23.6   FURTHER READING

Stanlake, G. F., *Macro-economics, an Introduction*, 2nd edition (Longmans, 1979).
Chapter 6: Investment

Livesey, F., *A Textbook of Economics* (Polytech Publishers Ltd, 1978).
Chapter 6: Investment.

24   Unemployment and Inflation

24.1   POINTS OF PERSPECTIVE

In this unit we introduce important theories which attempt to explain the twin economic evils of unemployment and inflation, and we also examine some suggested policy solutions. Firstly, however, we shall take a general look at the very different approaches adopted by some of the major schools of economic thought to these two problems.

1 The Pre-Keynesian View

The **neo-classical economists** who preceded Keynes (and whom Keynes rather confusingly labelled as 'classical') regarded the level of employment as being determined by the **'real forces'** of supply and demand in one large competitive labour market, whilst the **quantity of money** determined the price level. They accepted that there would always be a certain amount of **frictional** and **structural** unemployment – these are terms we shall define later – but believed that, provided that real and money wages were flexible, in a competitive economy *market forces* would always tend to bring about a long-run equilibrium at a minimum level of unemployment. (We shall later explain how, in recent years, **monetarists** have labelled this the **natural rate of unemployment**.)

The neo-classical theory of aggregate employment originates in the micro-economic theory of the **diminishing marginal productivity** of labour. We saw in Unit 15 how in **competitive labour markets** a firm's equilibrium employment of labour is determined where the marginal product of labour equals the real wage. In conditions of diminishing marginal returns, firms will only **voluntarily** employ additional workers if there is a fall in the real wage. If markets are sufficiently competitive, the **excess supply** of labour will cause the real wage to fall until unemployment is eliminated. The pre-Keynesians explained persistent mass unemployment in terms of un-competitive forces such as trade unions which prevent wages from falling. In this sense they viewed such unemployment as essentially **voluntary**. The work-force as a whole is to blame for the unemployment of some of its members, not because they are work-shy, but because of the refusal of those workers in employment to accept lower real wages.

For the neo-classicals, the determination of the **price-level** was completely separate from the determination of the level of employment. While the 'real forces' of supply and demand determine **levels of output and employment** and the equilibrium values of *relative* prices, **monetary forces** determine the price level (via the **quantity theory of money** which we shall shortly explain). Thus if the quantity of money doubles, relative prices and levels of output and employment remain the same, but all prices double.

2 The Keynesian View

Keynesians reject the older view that 'real' and 'monetary' forces are separate. Money provides a vital linkage between the markets of the real economy, and when this linkage breaks down, unemployment can result. Keynesians place great emphasis on the **store of value** function of money, arguing that **demand-deficient unemployment** can result when money incomes are stored in idle holdings of money rather than spent (Unit 16). In contrast the pre-Keynesians had never seriously entertained the possibility of such a **lack of aggregate effective demand**, accepting instead **Say's Law** that 'supply creates its own demand'. Keynes actually reversed Say's Law: instead of 'supply creating its own demand', Keynesian theory is based on the idea that 'demand creates its own supply'.

Keynes also claimed that the neo-classical theory of employment is guilty of the **fallacy of composition**. What is true for a single firm or market is not necessarily true for the economy taken as a whole. If the **money wage** paid by **one** firm falls, it will indeed be prepared to employ more workers, but if all money wages fall by the same proportion it does not follow that, collectively, **all** employers will employ more labour. Consider two possibilities. In the first place, prices of goods may fall as much as money wages. If all money wages and prices fall by the same proportion, the **real wage** will remain the same. Secondly, if prices fall by less than the money wage, the real wage will indeed fall, but a general fall in real incomes may reduce aggregate demand. If unemployment is already being caused by too little demand, a wage-cut policy may cut demand still further. Keynes argued that, far from curing mass unemployment, a wage-cut policy could make matters worse!

Keynes also rejected the **quantity theory of money**, the cornerstone of the pre-Keynesian (and the monetarist) theory of inflation. We shall explain shortly why the Keynesians reject this theory, and how Keynes adapted his theory of mass unemployment caused by **deflation** and **deficient demand** to the conditions of **inflation** and **excess demand** in the fully employed economy of World War II.

3 The Monetarist View

In many ways monetarism, or the **'New Classical Macro-economics'** as some versions of monetarism are now known, is simply a revival of the old pre-Keynesian economics. Keynes had written the *General Theory* in order to construct what he thought was a better and more general explanation than that provided by neo-classical theory of the outstanding problem on the agenda in his day: deflation or mass unemployment. Keynesian economics 'ruled' as long as its policy prescriptions ensured relative full employment, growth and price stability, although monetarist critics of Keynesianism now argue that full employment was **coincidental with**, and not **caused by**, Keynesian economic management. When, from the late 1960s onward, there was a simultaneous failure to achieve these objectives in the British economy, Keynesianism became vulnerable to attack from, amongst others, a revival of the 'old economics'. Monetarism essentially accepts the old **'Classical Dichotomy'** that the **real and monetary economy are separate**; the real forces of supply and demand determine 'real things' – output, employment and relative prices – whilst money, a **veil** behind which the real economy operates, determines 'money things' – the overall price level. Thus, growing unemployment is explained by monetarists largely in terms of workers **voluntarily** pricing themselves out of jobs, whilst, via a revival of the old quantity theory of money, irresponsible governments creating too much money are blamed for inflation.

24.2 Underlying concepts

1 Types of Unemployment

The most important distinction to be made between types of unemployment is between the concepts of **voluntary** and **involuntary** unemployment. According to both the pre-Keynesians and latter-day monetarists, persistent mass unemployment is **voluntary**, explained by workers **choosing** higher real wages and fewer jobs. In contrast, Keynesians explain a part at least of mass unemployment in terms of **demand deficiency** outside the control of workers. In this sense, such unemployment is **involuntary**. Before taking the discussion further, we shall firstly introduce a more detailed classification of specific types of unemployment:

(i) Frictional Unemployment (Transitional Unemployment) results from the time-lag involved in the move from one job to another – note the assumption that an **unfilled vacancy** exists elsewhere. Frictional unemployment is directly related to the **geographical and occupational immobility of labour**. Factors such as the lack of information or the required skill, and the cost of moving, can prevent a worker from filling a job vacancy. Consequently the number of unfilled vacancies can be used as a measure of frictional unemployment.

(ii) Casual Unemployment, which is a special case of frictional unemployment, occurs when labour is employed on a short-term basis in trades such as tourism, catering, building and agriculture. When casual unemployment results from regular fluctuations in demand or weather conditions, it can be called **seasonal unemployment**.

(iii) Structural Unemployment arises when a firm or industry suffers a **structural decline**, having become uncompetitive in the face of either changing costs and technology or changing demand. The growth of international competition is a particularly important cause of structural unemployment. For many years in the 1950s and 1960s, structural unemployment in Britain was regionally concentrated in areas of declining staple industries. Such **regional unemployment** was more than offset by the growth of employment in other industries and services which took the place of the declining industries. However, in more recent years structural unemployment has afflicted all parts of the UK, spreading right across the manufacturing base. We shall argue that the return of mass unemployment in the 1970s and 1980s is explained in large part by the re-emergence of structural unemployment in the **deindustrialization** process.

(iv) Technological Unemployment is a special case of structural unemployment resulting from the successful growth of new industries using labour-saving technology such as **automation**. In contrast to **mechanization**, automation involves machines rather than men operating other machines. Whereas the growth of mechanized industry usually involves an absolute increase in the demand for labour, automation of production can lead to the shedding of labour even when industry output is growing.

(v) Demand-Deficient Unemployment (Keynesian or **Cyclical Unemployment)** is the type of unemployment identified by Keynes as the cause of persistent mass unemployment between the wars. Economists generally agree that some unemployment may be caused by lack of demand in the downswing of the business cycle, but Keynes went further. He argued that the economy could settle into an underemployment equilibrium caused by a continuing lack of effective aggregate demand (see Units 21 and 22).

(vi) Residual Unemployment covers any other cause of unemployment. It includes the **work-shy** (not be be confused with **voluntary** unemployment in the sense used earlier) and the **unemployable**. It is now recognized that **long-term unemployment** in itself may cause a worker to become unemployable, as a result of both the erosion of job skills and work habits, and of the employer's perception that a worker with more recent job experience is a 'better bet'. We should also mention **hidden unemployment**, which strictly is not unemployment at all but a measure of **overmanning**. Hidden unemployment occurs when firms could produce the same output with fewer workers. It can be caused by trade union pressure and restrictive practices, the high costs of making workers redundant, or by the desire of firms to hang on to skilled workers in a recession in the belief that the workers will be needed when demand picks up.

2 Inflation, Deflation and Reflation

Inflation is usually defined as a **persistent or continuing tendency for the price level to rise**. Although **deflation** is strictly the opposite – a **persistent tendency for the price level to fall** – the term is usually used in a rather looser way to refer to a reduction in the level of activity or output. In this sense, a **deflationary policy** reduces the level of aggregate demand in the economy. Some economists find the terms **disinflation** and **disinflationary policy** preferable. Likewise, **reflation** refers to an increase in economic activity and output, and a **reflationary policy** stimulates aggregate demand. In a sense inflation is reflation 'gone wrong', increasing the price level rather than real output.

3 Types of Inflation

(a) Suppressed Inflation Although inflation involves the **tendency** for the price level to rise, it is not inevitable that prices will actually rise. Strong governments may successfully introduce tough price controls which prevent the price level from rising without at the same time abolishing the underlying inflationary process. The suppression of rising prices diverts the inflationary process into quantity shortages, queues, waiting-lists and black markets.

(b) Creeping Inflation The inflation rate experienced by most industrialized countries in the 1950s and early 1960s was fairly stable from year to year, averaging less than 5%. However, throughout the period it gradually crept upwards, developing into a **strato-inflation** in many countries in the late 1960s and early 1970s.

(c) Strato-inflation Whereas creeping inflations were typical of industrial countries in the post-war period, strato-inflation was the experience of developing countries, particularly in Latin America. In a strato-inflation the inflation rate ranges from about 10% to several hundred per cent, and it may be particularly difficult to **anticipate**.

(d) Hyper-inflation The transition from a creeping inflation to a strato-inflation in the early 1970s raised fears of an acceleration into a hyper-inflation. The famous German inflation of 1923 was a hyper-inflation, and similar but less publicized hyper-inflation occurred in other countries in central and eastern Europe at the end of both World Wars. However, hyper-inflations are usually short-lived and they should not be regarded as typical. A hyper-inflation usually occurs in a severe political crisis when a government turns to the printing press to create money to pay its debts. Inflation can accelerate to a rate as high as several thousand per cent a year. During the hyper-inflation, money ceases to be a medium of exchange and a store of value, and normal economic activity may completely break down.

(e) Stagnation (or Slumpflation) In the 1970s the incidence of both relatively high rates of inflation and increasing unemployment in the developed world led economists to coin the word 'stagflation'. It combines **stagnation** in the economy (low or negative increases in output) with **price inflation**. As we shall see, its existence made conventional Keynesian demand management policies seem inappropriate and politically damaging as a means of controlling either unemployment or inflation.

24.3 ESSENTIAL INFORMATION

1 The Adverse Effects of Inflation

The seriousness of the adverse effects of inflation greatly depends on whether the inflation is **anticipated** or **unanticipated**. It was relatively easy to anticipate more or less fully the creeping inflation of the 1950s and 1960s. Indeed in these years it was sometimes argued that a mild amount of inflation was harmless or even perhaps beneficial. This was because creeping inflation accompanied an expanding economy and became associated by businessmen with growing markets and healthy profits. This view may well explain why the control of inflation was regarded as a relatively minor policy objective.

In contrast, it is very difficult for people fully to anticipate a strato-inflation as the actual inflation rate varies substantially from year to year. The adverse effects will be much more severe and may completely destabilize the economy. Generally speaking, the main adverse effects of inflation are:

(i) It can be unfair. Weaker social groups in society such as old people on fixed pensions lose, while others in stronger bargaining positions gain. This is an example of how inflation affects the distribution of income and wealth. Nevertheless the **indexing** of pensions has reduced this particular disadvantage of inflation. In the absence of indexation, inflation also raises the average rate of taxation through the process of **fiscal drag** (see Unit 17).

(ii) A second important distributional effect occurs between borrowers and lenders. Inflation tends to redistribute wealth from lenders or creditors to borrowers or debtors. In an inflation the rate of interest may well be below the rate of inflation. This means that lenders are really paying a negative real interest rate to borrowers for the doubtful privilege of lending to them! The biggest borrower of all is usually the government. Inflation can be thought of as a hidden tax that re-distributes wealth to the government and reduces the real value of the national debt. This suggests that governments may not always be as keen as they pretend to control inflation completely!

(iii) Inflation distorts many types of economic behaviour and imposes costs upon economic agents. It can distort consumer behaviour by causing people to bring forward their purchases if they expect the rate of inflation to accelerate. This would probably affect sales of consumer durables such as washing-machines and it might also lead to the hoarding of goods such as groceries. If this were the case the **savings ratio** might be expected to fall as people borrowed or used up savings in order to finance consumption. However, an interesting feature of the inflation in the 1970s was the sharp rise in the savings ratio. This suggests that greater uncertainty may have caused people to save more. A large part of savings is intended to finance old age and retirement. If the inflation rate suddenly accelerates, existing planned savings become inadequate to finance retirement and people increase their savings to top up or supplement their existing stock of accumulated savings, in an attempt to restore the real value of accumulated savings.

(iv) Similar uncertainties affect the behaviour of firms and impose costs upon them. Long-term planning becomes very difficult. Firms may be tempted to divert investment funds out of productive investment into commodity hoarding and speculation. Profit margins may be severely squeezed in a cost inflation and firms can attempt to avoid this by making capital gains on property, land and even fine art and antiques rather than by using their funds in normal production.

(v) In a severe strato-inflation money becomes less useful as a medium of exchange and a store of value. More money may be needed to finance the buying of goods at higher prices, but this is countered by the disadvantages of holding money which is falling in value. In a hyper-inflation the use of money may completely break down and be replaced by less efficient *barter*. This imposes extra costs on most transactions.

2 Theories of Inflation

(i) The Quantity Theory of Money Old theories seldom die; they reappear in a new form to influence a later generation of economists and politicians. This is certainly true of the **quantity theory of money**, which is the oldest theory of inflation. From the 18th century to the 1930s, it was *the* theory of inflation. The quantity theory went out of fashion in the Keynesian era, but modern monetarism has restored the quantity theory to a central place in the current controversy on the causes of inflation.

Early or **'naive'** versions of the quantity theory are usually distinguished from the revival of the quantity theory in a more sophisticated form by Milton Friedman in the 1950s. However, all versions of the quantity theory, old and new, form a **special case of demand inflation** in which rising prices are caused by **excess demand**. The distinguishing characteristic of the quantity theory is the location of the source of excess demand in **monetary** rather than **real forces** – in an **excess supply of money** created or condoned by the government.

At its simplest, the quantity theory is often stated as **'too much money chasing too few goods'**. Indeed to some this is a definition of inflation, though as a definition it rather begs the question of the cause of a rising price level. The theory can also be written as a simple equation:

$$MV = PT$$

This says that the **Money supply** times the number of times money changes hands **(the Velocity of circulation)** equals the **Price level** times the **total number of Transactions**. This is the famous Fisher **equation of exchange**, devised by the American economist Irving Fisher. In the Fisher equation, T includes second-hand purchases of goods and services. Strictly these should be omitted from a measure of national income or output, so it is usually better to rewrite the **equation of exchange** as:

$$MV = Py$$

in which y is a measure of transactions involving currently produced output or **real national income**. Py is thus money national income. In this form the equation of exchange is known as the **Cambridge equation**.

The equation of exchange illustrates the very important difference between an **identity** and a **behavioural equation**. As the equation stands, it is merely an identity or truism implying very little more than that the amount bought always equals the amount sold. To convert the equation into the quantity theory two strong assumptions have to be made and the theory stands or falls with these assumptions:

(a) The price level is determined by the money supply and not vice versa, or:

$$P = f(Ms)$$

where Ms is the money supply, to be distinguished from the demand for money (Md). Keynesians in particular have attacked this assumption. They argue that the money supply passively adapts or accommodates itself to finance the level of transactions taking place at the current price level. To generalize, monetarists believe that the money supply actively determines the price level whereas Keynesians have argued that the **price level determines the money supply**. Keynesians agree with what they consider to be the trivial point that an expansion of the money supply is needed if inflation is to occur, but they argue that if the money supply is restricted so that the current level of transactions cannot be financed, then a drop in output and employment will occur. **Near monies** may take on the function of money, thus rendering control of the money supply ineffective. This (extreme?) Keynesian view can be summarised as:

$$Ms = f(P)$$

(b) Rewriting the Cambridge equation as:

$$Ms = \frac{1}{V}Py$$

and accepting the first assumption, it is easy to see that an increase in the money supply Ms will feed through to an increase in the price level P **provided that V and y are relatively constant**. Keynesians have attacked the quantity theory by attacking this assumption. They have argued that even if the assumption that the money supply influences the price level is correct, then the influence could be very small if an increase in the supply of money was 'absorbed' in a lower velocity of circulation, V, rather than in an increase in the price level. Monetarists have claimed that recent empirical studies support their view that the short-run velocity of circulation is constant.

This dispute extends into an argument about the **transmission mechanism** through which an increase in the money supply is supposed to increase the price level. Modern versions of the quantity theory are usually stated in terms of the **demand** for money:

$$Md = \frac{1}{V}Py$$

Monetarist believe that the demand for money is a **stable** function of the level of money income, money being required solely for transactions purposes (the **transactions demand for money**). When the government increases the money supply, people find themselves possessing larger money balances than they wish to hold. They simply spend their excess money holdings, thereby providing the mechanism by which prices are pulled up. Keynesians attack this **cash balance mechanism**, arguing that since people hold money for **speculative reasons** – the **speculative demand for money** – it does not automatically follow that an increase in the money supply is spent. If the demand for money is **unstable**, the effects of an increase in the money supply are **unpredictable**.

Even if it is agreed that the velocity of circulation is constant and that the demand for money is a stable function of money income, Keynesians have a third line of attack. An expansion of the money supply may increase **real output**, y, rather than the price level P, particularly if there is substantial spare capacity in the economy. Thus the Keynesians stress the reflationary **potential** of monetary policy, though because it is **unpredictable** it should be used as a supplement or 'back-up' to **fiscal policy**. Milton Friedman has admitted that monetary expansion can increase real output, but he argues that the effect is short-lived and that the main long-term effect is on the price level.

(ii) The Keynesian Demand-pull Theory of Inflation In an influential pamphlet published at the beginning of the Second World War, Keynes adapted his theory of **deficient demand** in a depressed economy to explain how inflation could be caused by **excess demand** in a fully employed economy. The theory is illustrated in Figure 24.1 in which the maximum level of **real output** the economy is capable of producing with existing capacity is Y_{FE}. However, the level of aggregate money demand exercised by the various sectors in the economy, shown by AMD_1, is greater than the output that can be produced. Excess demand pulls up prices, resulting in an equilibrium level of **money national income at** Y_1. A sustained reduction in aggregate demand to AMD_2 is necessary to close the **inflationary gap** so as to achieve full employment without inflation.

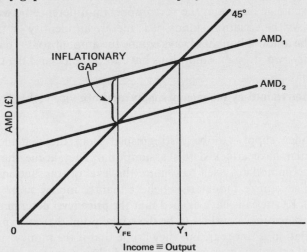

Fig 24.1 The Keynesian 'Demand-Pull' theory of inflation

Although the monetarist and the Keynesian theories are both demand theories of inflation, the Keynesian theory locates the engine of inflation firmly in the 'real' economy. Taken together, the combined **claims** on output of households, firms, the government and the overseas sector are greater than the output that can be produced. Thus inflation is explained by the real forces which determine how people behave. In the British economy of the post-war years in which governments were committed to pursue the objective of full employment, people could behave both as **workers** and as **voters** in an inflationary way. As workers, they could bargain for money wage increases in excess of any productivity increase without the fear of unemployment, while in the political arena they could add to the pressure of demand by voting for increased public spending and budget deficits. We have already noted how in a trivial sense Keynesians admit that inflation is a monetary phenomenon, since the money stock must expand to accommodate and sustain a rising price level. But Keynesians dispute that inflation is caused by a simple prior increase in the money supply; they believe that the real causes lie much deeper.

(iii) Cost Theories of Inflation During the post-war years creeping inflation continued even in years when there was little or no evidence of excess demand in the economy. This prompted many Keynesians to switch their allegiance away from the demand theory of inflation to **cost-push** or **structuralist** theories which explain inflation in terms of the structural and institutional conditions which prevail on the **supply side** of the economy.

Cost-push theorists argue that growing monopoly power in both labour and goods markets has caused inflation. Strong trade unions are able to bargain for money wage rises in excess of any productivity increase. Monopoly firms are prepared to pay these wage increases partly because of the costs of disrupting modern continuous-flow production processes, and partly because they believe they can pass the increased costs on to the consuming public in higher prices. It is often assumed in the cost-push theory that prices are formed by a simple **'cost-plus' pricing rule**. This means that monopoly firms add a standard profit margin to their costs when setting their prices.

The cost-push theory has become a very popular theory with newspapers and the general public. It suggests the simple conclusion that trade union 'pushfulness' and perhaps 'big business' are responsible for inflation. However, the question is often begged as to why unions have become more militant. Marxist versions of the cost-push theory locate the reason for increased labour militancy in a defensive struggle by workers to restore their real wages which are being squeezed by capitalists attempting to maintain the rate of profit. Some Marxists regard inflation as the outcome of a distributional struggle within the 'crisis of capitalism'. Other cost-push theorists argue that changed conditions in the labour market have led to aggressive rather than defensive union behaviour. The 'guarantee' of full employment by the state in the post-war years and the provision of a 'safety net' of labour protection legislation are said to have created conditions in which unions can successfully be more militant.

In explaining inflation, cost-push theorists place great emphasis on the roles of **pay relativities** and **different rates of productivity growth** in different industries. Suppose there are two sectors within an economy; one with a fast rate of growth of labour productivity and the other with a zero rate. Firms in the high productivity sector are prepared to pay wage increases equal to the rate of growth of productivity. Cost inflation need not therefore occur in this sector. However, workers with similar skills in the zero growth sector bargain for the same wage increases in order to maintain their comparability or to restore the differential relative to less skilled workers. Cost inflation thus occurs in the sector with zero productivity growth as the firms pass the increased wage costs on to consumers in higher prices.

A **wage-price 'spiral'** is unleashed as each group of workers attempts in a leap-frogging process to maintain or improve its real wage and its position in the pay 'league table'. Cost-push theorists essentially view the labour market not as one large competitive market but as a collection of non-competitive and separated markets for different trades and skills. Although workers realize that if **all** wages rise at the same rate as productivity, then inflation will probably fall, they also realize that what is in the interest of workers **collectively** need not be in the interest of a single group acting in isolation. A group that accepts a wage increase lower than the current rate of inflation will probably suffer if other workers do not behave in a similar fashion. Thus a group acts to preserve its relative position in the pay 'pecking order', even if its members know that by fuelling inflation a large **money wage increase** may be only a small **real wage increase** or even a decrease.

3 The Rise of the Phillips Curve

In the late 1950s and the early 1960s a great deal of energy was spent by economists in debating whether inflation is caused by **excess demand** or by **cost-push** forces. After 1958 the debate was conducted with the aid of a recently discovered statistical relationship, the **Phillips Curve**, which is illustrated in Figure 24.2.

The Phillips Curve purported to show a **stable** but **non-linear** relationship between the rate of change of wages (the rate of **wage inflation**) and the percentage of the labour force unemployed. Taking the rate of growth of productivity into account, Phillips estimated that in the UK an unemployment level of about 2.5% was compatible with price stability (or zero inflation), and that an unemployment level of 5.5% would lead to stable money wages. Economists grasped on the supposed **stability** of the Phillips relationship over a period of nearly one hundred years to argue that it provided statistical support for the existence of a 'trade-off' between inflation and employment. Using the Phillips Curve, economists believed that they could advise governments on the **opportunity cost** in terms of **inflation** of achieving any **employment** target. In offering this advice, the **non-linearity** of the curve was significant. At low levels of unemployment a further reduction in unemployment would incur a much greater cost in terms of increased inflation than a similar reduction at a higher level of unemployment. Indeed, the Phillips curve appeared to

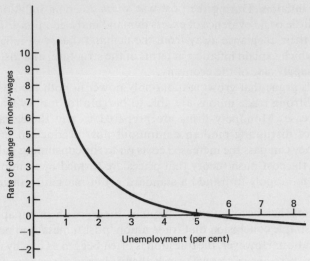

Fig 24.2 The Phillips curve

justify the Keynesian view that an **unemployment rate of about 1½% should be regarded as full employment**; any lower level of unemployment, or 'over-full employment' would be associated with an excessive cost in terms of inflation.

Nevertheless, the Phillips curve was never, in itself, a theory of inflation. In its early years the Phillips curve was most often used by Keynesians of the demand-pull school to illustrate how the rate of inflation varied with the amount of excess demand in the economy. In the demand-pull interpretation, the level of unemployment was used as a measure of excess demand which served to pull up money wages in the labour market. However, the Phillips curve was also accommodated in the cost-push theory, the level of unemployment being interpreted as a measure of trade union 'pushfulness'. The Phillips curve could illustrate and provide statistical support for both theories of inflation, but it could not decide between the two.

4 The Fall of the Phillips Curve

Around 1970 a growing level of unemployment accompanied by a much higher rate of inflation appeared to signal the breakdown of the Phillips relationship. According to the monetarists, this greatly damaged the credibility of both the cost-push theory of inflation and the demand-pull theory, at least in its Keynesian version. It is worth noting, however, that many Keynesians now claim that the Phillips curve was never a 'true' part of Keynesianism, merely excess baggage added on, the rejection of which does not destroy essential Keynesian theory. Nevertheless, neither the demand-pull nor the cost-push theorists had predicted the emergence of the **stag-flation** or **slumpflation** of the 1970s. Yet a leading monetarist, Milton Friedman, had predicted the breakdown of the Phillips relationship a number of years before it actually happened. It is not surprising, therefore, that the simultaneous appearance of increased unemployment and accelerating inflation greatly boosted monetarism.

There are at least two competing theories of what has happened to the Phillips relationship. In the version favoured by some cost-push theorists, the inverse relationship between inflation and unemployment still exists, but the trade-off is now at much higher rates of inflation and levels of unemployment. The continuing growth of non-competitive forces in the structure and insti-tutions of the economy are blamed for a rightward shift of the Phillips relationship. The cost-push school favours the use of an **incomes policy** as the only method which can once again achieve both a lower inflation rate and a lower level of unemployment.

In contrast, monetarists argue that even at the height of the Keynesian era there was never a **stable** relationship allowing a **long-term** trade-off between inflation and employment. The statistical relationship identified by Phillips is at best **short-run** and **unstable**. According to monetarists, the 'true' long-term relationship between unemployment and the rate of inflation lies along a vertical line, on which no trade-offs are possible, running through the **natural rate of unemployment**. This is depicted in Figure 24.3

To understand this conclusion we need to introduce two theories, one old and one relatively new, to help explain the monetarist view of 'how the economy works'. The old theory, the **monetarist theory of aggregate employment**, is essentially the pre-Keynesian employment theory discussed earlier in the unit, whilst the new theory introduces the **role of expectations** into the inflationary process. According to the monetarist theory of employment, the **'natural'** levels of employment and unemployment (U* in Figure 24.3) are determined at the equilibrium **real wage** at which workers **voluntarily** supply exactly the amount of labour that firms voluntarily employ.

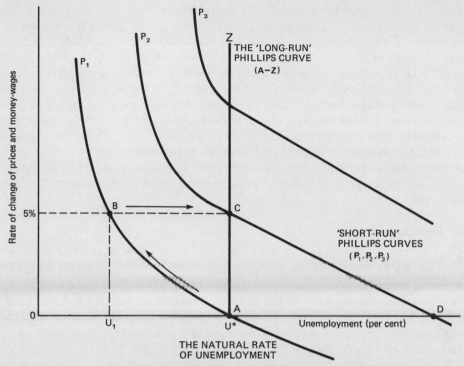

Fig 24.3 The expectations-augmented Phillips curve

Since monetarists do not recognise **demand-deficient unemployment** it follows that, at the natural rate, unemployment is composed largely of **voluntary frictional unemployment**, together with some **involuntary structural** unemployment.

We now introduce the **role of expectations** into the inflationary process. In order to keep the analysis as simple as possible, we shall assume that the rate of productivity increase is zero. Thus, the vertical axis in Figure 24.3 measures the rate of increase both of **money wages** and of **prices**. Suppose that the economy is initially at point A. Unemployment is at the natural rate U*, and the rates of increase of prices and money wages are zero and **stable**. In these circumstances, workers may **expect** the future inflation rate also to be zero. If the government is dissatisfied with the level of unemployment at U* and expands demand, it may believe that it can successfully trade-off along the Phillips curve P_1 to a point such as B. The cost of achieving U_1 appears to be an inflation rate of 5%. But will the new situation be stable? Not so, say the monetarists. Workers are only willing to supply *more* labour beyond the natural level of **employment** if the **real wage** rises, but a rising real wage causes employers to demand **less** labour! Initially, more workers may enter the labour market in the false belief that a 5% increase in the **money wage** is also a **real wage** increase. Similarly, if firms falsely believe that revenues are rising faster than labour costs, they will employ more labour. In other words, an increase in employment beyond the natural rate can only be sustained if workers and employers suffer **permanent money illusion** in equal but opposite directions!

Gradually both workers and employers will realize that they have confused money quantities with real quantities and that they have suffered from money illusion. Without permanent money illusion, employment can only stay above the natural level if inflation accelerates to keep employees' **expectations** about the rate of inflation consistently below the **actual** rate. As workers continuously adjust their **expectations of future inflation** to the **actual rate** and bargain for ever higher money wages, the **short-run** Phillips curve shifts outward from P_1 to P_2 and so on. Thus a level of unemployment below the natural rate can only be sustained if the government finances and accommodates the accelerating inflation by expanding the money supply. But even in these circumstances the inflation will eventually accelerate into a hyper-inflation and into a breakdown of economic activity, causing unemployment to rise **above** the natural rate. According to this logic, any attempt to reduce unemployment below the natural rate involves the short-run cost of accelerating inflation, whilst eventually having the perverse effect of increasing unemployment above the neutral rate to an unnecessarily high level.

The theory just described is sometimes known as the theory of the **'expectations-augmented Phillips curve'**. Supporters of this theory, which was originally conceived by Milton Friedman, tend to take the view that the economy must suffer rather a long period of unemployment **above** the natural rate to rid the economy of the effect of expectations built up while unemployment was **below** the natural rate.

Suppose, once again, that the government has expanded demand and the money supply, moving the economy to point B in Figure 24.3. Unemployment is U_1. It now realizes its 'mistake', and refuses to allow the money supply to grow by more than 5% a year. According to the Friedmanite school, the economy now moves to point C as workers and employers gradually realize that the real wage has not changed. Inflation has **stabilized** at 5%. But if the government wishes to get back to point A, it must get there via point D, which is at a much greater level of unemployment. This journey is necessary in order **gradually** to reduce expectations of inflation. Just as inflation **accelerates** whenever unemployment is below the natural rate, so it **decelerates** when unemployment is above the natural rate. In each case this is explained by economic agents gradually adapting their expectations of inflation to the actual rate. Above the natural rate of unemployment, actual inflation is always below expected inflation.

Accordingly, expectations are continuously revised downwards and the economy can only return to zero inflation **and** unemployment at the natural rate when the expected inflation rate has fallen to zero.

5 Rational Expectations

The message of the 'expectations-augmented Phillips curve' is gloomy. The economy must experience a **lengthy** period of deflation and unemployment above the natural rate as the penalty to be paid for an 'irresponsible' reduction in unemployment below the natural rate. However, in recent years many monetarists have tacked on to the Friedmanite concept of the natural rate of unemployment, an alternative theory of how expectations are formed.

According to this theory, it is unrealistic to assume that a rational economic agent acting in its self-interest will form expectations of future inflation only on the basis of past or experienced inflation. If economic agents on average **correctly forecast** the results of events taking place in the economy now, it is in their self-interest **quickly** to modify their economic behaviour so that it is in line with their expectations. Thus if workers **believe** that the government means business in reducing the money supply and the rate of inflation, they will immediately build a lower expected rate of inflation into their wage-bargaining behaviour. In this way, inflation can be reduced relatively painlessly without a lengthy period of unemployment above the natural level.

In recent years an important division has developed between **monetarists of the Friedmanite school** and those of the **rational expectations school**. According to the Friedmanites, governments can reduce unemployment below the natural rate as long as workers and employers suffer from money illusion. However, according to the rational expectations school, workers and employers instantly realize their mistakes; demand management policies can never succeed in reducing unemployment below the natural rate even in the short run. Monetarists of both schools usually agree that although the government cannot in the long run reduce unemployment below the natural rate, it can reduce the natural rate itself by policies designed to make the labour market more competitive, hence policies to reduce trade union power and to abolish the closed shop.

24.4   LINKS WITH OTHER TOPICS

The monetarist theories of inflation, the quantity theory of money, the rational expectations hypothesis, and the concept of the natural rate of unemployment, have had a great influence on British government policy in the 1980s, and in particular on the monetary policy discussed in Unit 19. In contrast, the authority of the Keynesian demand-pull theory of inflation has greatly diminished, at least in monetarist circles. This theory originates out of the Keynesian income/ expenditure model of the economy described in Unit 21. Yet the other inflation theory favoured by Keynesians – the cost-push theory with all its implications for the effectiveness of incomes policy (Unit 25) – waits in the wings, ready to re-emerge if and when monetarist theories suffer a decline.

In this unit we have omitted any discussion of the **international nature** of inflation and, in particular, of the role of the **exchange rate** in the inflationary process. This defect will be remedied in Units 25 and 28. Nevertheless, we should not conclude this unit without mentioning the monetarist argument that cost-push theories suffer the defect of explaining inflation solely in terms of institutional conditions in **domestic** markets. According to the monetarists, such theories inadequately explain why similar increases in the rate of inflation have occurred in a large number of countries with widely different domestic conditions and institutions.

24.5   QUESTION PRACTICE

Essay Questions

Question 1 Explain what is meant by the quantity theory of money. Discuss how well this theory lends itself to an explanation of price inflation.

(JMB: June, 1977)

Understanding the Question The question is in two fairly equal parts. The first part calls for a description of at least one version of the quantity theory; either the Fisher equation of exchange, or more modern versions of the theory developed from the Cambridge equation as a theory of the demand to hold money balances. Some discussion could then follow on the transmission mechanism through which an increase in the money supply leads to a rise in the price level.

The second part of the question invites you to show some knowledge of the controversy between the monetarist and Keynesian schools on the causes of inflation. The Keynesians attack the quantity theory by attacking its assumptions: these should be clearly explained.

Answer plan

1 Briefly describe the quantity theory in general terms – inflation is caused solely by a prior increase in the money supply.

2 Introduce the Fisher equation, or one or more versions of the quantity theory.

3 The strength of the theory depends on the validity of the assumptions of:
 (a) causality running from money supply to the price level and not vice versa;
 (b) a stable velocity of circulation of money;
 (c) the main effect being on the price level rather than on real output (the separation of 'money' and 'real' forces);
 (d) the transmission mechanism.

4 Explain how Keynesians attack these assumptions, and how they argue that the true cause of inflation is located in the 'real' economy.

5 Modern monetarists do not rely on the quantity theory as the *complete* explanation of inflation. The way expectations are formed in the real economy is also an important part of the inflationary process.

Question 2 (a) What do you understand by the term 'economic recession'? **(5)**
(b) What are the arguments for and against the idea that a country can 'spend its way out of a recession'? **(20)**
(SEB 1981)

Understanding the Question The allocation of five marks to part (a) indicates that while not much development is required in the answer, something more than a one line definition of the term is required. Candidates should attempt to show their understanding of the term recession as illustrated by the various quantifiable indicators e.g. increases in the rate of unemployment, reductions in gross domestic product, a slow down in the rate and volume of investment, falling numbers of housing starts, downward trends in the retail price index, etc.

Part (b) calls for a discussion of the arguments for and against the Keynesian theory of employment. The first essential would be a clear presentation of the basic Keynesian macro-model and the Multiplier concept. You should follow this with a comparison of the Keynesian view of the **'crowding in'** effects of public spending and the monetarist **'crowding out'** viewpoint. According to the Keynesians, public spending stimulates the private sector, many firms in the private sector depending on government orders for their output. Essentially the Keynesians believe in high values for the government spending multiplier, whereas monetarists believe its value is very low or even negative in terms of the increase in real output rather than prices that follows from an increase in government spending.

Answer plan

1 Define a recession.

2 Develop arguments in support of the quotation e.g. strong multiplier effects, the reflation of demand, 'crowding in' etc.

3 Develop the opposite demand-pull inflation and 'crowding-out' arguments.

Question 3 'The Phillips curve is no longer a useful guide to economic policy'. Discuss.
(London: January, 1979)

Understanding the Question You could usefully beg the question by noting that some economists, both Keynesian and monetarist, argue that the Phillips curve has **never** been a useful guide to economic policy. However, all answers must show how the Phillips curve was used to justify a demand management trade-off between employment and inflation. You must then go on to discuss the apparent breakdown of the relationship and one or more explanations of the breakdown.

Answer plan

1 With the aid of a diagram, explain the Phillips curve. Be careful with your labelling of the axes: the vertical axis must show the *rate of change* of wages or prices, not the wage or price *level*.

2 Discuss the policy trade-off implied by the curve, and its interpretation in both the demand-pull and the cost-push theories of inflation.

3 Describe the breakdown in the relationship, offering at least one explanation.

Question 4 In 1938 and 1978 there were about a million and a half people unemployed in Britain. To what extent do you think that the remedies for, and the character, causes, and consequences of, unemployment have changed since the 1930s?
(JMB: June, 1979)

Understanding the Question According to received Keynesian orthodoxy, most unemployment in the 1930s was caused by **deficient demand**, though it is worth noting that monetarists dispute this explanation. The question is seeking some discussion of whether you think that modern unemployment is caused in part or in whole by demand deficiency and whether it is **voluntary** or **involuntary**. Obviously, identifying the correct cause of unemployment is vital, since different policy solutions may suit different forms of unemployment. Indeed one of the consequences of wrongly identifying the cause may be the implementation of a policy 'solution' which perversely increases unemployment or which worsens some other problem. For example, monetarists argue that demand deficiency is not the cause of modern unemployment, and that a fiscal or monetary policy which expands demand eventually increases unemployment beyond the **natural rate**.

Most economists agree that a large part of modern mass unemployment is explained by an increase in **structural** unemployment, caused by industrial uncompetitiveness and the difficulties of adjusting to changes in demand and technical progress. Some economists, and particularly those of a monetarist persuasion, argue also that a growth in **voluntary frictional unemployment** has increased the natural rate of unemployment. It has become fashionable to use **search theories** to explain such unemployment. Suppose that a worker earning £200 a week loses his job and that vacancies exist which pay £100 a week, other conditions of work being similar. The worker may **choose** to remain unemployed rather than to fill the vacancy because (i) the wage does not meet his **aspirations**, and (ii) he is uncertain whether better-paid vacancies exist which he does not know about. Accordingly, unemployment is a **search period**. It ends either when the worker finds a vacancy which meets his aspirations, or when he reduces his aspirations sufficiently to accept the vacancy he knew about in the first instance. The length of the search period is strongly influenced by such factors as the level of unemployment benefits.

Search theorists suggest that voluntary frictional unemployment has increased for two reasons. In the first place, the state has created a welfare 'safety net' which allows the unemployed to use unemployment pay, redundancy payments and supplementary benefit to finance a longer voluntary search period. Secondly, they argue that a narrowing of the gap between the disposable income of the low-paid in **work** and that of the unemployed has occurred. If this is so, then the incentive for many of the unemployed to find work disappears.

The weakness of search theories lies in the assumption that unfilled vacancies exist. Although they may explain some unemployment, they can hardly explain all or most of the growth in unemployment in the 1970s and 1980s. Nevertheless they carry the political implication that reductions in unemployment pay will 'cure' unemployment. The growth in structural unemployment remains the principal cause of modern mass unemployment.

Answer plan

1 **Briefly** list and define the major types of unemployment.
2 State the Keynesian view that inter-war unemployment was caused by deficient demand.
3 If modern unemployment is of the demand-deficient type, expansionary fiscal policy could provide the remedy.
4 But if modern unemployment has other causes, other remedies will be appropriate.
5 Discuss the extent to which modern unemployment is caused by demand deficiency, structural and technological, or frictional reasons.
6 Discuss the character of structural unemployment and suggest policies which could reduce it – e.g. **market-orientated** policies to speed up market adjustments or **market-replacing** policies such as import controls, state funding of new investment, etc.

Multiple Choice Questions

Questions 5, 6 and 7
(a) if both statements are true and the second is a correct explanation of the first
(b) if both statements are true but the second is NOT a correct explanation of the first
(c) if the first statement is true but the second is false
(d) if the first statement is false but the second is true

	Assertion	*Reason*
Question 5	Inflation eases the burden of the existing National Debt to the government	Inflation increases the real value of a debtor's obligations
Question 6	Increased government spending increases inflation under all conditions	Increased government spending is an injection of demand into the economy
Question 7	During a sustained inflation, the money supply usually increases	Economists agree that inflation is caused by a prior increase in the money supply

Understanding the Questions The answer to Question 5 is **(c)**; the real value of the National Debt falls in a period of inflation since the maturity value of only a small part of the debt is index-linked. Thus the second statement is patently false. In Question 6, the second statement is true and the first is false. Economists agree that increased government spending can increase inflation, but none would assert that it will do so under all conditions. The answer is therefore **(d)**. **(c)** is again the answer to Question 7. The first statement is uncontroversial, but the second statement of course separates the monetarists from the Keynesians.

Data Response Questions

Question 8 Given below are some price indices for three years.

	1968	1973	1978
Retail prices	100	143	302
of which:			
Food	100	158	358
Input prices (basic materials & fuel)	100	158	389
Average price of new dwellings (on mortgage)	100	231	381
Import prices	100	150	357
Export prices	100	138	335
Terms of trade	100	92	94
Average weekly earnings of males in manufacturing industry	100	176	359

(Source): *The British Economy in Figures*, Lloyds Bank Ltd., 1979.)

(a) 'These indices clearly show that the average adult male in manufacturing industry has gained during a period of inflation and, therefore, inflation is in the general interest'. Discuss.

(b) Evaluate, in the light of these figures, the effect of inflation on house buyers.

(London: June, 1981)

Understanding the Question

(i) The figures do show that **pre-tax** earnings rose faster than the Retail Price Index over the ten-year period. However, the figures also indicate that the RPI was rising faster than earnings in the latter half of the period, so it is doubtful whether any very strong conclusions can be drawn. It is worth pointing out that while some sections of the population will gain from inflation, this does not mean that inflation is in the general interest. Inflation was clearly accelerating over the period, and the adverse effects of an accelerating inflation are likely to exceed any benefits.

You must attempt to use as much of the data as possible in answering the question. Thus the fact that input and import prices rose faster than the RPI, while the terms of trade deteriorated, implies that manufacturers suffered increasing costs which they were unable fully to pass on as price increases. Presumably, therefore, earnings rose at the expense of profits. You could debate whether this is in the general interest. You should also observe that changes are likely to have taken place that are not indicated by the data, for example redistribution of income away from those in weak bargaining positions, and the possibility of **fiscal drag** having reduced the rise in **post-tax** earnings.

It would also be useful to possess information on other factors helping to determine whether workers have gained during a period of inflation, for example, information on levels of employment and hours worked, other forms of income such as perks; and the real value of government benefits such as child benefit.

(ii) The data only provide information on newly built dwellings, though it is unlikely that the movement in the prices of existing housing was very much different. House prices rose faster than earnings, though the greatest divergency in growth rates occurred in the first half of the period, illustrating how data affected by inflation can 'catch up'. Thus the data indicate a rise in the real cost of new housing bought by first-time male buyers employed in manufacturing industry. It is impossible to tell whether **second-time buyers** gained, since they would sell a house at the same time as they purchased a new property. However, most buyers benefit from inflation once a house has been purchased. In the first place they benefit from the **capital appreciation** of the asset, while, secondly, inflation erodes the real value of the house-buyer's mortgage.

24.6 FURTHER READING

Morris, D., editor, *The Economic System in the UK*, 2nd edition (Oxford University Press, 1979). Chapter 7: Inflation.

Trevithick, J. A., *Inflation, A Guide to the Crisis in Economics*, 2nd edition (Penguin Books, 1980).

25 Keynesianism and Monetarism

25.1 POINTS OF PERSPECTIVE

In the preceding units, frequent mention has been made of Keynesian and monetarist views and of points of controversy and disagreement which separate economists of the two schools. In this unit we firstly gather together and summarize some of the themes of the earlier units, before extending the discussion to other aspects of the controversy such as the role of incomes policy and the international nature of inflation. Besides emphasizing that **Keynesianism** and **monetarism** are broad labels which encompass a wide variety of different viewpoints, we shall also note the existence of another school of thought, the self-styled **'radical'** or **neo-Marxian** school which rejects both Keynesianism and monetarism.

25.2 UNDERLYING CONCEPTS

1 Keynesianism

Keynesianism is a label attached to the theories and policies of those economists who claim to have inherited the mantle of the great English economist, **J. M. Keynes**. In *The General Theory of Employment, Interest and Money* published in 1936, Keynes created a theory of the working of the **whole economy**, and from this foundation modern macro-economics developed. Keynes argued that no automatic tendency exists for unregulated market forces to bring about full employment and that **persistent mass unemployment** could be caused by **deficient demand**. Before his death in 1946, Keynes adapted his theory of **deflation** and deficient demand to the problem of **inflation** caused by **excessive demand**. However, although he did not live to see it, the 'true' **Keynesian era** dawned in the years after 1945 when, in the United Kingdom in particular, Keynesianism became the new economic and political orthodoxy. Essentially, Keynesianism became associated with an **increased level of government intervention** in the economy, especially through **budget deficits** and **fiscal policy**, to 'fine-tune' or manage aggregate demand to a level consistent with achieving relative **full employment** and **economic growth** without excessive costs in terms of **inflation** or **Balance of Payments** crises.

2 Monetarism

Monetarism takes its name from the belief held by all monetarists that inflation is explained by the **quantity theory of money**; according to monetarists **all** inflation is caused by a prior expansion of the money supply. In fact, monetarism means rather more than this, extending to encompass a large part of the pre-Keynesian or 'classical' view of how the economy works. Indeed, **'the New Classical Macro-economics'** is probably a better descriptive label than monetarism of the true roots of the views held by many members of the monetarist school.

3 Some fundamental issues of dispute

Later in the unit we shall examine some of the issues of dispute between Keynesians and monetarists on particular aspects of government policy. First, however, we shall look at some rather more fundamental differences in the views held by the two schools on the essential nature of the economy:

(i) The separation of 'real' and 'monetary' forces Many monetarists appear to accept the old 'classical' view (known as **the Classical Dichotomy**) that **real** and **monetary** forces in the economy are separate. Via the quantity theory of money, an increase in the money supply causes the price level to rise, but it leaves unaffected the **equilibrium** values of relative prices and levels of output and employment. This view, which is completely rejected by Keynesians, carries the implication that a policy of monetary expansionism will in the **long run** increase prices but not output and employment, though in the **short run** (a period of up to five or ten years according to Milton Friedman) monetary changes can primarily affect output.

(ii) The stability of market forces Monetarists see a market economy as a calm and orderly place in which the market mechanism, working through **incentives** transmitted by **price signals** in **competitive markets**, achieves a better or more optimal outcome than can be attained through government interventionism. In essence, risk-taking businessmen who will gain or lose through the correctness of their decisions in the market-place 'know better' what to produce than civil servants and planners cocooned by risk-free salaries and secured pensions. And providing that markets are sufficiently competitive, what is produced is ultimately determined by the wishes of consumers, who also know better than governments what is good for them. According to this philosophy the correct economic function of government is to act as 'nightwatchman' by maintaining law and order, to provide public goods where the market fails, and generally to ensure a suitable environment in which 'wealth-creating' private enterprise can function in competitive markets subject to minimum regulation.

This view of the correct economic role of government leads monetarists generally to **reject discretionary intervention** in the economy as a means of achieving goals such as reduced unemployment. At best, such intervention will be ineffective, at worst it will be destabilizing and damaging. To ensure that such intervention does not take place, governments should adopt, if necessary by law, **fixed** or **automatic policy rules**. Many monetarists recommend the adoption of a

fiscal rule to balance the budget or reduce the PSBR to a fixed percentage of GDP; a **monetary rule** to expand the money supply in line with the growth of real GDP; and an **exchange rate rule** either to keep to a fixed exchange rate or to allow the exchange rate to float freely. (The debate between Keynesians and monetarists on the respective merits and demerits of discretionary policy and automatic rules is sometimes conducted in terms reminiscent of a motor manual. Thus Milton Friedman argues the advantage of a 'fixed throttle' increase in the money supply, rejecting the 'fine-tuning' of demand advocated by the Keynesians.)

In contrast, Keynesians adopt a rather different view of the functioning of an unregulated market economy. In particular, they stress:

(i) the **imperfect** nature of generally **uncompetitive markets**, the growth of **monopoly power** and **producer sovereignty**, and the importance of **uncertainty about the future** and **lack of correct market information** as potentially destablizing forces;

and

(ii) the possible breakdown of **money linkages** between markets. In market economies money is used as a means of payment for market transactions, but people receiving money incomes from the sale of labour in the **labour market** may not necessarily spend their income on the purchase of goods and services in the **goods market**. Instead they may decide to hold idle money balances. Thus Say's Law that 'supply creates its own demand' breaks down and **deficient demand** causes **involuntary unemployment** of labour and other resources.

Thus monetarists emphasize the optimal aspects of a **competitive** economy in a state of **general** (and **fully employed**) equilibrium, and the role in attaining such an equilibrium of **private economic agents** reacting to **price signals** in conditions of near-perfect market information. In competitive markets the market mechanism working through **flexible** prices will move the economy towards a full employment equilibrium. In contrast, the Keynesians emphasize the **inflexible** nature of prices and particularly wages. They also see the economy in terms of **disequilibrium** rather than equilibrium. The economy is subject to the uncertainty of **random 'shocks'** or **autonomous changes** which, by inducing **destabilizing multiplier effects**, hold no guarantee of a smooth and orderly movement to a full employment equilibrium. By **managing the level of demand** the government can 'know better' than unregulated market forces. It can anticipate and counter the destabilizing forces existent in the market economy, achieving a better outcome than is likely in an economy subject to market forces alone.

In summary, therefore, monetarists lay great stress on the essentially **stabilizing** properties of market forces, seeing discretionary government intervention as **destabilizing** and **inefficient**. Conversely, Keynesians justify discretionary interventionism on the grounds that it **stabilizes** an inherently **unstable** market economy.

25.3 ESSENTIAL KNOWLEDGE

1 Keynesian Instruments and Objectives

In order to explain the principal points of difference between Keynesian and monetarist **policies,** we shall adopt an **instruments and objectives approach.** First we must identify the objectives, goals or targets which governments or their policy-makers wish to achieve. Once we have specified the **objectives,** the next stage is to **assign** a particular **policy instrument** to a particular objective.

In the earlier part of the Keynesian era, and especially in the 1950s and early 1960s, the Keynesian policy-makers in the United Kingdom relied on **one principal policy instrument** – the use of **discretionary fiscal policy.** Fiscal policy was used to achieve **three** policy objectives: **full employment, a satisfactory balance of payments** (and the **protection of a fixed exchange rate**), **and control of inflation**. In order to create full employment, tax cuts and increases in public spending resulting in a budget deficit were used to **expand demand.** However, an increased level of demand also raised imports and pulled up the price level. Eventually, either a balance of payments crisis or an unacceptable rise in the inflation rate, or both, would cause the policy-makers to initiate a reversal of policy in which fiscal policy would be used to **deflate** demand in order to protect the exchange rate or to reduce inflation. Thus Keynesianism became associated with 'stop-go' management of the economy.

It is worth noting that in this era discretionary fiscal policy was used as the principal tool of demand management, partly because the Keynesians believed it to be more effective than discretionary **monetary policy**, but also because monetary policy was in the main assigned to **another objective,** that of **National Debt management.** Nevertheless, the role of monetary policy was not absolutely clear; it was also used as a **supplementary tool** of demand management to 'back up' fiscal policy, and as a means of protecting the exchange rate through high interest rates in the recurrent balance of payments crises of the era. In a credit squeeze, demand would be deflated through the use of monetary policy instruments such as open-market operations and the raising of interest rates.

During this first period of Keynesian management of the British economy, successive British governments were committed to preserving a fixed exchange rate. The **exchange rate** was thus a **target** rather than an **instrument** of the policy. But in the latter part of the Keynesian era in the later 1960s and the early 1970s, many Keynesians came to the conclusion that if 'stop-go' was to be avoided a **separate policy instrument** must be assigned to each of the **three principal objectives** of policy. Accordingly, the Keynesian **assignment rule** became:

INSTRUMENT		OBJECTIVE
Fiscal policy	:	Full Employment and Growth
Exchange Rate policy	:	Balance of Payments
Incomes policy	:	Control of Inflation
Monetary policy	:	National Debt Management

2 Keynesians and the Exchange Rate

The Keynesians believed that their ability to achieve sustained full employment and economic growth by means of expansionary demand management policies was severely **constrained** by the tendency of the Balance of Payments to go into serious deficit whenever full employment was approached. Increasingly in the early 1960s Keynesians argued in favour of abandoning the commitment to maintain a fixed exchange rate. **Devaluation** should be used as a policy instrument to 'look after' the Balance of Payments, leaving fiscal policy free to pursue the objective of full employment. (You should refer to Units 27 and 28 for a detailed explanation of the effects of a change in the exchange rate on the Balance of Payments.) The ideas of **'export-led growth'** and of the existence of a **'virtuous circle'** became fashionable amongst Keynesians in the 1960s. They argued that a devaluation (or downward float) of the exchange rate improves the competitive position of exports and worsens that of imports. The improved Balance of Payments position then stimulates growth which in turn stimulates productivity. The competitive position of exports then further improves as a result of falling average costs of production. The process continues, with exports stimulating growth, stimulating competitiveness and so on. Conversely, it was believed that an **overvalued exchange rate** could explain Britain's predicament in the 1960s, trapped in a **vicious circle** of uncompetitive exports, slow growth, and a worsening Balance of Payments position.

Nevertheless, neither the 1967 devaluation of the £ nor its floating in 1972 succeeded in achieving for Britain the 'miracle' of export-led growth. Against this background, economists of the Keynesian persuasion increasingly turned their attention to **incomes policies**, and even to **import controls**, in the search for additional policy instruments with which to manage the economy successfully.

3 Keynesians and Incomes Policy

As it became increasingly clear that, on its own, discretionary fiscal policy or demand management was unable to secure both full employment and price stability, Keynesians of the cost-push school turned their attention to **incomes policy** as the appropriate instrument to reduce inflation. However, many economists dispute the idea that an incomes policy should be regarded as a well-defined policy instrument. They argue that 'incomes policy' has become a label for a wide variety of **statutory** and **voluntary, short-term** and **long-term** policies for the **freezing, restraint** or **'planned growth'** of **wages, incomes,** and even **prices.** Incomes policies can vary from emergency ad hoc measures, usually of short duration in response to a panic or crisis, to the long-term forward planning of the growth of incomes, based on some social consensus.

Other economists take the view that the **control of inflation** is not necessarily the main objective of an incomes policy. Many Marxists argue that its main function is to **squeeze wages** so as to alter the distribution of income in favour of profits. A popular view is that incomes policies should be used to pursue a **'social fairness' policy** in which job evaluation replaces market forces as the determinant of wages. One result of this proliferation of interpretations as to what is meant by incomes policy is that it is exceedingly difficult to evaluate the effectiveness of incomes policies in controlling inflation. This is because it is almost impossible to compare a **'policy-on' period** with a period of **'policy-off'** as no one can agree on what exactly constitutes an incomes policy.

Nevertheless, the incomes policies introduced by successive British governments in the 1960s and 1970s went through four identifiable stages in the cycle of their rather short lives:

(1) Incomes policies have almost always been introduced as unthought-out and temporary measures by governments elected to office on an anti-incomes policy platform. Indeed, in the first months in office the government may well have been busy dismantling an earlier policy inherited from its predecessor. The first stage of an incomes policy has usually been a **wage freeze** introduced in response to a crisis – either of inflation or in the Balance of Payments. **Free collective bargaining** may be suspended for the duration of the wage freeze.

(2) Traditionally, governments have used the wage freeze as a breathing space for thinking out the detailed strategy of the second or **'planned growth of incomes'** stage. In this critical stage of an incomes policy, the government allows market forces to work but imposes constraints on their operation, particularly in the labour market. A **statutory** incomes policy imposes legally binding limits on free collective bargaining, and sometimes on prices as well. In contrast, a **voluntary** incomes policy will rely on exhortation, an appeal to the national interest and national unity, or to some form of **social contract** between government, employers and unions.

Restraint on the wage-bargaining process may take the form of a **maximum limit** for wage rises. Usually the government chooses a wage ceiling on the basis of the estimated rate of growth of productivity. For example, if productivity grows at 3 per cent, a limit on wage rises of 7 per cent should be consistent with 4 per cent inflation. In practice, however, an **upper limit** on wage rises becomes interpreted as the **norm**, or even as a **lower limit** which every self-respecting union negotiator must attempt to exceed.

(3) The second stage of an incomes policy has usually lasted as long as it is accepted as **socially fair** by the people upon whom it is imposed. In the third stage, the incomes policy begins to **disintegrate** when this consensus breaks down. Workers begin to resent and fight against the incomes policy when they see other groups in society successfully evading the policy. **Wage-drift** provides one form of evasion. In a period of incomes policy, workers may try to negotiate locally at the plant level rather than through national collective bargaining. It is usually much more difficult for the government to 'police' thousands of local agreements than the much smaller number of national collective agreements. Thus **total earnings** drift away from **basic wage rates** which are still usually negotiated nationally, but only certain groups of workers will benefit from the process. Other methods of evasion include **job re-gradings** and the tendency for higher-paid workers – particularly managers – to take a larger part of their real income in the form of **fringe benefits** or **perks**. The feeling of social unfairness will also intensify if certain types of income, such as profits and the income of the self-employed, are outside the bounds of the incomes policy, or if there is no restraint on prices.

In the third stage of incomes policy, workers begin to claim, and the government begins to allow, **special case treatment**, whereby certain groups of workers bypass or exceed the limits on pay rises. Some groups, usually the higher paid, claim **special case** status on the grounds of a higher than average rise in productivity, whereas others, usually the lower paid, argue that they merit special treatment on the basis of 'social fairness'.

(4) Incomes policies in the UK have **finally collapsed** under one of two sets of circumstances. Either the government, having lost its resolve, has allowed the policy to fade away in a spate of 'special cases', or the election of a new government has defeated the policy at the ballot-box. However, before too long an incoming government has usually found it necessary to reintroduce an incomes policy despite its avowed intentions. Even the monetarist Conservative Government elected in 1979 operated an **informal incomes policy** applied to wages in the public sector where the government is the employer! This incomes policy was a logical consequence of the **cash limits** and **external financing limits** imposed respectively upon government departments (and local government) and nationalized industries. Wage increases exceeding these limits would not be compatible with the government's achieving its PSBR and money supply targets.

Immediately following the final collapse of an incomes policy, there is usually a **'catching-up' period** in which workers frantically attempt either to make up what they see as lost ground, or to restore differentials. Indeed, the sudden rise in the inflation rate which occurs in the catching-up period creates precisely the conditions in which a 'new' incomes policy is introduced to reduce the rate of inflation. Thus, because of the catching-up period between incomes policies, it is very difficult to assess just how effective incomes policies have been in reducing inflation.

4 Monetarists and Incomes Policies

Most monetarists completely oppose the use of an incomes policy except as an **informal policy** to control pay increases in the public sector, where the state is the employer. As we have explained, monetarists accept the neo-classical tradition of the allocative efficiency of market forces and retain a suspicion of the economic power of the state. Incomes policies are undesirable because they **interfere** with and **distort** the working of the market mechanism, and **extend the economic**

role of the state. Nevertheless, some economists take up a more **eclectic** or **pragmatic** position between the extremes adopted by cost-push Keynesians and monetarists. The **eclectics** argue that an incomes policy may **sometimes** have a useful role in reducing inflationary expectations, without at the same time greatly distorting market forces.

5 Monetarist Instruments and Objectives

While the Keynesians have consistently searched for an ever-wider range of policy instruments with which to conduct the management of the economy, the monetarists have argued that the correct role of government is to minimize its intervention in the economy. While monetarists usually believe that **discretionary** monetary policy has a more powerful influence on the level of money national income than fiscal policy, it is wrong to draw the conclusion that monetarists advocate its use in the management of the level of demand. Not only would a discretionary monetary policy be **unpredictable** in its effects, the main effect of monetary expansion would be a **rising price level** rather than a growth of real output. Monetarists usually reject the use of **discretionary** economic management policies of any kind – fiscal policy, monetary policy, incomes policy and exchange rate policies. Instead, they argue that the economic function of government is to create the conditions in which market forces, working through price signals and private incentives, can properly operate. Nevertheless, it is still useful to analyze monetarist economic policy in terms of instruments and objectives, even though the monetarists prefer the announcement of **firm policy rules** to a discretionary intervention in the working of the economy:

(i) The **ultimate objective** of monetarist policy is to create conditions in which market forces and private enterprise can ensure full employment and economic growth.

(ii) **Control of inflation** is seen as a necessary condition or **intermediate** objective which must be achieved before market forces can work properly.

(iii) Monetarists believe that inflation is caused by an excessive rate of growth of the money supply. Therefore **control of the money supply** is a necessary intermediate (or immediate) objective of policy. Nevertheless, control of the money supply may be difficult to achieve. Some monetarists believe that it should be regarded as a general **indicator** of whether or not the policy is 'on course', and used in conjunction with other indicators or intermediate targets such as the **exchange rate** and the **rate of growth of Money GDP**.

(iv) Monetary policy cannot be separated from the **fiscal stance** adopted by the government. At the root of monetarism is the belief that the **levels of public spending and the PSBR** must be used as a policy instrument to achieve control over the rate of growth of the money supply. A tight fiscal stance and the reduction of both public spending and the PSBR as a proportion of GDP will also reduce undesirable 'crowding out' in the economy by freeing a greater volume of resources for use and employment in the private sector.

(v) Monetarists place considerable emphasis on **supply side** or **micro-economic** policies which have the general objective of making markets more competitive. **Competition policy** and **industrial relations policy** (perhaps a euphemism for anti-trade union policy) are examples.

6 Monetarists and the Exchange Rate

Practical monetarism thus involves the adoption of **two automatic policy rules:**

(i) A **fiscal rule** to balance the budget or to reduce public spending and the PSBR as proportions of GDP;

and

(ii) A **monetary rule** to allow the money supply to grow at some predetermined rate, for example based on the rate of growth of real GDP.

There is much less agreement amongst monetarists on the form of a **third rule** to be adopted for the **exchange rate**. Monetarists generally fall into one of two camps, advocating either a **fixed** or a **freely floating** exchange rate, the former group being called **International monetarists**.

Many monetarists prefer a completely free or cleanly floating exchange rate because this is consistent with their view that market forces and not the government should determine as far as possible the level of activity within the economy. As in the case of other forms of government intervention, monetarists believe that an attempt by government to **manage the exchange rate** will create distortions and inefficiencies and is in any case in the long run unable to defy market forces. We develop this theme in Unit 28. Additionally, a floating exchange has the advantage, in theory at least, of **isolating the economy from international inflationary pressure**. In the absence of a floating exchange rate, a country may **'import' inflation from the rest of the world**. Many monetarists, and also many Keynesians, argue that this is what happened in the 1960s when the USA expanded its domestic economy and built up a huge balance of payments deficit against the rest of the world. Because the dollar was the cornerstone of the **Bretton Woods system of fixed exchange rates** (to be explained in Units 27 and 28), the Americans managed to persuade other countries to maintain their fixed exchange rates against the dollar and to accept dollars in payment for US imports from the rest of the world. The resulting outflow of dollars from America into the reserves of the rest of the world greatly swelled international demand and, in the monetarist interpretation, added to the excessive rate of growth in the money supply within other countries. If, instead, other exchange rates had freely floated against the dollar, the rest of the world would not have imported the dollars created by the American authorities. The American Balance of Payments deficit would simply have resulted in an excess supply of dollars on foreign exchange markets which would then have caused the exchange rate of the dollar to fall until the US deficit had been eliminated.

Nevertheless, the experience of floating exchange rates in the 1970s and 1980s has convinced many monetarists – and Keynesians as well – that a **floating exchange rate contributes to the inflationary process**. They argue that a **completely** fixed exchange rate provides a source of **discipline** for workers and business enterprises within the domestic economy. If, for example, workers bargain for wage increases of 10% when the average rate of growth of productivity is only 4%, then the domestic price level is almost sure to rise. But in a regime of freely floating exchange rates, international competitiveness need not be adversely effected. The exchange rate may simply fall to maintain the initial **relative price** of British goods compared with foreign goods. But the inflation process does not stop here. Workers may respond to the rising **money price** of imports by demanding even higher money wages in an attempt to increase the real wage. This causes a further rise in prices, followed by a fall in the exchange rate and further wage increases in a vicious inflationary spiral accompanied by a plummeting exchange rate.

The floating of the exchange rate may also remove a source of discipline from the behaviour of governments. Indeed, the acceleration in the rate of inflation experienced simultaneously by many countries in the 1970s has been explained in terms of the breakdown of the Bretton Woods system of fixed exchange rates in 1971 and 1972. Governments apparently felt free to reflate demand, hoping that a floating exchange rate would 'look after' the Balance of Payments. They also hoped that in a regime of floating exchange rates there would no longer be a need periodically to deflate demand in order to support the exchange rate. As a result simultaneous reflation by many countries in the early 1970s caused a world-wide increase in demand which world output was incapable of meeting, and inflation resulted.

Thus many economists, both monetarist and Keynesian, have swung round to the opinion that a fixed exchange rate is needed to impose the necessary **discipline** upon the behaviour of workers and firms in the setting of wages and prices, and upon government in avoiding the temptation to reflate demand 'irresponsibly'. Some monetarists even go as far as to recommend a return to a **gold standard system** of fixed exchange rates similar to the system that operated in the 19th century.

7 'New School' and 'Old School' Keynesians

We have already mentioned that Keynesians of the cost-push school favour the use of an incomes policy as a means of controlling inflation. One group of Keynesians whose members suscribe to the cost-push theory of inflation is the **Cambridge Economic Policy Group** (CEPG). The members of the CEPG are also known as the **'New School' Keynesians**, a title which distinguishes them from the more traditional **'Old School'** supporters of demand management and discretionary fiscal policy. In common with monetarists, New School Keynesians are doubtful of the virtues of **short-term discretionary management** of the economy. Instead, they prefer a more **medium-term policy**, aimed at improving the **structure or supply side** of the economy. Nevertheless, in contrast to monetarists, the New School shares with the older school of Keynesians a belief in the need to increase rather than to reduce government intervention in the market economy. Members of the CEPG have argued that a close link exists between the **budget deficit** and the **Balance of Payments**; in short, that a larger budget deficit has an adverse on the Balance of Payments. In consequence, the government's **fiscal stance** should be used to achieve a desired Balance of Payments target. This would mean that fiscal policy is unavailable for use as a policy instrument to secure the domestic target of full employment. The New School has at times recommended the use of **import controls**, not so much as a means of protecting the Balance of Payments, but as a policy instrument to achieve full employment by increasing the volume of domestically produced output.

To complete the picture, both incomes policy and the exchange rate have been recommended by various members of the New School as appropriate policy instruments to control inflation. However, different members of the New School hold different views which have been subject to frequent change and adjustment. New School views have had a significant influence on the **Alternative Economic Strategy** adopted as **Labour Party economic policy**. As with the Old

School of Keynesians, the New School attaches a relatively small importance to monetary policy in its assignment of policy instruments to policy objectives.

8 A Criticism of Keynesian and Monetarist Economics

With the decline of traditional or Old School Keynesianism, both monetarism and the New Keynesian School have had an influence upon the conduct of economic policy in the UK. The influence of the monetarist school has of course been considerable and often dominating. Nevertheless we should not conclude this unit without mentioning, albeit briefly, the arguments of another school of thought which attacks and rejects both Keynesianism and monetarism. This is the **'radical'** or **Neo-Marxian school**, which has experienced something of a revival at the academic level in some British universities, but which has had absolutely no influence upon the conduct of UK policy. Marxists analyze the problems of the British economy in terms of the historical development of **capitalism** as an **economic system**, and of the particular stage of development in which the British economy finds itself.

According to the Marxist view, Keynes made respectable the extension of the economic role of the state in a non-socialist economy. Government intervention could make the capitalist economy function better, without changing the fundamental nature of capitalism as an economic system. For a time Keynesian economic management did indeed contain and reduce the inconsistencies and contradictions within the capitalist system, but it did not eliminate them. Marxists argue that this is demonstrated by the role of the state in capitalist economies such as the UK. On the one hand, the state provides necessary services which allow private capital to be more profitable. These services include the **management of demand**, the provision of **external economies**, and the maintenance of **social order**. But on the other hand, most of the economic functions of the modern state are not directly productive and the growth of the state imposes an increasing burden of taxation upon private capital. Marxists argue that in the short run the state has been able to reduce this burden and to achieve full employment, but only at the expense of pursuing inflationary policies. The modern state now finds itself in an impasse, with capitalism in a state of crisis. A further extension on Keynesian lines of the role of the state to restore full employment will either add to inflationary pressure or, by increasing the burden of taxation, it will erode the vital requirement for capitalist accumulation – the rate of profit.

Yet if the monetarists' alternative is adopted and the state 'rolled back' to become a mere 'nightwatchman' over the economy, the necessary functions of the state for private capital will not be performed. Thus Keynesian economic management will produce runaway inflation and declining profitability, whereas monetarism will result in mass unemployment and social conflict. According to Marxists, neither Keynesian nor monetarist economic management can deal with the true causes of the crisis, which lie within the nature of capitalism itself. The controversy between Keynesians and monetarists is irrelevant; only a change in the system, to **socialism**, will eliminate the crisis in capitalism. Needless to say, most 'orthodox' Keynesians and monetarists dispute the Marxian analysis, though some would accept that it usefully adds to the discussion about the current problems facing the economy. However, there is a widespread dismissal by Keynesians and monetarists of the Marxist view that the problems would somehow be eliminated or reduced if the capitalist system was replaced with socialism.

25.4 LINKS WITH OTHER TOPICS

In this unit, which concludes our main section on macro-economic theory and policy, we have attempted to draw together many of the themes introduced in earlier units from Unit 16 to Unit 24. The essentials of the Keynesian national income-expenditure model are covered in Units 20 to 23. Units 16 to 19 cover areas of monetary and fiscal dispute between Keynesians and monetarists, including the topical issue of the importance of the PSBR and its effects upon the economy. Unit 24 concentrates on the dispute about the causes of unemployment and inflation.

We have made some mention in this unit of the impact that the Balance of Payments and the exchange rate have on the task of domestic economic management. This theme is developed in more depth in Unit 27 on the Balance of Payments and Unit 28 on the exchange rate.

25.5 QUESTION PRACTICE

Essay Questions

Question 1 'Monetary policy is superior to fiscal policy as a method of controlling the economy'. Discuss.

(AEB: November, 1980)

Understanding the Question The short answer is that Keynesians believe that fiscal policy is a more **effective** and **predictable** method of controlling **the level of demand** in the economy, while monetarists doubt whether either should be used in a **discretionary** way to manage demand. Nevertheless, the monetarist view is that monetary policy has a greater effect upon the level of money national income, but that the main long-term effect is upon **prices** rather than upon **real output**. Increasingly, both Keynesians and monetarists agree that the real problems in the economy lie on the **supply side** rather than on the **demand side**, so that even if fiscal policy is **an** appropriate method of controlling the economy, it is insufficient to use it as the single policy instrument for achieving all the desirable policy objectives. (See also the notes on Question 5, which is closely related to this question.)

Answer plan

1 Explain how Keynesian fiscal policy attempted to manage the level of demand through changes in government spending, taxation, and the budget deficit. Keynesians have believed that **large fiscal multipliers** make the policy effective.

2 Explain how a **discretionary monetary policy** can be used to manage demand, or alternatively it can be assigned to other objectives such as **national debt management** or **protecting the exchange rate**. Keynesians believe that its main effect on demand occurs through changes in interest rates, but that, in practice, interest rates can seldom fluctuate sufficiently to have a great effect on businessmen's investment decisions. Keynesians believe that other factors such as business confidence may be more important than the rate of interest in determining investment. Indeed, in a **liquidity trap** a change in the money supply will have no effect on the rate of interest, and hence no impact on the economy. In contrast monetarists emphasize the effects on the price level rather than upon real output, via the quantity theory of money, of an expansionary monetary policy.

3 Monetarists throw doubt on the value of the fiscal multiplier, emphasizing the indirect monetary effects of fiscal policy that result from the borrowing which finances the budget deficit. They argue that increased budget deficits can increase either the money supply or interest rates, causing inflation and 'crowding-out'. They also argue that discretionary policy **destabilizes** rather than stabilizes the economy. Therefore **fiscal and monetary rules** should be used, not to control the economy, but to create the conditions in which market forces can properly function. Monetarists attempt to achieve money supply targets via their fiscal policy of controlling the level of public spending and the PSBR.

Question 2 'It is obvious that even a government with monetarist objectives must have some sort of incomes policy'. Do you agree?

(O & CSEB: June, 1981)

Understanding the Question We have explained how in its **extreme form** monetarism rejects the use of an incomes policy. Nevertheless, monetarists also believe that market forces will only achieve an equilibrium at a minimum level of unemployment provided that all markets, including the labour market, are sufficiently competitive. Thus in one sense a monetarist 'incomes policy' involves the adoption of those policies which have the general aim of making the labour market more competitive. Monetarists place great emphasis on policies to reduce restrictive practices and to 'educate workers about the reality of the market place'.

While it is certainly true that monetarists reject **formal statutory incomes policies** that directly prevent the free working of market forces, they nevertheless favour the imposition of wage restraint in the public sector where the state is the employer, and the announcement of the rate of wage increases in the economy as a whole that they believe is compatible with the government's inflation rate target.

We have explained how economists of many schools of thought now place considerable emphasis on how expectations are formed in the economy. This has caused some economists of a generally monetarist persuasion to accept that a temporary incomes policy might in certain circumstances have a useful function in ridding the economy of inflationary expectations.

Answer plan

1 Explain why monetarists reject the use of a formal statutory incomes policy.

2 Nevertheless, there is no single way of defining an incomes policy. In the sense that **all** governments have a 'policy towards incomes', even monetarists have an incomes policy.

3 Explain why a monetarist government is likely to have a policy towards public sector incomes.

4 Some monetarists believe that incomes policies may have a limited role in reducing expectations of inflation.

Multiple Choice Questions

A	B	C	D
1, 2, 3 all correct	1, 2 only correct	2, 3 only correct	1 only correct

Question 3 Which of the following statements might represent the views of a monetarist economist?

1 Inflation is primarily caused by trade union behaviour.

2 An increase in government spending is likely to reduce spending by the private sector.

3 In the long term governments cannot reduce unemployment below the natural rate.

Understanding the Question The first statement is wrong since monetarists believe that **governments** cause inflation by expanding the money supply and by attempting to reduce unemployment below its natural rate. However, according to monetarists, trade unions may cause unemployment by refusing to accept a real wage at which employers will voluntarily employ all the labour force at the 'natural' rate of employment. Unemployment can temporarily be reduced below the natural rate of unemployment, but only at the expense of an accelerating inflation that will eventually make the level of employment unsustainable. Thus statement three is a correct summary of an important monetarist view. Statement two is also correct: monetarists believe that expenditure by the state often 'crowds out' private spending. Since 2 and 3 are correct, the answer is therefore C.

Question 4 The main areas of dispute between monetarist and Keynesian economists include:
1 whether statutory incomes policies should be used to control inflation;
2 whether changes in the money supply cause changes in the price level;
3 whether government policy should attempt to make the economy more competitive.

Understanding the Question The answer to this question is B since only the first two statements are correct. Monetarists reject the use of statutory incomes policies, while many Keynesians recommend that an incomes policy be used as the principal instrument to control inflation. The second statement relates to a major area of controversy between monetarists and Keynesians; a popular Keynesian view is that the money supply *responds* to rather than *causes* changes in the price level. In contrast, there is no general dispute between Keynesians and monetarists on the virtues of competition policy, though monetarists probably place a greater emphasis upon it.

Data Response Questions

Question 5
'In the 1950s and early 1960s there was virtual unanimity that fiscal and monetary policy (particularly fiscal policy) could be used to regulate the quantity of spending and thus the level of output and employment.

This unanimity no longer exists. Monetarist economists broadly speaking maintain not only that monetary policy is more powerful than fiscal policy in influencing expenditure but also that changes in fiscal policy while the money supply is held constant will result in the long run only in a different level of interest rates, and thus in a different balance between consumption and investment rather than in changes in the total level of real expenditure. In other words they consider that one of the causes of companies' problems in recent years has been the high level of interest rates which has deterred private investment, and that these interest rates are the result of the large public sector deficit and the even larger public sector borrowing requirement.'

Extract from the *'Report of the Committee to Review the Functioning of Financial Institutions,* Cmnd 7937, HMSO 1980.

(a) Outline the reasoning behind the monetarist view that monetary policy is more powerful than fiscal policy in influencing expenditure.   **(10 marks)**
(b) Explain the relationships between the public sector borrowing requirement, interest rates and private investment.   **(10 marks)**

(AEB: June 1982)

(a) Monetarists explain the influence of monetary policy on expenditure in terms of the quantity theory of money. They argue that an increase in the money supply causes people to possess larger money balances than they wish to hold for transactions purposes, and that they simply spend their excess money holdings. They further argue that the main effect is to **inflate the price level** rather than to **reflate real output**. Thus an expansionary monetary policy results in **powerful but undesirable** effects.

In contrast, monetarists doubt whether the value of the government spending multiplier is significantly above zero. The lower the multiplier, the less effective is fiscal policy.

(b) The answer to this second part of the question develops the last point we mentioned in the context of part **(a)**. An expansionary fiscal policy usually requires a larger budget deficit and hence a larger PSBR. Monetarists place great emphasis on the effects which result from the increased public borrowing requirement. If the government borrows from the general public rather than from the banks, the rate of interest may have to be raised to make gilts attractive and so funds flow to the government rather than to the private sector. This is one mechanism through which 'crowding-out' can take place. According to the monetarists, fiscal policy is ineffective because an increase in public spending displaces private spending. It is also likely that businessmen will undertake few investment projects, particularly if they are responsive to changes in the cost of borrowing.

25.6 FURTHER READING

Morris, D., editor, *The Economic System in the UK,* 2nd edition (Oxford University Press, 1979) Chapter 9: Objectives and Instruments.

Trevithick, J. A., *Inflation, A guide to the Crisis in Economics,* 2nd edition (Penguin Books, 1980)

Glyn, A., and Harrison, J., *The British Economic Disaster,* (Pluto Press, 1980).

26 Trade

26.1 POINTS OF PERSPECTIVE

The underlying basis for trade is the same whether trade takes place between individuals or business enterprises, on a regional basis **within** a country or **internationally** between countries. Although in this unit we shall concentrate on international trade, the basis for all voluntarily undertaken exchange and trade is the belief that both parties can gain. Trade begins when an individual productive enterprise produces an output that is surplus to its own needs, which it is able to exchange for the surplus of some other individual or productive enterprise, increasing the **welfare** of both. Before the development of money, the exchange was achieved through barter. Nowadays, a commonly accepted currency serves as the medium of exchange for internal trade within a country, but **payments difficulties** prevent the full development of international trade. Countries may lack a means of payment acceptable to other countries, and risks and uncertainties about **exchange rates** may reduce trade. Deliberately imposed restrictions on trade, such as **tariffs**, and other forms of **import control** may create further **barriers to trade**.

World trade is dominated by the advanced industrial nations, whose exports and imports usually exceed 20 per cent of GDP. Because of the size of its huge domestic market the USA is somewhat of an exception, with the value of US exports and imports equalling only about 8 per cent of GDP. The largest proportion of the trade of industrialized countries (the **'North'**) is with each other, rather than with the less developed countries (LDCs or the **'South'**). A considerable growth in 'North/South' trade may be necessary if the development gap between the countries of the world is to be reduced.

26.2 UNDERLYING CONCEPTS

1 The case for specialization and trade

The general case for specialization and trade centres on the proposition that countries or regions can attain levels of production, consumption and economic welfare which are beyond the **production possibility frontier** open to them in a world without trade. Assuming full employment of all factors of production, a country can only increase the production of one good or service by diverting resources away from the production of other goods. Whenever resources are scarce, the **opportunity cost** of increasing the output of one industry is the alternative output foregone in other industries in the economy. If, however, a country concentrates scarce resources and factors of production into producing the goods in which it is most efficient, total world production can increase. Gains from specialization and trade are possible if countries can agree to exchange that part of the output which they produce that is surplus to their needs. Having stated the general case for trade, we shall now examine some more specific arguments in favour of specialization and trade.

2 The benefits of competition

In Unit 6 we explained how market forces operating in a perfectly competitive market economy can, subject to rather strong assumptions, achieve a state of **economic efficiency**, defined as a combination of **productive** and **allocative efficiency**. Within an isolated and relatively small economy, markets may be too small to be competitive and monopoly may predominate. Exposure to international competition is likely to make markets more competitive and hence more efficient.

3 The benefits of economies of scale and division of labour

The benefits of the division of labour were first recognized in the 18th century by the great classical economist Adam Smith. Smith discussed the division of labour in the context of workers specializing in **different productive tasks** within a factory which itself specialized in producing a particular type of product. He then went on to extend the analysis to specialization between regions and countries. Thus, it should be stressed that there are many different levels at which the benefits of the division of labour can be attained: division of labour within a plant; division between plants within a firm; division between firms within an industry; division between industries within a country; and finally division of labour between countries.

Adam Smith suggested three reasons why division of labour increased production and efficiency:

(i) workers become better at a particular task – 'practice makes perfect';
(ii) time, which would be lost when workers move between tasks, is saved;
(iii) more and better capital can be employed in production.

The latter advantage cited by Smith is particularly important, since it is closely related to the benefits of economies of scale. If a country specializes in producing the goods in which it is already most efficient, a large scale of production may allow it to benefit from increasing returns to scale and economies of scale. In other words, its industries become even more efficient, when, for example, long production runs allow firms to introduce more advanced forms of machinery and improved technology. In the absence of international trade, the limited extent of the domestic market may prevent a country from benefiting from economies of scale. Thus, by **extending the market**, international trade and specialization allows the full benefits of the division of labour and economies of scale to be achieved (though we should also note that the possibility of **diseconomies of scale** and other disadvantages of the division of labour form the basis of a case against trade).

5 Increasing the range of choice

The **international immobility** of some factors of production and the **unique allocation of natural resources** in each country mean that the production possibilities open to each country are different. In the extreme, the production of some goods or services may be exclusive to a particular country. A simple example will show in this situation how wider choice can result from trade. If there are just two nations (A and B) and one can only produce bread and the other jam, then if each country's production exceeds its needs, both countries can gain by trading their surplus rather than letting it rot. Thus the welfare of each nation is increased as they both have bread **and** jam, rather than bread **or** jam.

26.3   ESSENTIAL INFORMATION

1 The principle of comparative advantage

Even when there are no economics of scale or increasing returns to scale, the theory of comparative advantage indicates that gains can still be realized from international trade. This is easiest to show when each country in our two-country model has an **absolute advantage** in producing either bread or jam, but is able to produce the other commodity if it wishes.

(i) **Absolute advantage** We shall assume:
(a) Factors of production are perfectly mobile **within** each country and they can be instantly switched between industries. However, factors are **immobile** between countries, though final goods and services can be traded.
(b) There are **constant returns to scale** and **constant average costs of production** in both industries in both countries.
(c) Both commodities, bread and jam, are in demand in both countries.
(d) The **limited** resources and factors of production in each country are fully employed.

Suppose now that each country has equal resources and devotes half of its limited resources to bread production and half to jam. The **production possibilities** are:

	Bread (units)	Jam (units)
Country A	10	5
Country B	5	10
	—	—
'World' total	15	15

The relative or **comparative cost** of bread production is lower in country A than in country B, but the position is reversed in the production of jam. Country A has an **absolute advantage** in bread production, whereas the absolute advantage in jam production lies with country B. If each country specializes in the production of the commodity in which it is most efficient and possesses the absolute advantage, we get:

	Bread (units)	Jam (units)
Country A	20	0
Country B	0	20
	—	—
'World' total	20	20

The gains from specialization and trade equal 5 units of bread and 5 units of jam, provided that there are no transport costs.

(ii) Comparative advantage It is less obvious that specialization and trade are also worthwhile even when a country can produce **all** goods more efficiently at a lower comparative cost than other countries. This phenomenon is explained by the principle of **comparative advantage**, or a comparison of the **relative efficiency** of production in different countries rather than their absolute efficiency.

Suppose that country A becomes more efficient in both bread and jam production. If each country devotes half its resources to each industry, the production totals are:

	Bread (units)	Jam (units)
Country A	30	15
Country B	5	10
'World' total	35	25

Country A possesses an absolute advantage in both industries, but whereas A is six times as efficient in bread production, it is only 50 per cent more efficient in jam production. Nevertheless, if country B produces an extra unit of jam, it need give up only half a unit of bread. In contrast, country A must give up two units of bread in order to increase production of jam by one unit. We say that a country's comparative advantage lies in the good which it can produce **relatively cheaply**, at a **lower opportunity cost** than its trading partner. Country A (which has the absolute advantage in both commodities) possesses a comparative advantage in bread production, whereas country B (with an absolute disadvantage in both) has the comparative advantage in jam production.

If each country specializes **completely** in the activity in which it possesses a comparative advantage, the production totals are:

	Bread (units)	Jam (units)
Country A	60	0
Country B	0	20
'World' total	60	20

You will notice that compared with the situation without specialization and trade in which each country devoted half its resources to each industry, there is a gain of 25 units of bread; but a loss of 5 units of jam. Thus in the case where one country is more efficient in both activities we cannot say, without some knowledge of demand and the value placed on consumption of bread and jam by the inhabitants of the two countries, whether a **welfare gain** will result from **complete** specialization. We can be more sure of a welfare gain if **at least as much of one good** and **more of the other** results from specialization and trade. We can obtain this result by devising a situation in which country A, the country with the absolute advantage in both goods, decides not to specialize completely, but to devote some of its resources to jam production. For example, if country A produces 5 units of jam with one-sixth of its resources and 50 units of bread with the other five-sixths, then the production totals are:

	Bread (units)	Jam (units)
Country A	50	5
Country B	0	20
'World' total	55	25

Compared with the situation without specialization and trade, there is a gain of 20 units of bread.

2 The Terms of Trade

The rate of exchange of bread for jam, or the **terms of trade**, will determine the benefits of trade for these trading partners. The **limits to the exchange** are set by each country's **opportunity cost ratio**. In the example where country A has an absolute advantage in the production of both goods, country A will be prepared to give up no more than 2 units of bread for 1 unit of jam, whilst country B will require at least $\frac{1}{2}$ a unit of bread for 1 unit of jam if trade is to be worthwhile. Thus the terms of trade must lie between $\frac{1}{2}$ unit of bread and 2 units of bread for 1 unit of jam. The exact rate of exchange, or the relative price of the two commodities, will be determined by the strength of demand.

In the real world where millions of goods and services are traded, a nation's average terms of trade are measured with **index numbers**. The average prices of exports and imports are calculated using **weighted indices** and the export index is divided by the import index to give the terms of trade index. A rise in the index indicates an **improvement** in a nation's terms of trade, indicating that a given quantity of exports now pays for more imports than previously. We shall examine the causes and effects of changes in the terms of trade in greater detail in Units 27 and 28. It is worth noting, however, that a rise in the exchange rate of the £, and a domestic inflation rate higher than that of our trading partners, can both 'improve' the terms of trade, but that the effects of the 'improvement' are not necessarily beneficial in other respects.

3 The case against trade

The case **for** specialization and trade is based on the proposition that all countries taken together will gain in terms of increased production, efficiency and welfare, providing that the terms of trade lie within the opportunity cost ratios. However, there is no guarantee that the gains are distributed equally amongst the trading countries. Although restraints on free trade will probably reduce world welfare, individual countries may feel that it is in their self-interest to restrict the freedom of trade. Not all the arguments put forward to justify restrictions on trade are strictly economic; social and political factors are also involved.

(i) Economic arguments:

(a) The protection of 'infant industries' This argument is quite strong when there is scope for industries to benefit from **economies of scale**. A newly established industry, in for example a developing country, may be unable to compete with other countries in which established rivals are already benefiting from economies of scale. Protection may be justified during the early growth of an 'infant industry'.

(b) To avoid the dangers of overspecialization The benefits which result from specializing in accordance with the principle of comparative advantage will not be obtained if the **disadvantages of the division of labour** outweigh the advantages. **Diseconomies of scale** may be experienced. Agricultural overspecialization can result in **monoculture**, in which the growing of a single cash crop for export may lead to soil erosion, vulnerability to pests, and falling agricultural yields in the future. Overspecialization can also cause a country to be particularly vulnerable to sudden changes in demand or in the cost and availability of imported raw materials or energy, or to new inventions and changes in technology which eliminate its comparative advantage. The greater the **uncertainty about the future**, the weaker the case for complete specialization. If a country is self-sufficient in all important respects, it is effectively **neutralized** against the danger of importing recession and unemployment from the rest of the world if international demand collapses.

(c) To cushion home employment The model of comparative advantage assumes that factors of production are both fully employed and perfectly mobile within countries. If large-scale unemployment exists, there is a case for using factors **inefficiently** rather than not to employ them at all. Countries may also regard as unacceptable the costs of **structural** unemployment resulting from complete freedom of trade. Structural unemployment occurs when old industries decline in response to changes in either demand or comparative cost and advantage. There is a case for **selective** and **temporary** import controls to ease the problems of adjustment to the new conditions, whilst still accepting that in the long run trade should be encouraged and that a country should adapt to produce the goods in which it possesses a comparative advantage. Indeed the **New Cambridge School** have argued that import controls will boost the economy to such an extent that, although the **structure** of imports will change, the **volume** of imports will not actually fall once growth has taken place. This is the **paradox of import controls**, a counter to the free-trade view that 'what keeps imports out, keeps exports in.'.

(d) To prevent dumping Exports are sometimes sold at a price below their cost of production and below the market price in the country of origin. Dumping may be motivated by the need to obtain foreign currency or a foothold in a foreign market, or by the hope of achieving productive economies of scale.

(e) To avoid 'unfair' competition It is sometimes claimed that low-wage countries in the developing world exploit local labour in order to produce cheap goods and that such activity is unfair. However, the developing countries are simply specializing in producing goods in which a plentiful supply of labour gives them a comparative advantage. It is essentially a value judgement whether this is 'fair' or 'unfair'.

(f) To raise revenue Tariffs are sometimes justified as a means of raising revenue for the government, but in modern economies this is a comparatively unimportant source of government revenue.

(ii) Political and social arguments:

(a) Economic sanctions Economic sanctions have been used for centuries to buttress political decisions. An **embargo** on trade may weaken a political enemy and it may also encourage co-operation between politically sympathetic countries. Embargos and other import controls are often imposed on trade in armaments and military goods.

(b) Restrictions are also commonly placed on the trade in harmful goods (demerit goods) such as narcotic drugs.

(c) Restrictions may be imposed for **strategic reasons,** to ensure that a country is relatively self-sufficient in time of war.

4 Arguments against Protectionism and restrictions on trade

We have already covered the principle arguments involved, in our explanation of the case for trade. We have shown that, subject to some rather strong assumptions about the full employment of resources and the nature of demand, welfare losses will result if countries fail to specialize in accordance with the principle of comparative advantage. Countries may use import controls and other restrictions on trade to gain a **short-term** advantage at the expense of other countries (the **'beggar my neighbour'** principle). However, **retaliation** by other countries is likely to cause a **long-term** welfare loss which is experienced by all countries, since protection props up inefficient and monopoly producers and redistributes income in favour of the protected.

5 Methods of Protection

The decision to protect is made deliberately by a government. The method chosen may affect demand, supply or price. The demand for goods can be influenced by **tariffs, subsidies** and **exchange controls**. Supply can be manipulated by **embargoes, quotas, administrative restrictions** and **voluntary agreement**.

(i) Tariffs Tariffs, which may be **specific** or **ad valorem**, are taxes placed on imported, but not on domestic, goods. The ability of a tariff to reduce imports depends upon its size and upon the **elasticity of demand** for the imported good. If the country which imposes the tariff produces **close substitutes,** demand for imports is likely to be price elastic. In these circumstances, a tariff will reduce imports by **switching** demand towards the domestically produced substitutes. Conversely, if demand for imports is price inelastic, the main effect of the tariff will be on import prices rather than on the quantity of imports. (Refer back at this stage to the analysis in Unit 17 on the various effects which follow an increase in expenditure taxes. A tariff is simply an example of an expenditure tax.)

(ii) Subsidies These are provided in many, often clandestine, forms to avoid GATT restrictions on subsidies and dumping. The provision of export credit, VAT remission and regional aid may reduce total costs for exporters and thereby distort trade by affecting market prices. The support given by government agencies, such as the Export Credit Guarantees Department and the British Overseas Trade Board, to British exporters is envied by her European rivals! At the same time, subsidies to domestic producers enable them to compete more easily with imported goods.

(iii) Exchange Control Some nations control the amount of currency which can be used for buying imports. Usually foreign currency earnings (from exports) are deposited with the central bank, which authorizes the withdrawals for the buying of imports. In this way, selective control of imports can be achieved. In Britain up to 1979 when exchange control was abolished, transfers of cash and overseas investment were limited to protect the balance of payments.

(iv) Embargoes As we have already mentioned, some goods are completely banned from entry into a country. This encourages smuggling and the development of black markets.

(v) Quotas The import of a certain quantity of goods may be allowed, usually via licensing arrangements, for example footwear into the UK. Although acting on supply rather than demand, a quota has the same effects as a tariff in that it raises prices and domestic output whilst cutting the volume of imports.

(vi) Administrative Restrictions Prices, documents and procedures are used by many nations as a covert method of protection. A Japanese trading practice considered by other countries to be unfair is the withholding of information on product specifications from foreigners but warning domestic producers of changes well in advance. Similarly, Britain refuses to admit poultry from countries which use vaccination rather than slaughter as the means of controlling foul pest.

(vii) Voluntary Agreements One government may try to persuade another to pressurize its exporters into limiting supplies to certain markets, for example Japanese government restraint over Japanese car exports to the UK in 1981.

6 The General Agreement on Tariffs and Trade (GATT)

Towards the end of the Second World War, the American and British governments decided to establish new international institutions which would have the general aim of preventing a breakdown of world trade similar to the collapse which had contributed to the inter-war depression.

The intention was to create an **International Trade Organisation** (ITO) to liberalize trade, and an **International Monetary Fund** (see Units 27 and 28) to supervise the post-war system of payments and exchange rates. Because the charter to establish the ITO was never ratified, GATT, which was originally a temporary substitute for the ITO, survived as the most important international forum for expanding world trade and seeking the **multilateral** reduction of tariffs and other barriers to trade.

The General Agreement which came into operation in 1948 was based on four principles:

(i) **Non-discrimination** The **'most favoured nation' clause** binds countries to extend reductions in tariffs to the imports of all GATT members.

(ii) **Protection through tariffs** Where protection is justified, it should only be through tariffs and not through import quotas and other quantity controls.

(iii) **Consultation between members**

(iv) **Tariff reduction through negotiation** GATT should provide the framework through which successive *rounds* of tariff reduction are negotiated.

The history of GATT can be divided into two. During the 1950s and the 1960s the economic climate was such that countries were willing to negotiate tariff reductions, culminating in the 'Kennedy Round' of 1967. In more recent years, the main achievement of GATT has been in preventing members from reintroducing protectionist measures rather than in achieving any further notable liberalization of trade. The main advantages of tariff cuts have accrued to the advanced nations. In order to extend the tariff reductions of GATT to developing countries and to help primary producers, the United Nations established the **United Nations Conference on Trade and Development** (UNCTAD). This started in 1964 and meets every four years. However, because the problems of the developing countries are so diverse, co-operative trade developments have been limited.

7 Regional Economic Groupings

(i) **Free Trade Areas and Customs Unions** GATT allows the continuation of any system of tariffs in operation when GATT was signed. It also allows the creation of either a **Free Trade Area** (FTA) or a **Customs Union** (CU), both of which aim to liberalize trade between members, without extending most favoured nation treatment to non-members. Members of a FTA, such as the **Latin American Free Trade Area** (LAFTA), are free to choose their trading policy with outsiders. Britain was a founder member of the **European Free Trade Area** (EFTA), but left in 1973 to join the **European Economic Community** (EEC). The EEC is a Customs Union, in which a **common external tariff** restricts members' freedom of action. A Customs Union usually involves a much closer economic integration between members, who adopt **common policies** additional to the common external tariff. Indeed, the formation of the EEC as a Customs Union in 1958 is seen by many as a first step to full **Economic Union**, and perhaps even **Political Union**. Common economic policies have been established which either considerably replace the freedom of separate policy action in member countries (the CAP and the Common Fishery Policy) or supplement the policies of individual members (Regional and Competition Policy). Most members of the EEC are also members of the **European Monetary System** (Unit 28), which has been interpreted as a step towards full **Monetary Union**.

The effect on a country of its joining a Customs Union will depend on the **size of the common external tariff**, on whether the tariff is applied to all traded goods, and on the **pattern** of the country's trade. If a growing proportion of the country's trade is with the members of the CU, then there may be a strong case for joining, particularly if the common external tariff is high. However, FTAs are more consistent with the philosophy of GATT than are Customs Unions. The latter are more likely to encourage trade between members by diverting trade from non-members. The distortive effects of the common external tariff on trade with the rest of the world can depend on the extent to which the CU is 'inward'- or 'outward'-looking. Customs Unions can be **trade-diverting** or **trade-reducing** rather than **trade-creating**. They do not take comparative advantage to its logical conclusion, favouring instead internal producers against lower-cost external producers. The members of the EEC claim to be outward-looking, citing for example the Lomé Convention of 1975, renewed in 1979, which enables sixty less developed countries to export duty free to the EEC, and without reciprocity.

(ii) **Suppliers' organizations** Occasionally, producing countries co-operate in order to exploit the world market, for example by forming an international **cartel**. Primary producing countries justify the formation of agreements such as that of the **Organization of Petroleum Exporting Countries** (OPEC) in order to countervail the market power of industrial countries. For most of the 20th century, the terms of trade have moved against primary producers and in favour of industrial countries.

Indeed, the adverse effects of the terms of trade on developing countries, together with profit remittances to developed countries, may far have exceeded the benefits of any **aid**. By creating a monopoly in the supply of a primary product, countries hope to reverse the movement in the terms of trade. International producers' cartels are most effective when governments can control supply, when there is unity of purpose and action amongst members, and when the demand of the industrialized countries is greatest.

8 British Trade

Britain accounts for about 10 per cent of the world exports in manufactured goods, a figure which is relatively high considering the size of the British economy, but relatively low compared with past importance, reflecting declining competitiveness. The **geographical pattern** of British trade illustrates the world trend for trade to grow fastest between similar industrial countries, and for increased competition in the old colonial markets.

Table 26.1

Visible Trade by Area	1980	
	Exports %	Imports %
EEC	43.5	41.4
Other West Europe	14.3	14.6
North America	11.3	15.0
Other developed	5.6	6.8
OPEC	10.1	8.6
Rest of the world	15.2	13.6

Source: *Lloyds Bank Economic Profile 1981*

Britain's **commodity** pattern of trade has also altered. Imports have significantly changed in the last twenty years with improvements in the standard of living. In 1960 food imports were over 30 per cent and basic materials over 20 per cent but Table 26.2 shows their relative decline and the rapid growth of manufactured imports. In contrast the pattern of British exports has adjusted only marginally.

Table 26.2

Visible Trade by Commodity	1980	
	Exports %	Imports %
Food	6.9	12.4
Basic materials	3.1	8.1
Fuels	13.6	13.8
Semi-manufacturers	26.6	24.0
Manufacturers	40.6	32.6
Others	9.2	9.1

Source: *Lloyds Bank Economic Profile 1981*

British trading performance reflects both the underlying trends of imports increasing as a percentage of GDP (a trend shared with most developed countries) and fluctuations associated with the business cycle. In a depression stocks are run down and production is cut whilst lower demand generally also cuts import demand. There has been a growing import penetration into British markets, particularly in consumer goods where Britain's **high income elasticity of demand** is significant. This has been explained by the low growth rate in the British economy which has rendered domestic firms unable to generate the **spare capacity** which could be used to meet surges in demand. As a result, imports fill the gap (for example motor vehicles, electronics).

It is usually claimed that British exports maintain their share of world trade during slumps but fall behind in periods of world expansion. Thus, over time Britain's share of world manufactured exports has declined. Reasons suggested include inadequate salesmanship, failure to meet delivery dates, poor after-sales service, lack of capital and higher rates of inflation resulting in price uncompetitiveness.

British exports of goods, excluding oil, have grown more slowly than imports in the 1970s. However, export services have been most successful and made a vital contribution to the Balance of Payments, as explained in Unit 27. Japan's **export-led growth** has been envied but not copied. The theory that expanding exports generate growth by increasing comparative advantage, productivity and profits, as propounded by Kaldor, Beckerman and others, is not wholly accepted. Some critics believe that causation runs from growth to exports, rather than vice versa.

26.4 LINKS WITH OTHER TOPICS

Although trade gives an international dimension to economics, the theory of trade is essential based on the concepts of scarcity, production possibilities and opportunity cost, division of labour and economies of scale which we first introduced in Units 1 to 6. We now examine some of the complications, distortions and barriers to trade which result from the fact that countries may lack an acceptable means of payment for trade (Unit 27 on the Balance of Payments), while in Unit 28 we see how exchange rates can cause further distortions and uncertainties.

26.5 QUESTION PRACTICE

Essay Questions

Question 1 Discuss the benefits to be obtained from the application of the principle of comparative advantage and show the operation of the principle by means of a numerical example.

(London: January, 1979)

Understanding the Question The principle of comparative advantage shows how countries can benefit from trade even if one country has an absolute advantage in producing most goods. The simplifying assumptions of the theory require explaining at the outset so that an example, as illustrated in the unit, can be devised. Each country **specializes** in producing the goods in which it is relatively most efficient. This specialization may yield further increases in output such as the benefits of economies of scale which do not directly result from the principle of comparative advantage.

A candidate must also mention that the **distribution** of the benefits will be determined by exchange rates, the strength of demand and income patterns, both within and between nations. Furthermore, discussion of the benefits implies consideration of the disadvantages associated with such specialization – loss of economic independence, intense susceptibility to world prices and events, growth of externalities. In addition, a critical examination of the theory's assumptions, regarding transport, trade and the mobility of factors, should be made.

Answer plan

1 Explain the general idea of comparative advantage, clearly distinguishing the principle from absolute advantage.
2 Elaborate the assumptions.
3 Calculate an example to show how it works.
4 Consider the benefits.
5 Comment on the defects.

Question 2 Many nations' economies are heavily dependent on primary production. Discuss some of the economic problems which these nations experience because of this dependence. **(25)**

(SEB 1981)

Understanding the Question The key to this question is the term primary production, that is, the production of food, minerals, raw materials, etc. Thus the question could relate to problems of richer countries like New Zealand, from the so-called developed world, or to the economies of the oil-rich states such as Saudi Arabia, as well as to the under-developed countries of the third world dependent on one or more cash crop, for example Brazil or Burma.

Strictly, the question should be answered from the standpoint of primary producers' **dependence** on a narrow range of products, and the often dramatic **fluctuations of world demand**, allied to **supply side problems** such as crop failure. However, at this level it is perfectly reasonable to develop an answer along the lines of the broader problems of less-developed countries, many of which coincide with those problems arising purely from dependence on primary products as above. Credit will also be earned from an attempt to clarify the meaning of the term 'dependence' in economics. This dependence might be reflected in the GNP, level of employment, or balance of payments, but the country does not have to be only a primary producer to be regarded as dependent on that sector. General problems of development, such as lack of technical expertise, capital, etc., are relevant to the question, while comments on such issues as over-population are not directly relevant. However, a good answer might touch on the trade-off between the desire to grow food for the indigenous population and the need to increase the volume of cash crop production to boost export earnings.

Answer plan

1 Definition of primary production, contrasting it with the other sectors of production.
2 A description with examples of dependent economies e.g. Bolivia (copper).
3 Economic problems – **(a)** dependence on the state of world trade, particularly the vulnerability to world recession and price fluctuations. **(b)** the difficulty of developing new markets; **(c)** problems of over-production; **(d)** difficulty of diversification in the face of competition from overseas; and **(e)** the development of synthetic substitutes. Examples will once again earn credit.

Question 3 Show how, in theory, free trade among nations leads to an increase in economic welfare. What justification, if any, can you find for the policy of selective import controls advocated by some economists in recent years for Britain?

(JMB: June, 1980)

Understanding the Question Free trade, in theory, leads to international specialization, the division of labour, large markets and economies of scale. There is efficient allocation of world's resources and output is maximized. The benefits of this can be translated into improved living standards, assuming a certain pattern of income distribution.

The second part of the question seeks a critique of the simplifying assumptions of the free trade model. For instance, trading nations are not equally powerful, persistent trade deficits occur in certain economies and income distribution patterns vary. Thus a nation may require protection, as it may suffer whilst 'the world' gains! 'Unfair' competition may occur in certain sectors of an economy and thus the 'selective' aspect to the question needs emphasizing. British industries such as textiles and shoes have sought and received protection against the low-cost imports from developing countries. You could also introduce the arguments put forward by the New Cambridge School justifying selective import controls on the basis that they eventually increase trade.

Answer plan

1 Explain what you understand by economic welfare, and how an increase in the world's production possibilities should increase welfare.

2 Briefly illustrate how specialization and free trade can increase production and hence welfare, in comparison with a situation in which countries impose import controls.

3 Selective import controls may seek to minimize disruption to free trade. They may be used where 'dumping' is suspected, or to protect industries facing rapid structural decline as a result of a sudden change in their competitiveness. They can be justified in order to reduce the costs of the adjustment process as industries adapt to changing demand.

4 Mention the disadvantages of selective import controls; they may protect inefficiency, provoke retaliation, or be the first move in a shift towards protectionism, endangering export industries.

Multiple Choice Questions

Questions 4 and 5 These refer to the following information:
In a simple model of international trade there are two countries, A and B, and two commodities, guns and butter. When each country divides its resources equally between the two products they produce as follows:

	Guns (units)	Butter (units)
Country A	600	400
Country B	800	200

Question 4 Assuming constant returns to scale, if each country specializes in producing the commodity in which it has a comparative advantage, total output will increase by:

(a) 200 units of guns
(b) 400 units of guns and 200 units of butter
(c) 200 units of guns and 200 units of butter
(d) 200 units of guns and 400 units of butter

Question 5 Which of the following would improve the terms of trade of country A?

(a) An increase in the world price of butter
(b) An increase in the world price of guns
(c) An increase in the volume of butter exports
(d) The imposition of a tariff on the exports of country B

Understanding the Questions This is a simple model of absolute advantage in which country B has an absolute advantage in the production of guns and A has an absolute advantage in butter. It is obviously the case that each country has a comparative advantage in the commodity in which it has an absolute advantage. Total 'world production' is 1400 units of guns and 600 units of butter without specialization, whereas output increases to 1600 guns and 800 units of butter when each country specializes in the activity in which it has a comparative advantage. The correct answer to Question 4 is therefore (c).

The terms of trade move in a country's favour if its export prices rise relative to the price of imports. Since country A exports butter, the commodity in which it has a comparative advantage, the answer to Question 5 is (a).

Data Response Questions

Question 6 Study the table below and answer the questions which follow;

United Kingdom Visible Trade Statistics

1970 = 100 Volume Indices		1970 = 100 Unit Value Indices			1970 Trade competitiveness index (i)	1970 = 100 World commodity prices index (ii)	Dec. 1971 = 100 Sterling effective exchange rate
	Exports	Imports	Exports	Imports	Terms of Trade			
1971	107	104	106	105	101	102	105	—
1972	107	117	111	110	101	103	116	95
1973	122	134	126	140	90	94	168	86
1974	132	136	163	217	75	93	295	84
1975	126	134	199	246	81	96	300	77
1976	136	134	241	300	80	95	385	65

(Source: *Economic Trends*, H.M.S.O. September, 1977)

(i) The ratio of UK to weighted average export (dollar) prices for major competitors in respect of manufactured goods.

(ii) Weighted average, in sterling terms, of United Nations Index numbers for primary commodities and non-ferrous metals.

(*a*) Comment briefly on the trend in Britain's net barter terms of trade. (4 marks)

(*b*) What effect would the changes in the terms of trade have had on the standard of living in the United Kingdom over the period 1971–1976? (4 marks)

(*c*) What other series listed in the table may help to explain movements in the volume and unit value of imports? (4 marks)

(*d*) Discuss the main factors determining the trade competitiveness of British manufacturing industry. (4 marks)

(*e*) What connections, if any, are there between movements in the exchange rate and changes in the other series? (4 marks)

(Cambridge: November, 1979)

Understanding the Question The terms of trade refer to the **price** of exports and imports rather than the volume. Britain's position has clearly declined over this period because import prices have risen faster than exports as the unit value indices show. The rising price of oil imports was a major cause of the deterioration in Britain's terms of trade in these years. When the terms of trade move against a nation, then, other things being equal, the standard of living will fall. The effect may be direct through the higher prices of imported finished products or indirect via raw materials raising domestic costs and eventually prices. There may also be secondary effects on wages. Since more goods must be exported to purchase a given volume of imports, less of the domestically produced output is available to support the citizens' standard of living.

You should note the relationships between the different columns in question (c) and (e). For instance, the volume correlates with trade competitiveness through the idea of elasticity. Also, the unit volume index and the world commodity prices index follow a similar pattern, indicating the importance of primary products in British imports.

If the rate of inflation in the UK is higher than that in other countries, export prices will rise relative to import prices and the terms of trade will improve. Unless the exchange rate falls, however, British exports will become increasingly uncompetitive, particularly if foreigners' demand for British exports is price elastic. British trade competitiveness will therefore be affected by the factors which determine British production costs, movements in the exchange rate, and the degree to which foreign goods are close substitutes for British exports. A fall in the exchange rate should make exports cheaper and imports more expensive, thus affecting the unit value index and intensifying the commodity prices problem. However, it should make British goods more competitive – the lack of correlation here suggests that the more fundamental problems of inflation and low productivity overpower the exchange rate advantage.

26.6 FURTHER READING

Livesey, F., *A Textbook of Economics* (Polytech Publishers Ltd, 1978).
Chapter 7: International Trade and the Balance of Payments

Lipsey, R. G., *An Introduction to Positive Economics*, 5th edition (Weidenfeld & Nicolson, 1979).
Chapter 42: The gains from International Trade
Chapter 44: Tariffs and the gains from Trade

27 The Balance of Payments

27.1 POINTS OF PERSPECTIVE

In Unit 26 we noted how the existence of **barriers to trade** such as import controls can prevent two countries from trading together even though they might both benefit from the exchange. We now go on in Units 27 and 28 to examine how **payment difficulties and uncertainties** can cause further barriers to trade, and how they can also affect the domestic economy and the government's economic management thereof. This unit concentrates on a country's **Balance of Payments**, while Unit 28 looks at the interrelated question of the **exchange rate**. We also introduce important aspects of the **international monetary system**, including the role of **reserve currencies** and other means of payment, and of **international institutions** such as the **International Monetary Fund** (IMF).

27.2 UNDERLYING CONCEPTS

1 The Balance of Payments as part of the system of National Accounts

Whenever trade takes place between nations, payment must eventually be made in a currency or means of payment acceptable to the country from whom goods or services have been purchased. The **Balance of Payments** is the part of the **National Accounts** which records payments to, and receipts from, the rest of the world. Although these payments and receipts are part of a **continuous flow** of currences between countries, it is conventional to measure the Balance of Payments over a time-period of either a single month, quarter, or year.

Since the Balance of Payments is an official record collected by the government, the presentation of the statistics depends upon how the government decides to group and classify the different

Table 27.1: Summary of the British Balance of Payments

1 CURRENT ACCOUNT	£m
(i) Visible exports	+
(ii) Visible imports	−
(iii) Balance of Visible Trade	A
(iv) Invisible exports	+
(v) Invisible imports	−
(vi) Balance of Invisible Trade	B
(vii) Current Balance	A + B
2 INVESTMENT AND OTHER CAPITAL FLOWS (THE CAPITAL ACCOUNT)	
(viii) Long-term capital flows (inflows +, outflows −)	net
(ix) Short-term capital flows (inflows +, outflows −)	net
(x) Total Investment and other capital flows	C
(xi) Balancing item (+ or −)	D
(xii) Balance for Official Financing	A + B + C + D
3 OFFICIAL FINANCING	
(xiii) Transactions with IMF and foreign central banks	net
(xiv) Foreign currency borrowing by public sector	net
(xv) Drawings on (+) or additions to (−) official reserves	net
(xvi) Total Official Financing	− (A + B + C + D)

items of payment. In recent years the British government has divided the Balance of Payments into the three categories which are summarized in Table 27.1. These are:

(1) The Current Account
(2) Investment and Other Capital Flows (also known as the Capital Account)
(3) Official Financing

2 The Balance of Payments on Current Account

This measures the flow of expenditure on **goods** and **services** and broadly indicates the income gained and lost from **trade**. The Current Balance is usually considered the most important part of the Balance of Payments, reflecting the international competitiveness of the UK economy and the extent to which the nation is living within its means. If receipts exceed payments there is of course a Current Account **surplus**. The Current Balance is obtained by simply adding the **Balance of Visible Trade** (A in Table 27.1) to the **Balance of Invisible Trade** (B in Table 27.1).

(i) The Balance of Visible Trade Although visible trade is the most important single item in the Balance of Payments, it is perhaps the most simple to define. The Visible Balance measures the value in **pounds sterling** of **goods** exported minus the sterling value of goods imported. The Visible Trade Balance is often referred to simply as the **Balance of Trade**, but this is rather a loose term which is also used to refer to the whole of the Current Account Balance, including invisibles.

(ii) The Balance of Invisible Trade In general terms this measures the sterling value of **services** exported minus the value of services imported. However, the Invisible Balance includes a number of rather disparate items. For example, invisible **exports** include:

(a) a large part of the earnings of the City of London, insurance and brokerage services, etc.;
(b) the overseas earnings of British shipping and aviation services;
(c) expenditure by overseas governments on embassies and military bases in the UK;
(d) spending by foreign tourists;
(e) gifts of money from overseas residents to British residents;
(f) dividends or profits remitted to British residents owning capital assets overseas – the difference between such profit inflows and outflows is sometimes known as **net property income from abroad**.

Conversely any payments from British residents to overseas residents for shipping services, tourism, the upkeep of embassies, etc., are **invisible imports**. In recent years Britain's **net contribution to the EEC budget** has developed into an important invisible import. Some forms of **aid to developing countries** are also classified in the invisible account.

3 The Changing Nature of the UK Current Account

For most of the 20th century the British Balance of Payments on Current Account displayed a **deficit** on the balance of visible trade and a **surplus** on the invisible balance, both of which could be explained by the **principle of comparative advantage**. The emergence of other competing industrial countries reduced or eliminated Britain's comparative advantage in many manufacturing industries, but she still retained her advantage in services. Whether the overall Balance on Current Account was in surplus or deficit in any single year depended on whether the invisible surplus was sufficient to offset the visible deficit.

In the 1970s and 1980s significant changes have occurred in the composition of the Current Account:

(i) The contribution of **North Sea oil revenue** moved the visible balance into surplus, both through import-saving and oil exports.

(ii) However, this disguised the continuing deterioration of the balance of **non-oil visible trade**, reflecting the growing **propensity to import** in the UK and the uncompetitiveness of British manufacturers. Indeed, it is useful nowadays to divide the visible balance into the separate categories of the **oil balance** and the **non-oil balance** of visible trade. The revenues of North Sea oil have been largely used to finance domestic standards of living through the import of consumer goods and foodstuffs. Indeed in 1982 for the first time ever, Britain's imports of manufactured goods began to exceed her exports of manufactures.

(iii) While the invisible balance is still in surplus, the surplus is proportionately smaller than it used to be. This reflects the growing importance of other financial centres competing with the City of London, the UK contribution to the EEC budget, and profit remittances to European, Japanese and American companies, including the oil companies which developed the North Sea. The decline in the relative importance of the invisible surplus points to serious problems which may emerge for the UK if and when North Sea oil runs dry.

4 Investment and Other Capital Flows

The **Capital Account** of the Balance of Payments indicates the extent to which the residents of a nation forgo consumption in order to acquire capital assets overseas that may earn income in the future. In order to understand the importance of the Capital Account it is useful to distinguish between **long-term** and **short-term** capital flows, although this distinction is no longer made in the official presentation of the UK Balance of Payments.

(i) Long-term Capital Flows We can explain long-term capital flows by invoking the principle of comparative advantage, which explained the nature of visible trade. A long-term capital flow occurs when residents of one country buy up or invest in the productive resources **within** another country. They will do so if they believe that their financial assets can be more productively and profitably employed in the other country.

A net outflow of long-term capital means that there is more investment by British citizens in other countries than there is foreign investment in Britain. Such an outflow includes both **real investment**, when for example a British company buys or creates a foreign subsiduary, and **portfolio investment**, when British residents purchase the shares of overseas companies or the securities of foreign governments.

(ii) Short-term Capital Flows Since changes in comparative advantage usually take place relatively slowly, the long-term capital flows tend to be stable and predictable. Movements in the Balance of Payments resulting from the changing pattern of either trade or of long-term capital flows are said to be **spontaneous** or **autonomous**. In contrast, short-term capital flows are neither stable nor predictable, and they frequently occur in response to a change in the autonomous part of the Balance of Payments. A growing proportion of the short-term flows is extremely volatile **'hot money'** which, by flowing in – and just as quickly out – of countries, can destabilize the Balance of Payments, the exchange rate, and indeed the international monetary system as a whole. Hot money is the name given to the pool of 'footloose' hard currencies owned by governments, banks, businesses and private individuals, usually outside the exchange controls of the currency's country of origin. A major cause of the growth of hot money flows lies in the emergence of the **Eurodollar market** after 1957.

The pool of Eurodollars grew dramatically in the 1960s and 1970s when the USA persuaded other countries to accept payment for the US Balance of Payments deficit in dollars. Some of these dollars were received in payment for American imports, but others arose from capital investment overseas by American firms and the growth of overseas bank deposits owned by American residents. The early growth of the Eurodollar market was prompted by the imposition of restrictions by the American monetary authorities upon the domestic banking system. In the absence of exchange controls, it became more profitable for American residents to keep their dollars in overseas bank accounts, often in the subsidiaries of US banks, rather than in deposits held within the USA.

From these origins in the late 1950s and 1960s the Eurodollar market has grown, hugely supplemented by the injection of 'petrodollars' after the oil crises in the 1970s when the OPEC countries accumulated large Balance of Payments surpluses matched by deficits in the oil-consuming industrial countries. The oil-producing countries placed a significant proportion of their oil revenues on deposit in the European banking system, thus adding to the pool of footloose hot money. Indeed the market is perhaps better called the **Eurocurrency market**. Although the dollar is still the most important currency deposited, other currencies such as sterling and the Deutsch Mark are also involved.

The European banks, including those in London, have developed a thriving business in the short-term borrowing and lending of international currencies, outside the exchange controls which may exist in their countries of origin. These Eurocurrency flows are extremely destabilizing because the sheer size of the hot money pool means that the financial markets and Balance of Payments of a single country can be overwhelmed by a sudden inward or outward flow which may often occur for essentially speculative reasons. A hot money flow into a country may be triggered by high rates of interest, by the belief that the exchange rate is undervalued, or by an event such as a Middle East war, when currencies are shifted into countries that are regarded as 'safe havens' for funds. The movement of funds into a country on a large scale itself puts upward pressure on the exchange rate since it creates a demand for the local currency on foreign exchanges, when for example government securities are purchased by the overseas owners of hot money. Conversely, a sudden outflow can cause a rapid deterioration in the Balance of Payments and downward pressure on the exchange rate.

5 The Current and Capital Accounts and Official Financing

Like all balance-sheets, the Balance of Payments must balance, at least in a strictly accounting sense. This means that all the items in the Balance of Payments must **sum to zero**. Thus if there is a Balance of Payments surplus on Current and Capital Account of + £200 million (the Balance for Official Financing), there must be **accommodating flows** in the final section of the Balance of Payments of exactly − £200 million. Intuitively you might feel that this accounting convention is rather strange. It seems more reasonable that the **additions to reserves** resulting from a Balance of Payments surplus should be shown as a positive figure. But this does not happen. In order to make the accounts exactly sum to zero, the additions to reserves resulting from a surplus are shown as a negative figure and the drawings on reserves which occur when the Balance is in deficit are shown as a positive figure.

Table 27.1 shows that changes in official reserves are only one of the possible methods of officially financing a deficit or surplus on Current and Capital Account. In fact the change in reserves will be a final **residual** financing after any official borrowing from the IMF or foreign central banks to finance a deficit, or the repaying of previous borrowing in the case of a surplus. Foreign borrowing (or its repayment) by nationalized industries to finance domestic investment is also included in the Official Financing section of the Balance of Payments.

Indeed, this illustrates an interesting but potentially misleading aspect of how the Balance of Payments is constructed. If a large deficit occurs on the Current Account, reflecting an uncompetitive trading position of the British economy, it can be financed **either** through a **Capital Account surplus** or through **Official Financing**, or through **both methods**. While it is usually difficult for the authorities to influence quickly the largely autonomous long-term capital flows (except through the imposition or removal of exchange controls and tax advantages), this is not true of the short-term capital flows. Thus the authorities may raise interest rates in order to engineer a hot money inflow as an alternative to the official financing of the deficit through drawing on reserves or borrowing from the IMF. Similarly, in the more recent case of a Current Account surplus the authorities may prefer to encourage a capital outflow rather than finance the surplus through the accumulation of official reserves.

This brings us to the very important point that a long-term capital outflow, while 'worsening' the Balance of Payments, can have considerable long-term advantages for a country. Overseas capital investment results in a country's residents' owning assets in other countries which will in future years yield a profit and dividend flow-back to the country. By creating a surplus on the invisible balance of trade in the Current Account, the profit inflow will allow the country's residents to benefit from standards of living and levels of consumption greater than could be sustained by the country's output level alone – broadly speaking the profit inflow can be used in future years to finance a deficit on visible trade. This is precisely the benefit which British residents have received during the 20th century from earlier capital investment.

A capital inflow can also have advantages if it is invested in assets which add to the country's productive potential and efficiency in future years. If, however, a capital inflow or official borrowing merely finances current consumption and standards of living – via the trade deficit that the inflows make possible – then trouble will most likely be built up for the future. The inflow will not have increased the country's productive potential, yet part of the nation's income will have to be sacrificed in interest payments on the foreign debt which has been incurred.

6 The Balancing Item

The official estimates of the Current and Capital Accounts will seldom be accurate because of the imperfect nature of data collection. The authorities may feel that the data on the accommodating flows in the Official Financing section are more accurate than the highly disparate data collected on trading and capital flows in the autonomous or spontaneous sections of the Balance of Payments. Therefore it is usual for a 'Balancing Item' – analagous to the residual error in the National Accounts – to be added or subtracted from the Balance on Current and Capital Account in order to make the Balance for Official Financing exactly equal (but with the opposite sign) to the Total Official Financing. In the years following the first publication of the Balance of Payments statistics for a particular year the figures are constantly revised. It is quite usual for all the figures to change and for the Balancing Item to become smaller as it is gradually 'allocated' to one or other of the 'real' items in the Balance of Payments.

27.3 Essential knowledge

1 Balance of Payments Equilibrium and Disequilibrium

Although in an accounting sense the Balance of Payments always balances, this can obscure the fact that a country's payments may not be in a state of equilibrium. **Balance of payments equilibrium** (or **external equilibrium**) is usually taken to mean that the **desired spontaneous** or **autonomous trade and capital flows** into and out of the country are equal over a number of years. A state of equilibrium in the Balance of Payments is perfectly compatible with the existence of **short-term** surpluses and deficits. But a **fundamental disequilibrium** in the Balance of Payments will exist if there is a persistent tendency for the autonomous flows out of the country to be greater or less than the corresponding inflows. When for example a persistent deficit occurs in the autonomous items in the Balance of Payments, it must be accommodated by a loss of reserves, by official borrowing in the Official Financing section of the Payments account, or by 'unofficial' borrowing via a hot money inflow in the Capital Account.

2 The Problem of a Balance of Payments Deficit

While a short-run deficit or surplus on either the Current or Capital Account of the Balance of Payments seldom poses a problem, the same is not true when a persistent imbalance indicates a fundamental disequilibrium. It is easy to see why a persistent deficit in the autonomous items in the Current and Capital Accounts is a problem, since the resulting loss of reserves and need for borrowing cannot be maintained indefinitely. However, the extent of the problem depends on a number of factors, including the **size of the deficit, its cause** and the **exchange rate regime**.

Obviously, the larger the deficit the greater the problem is likely to be, but it also depends upon which items are in deficit. For example, an overall deficit caused by a long-term capital outflow may produce the long-term benefit of an eventual profits inflow in the invisibles section of the Current Account. In contrast, if the cause of the deficit lies in the Current Account the problem may be more serious. Although a trade deficit allows the country's residents to enjoy a higher standard of living than would be possible from the consumption of the country's output alone, it may also reflect the uncompetitiveness of the country's goods and services.

In the next unit we shall examine in some detail the effect of different exchange rate regimes upon the Balance of Payments. In this unit we can merely note that a payments deficit is usually considered more of a problem under **fixed exchange rates** than when the exchange rate is **freely floating**. In a floating regime the market mechanism may eliminate the cause of export uncompetitiveness and restore an equilibrium in the Balance of Payments. In contrast, when the exchange rate is fixed the government usually has to take action through **deflation, import controls, devaluation** of the exchange rate, or a combination of all three.

In the 1960s and 1970s it was widely believed that the British Balance of Payments posed a problem in the sense that in a fixed exchange rate regime the exchange rate was 'unavailable' as a policy instrument to cure the persistent payments deficit that Britain experienced at that time. This meant that the **internal** policy objectives of full employment and growth had to be sacrificed to the **external** objective of protecting the Balance of Payments and supporting the exchange rate, which imposed a serious **constraint** on the sustained achievement of the domestic policy objectives. Floating the exchange rate was regarded as an 'escape route' from this constraint; a floating exchange rate would 'look after' the Balance of Payments, allowing economic policy to be devoted to the internal policy objectives.

However, the experience of floating exchange rates after 1972 – albeit **dirty** or **managed** floating rather than **clean** or **freely floating** exchange rates – has led to considerable disenchantment with this view. Countries have still intervened to protect the Balance of Payments and to support the exchange rate. In particular there has been a growing awareness of the effects of a falling exchange rate on the domestic inflation rate and the pursuit of internal policy objectives. It is now generally accepted that even with a floating exchange rate the Balance of Payments cannot be completely isolated from the pursuit of internal economic policy. These issues are discussed further in Units 26 and 28.

3 The Problem of a Balance of Payments Surplus

While it is generally accepted that a persistent Balance of Payments deficit is a problem, it is much less obvious that a surplus can also pose problems. Indeed, because a surplus is often regarded as a symbol of national economic success, many people argue that the bigger the surplus, the more successful the country must be. Nevertheless there are a number of reasons why a persistently large surplus is undesirable, even though a small surplus may be a more justifiable objective of policy:

(i) One country's surplus is another country's deficit It is impossible for all countries simultaneously to run surpluses. If countries refuse to reduce their persistently large surpluses, then deficit countries will find it difficult, and even impossible, to reduce their deficits. The danger then arises that deficit countries will resort to import controls and all countries may suffer from a consequent reduction or collapse in world trade. In recent years the danger posed to the development of world trade by excessive surpluses and deficits has been well illustrated by the problem of recycling the surpluses of the oil-producing countries.

(ii) The 'Dutch disease' effect The growth of Britain's own oil trade surplus in the 1970s and 1980s illustrates another way in which a surplus can create a problem. In 1980 and 1981 the Current Account surplus, reinforced by hot money inflows on the Capital Account, caused the exchange rate to rise to a level which decreased the competitiveness of non-oil visible exports in world markets, and increased the competitiveness of imports in the UK economy. This accelerated the **de-industrialization** of the British economy and caused much of the benefit of North Sea oil revenues to be 'lost' in financing imports and the upkeep of the growing number of unemployed. The effect of the Balance of Payments surplus upon the exchange rate and the domestic economy is called the **'Dutch disease'** after the experience of the Netherlands following the discovery and development of natural gas in the 1950s and 1960s.

(iii) In Keynesian terms, a Balance of Payments surplus represents an **injection of demand** into the economy, causing **demand-pull inflation** if output cannot be raised to meet demand.

(iv) The money supply and a Balance of Payments surplus In an open economy the domestic money supply is affected by the Balance of Payments; a surplus tends to increase and a deficit to decrease the money supply unless the exchange rate is freely floating. When the Balance of Payments is in surplus, the country's currency is in short supply on foreign exchange markets. If the authorities wish to prevent the exchange rate from rising in response to the excess demand, they must buy the foreign currencies being offered in the market, giving their own currency in exchange. The nation's foreign currency reserves expand, but only at the expense of an increase in the money supply. The process of selling the country's own currency and buying reserves in order to prevent the exchange rate from rising is an example of **exchange equalization**.

The extent to which a Balance of Payments surplus (or deficit) leads to an increase (or decrease) in the money supply depends upon the exchange rate policy being pursued. A 'clean' or pure float can eliminate the external imbalance with little or no change in either the reserves or the money supply, but if the exchange rate is fixed or managed quite large changes in both can result. The impact of the Balance of Payments upon the domestic money supply clearly poses a problem for **monetarist economic policy**, with its emphasis on the need to control the rate of growth of the money supply.

This also explains why monetarists sometimes prefer **Domestic Credit Expansion** to monetary aggregates such as M1 or Sterling M3 as a measure of monetary growth in the **domestic** economy. DCE is broadly defined as Sterling M3 plus (or minus) the Balance of Payments deficit (or surplus). Thus when the Balance of Payments is in surplus, Sterling M3 is greater than DCE, but the reverse is true when the Balance of Payments is in deficit.

4 Policies to Cure a Fundamental Disequilibrium in the Balance of Payments

We shall now discuss in more detail the various policy measures of **deflation**, the imposition of **import controls**, and **devaluation** (or a **managed** or **'dirty' downward float**), which can be used to correct a persistent Balance of Payments deficit. (In Unit 28 we shall discuss how a payments disequilibrium is **automatically** corrected without the need for government intervention under **freely floating** and **rigidly fixed (gold standard)** exchange rates.)

(i) Deflation Both **fiscal policy** and **monetary policy** can be used to deflate the level of demand in an economy in order to correct a payments deficit. Deflation is primarily an **expenditure-reducing policy** which cures a deficit by reducing the demand for imports. The increase in unused capacity produced by the deflation may also encourage firms to seek extra export orders, though many economists argue that a sound and expanding home market is necessary for a successful export drive since exports are usually less profitable than domestic sales. A deflation can also have a subsidiary **expenditure-switching effect** upon the Balance of Payments. Successful deflation results in the domestic inflation rate falling relative to that in other countries, thereby increasing the **price competitiveness** and demand for British exports, while reducing the demand for imports.

However, a deflationary policy usually involves severe costs, since in modern economies **output** and **employment** fall rather than the **price level**. For this reason, governments may use the **expenditure-switching policies** of import controls and devaluation as alternatives to expenditure-reducing deflation.

(ii) Import Controls Import controls have a direct **expenditure-switching** effect upon the Balance of Payments. **Quotas** and **embargoes** reduce or prevent expenditure on imports, while **tariffs** or **import duties** discourage expenditure by increasing the relative price of imports. However, import controls do not deal with the underlying cause of imbalance – usually the uncompetitiveness of a country's industries – and they may provoke retaliation with an undesirable decrease in world trade and specialization. In any case, import controls may be 'unavailable' because of membership of a trading body such as GATT which discourages their use.

(iii) Devaluation The 'unavailability' of import controls as an effective instrument to correct a payments deficit has meant that the real policy choice has usually been between **deflation** and **devaluation**. Devaluation of a fixed exchange rate, or a managed or 'dirty' downward float, is essentially an **expenditure-switching** policy. By increasing the price of imports relative to the price of exports, a successful devaluation switches demand away from imports and towards domestically produced goods. Similarly, foreign demand for the country's exports increases in response to the fall in price.

However, the effectiveness of a devaluation (and of any expenditure-switching policy) depends in large part upon the **price elasticities of demand for exports and imports**. It is easy to see that when the demands for exports and imports are both highly elastic, a devaluation will improve the Balance of Payments. Overseas residents will spend more on British exports following a fall in their relative price, while British residents will spend less on imports. But it is rather more difficult to see what will happen if the demands are less elastic. Providing, however, that the **sum of the export and import elasticities is greater than unity**, it can be shown that a devaluation or downward movement of the exchange rate will reduce a payments deficit (and that a **revaluation** will reduce a **surplus**). This is known as the **Marshall-Lerner condition** or criterion for a successful devaluation or revaluation.

5 Expenditure-reducing versus Expenditure-switching policies

While the Marshall-Lerner condition is a **necessary condition** for a successful expenditure-switching devaluation, it is not a **sufficient condition**. A devaluation could fail if there were insufficient spare capacity within the domestic economy. Spare capacity is needed in order to **increase supply** so as to meet the switching of overseas and domestic demand away from foreign goods and towards the home-produced output. Thus it is far better to regard an **expenditure-reducing deflation** and an **expenditure-switching devaluation** as *complementary* rather than as *substitute* policies in curing a payments deficit. Deflation alone may be unnecessarily costly in lost output and employment, yet may still be necessary to create the spare capacity and 'prepare the way' for a later successful devaluation.

6 The J-Curve Effect

Even if an expenditure-reducing deflation creates the spare capacity, a country's industries may still be unable **immediately** to increase supply following a devaluation. It may also be that the Marshall-Lerner condition is not met in the immediate period, since the demand for exports and imports is likely to be much more inelastic in the short run than in the long run. Thus the Balance of Payments may actually deteriorate before it improves. This is known as the **J-curve effect**. The deterioration in the Balance of Payments may reduce confidence in the eventual success of the policy, leading to capital outflows which destabilize both the Balance of Payments and the exchange rate. The existence of the J-curve effect, which can perhaps be minimized by an expenditure-reducing deflation prior to the devaluation, reduces the attractiveness of exchange rate adjustment as a policy to cure a payments deficit. And even when the benefits of the devaluation are realized, they may be relatively short-lived. The advantages of price competitiveness produced by the devaluation may be lost as a result of increased import prices raising the country's inflation rate.

7 The Absorption Approach to the Balance of Payments

Whereas the Marshall Lerner condition illustrates the **elasticities approach** to the Balance of Payments, the need to deflate domestic demand in order to prepare for a later successful devaluation reflects the **absorption approach**. This examines the Balance of Payments in an essentially Keynesian way in terms of aggregate demand **absorbing**, or failing to absorb, a country's output. In Unit 21 we wrote the equilibrium condition for National Income as

$$Y = C + I + G + X - M$$

Rewriting the equation, we get:

$$X - M = Y - (C + I + G)$$

Thus the Balance of Payments (X − M) will be in deficit if the economy consumes or **absorbs** more goods and services than it produces: if (C + I + G) is greater than Y.

To put it another way, the Balance of Payments equals national output less national absorption. If unemployed resources exist, an expenditure-switching devaluation can reduce a payments deficit without having to reduce absorption, but if full employment exists, Y cannot increase. The Balance of Payments can only improve if the economy is deflated and domestic absorption reduced.

27.4 LINKS WITH OTHER TOPICS

The Balance of Payments is one part of the **National Income Accounts** which have been considered in Unit 20. The major **macro-economic issues and policies** considered in Units 17–19 and 21–25 all influence, and are often influenced by, the payments position. Similarly world trade (Unit 26) and international exchange rates, which we consider in Unit 28, have a significant impact upon a nation's Balance of Payments position and performance.

27.5 QUESTION PRACTICE

Essay Questions

Question 1 'A deficit on the Balance of Payments Current Account has favourable short-run but unfavourable long-run consequences.' Discuss.

(AEB: June, 1981)

Understanding the Question A Current Account deficit means that an economy is obtaining certain goods and services (imports) without paying for them out of existing income. The payment for the excess of spending over income is met out of reserves or by borrowing.

In the short run, which in Balance of Payments terms means a number of months or at most one or two years, a country can gain by consumption or investment beyond its means. The standard of living may improve through extra consumption in the short run, while in the long run increased investment may enhance growth potential. Whilst confidence in the currency remains, a small deficit may not be too unfavourable even in the long run, particularly if capital inflows support the exchange rate.

However, if the deficit is both large and persistent, the economy may suffer in the long run although the manner may vary according to how the deficit is financed and dealt with. A loss of reserves may lead to loss of confidence in the economy, thereby weakening the currency and reducing the attractiveness of inward investment. Thus the Capital Account may in turn become less favourable. External currency borrowing may lead to foreign interference in domestic economic policy, as Britain found in 1976 when obtaining credit from the IMF. Generally, however, a government will take action to reduce the payments deficit. In Britain's case this has almost always involved deflation with the undesirable side-effects of reducing growth, output and employment levels.

Answer plan

1 Briefly explain the Current Account Balance and illustrate how a deficit may arise.
2 Consider the short-run favourable effects in terms of increased living standards.
3 There may also be long-run benefits if the deficit is used to finance investment and growth.
4 Explain how in the long run a persistently large deficit is likely to have unfavourable effects.
5 The policies required to cure a long-run deficit may also have unfavourable effects. Discuss whether floating the exchange rate will cure the deficit 'painlessly', or whether it would involve costs of its own such as increasing domestic inflation.

Question 2 Outline the circumstances under which a government may seek to reduce a Balance of Payments surplus and discuss the measures which it might employ to bring this about.

(London: June, 1978)

Understanding the Question In answering this question you need to make clear that the Balance of Payments refers to the Balance on Current **and** Capital Account – or the Balance for Official Financing – because the Current Account is not specifically stated. Thus a surplus can arise from several sources, according to performances on visible trade, invisibles and long-term or short-term capital movements as illustrated in Table 27.1. There are many combinations of these four variables which may create an overall surplus.

Generally, however, the impact of the surplus is to increase demand for the country's output. In Keynesian terms this is represented by an injection of demand into the economy with consequent multiplier effects. If the economy is below full employment, a desirable increase in output may occur, but if the economy is fully employed or if there are production bottlenecks, the main effect may be inflationary. Monetarists emphasize the impact on the domestic money supply of the currency inflow associated with the surplus, also stressing the inflationary consequences.

We have described in the unit some of the other reasons why a large surplus may not be desirable – namely the effect on deficit countries and the 'Dutch disease' syndrome. Generally, however, there is less international pressure to reduce a surplus than a deficit, and a country may only take action if the undesirable effects on its own economy are obvious.

The policies to cure a surplus are the reverse of those to remedy a deficit, namely **reflation, revaluation** (or allowing the exchange rate to float upward) and the **removal of import controls**. You might also mention that if the surplus is on the Current Account, the **removal of exchange controls** might encourage a capital outflow which will counter the trading surplus.

Answer plan

1 Explain the meaning of a Balance of Payments surplus and its possible origins.
2 Outline why a government may wish to remove or reduce such a surplus. It is worth pointing out that a surplus is a success symbol and that most governments are reluctant to remove them.

3 Explain the main measures and how they will operate on the payments position. Reflation is mainly **expenditure-increasing** while other policy measures are **expenditure-switching**.

Question 3 Define (a) the terms of trade and (b) the Balance of Payments on Current Account. Discuss the possible relationships between the two concepts.

(AEB: November 1979)

Understanding the Question Examination candidates frequently confuse the **terms of trade** with the **balance of trade** (the Balance of Payments on Current Account). However, the two concepts are completely separate though a movement in the terms of trade usually has a definite impact upon the Balance of Payments and the balance of trade.

The terms of trade is simply the ratio between an index of average export prices and a similar index for import prices. An 'improvement' or 'favourable' movement in the terms of trade means that export prices have risen faster than import prices. The two most likely causes are (i) a higher rate of domestic inflation than in the rest of the world and (ii) an upward movement in the exchange rate. In the first case it is the movement in the **internal** price level which is responsible, whereas in the latter case it is a change in the **external** price of the currency.

Whether a favourable movement in the terms of trade leads to an improvement or deterioration in the Current Account of the Balance of Payments depends upon the elasticities of demand for exports and imports. We have explained in the unit how if the Marshall-Lerner condition is met (the sum of the elasticities is greater than unity) a devaluation will improve and a revaluation worsen the Balance of Payments. It follows therefore that a favourable movement in the terms of trade will cause an adverse movement in the Current Account if the Marshall-Lerner condition is met, and a favourable movement if it is not. A change in the terms of trade caused by differing inflation rates may also initiate less predictable short-term flows in the Capital Account, in expectation for example of compensating exchange rate movements. However, you are not expected to include these relationships in your answer.

Answer plan

1 Define and carefully distinguish between the two concepts.
2 Explain the possible causes of an improvement in the terms of trade.
3 Carefully show how the effect of an improvement in the terms of trade upon the payments Current Account depends upon elasticities of demand. Introduce the Marshall-Lerner condition.

Multiple Choice Questions

Question 4 'Expenditure-switching' policies to improve the Current Account Balance include all of the following **except**:
(a) Customs duties
(b) Deflation
(c) Export credits
(d) Export subsidies

Understanding the Question Measures to improve the Balance of Payments can be classified as either **'expenditure-reducing'** or **'expenditure-switching'**. Of those in this question, deflation is the only expenditure-reducing one as it seeks to lower the growth of national income and thus demand for imports. The introduction of customs duties, export credits and export subsidies all attempt to give British goods a price advantage which will cause consumers to switch expenditure to British goods, thereby benefiting the payments position. Thus, alternative (b) – deflation – is the correct alternative.

Question 5

Selected Balance of Payments Figures 1980 – UK

	£m
Visible Balance	+ 1177
Invisible Balance	+ 1560
Balance for Official Financing	+ 1192

It is possible to conclude from these figures that in 1980 there was:
(a) an unfavourable balance of trade
(b) a Capital Account deficit
(c) a Current Account deficit
(d) a fall in Official Reserves

Understanding the Question The Balance of Trade is sometimes taken to mean the Balance of Visible Trade and sometimes the whole of the Current Balance, including invisibles. It does not matter which interpretation is used here, as visibles, invisibles and the combined Current Balance are all in surplus. Thus **(a)** and **(c)** are clearly incorrect. As the Balance for Official Financing is also in surplus, official reserves will have risen rather than fallen, so **(d)** is incorrect. This leaves **(b)** as the correct answer: the fact that the Balance for Official Financing is in less of a surplus than the Current Account indicates a Capital Account deficit.

Data response Questions

Question 6 The following is the summary of the UK balance of payments for 1976 and 1977.

	1976	1977
Current Account		
Visible balance	− 3589	− 1709
Invisible balance	+ 2452	+ 1998
Current balance		
Investment and other capital transactions	− 2896	+ 4410
Balancing item	+ 404	+ 2662
Balance for official financing		
Official financing		
Net transactions with overseas monetary authorities	+ 984	+ 1113
Foreign currency borrowing (net):		
by HM Government	–	+ 871
by public sector under exchange cover scheme	+ 1792	+ 243
Official reserves (drawings on +/ additions to −)		

(a) Calculate for each year (i) the Current balance (ii) the Balance for official financing (iii) the drawings on or additions to the Official reserves   [7]

(b) Explain how the Visible balance is calculated.   [2]

(c) Which items make up the Invisible balance?   [3]

(d) What is the Balancing item?   [1]

(e) What are the Net transactions with overseas monetary authorities?   [1]

(f) What is Foreign currency borrowing (net) by public sector under exchange cover scheme?   [1]

(g) Comment on the structure of the UK balance of payments for these two years pointing out the strengths and weaknesses.   [10]

(O & CSEB: June 1980)

Understanding the Question Part (*a*) is relatively easy in that there are gaps in the data which show you what to calculate. In calculating (iii) you must ensure that the Total Official Financing equals (but with the opposite sign) the Balance for Official Financing; in 1976 there were drawings on reserves but in 1977 the reserves were replenished. You must make sure that you explain to the examiner what you are trying to do at each stage in your calculations, so that you can earn at least some marks in the event of an arithmetical error.

All the items have been covered in this unit except (*f*). The net foreign currency borrowing by the public sector under the exchange cover scheme refers to the difference between the public corporations' borrowings and repayments in the Eurodollar market.

As the marks indicate, the last part of the question is the main part. The principal points to identify about the structure of the Balance of Payments are:

1 The visible deficit indicates competitive weakness. (These years were just before the major impact of North Sea oil revenues on the Balance of Payments.)

2 The invisible surplus indicates a trading strength and the importance of profit inflows.

3 There are dramatic changes in investment and capital movements which make the Capital Account so volatile. This is destabilizing and a possible weakness, particularly as the Capital Balance exceeds the Current Balance in both years, in deficit in one year but in surplus in the other.

4 Official financing by borrowing is relatively stable, but the reserves are subject to particularly violent changes.

5 A large Balancing Item, which is essentially a residual, throws doubt on the accuracy of the 'real' figures. Indeed it is quite common for a deficit which appears in an early estimate of the accounts for a particular year to be transformed later into a surplus (and vice versa) as the balancing item is gradually allocated to one or other of the 'real' items in the payments accounts.

27.6 Further reading

Cobham, D., *The Economics of International Trade* (Woodhead-Faulkner, 1979)

Nevin, E., *Textbook of Economic Analysis,* 5th edition (Macmillan, 1981)
Chapter 31: The Balance of Payments.

Davies, B., *The United Kingdom and the World Monetary System* (Heinemann, 1979)

Burningham, D., editor, *Understanding Economics, An Introduction for Students* (Macmillan, 1978)
Chapter 17: The Balance of Payments and its Adjustment.

28 Exchange Rates

28.1 POINTS OF PERSPECTIVE

In Unit 27 we emphasized how the method of restoration of equilibrium in the **Balance of Payments** depends in large measure upon the type of exchange rate that exists. In this unit we examine in greater detail the mechanisms through which **freely floating** and **completely fixed** exchange rates operate, before investigating various types of **managed exchange rates** that have existed in the world economy since 1945. We shall introduce the role of the **International Monetary Fund** (IMF) in providing the institutional framework within which modern exchange rates operate, and we shall comment on the **international payments difficulties** and the **problems of world liquidity** which exist today.

28.2 UNDERLYING CONCEPTS

1 The Simple Theory of a Freely Floating Exchange Rate

Exchange rates and the existence of a **foreign exchange market** are necessary because different countries use different currencies to pay for **internal** trade. An exchange rate is simply the **external price** of a currency expressed in terms of gold, another currency such as the US dollar, or a weighted average of a sample of important trading currencies. For the sake of simplicity, we shall for the most part follow the convention of expressing the exchange rate of the pound sterling in terms of the dollar, but we shall also note when other expressions of the exchange rate are more appropriate.

In a regime of **freely** (or **cleanly**) floating exchange rates, the currency of a country is regarded as a simple commodity to be traded on foreign exchange markets, its price or exchange rate being determined by the forces of supply and demand. For the time being we shall assume that a currency is demanded on foreign exchanges only for the payment of trade (we are ignoring the complications caused by **capital flows** and **speculation**), that a country needs another country's currency to purchase imports from that country, and that all countries will immediately sell on the foreign exchange market any holdings of foreign currencies that are surplus to their requirements.

As in any market, the **demand** and **supply** curves for a currency (in this case the pound sterling) show the amounts of the currency which traders wish to buy and sell at various possible prices or exchange rates. Since we are assuming that people wish to hold foreign currency only for the purpose of financing trade, the slopes of the demand and supply curves for a currency will depend on the levels of exports and imports that are desired at each exchange rate. The lower the exchange rate of the pound, the more competitive are British exports when priced in foreign currencies and the greater the volume of exports. Thus the lower the exchange rate, the greater the demand for pounds on foreign exchange markets, since foreigners need more pounds to buy a greater

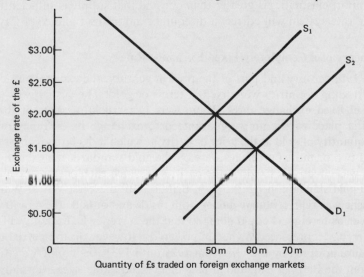

Fig 28.1 Exchange rate adjustment in a system of freely floating exchange rates

volume of British exports at their current sterling price. The result is the downward-sloping demand curve for pounds illustrated in Figure 28.1.

While exports generate a demand for pounds on foreign exchange markets, imports generate the supply of sterling needed to purchase the foreign currencies required to pay for the goods and services demanded. A fall in the exchange rate will reduce the competitiveness of imports when priced in sterling. Provided that the demand for imports is elastic, the quantity of pounds being supplied to pay for imports decreases as the exchange rate falls – and increases as the exchange rate rises – resulting in the upward-sloping supply curve of sterling in Figure 28.1.

Figure 28.1 illustrates an initial exchange rate of £1 = $2.00, the demand curve for sterling being D_1 and the supply curve of sterling S_1. Clearly this is an **equilibrium exchange rate** at which the demand for and the supply of sterling are equal. Since the value of exports (paid for in pounds) equals the value of imports (paid for in foreign currencies), the **Balance of Payments** is also in equilibrium! This point is well worth stressing: **exchange rate equilibrium** implies **Balance of Payments equilibrium** and vice versa. Indeed, the two concepts are merely different sides of the same coin, the one an equilibrium stated in terms of an equilibrium price (the exchange rate), and the other an equilibrium of quantities (currency flows). If the Balance of Payments is in equilibrium there will be no pressure for a change in the exchange rate.

Suppose now that for some reason, such as an increase in the quality competitiveness of foreign goods, the desire to buy imports increases at all existing prices expressed in sterling. More foreign exchange is demanded in order to purchase imports and the supply curve of sterling in Figure 28.1 shifts rightwards to S_2. $2.00 is no longer an equilibrium exchange rate, since foreigners now accumulate sterling holdings of £70m., whereas they only require £50m. to pay for their own purchases of British exports at this exchange rate. The market mechanism now operates to restore simultaneously equilibrium in the Balance of Payments and an equilibrium exchange rate. The sale by foreigners of the **excess supply** of pounds depresses or **depreciates** the exchange rate, thereby increasing the price competitiveness of British exports and reducing that of imports. The process continues until the new equilibrium exchange rate of $1.50 is reached. Conversely if the initial equilibrium is disturbed by an event such as the production of North Sea oil which moves the Balance of Payments into surplus, the exchange rate will rise or appreciate until the **excess demand** for sterling is eliminated and a new equilibrium is achieved.

2 The Marshall-Lerner condition and Exchange Rate stability

It is important to stress that the result illustrated in Figure 28.1 depends critically upon our assumption that the demand for imports is elastic. If demand is inelastic, more pounds will be needed as the exchange rate falls in order to pay for imports. The fall in the quantity of imports at lower exchange rates is insufficient to offset the effects of the higher sterling price of each unit of imports. In these circumstances a **downward-sloping (perverse** or **backward-bending)** supply curve for sterling results. The equilibrium exchange rate is still determined where the demand and supply curves intersect, but the equilibrium may not always be stable. The **stability condition** is provided by the **Marshall-Lerner criterion** which we introduced and explained in Unit 27. Provided that the sum of the elasticities of foreigners' demand for British exports and British demand for imports is greater than unity, there will be a tendency to move towards a stable equilibrium exchange rate. Even if the demand for imports is inelastic, provided that the **sum** of the export and import elasticities is greater than one and that supply is sufficiently elastic, then a floating exchange rate system will correct a disequilibrium in the Balance of Payments.

3 The Simple Theory of a Completely Fixed Exchange Rate

For much of the 19th century and part of the present century, the exchange rates of the world's most important trading countries were fixed in terms of gold. The system was known as a **gold standard system of fixed exchange rates**. There were two crucial aspects of the gold standard system. In the first place each country guaranteed to exchange its currency on demand for a certain physical quantity of gold at the **price** or **parity** at which it declared its currency on the gold standard. Thus if two or more currencies were on the gold standard, the exchange rate of one in terms of another was effectively fixed via the parities at which each currency could be exchanged for gold. The **full gold standard** in operation in Britain until the First World War meant that the country's note issue was **representative money** both inside and outside the country. The country's own citizens as well as foreigners could demand that the currency be exchanged for gold. Ownership of paper currency represented ownership of gold. However, in the **partial gold standard** or **gold bullion standard** adopted by the UK from 1925 until 1931, the country's citizens could only purchase gold from the Bank of England in bars of a considerable size. Internally, because of the shortage of it gold had been effectively **demonetized**.

The second essential feature of the gold standard system as a **mechanism for correcting Balance of Payments disequilibrium** was that a country on the gold standard agreed to the inflow and outflow of gold in payment for trade. Assuming that one country on the gold standard experienced a Balance of Payments deficit and another country simultaneously experienced a surplus, the following sequence of events was expected to take place:

(i) Gold would be shipped out of the deficit country and into the surplus country.

(ii) The money stock in the deficit country would automatically contract, directly in the case of gold coins and paper currency backed by gold; indirectly in the case of fractionally backed bank deposits. Conversely, there would be an automatic expansion of the money stock in the surplus country.

(iii) This would be followed by an automatic deflation of the price level (via the **quantity theory of money**) in the deficit country and an automatic inflation in the surplus country.

(iv) The falling **internal** price level of the deficit country would increase the competitiveness of its exports, while the rising price level within the surplus country would reduce its export competitiveness.

(v) The process would then continue until the restoration of equilibrium in the Balance of Payments of both countries.

4 The Weaknesses of the Gold Standard mechanism

The 19th century gold standard displayed a number of weaknesses which make it extremely unlikely that it will ever be adopted again in pure form, though a minority of monetarist economists have called for its revival. The principal weaknesses in the gold standard were:

(i) The gold standard adjustment mechanism worked only very slowly. Internal price levels within countries did not respond quickly to gold inflows and outflows in the manner suggested by the simple quantity theory of money. Although a gold inflow might have an inflationary effect in a surplus country, prices and wages were usually 'sticky downwards' in a deficit country. Instead of **prices** falling in the deficit country, the main **deflationary effect** was **lost output** and **increased unemployment** which could persist for many years as a result of too high an exchange rate against gold. If the country's currency was overvalued against gold, only deflation would cure the payments disequilibrium.

(ii) Although the length of the adjustment period partly explains why deficit countries tended to run out of gold, an increasing shortage of monetary gold also contributed to the weakness of the gold standard system, despite the adoption of a **partial gold standard**, which allowed a greater proportion of a country's monetary gold to be available as an international means of payment. However, world trade expanded despite the world shortage of monetary gold largely because sterling took on the key role of a reserve currency, thereby supplementing gold and becoming an important source of world liquidity. The gold standard became a **gold exchange standard** in which key currencies on the gold standard, notably sterling, occupied a growing proportion of world reserves.

However, the reserve currency role of sterling involved a **contradiction** which eventually led to the downfall of the gold standard system in the 1930s, just as the contradictory role of the dollar later contributed to the collapse of the Bretton Woods system of fixed exchange rates in the 1970s. In order to become a reserve currency, and thereby provide the liquidity to finance the continuing growth of world trade, a key currency must be **transmitted** into the reserves of other countries. Only a large **Balance of Payments deficit** over a long period of time can provide the required **transmission mechanism**. In effect the other countries with whom a deficit country trades agree to accept payment in that country's currency without the country being required to reduce its deficit. The other countries then hold the 'excess supply' of the currency in their reserves for use as a means of payment. To be acceptable as a reserve currency, countries must be confident of the exchange value of the currency, yet the Balance of Payments deficit required as a transmission mechanism eventually destroys this very state of confidence. In the case of sterling in 1931 (and latterly of the dollar which was also on the gold standard), the currency eventually became vulnerable to speculative runs when external holdings of the currency, held both privately and officially in other countries' reserves, far exceeded the British (and American) gold reserves.

Thus the **liquidity-confidence problem** which forced the pound off the gold standard in 1931 led to the collapse of the gold standard system of fixed exchange rates as, one by one, most other leading trading countries followed suit. For the rest of the 1930s exchange rates either floated freely or were artificially depressed as countries attempted to escape from the Great Depression by gaining a competitive advantage at the expense of the rest of the world. This era established a bad reputation for floating exchange rates just as the experience of the 1920s had diminished the reputation of the Gold Standard. It is not surprising, therefore, that by the end of the Second

World War, when the new **Keynesian orthodoxy** was advocating the **extension of economic management within countries**, its logic should be extended to the **management of exchange rates** and of the system of world payments **between** countries.

28.3 ESSENTIAL INFORMATION

1 Exchange Rates and Balance of Payments Adjustment

Before we investigate the advantages and disadvantages of freely floating and fixed exchange rates, we shall present a simple summary of the critical difference between the Balance of Payments adjustment mechanism under the two exchange regimes. Under a system of floating exchange rates, the *external price* of the currency (the exchange rate) moves up or down to correct a payments imbalance, without requiring an adjustment in domestic output or the *internal price level*. In contrast, under a system of fixed exchange rates it is the internal price level (together with the levels of domestic output and employment) which adjusts to cure the imbalance, the external price of the currency remaining unchanged.

2 The Advantages of Floating Exchange Rates

(i) An important advantage of a **freely floating** (or **flexible**) exchange rate stems from the nature of the adjustment mechanism just described. According to the simple theory of a freely floating exchange rate, the exchange rate should never be over- or undervalued for very long. In the event of a 'too-high' exchange rate causing export uncompetitiveness and a payments deficit, market forces should quickly adjust towards an equilibrium exchange rate which also achieves equilibrium in the Balance of Payments – provided of course that the Marshall-Lerner condition holds.

(ii) Correctly valued exchange rates are necessary if the world's resources are to be efficiently allocated between competing uses. If efficient resource allocation and use are to be achieved in a constantly changing world, market prices must be free to reflect the shifts in **demand** and **comparative advantage** that result from such events as resource discoveries and changes in technology and labour costs. A freely floating exchange rate may automatically adjust to gradual changes in demand and comparative advantage, whereas in a fixed exchange rate system a currency may become gradually over- or undervalued when demand or comparative advantage move either against or in favour of a country's industries.

(iii) It has been argued (rather naively as we shall later see) that when the exchange rate is freely floating, the state of the Balance of Payments ceases to be both a **'policy problem'** and a **constraint** upon the pursuit of domestic economic objectives. Governments can leave market forces to 'look after' the Balance of Payments while they concentrate on achieving full employment and growth. If the pursuit of domestic objectives causes the inflation rate to rise out of line with other countries, then, according to the **purchasing power parity theory**, the exchange rate will simply fall to exactly compensate for the higher inflation rate. In this way the competitiveness of the country's exports is always maintained. In a fixed exchange rate system, the country would **'import' unemployment** from the rest of the world as a result of its deteriorating competitiveness and because of the need to deflate the domestic economy in order to correct the payments deficit.

(iv) Equally, a 'responsible' country with a lower than average inflation rate benefits from a floating exchange rate which insulates it from **'importing' inflation** from the rest of the world. There are two ways of explaining this. If the rest of the world is inflating at a faster rate, a fixed exchange rate causes a country to 'import' inflation through the rising prices of goods it purchases abroad. Alternatively under fixed exchange rates, excess demand in countries with persistent Balance of Payments deficits causes inflationary pressure to be 'exported' to surplus countries. The deficit countries escape the full inflationary consequences of the excess demand generated by their economies.

(v) When the exchange rate is floating, a country's monetary policy (as well as its fiscal policy) can be completely independent of external influences. This is because the country has no need to keep official reserves to finance a payments deficit or to support the exchange rate. If for example the deficit increases, the exchange rate simply corrects the disequilibrium without any loss of reserves. The country's domestic money supply is unaffected by a change in the official reserves, and interest rate policy is not determined by the need to protect the exchange rate.

(vi) Because a country has no need to hold large official reserves of foreign currencies, resources which would otherwise be tied up in the reserves can be used more productively elsewhere.

3 The Disadvantages of Floating Exchange Rates

(i) It is often argued that floating exchange rates **increase business uncertainty** and lead to less specialization, trade, and investment than would otherwise take place. However, uncertainty is probably not the most serious problem that results from a floating exchange rate. Indeed, **hedging**, which usually involves the purchase or sale of currency three months in advance in the **'forward'** market, can considerably reduce the business uncertainties caused by floating exchange rates. It is also the case that fixed and managed exchange rates can on occasion be just as uncertain as floating rates, particularly when a currency is obviously overvalued, and a devaluation is expected.

(ii) It is also asserted that a floating exchange rate promotes an increase in **currency speculation** with all its **destabilizing** effects. There are a number of interesting aspects to this question. While it is undoubtedly true that there has been a growth in currency speculation in the modern era of 'dirty' floating, it may be less related to floating than to the growth of the pool of footloose 'hot-money' – itself a response to the role of the dollar in the Bretton Woods system of managed exchange rates. Secondly, there is far more scope for speculators to 'win' at the expense of governments in a managed exchange rate system than in a freely floating system. In the former case, a speculator engages in the 'one-way option' of selling currency to the central bank defending the currency, hoping to force a devaluation and to realize a capital gain when the currency is bought back at a lower price. If the pressure fails, the speculator will only make a small loss since he can buy back the currency at or near the original price. In a freely floating system, however, a speculator wishing to sell must find another wishing to buy – and in the consequent trading the speculator who guesses correctly gains at the expense of the one who guesses wrongly. The successful speculators are those who correctly sell when the exchange rate is too high and buy when it is too low. Their activity speeds the process of adjustment to an exchange rate equilibrium, stabilizing rather than destabilizing, and smoothing out rather than reinforcing temporary fluctuations.

Nevertheless it is undoubtedly true that in the present-day regime of dirty floating, massive, essentially speculative, short-term capital flows or hot money movements have had seriously destabilizing effects upon the exchange rates, Balance of Payments and indeed the structure of the domestic economy of a number of countries. During 1980 and the early part of 1981, hot money flows into the United Kingdom forced the exchange rate to a level above $2.40 at a time when the British inflation rate was above that of her main trading competitors. This massive rise in the exchange rate could certainly not be justified by the export competitiveness of British industry. Indeed, the high exchange rate accelerated the deindustrialization process and increased the already high level of unemployment. Nor could the exchange rate appreciation be explained solely by the impact of North Sea oil revenues on the Current Account, since there was an equally massive fall in the exchange rate later in 1981 when the contribution of oil revenues to the Balance of Payments was still growing. A major part of these fluctuations can only be explained by the destabilizing effects of essentially speculative hot money movements, themselves a response both to interest rate differences between countries and to expectations that exchange rates might rise or fall.

(iii) We have already noted how fixed exchange rates have been blamed for the 'export' of inflation from one country to another. However, other economists believe that floating exchange rates are to blame for inflation and that fixed exchange rates in fact possess a **deflationary bias** which reduces inflation. If a country allows its inflation rate to exceed that of its trading competitors, its Balance of Payments will move into severe deficit. A growing export uncompetitiveness and import penetration will 'discipline' the domestic causes of cost-push inflation through an increase in the level of unemployment and the number of bankruptcies. At the same time the loss of reserves will put pressure on the deficit country to deflate its domestic economy in order to cure the imbalance, but the system is asymmetrical since no equivalent pressure is put upon the surplus country to cure its surplus.

In a floating exchange rate system no such discipline exists to make a country reduce its inflation rate. (Indeed we argued earlier that the lack of such a discipline is regarded by some as one of the virtues of floating exchange rates, allowing a country to pursue domestic objectives unconstrained by the need to support the Balance of Payments or the exchange rate.) In fact, however, a policy of pursuing domestic objectives irrespective of their effects on the exchange rate contains two serious dangers. In the first place, through the effects of a falling exchange rate upon import prices and hence upon domestic inflation, such a policy may unleash a **vicious circle** or **cumulative spiral** of ever faster **inflation** and **exchange rate depreciation** which eventually destabilizes large parts of the domestic economy and prevents growth and full employment from being attained. Secondly, a simultaneous expansion of demand in a large number of countries untrammelled by the consequences upon the exchange rate can add to excess demand and fuel inflation on a world-wide scale. In an individual country such inflation may be explained in cost-push terms since it appears to originate in increased import prices, but the true causes probably lie deeper in an international increase in money demand which far exceeds the short-run ability of industries, and particularly primary producers, to increase world supply.

4 The Advantages and Disadvantages of Fixed Exchange Rates

The advantages and disadvantages of fixed exchange rates are closely but oppositely related to the disadvantages and advantages of floating exchange rates which we have already covered in some detail. In summary, we can state that the main advantages usually cited for fixed exchange rates are (i) certainty and (ii) the 'discipline' imposed on a country's domestic economic management and upon the behaviour of workers and firms. In contrast, the main disadvantages are (i) in some circumstances uncertainty may actually be increased, (ii) a currency may be over- or undervalued, in which case (iii) severe costs in terms of unemployment and lost output may be imposed on deficit countries, and (iv) in a rigid gold standard system there may not be an adequate adjustment mechanism successfully to cure a payments imbalance.

5 The Experience of Managed Exchange Rates

(i) The Bretton Woods System In earlier units we noted how in the 1940s **Keynesian economic policies** were first adopted **within** many countries to pursue growth and full employment through demand management and government interventionism. It is not surprising, therefore, that it was also the decade in which interventionism was extended to the international economy through the creation at the **Bretton Woods Conference** in 1944 of the system of **managed exchange rates** that came into full operation in 1947. Indeed Keynes himself was a principal architect of the new system, and of the **International Monetary Fund** (IMF) set up to supervise the post-war exchange rates. (The other functions of the IMF are explained in more detail in one of the questions at the end of this unit.)

By the 1940s it had become generally agreed that the **Great Depression** experienced by most countries in the 1930s had been deepened, if not caused, by a collapse of world trade. The collapse of trade was itself related to the failures of, firstly, the gold standard and, after 1931, of floating exchange rates to cure payments imbalances and to provide adequate world liquidity.

The United States and United Kingdom therefore decided to create a post-war system of managed exchange rates which they hoped would possess the **advantages of both fixed and floating exchange rates** with the disadvantages of neither system. They hoped that the Bretton Woods system would be both **more flexible** than the gold standard and **more stable** than the floating exchange rates of the 1930s.

The gold standard had failed for two main reasons: the shortage of gold and the lack of an adequate adjustment mechanism to correct a 'wrongly' valued currency. In the new system the dollar became the principal international reserve asset supplementing gold, being transmitted into other countries' reserves through the mechanism of the US payments deficit. The dollar also became the **pivot** or **fulcrum currency** in the new system. (Nevertheless, because the dollar remained on the gold standard, the 'new' system was still essentially a **gold exchange standard** in which other exchange rates were fixed, via the dollar, against gold.) The **adjustment mechanism** in the Bretton Woods system worked through the creation of a **zone of flexibility** around an **adjustable peg** exchange rate. **Market forces** were free to determine the day-to-day exchange rate of a currency within a **ceiling** and **floor** 1% each side of an agreed par value or 'peg'. A temporary Balance of Payments surplus would cause the exchange rate to rise towards the ceiling, whereas a deficit would depress the rate towards the floor.

Each country agreed to intervene in the foreign exchange market to keep the exchange rate within the zone of flexibility. This was achieved through a process of exchange rate management or **exchange equalization**. If the exchange rate was tending to rise through the ceiling, the country's central bank artificially increased the supply of its own currency by selling it on the foreign exchange market and buying reserves, Conversely, it would sell reserves and buy its own currency when the exchange rate was falling through the floor. A persistent tendency for the exchange rate to leave the zone of flexibility would indicate a fundamental disequilibrium in the Balance of Payments and a 'wrongly' valued exchange rate. In these circumstances the IMF rules allowed a country to adjust the par value of its exchange rate: to **revalue** in the case of a surplus and to **devalue** in the case of a deficit.

In this way it was hoped that countries could benefit from **'managed flexibility'**, but as time went by the system increasingly displayed signs of **'managed inflexibility'**. It suffered from many of the disadvantages of the gold standard and fixed exchange rates that we have already described. The IMF interpreted its rules in such a way that devaluation became effectively ruled out, except as a last resort, for countries suffering from persistent payments deficits. Such countries were expected to deflate, but this could be unsuccessful without a simultaneous pressure on surplus countries to reflate.

A number of factors eventually contributed to the final collapse of the Bretton Woods system in 1971/72. In the first place, it is exceedingly difficult to maintain relatively fixed exchange rates if the inflation rate in deficit countries is markedly higher than in surplus countries. It is no accident that the system worked best in the 1950s when inflation rates in the developed world were remarkably similar. In contrast the greatest strains on the system began to occur in the 1960s when divergent inflation rates began seriously to alter the relative export competitiveness of the world's major trading countries. As a result, pressures began to mount in many countries, including the UK, to use the exchange rate as a **discretionary policy instrument** to be specifically assigned to Balance of Payments management, leaving the country supposedly free to pursue its own internal objectives.

The final weakness in the Bretton Woods system concerned the contradictory role of the dollar as a reserve currency. We have already explained how, in the context of the reserve role of sterling in an earlier era, a reserve currency is transmitted into the ownership of other countries via the mechanism of a payments deficit in the country of origin, and how eventually this weakens or **softens** the currency, making it less desirable or acceptable as a reserve asset and means of international payment. For the dollar, this stage had been reached by the late 1960s when dollars held outside the USA far exceeded American gold reserves. Being the pivot currency of the Bretton Woods system, it was impossible to devalue the dollar so as to restore American trading competitiveness against other countries and to stem the speculative runs which were taking place against the dollar. The dollar could only be devalued against gold, and when in 1971 a series of dollar crises culminated in the dollar being taken off the gold standard and allowed to float, the Bretton Woods system collapsed at a stroke.

(ii) Dirty Floating Since the breakdown of the Bretton Woods system of managed exchange rates in 1971/72, countries have frequently intervened in the foreign exchange market by buying or selling their own currency in order to influence its exchange rate. At one extreme this can simply be regarded as a **smoothing operation** in a regime of otherwise clean or freely floating exchange rates, but when the intervention is designed to secure an **'unofficial' exchange rate target** it is better described as **dirty floating**. After an attempt in the **Smithsonian Agreement** of 1971 to patch up the Bretton Woods system of fixed exchange rates, the modern era of dirty floating was initiated in 1972 by the British decision to float the pound so that domestic economic objectives could be achieved without the need to defend the exchange rate. Most other currencies then quickly followed suit.

The British experience of dirty floating in the 1970s exhibited two interesting phases. In the initial stage up to about 1977, market forces aided by massive hot money movements out of sterling tended to depress the exchange rate. Since the British inflation rate was higher than that of most of her competitors, this was in line with the predictions of the **purchasing power parity theory**. However, the British government considered the fall in the exchange rate to be excessive and tried to intervene (unsuccessfully in the sterling crises of 1975 and 1976) to prevent the exchange rate falling beneath an unofficial exchange rate target (or **floor**) which the government had chosen. Both sterling crises culminated in the abandonment of the authorities' unofficial target, and the pound fell to a 'low' of about $1.55 in 1976.

In the late 1970s the authorities had to intervene in the market to try to prevent the exchange rate from rising. Hot money now moved into sterling because of North Sea oil revenues and the continued weakness of the dollar. Again the intervention was largely unsuccessful. A 'trade-off' appeared between the successful control of the domestic money supply and the exchange rate target. The authorities gave up the attempt to control the exchange rate because the sale of sterling involved was increasing the domestic money supply at an unacceptable rate. Thus the pound floated upward, becoming severely overvalued at a rate of over $2.40 early in 1981. This phase of recent history illustrates the consequences of domestic fiscal and monetary policy upon the exchange rate. A tight fiscal and monetary stance pushes up interest rates, attracts hot money, and therefore pushes up the exchange rate.

By the late 1970s the UK authorities were facing the dilemma of choosing between a **'low pound' target** (below $2.00) and a **'high pound' target** (above $2.00). A high exchange rate might reduce domestic inflation (a) through cheaper import prices and (b) through 'disciplining' domestic causes of cost-push inflation. However, this could also be a disadvantage if the 'discipline' led to an unacceptable loss of output and employment and to an acceleration of the deindustrialization process. In contrast, a 'low pound' target would increase the competitiveness of British industry, but it might fail to discipline inflation. Indeed it might lead to a vicious downward spiral of cumulative inflation and exchange rate depreciation.

As it happened, market forces and capital movements caused a rapid fall in the exchange rate in 1981. The British government then appeared to settle for an exchange rate target of about $1.80 to $1.90 (or 90% of its 1975 value against a trade-weighted average of leading currencies) and it began to operate its domestic policies so as to sustain an exchange rate roughly within this range. Indeed, the exchange rate target began to assume the role of an **indicator of the degree of tightness or slackness in the fiscal and monetary stance of the government**, supplementing such indicators as Sterling M3 and the PSBR.

28.4 Links with other topics

The nature of a country's exchange rate and the system of exchange rates in operation amongst the trading countries of the world has a great effect upon the development of world trade (described in Unit 26) and upon the adjustment of the Balance of Payments (Unit 27). They also considerably influence the conduct of macro-economic policy in an open economy, affecting both the level of demand (Units 21 and 22) and the inflationary process (Unit 24). The exchange rate is also an issue of controversy between Keynesians and monetarists (Unit 25); Keynesians usually advocate government intervention to secure an exchange rate target, whereas monetarists are split between supporting a gold standard and a freely floating market mechanism.

28.5 Question practice

Essay Questions

Question 1 Explain why the government might intervene to prevent exchange rates from floating freely, and discuss the relative merits of any two intervention mechanisms.

(AEB: November, 1980)

Understanding the Question Intervention to prevent the exchange rate from freely floating can take a number of forms. At one extreme it can involve a complete commitment to a gold standard or an equivalent regime of rigidly fixed parities in which the exchange rate is never allowed to vary. At the other extreme a country may nominally support a completely free rate, but secretly intervene in the foreign exchange market to depress the exchange rate artifically in order to gain a competitive advantage in world trade. Many countries indulged in such behaviour in the 1930s. In between these extremes are the managed exchange rates of the Bretton Woods system and the dirty floating of the years since 1972. In the gold standard system, governments always agreed to exchange their currency for a fixed amount of gold, whilst in the managed exchange rates of the post-war years, exchange equalization has been used to support the exchange rate by official intervention in the foreign exchange market.

Except when a government secretly depresses the exchange rate, it will intervene either (a) if it believes that a fixed exchange rate possesses more advantages than a freely floating rate or (b) if it accepts the principle of a floating rate but believes that a completely freely floating rate will be unduly destabilized by capital flows.

You can answer the second part of the question by comparing the gold standard mechanism with exchange equalization, but an alternative – and probably the expected – approach is to compare the mechanism of dirty floating with the adjustable peg exchange rate system.

A dirty floating regime may be more responsive to market forces and avoid the need to deflate an economy in order to cure a payments deficit. However, it does tempt each country to use the exchange rate to gain at the expense of others. It is worth concluding that no exchange rate system is demonstrably superior to all others; it is on the wisdom and skill with which the system is operated that it depends for its relative success or failure.

Answer plan

1 Briefly describe the different types of exchange rate that are possible besides a freely floating exchange rate regime.

2 Explain how the reasons for intervention can range from a belief in the virtues of fixed exchange rates, to a wish to gain at the expense of other countries. It is also worth mentioning that many countries may simply accept the exchange rate system agreed by other more powerful countries or international bodies such as the IMF.

3 Briefly describe the advantages of fixed exchange rates and/or the disadvantages of freely floating rates.

4 Explain that the advantages of **certainty** and the **disciplining of domestic inflationary pressures** are probably greatest in a rather rigid system of fixed exchange rates when a country is forced to deflate its domestic economy in order to remedy a payments deficit. However, the disadvantages created by overvalued and undervalued currencies may result.

5 Compare two adjustment mechanisms e.g. formal adjustments (de- and re-valuation) versus dirty floating.

Question 2 Discuss the case for and against floating exchange rates.

(AEB: November, 1981)

Understanding the Question Since exchange rates were floated in the early 1970s examination questions have more frequently appeared on floating than on fixed exchange rates. A question of this type can be answered by drawing on the advantages and disadvantages we have already listed earlier in the unit. Once again, however, it is well worth arguing that there may be no inherent reason why a floating exchange rate is superior or inferior to a fixed system; the advantages and disadvantages depend upon how skilfully each system is operated.

Answer plan

1 Briefly describe how in theory a *freely* floating exchange rate prevents or cures a payments imbalance.
2 List and briefly explain the advantages, which include:
   (i) A currency should never be wrongly valued, except possibly temporarily.
   (ii) A government is freed of the need to keep reserves to support the exchange rate in the event of a payments deficit.
   (iii) It is also freed of the need to sacrifice domestic policy objectives to support the exchange rate and the Balance of Payments, and it is spared the problem of guessing the required de- or re-valuation if the exchange rate is obviously wrongly valued.
3 List and briefly explain the disadvantages, including:
   (i) Business uncertainty.
   (ii) Exchange rate fluctuations may be destabilizing because of speculative capital flows, and the Marshall-Lerner condition not being met.
   (iii) The removal of a source of discipline from the domestic causes of inflation, triggering the vicious circle of cumulative inflation and a falling exchange rate.
4 Evaluate the relative importance of the advantages and disadvantages.

Question 3 Evaluate the role of the International Monetary Fund in the last two decades.

(O & CSEB: June, 1980)

Understanding the Question The IMF should be evaluated in terms of its success or failure in promoting a growing and freer system of world trade and payments. To achieve this general objective, the original Articles of Agreement of the International Monetary Fund specified that the IMF should:

1 promote international monetary co-operation;
2 promote stable exchange rates, maintain orderly exchange arrangements and avoid competitive exchange depreciation;
3 encourage full convertibility between currencies and an ending of exchange controls:
4 lend its resources to countries to enable them to correct payments imbalances without resorting to harmful restrictions on trade;
5 shorten periods of disequilibrium in the Balance of Payments of member countries.

Essentially the IMF has adopted **three roles**:

(i) An advisory role acting as a consultant and giving expert advice to members.

(ii) 'Policing' the Bretton Woods system of exchange rates We have already described the system of exchange rates introduced at Bretton Woods in 1944 which was operational from 1947 to 1971. In summary, the system worked well until about 1960, but came under an increasing strain in the 1960s when inflation rates began to diverge and the dollar weakened. The system collapsed in 1971/72, since when the IMF has rather ineffectively attempted to produce orderly conditions in a world of dirty floating. In particular the IMF has discouraged countries from artificially depressing the exchange rate in an attempt to gain a competitive advantage at the expense of the rest of the world.

(iii) A banking role The Bretton Woods Agreement aimed to promote the orderly development of world trade by providing an adequate supply of **international liquidity** to tide deficit countries over **temporary** payments difficulties. We have already seen how the dollar provided the main source of **primary liquidity**, and how it eventually contributed to the downfall of managed exchange rates. Specially created **IMF reserves** were to provide a source of **secondary liquidity** to supplement the reserves held by individual countries. When the IMF was initially established, each member paid a **quota** (75% in its own currency and 25% in gold) into the IMF 'pool' of currency reserves which were to be available for member countries to draw upon in the event of a payments deficit. A deficit country could then draw upon the IMF currency 'basket' to supplement its own reserves when financing a temporary payments imbalance. The first part of a country's drawing entitlement is automatic, but beyond a certain limit the IMF can impose conditions upon any further loan. At regular intervals, the size of quotas and the Fund's overall reserves have increased.

Other methods of expanding the IMF's lending ability have included (a) the creation of **stand-by credits** in the mid-1950s; (b) **currency swaps**, and the **General Agreement to Borrow** in 1962, under which ten leading industrial countries (the **Group of Ten**) agreed to support each other's currencies through a supplementary IMF pool; and (c) the **Special Drawing Rights** (SDRs) scheme initially operated in 1970.

The creation of SDRs illustrates a most important aspect of the IMF's banking function. The Bretton Woods Agreement was essentially a compromise between the radical **Keynes plan** advocated by Britain and the more conservative **White plan** suggested by the USA. Keynes had envisaged a **world 'super bank'** issuing its own **world trading currency** (to be called **bancor**) which would effectively replace gold and national currencies in financing world trade. If the Keynes plan had been adopted, the IMF might have been able to expand the supply of world liquidity to meet demand without having to use national currencies such as the dollar. Because world trade grew much faster than the supply of IMF reserves, the burden of financing world trade was thrust upon the dollar, with the consequences we have already described.

Before the creation of SDRs, the IMF's lending ability was restricted by the size of the basket of currencies deposited by members. The Fund could only lend what it possessed, and many of the currencies it held were not very useful for the purpose of paying for trade. With the creation of SDRs or **'paper gold'**, the IMF could for the first time expand its lending ability without facing the constraints imposed by the size and composition of its currency basket. SDRs are essentially **book-keeping units of account** allocated by the IMF to each member. The allocation of SDRs can be expanded to keep pace with the growth of world trade. However, the usefulness of SDRs depends upon their acceptability. The creation of SDRs has not really solved the problem of world liquidity, since many countries lack trust in both the IMF and in SDRs. They regard SDRs as artificial man-made assets, far inferior to gold, an asset which has proved its value over thousands of years.

Thus opinions on the IMF are divided. One school of thought wishes to continue to expand both its regulatory or 'policing' powers and its role as a major source of world liquidity, while the opposing school regards the IMF as an unnecessary institution in a world in which the necessary discipline upon individual countries should still be imposed by gold.

Answer plan

1 Describe the functions of the IMF.
2 Explain how the early years of the 1970s mark a critical division between (i) the Bretton Woods system of exchange rates and 'dirty' floating and (ii) the development of the IMF's banking function before and after the creation of SDRs.
3 Evaluate the IMF's role in policing exchange rates.
4 Evaluate the banking role. Some economists argue that countries should possess a much greater automatic right to borrow from the IMF. They argue that the IMF wrongly insists on 'free market' domestic policies as a condition for lending. Other economists take the opposite view, arguing that as a banker the IMF has a duty to impose stiff conditions in order to ensure 'responsible' behaviour.
5 Discuss the criticism that the IMF is a 'rich man's club', assisting developed countries with their payments problems, while being insufficiently attentive to the needs of developing countries. In recent years the IMF has attempted to meet this criticism by expanding the facilities available to developing countries.
6 Lastly, explain that since the oil crises of the 1970s the liquidity problem facing the IMF may be less a problem of **shortage** of world liquidity than of its **distribution**, including the problem of **recycling oil revenues**.

Question 4 What would be the probable costs and benefits of the United Kingdom joining the European Monetary System?   *(SUJB: June, 1980)*

Understanding the Question The **European Monetary System** (EMS) which began operations in 1979 was initially a **'joint float'** of (mainly) EEC currencies against the currencies of the rest of the world, though it was intended eventually to create a **European Monetary Fund**. Indeed, some people believe that the EMS is the first step along a path to a **full monetary union** within the EEC, including the adoption of a common currency.

The currencies of the member countries of the EMS are fixed against each other, but with rather wider zones of flexibility than under the old Bretton Woods system, and exchange rates are also fixed against a **European currency unit** (ECU). Within the EMS, currencies can move within the relatively wide zones of flexibility, and, in theory at least, EMS rules require action by both surplus and deficit nations to keep the currencies within the permitted bands.

Initially, the United Kingdom decided to remain outside the system, but this decision contradicts the spirit if not the rules of Common Market membership. The EMS was established because it is difficult, if not impossible, to implement the **common economic policies** of the EEC in a world of erratically floating exchange rates. The costs or benefits of joining the EMS are thus closely associated with the costs and benefits of Community membership.

A major benefit of EMS membership might be the ability to draw on the help of other members to deter destabilizing hot money movements into and out of the country. Britain might also benefit if a successfully established EMS eventually creates a new source of world liquidity which is able to take pressure off the reserve role of the dollar.

However, Britain might also be expected to suffer the disadvantages of any system of relatively fixed exchange rates. The EMS has tended to become a 'Deutsch Mark area' in which the West German mark is the key currency. A strong DM might pull up the fixed values of the other currencies, leading to their overvaluation against the rest of the world. Although the zones of flexibility are designed to prevent this, great pressure could still be placed on the exchange rates of the other currencies, particularly if countries continue to experience highly divergent inflation rates. In Britain's case, the domestic costs of lost output and increased unemployment resulting from the deflationary policies necessary to reduce the inflation rate may be deemed too high; indeed many commentators felt that the severe deflationary policies of the early 1980s were 'preparing the way' for entry into the EMS.

Lastly, the **reserve role of sterling** might create severe problems, as the volume of sterling owned overseas and the attractiveness of London as a centre for hot money operations have caused much greater fluctuations in the exchange rate of the pound than in most other European exchange rates. This might place even greater pressure on the UK to deflate its economy in order to keep the sterling exchange rate steady against the EMS currencies.

Answer plan

1 Describe the main elements in the EMS.
2 Assess the advantages of membership to the UK:
  (i) the advantages of fixed exchange rates;
  (ii) European co-operation and the implementation of common economic policies;
  (iii) advantages resulting from a new source of world liquidity.
3 Assess the disadvantages:
  (i) the disadvantages of fixed exchange rates;
  (ii) the DM pulling up and overvaluing the other exchange rates;
  (iii) the domestic deflationary costs might be too high.

Multiple Choice Questions

Question 5 Other things being equal, which of the following is (are) likely to lead to a fall in the exchange rate of the pound sterling?

1 A fall in UK interest rates.
2 The Bank of England selling sterling for foreign currencies.
3 An increase in the UK inflation rate.

A	B	C	D
1, 2, 3 correct	1, 2 only	2, 3 only	1 only

Understanding the Question The answer is A since all three are correct. A fall in British interest rates relative to those in other countries would lead to a capital outflow, deteriorating the Balance of Payments and causing the exchange rate to fall. Likewise a deliberate policy by the Bank of England of selling sterling on the foreign exchange market will increase the supply of sterling relative to demand, thereby depressing its price. An increase in the inflation rate relative to that in other countries will worsen the Current Account of the Balance of Payments, causing the exchange rate to fall via the Purchasing Power Parity theory.

Question 6 (Use the table above) Revaluation must have the effect of:

1 Improving the terms of trade.
2 Improving the Balance of Payments.
3 Increasing the country's official reserves.

Understanding the Question Revaluation inevitably improves the terms of trade since export prices expressed in the country's own currency rise relative to import prices. However, if the Marshall-Lerner condition is met, the Balance of Payments will deteriorate, though there may be a temporary improvement immediately after the revaluation – a **'reverse J-curve effect'**. If the Balance of Payments deteriorates following a revaluation, official reserves will tend to fall. Therefore the correct answer is D.

Data Response Questions

Question 7 In the summer and autumn of 1976 there was a persistent fall in the sterling exchange rate which conventional textbooks would predict should lead to an increase in exports and possibly to an improvement in the balance of payments.

A correspondence commenced in *The Times* newspaper and the following is an extract from part of it:

'Real changes in the exchange rate mean those which more than offset changes in *some index of relative inflation*. The greater part of exchange rate changes in many cases merely offsets relative differences in rates of inflation. The view that the UK's exports should be growing rapidly because the pound has been depreciating or that Germany's ought to be growing slowly because the mark has been appreciating errs by neglecting the much slower rate of inflation in Germany.

However, once one attempts to allow for relative rates of inflation, as well as for many other factors which are relevant (time lags, tariff changes, changes in the pressure of demand, to give a few examples), it soon becomes extraordinarily difficult to assess the effect of exchange rate changes on trade.'

(i) Explain what the authors mean by the phrase *some index of relative inflation*. What problems are there in constructing such an index?

(ii) Using simple numerical examples, explain the importance of the point made in the first paragraph of the question.

(iii) Comment on the significance of the terms underlined in the passage. *(London: January, 1979)*

Understanding the Question

(i) Most examination candidates know how a **cost of living index** (or **price index**) such as the **Retail Price Index** (RPI) is used to measure the rate of inflation **within** a **single** country. However, the RPI must not be confused with an **index of relative inflation** which would compare the inflation rates in **different** countries. The problems in constructing such an index are broadly the same as those for an inflation index within a single country, namely (a) choosing a **representative sample of goods** in order to measure changes in their prices; (b) allocating **weights** to each good in the sample according to its relative importance; and (c) choosing a **suitable base year** for the index. Nevertheless, these problems are likely to be much greater when constructing an index to measure the inflation rates in several countries, particularly if the type of goods and services consumed vary significantly. The composition of a representative sample of goods will be very different in a high-income, developed country on the one hand and a poor subsistence economy on the other. There will even be significant difference between developed countries; for example, expenditure on home heating may be expected to vary between a temperate country such as Italy and a much colder country such as Sweden. Exchange rates may also complicate the construction of the index – an overvalued rate making imported foodstuffs, raw materials and finished goods appear artificially cheap.

(ii) The first paragraph in the question relates to the Marshall-Lerner condition, which states that when the sum of the elasticities of demand for exports and imports is greater than unity, a fall in the exchange rate will improve the Balance of Payments. You can illustrate this numerically by assuming particular elasticities of demand and showing the effects on import and export revenues of a change in the exchange rate.

(iii) The author of the passage is asserting that the effects of a devaluation on the Balance of Payments are difficult to separate from the effects of the other policy measures, **deflation** (which reduces the pressure of demand) and **import controls** (of which tariffs are an example). The problem of time lags refers to the **J-curve effect** whereby the Balance of Payments may be expected to deteriorate before it improves, following a devaluation. This part of the passage is a good example of the **violation of the** *ceteris paribus* **assumption**: we cannot easily isolate the effects of one variable upon another because other variables which may be expected to have an impact are also constantly changing.

The passage in the question illustrates the important difference between **nominal** and **real** changes in the exchange rate. Suppose that the exchange rate of sterling depreciates by 10% at a time when the British inflation rate is 10% greater than the average rate in our trading competitors. Although the nominal rate has fallen by the full 10% (the amount consistent with the purchasing power parity theory), the real exchange rate has stayed the same. In this example, the nominal rate would have to fall by more than 10% in order to cause a fall in the real rate, thereby increasing the real competitiveness of British exports.

28.6 FURTHER READING

Davies, B., *The United Kingdom and the World Monetary System*, 3rd edition (Heinemann, 1979).

Burningham, D., editor, *Understanding Economics, An Introduction for Students* (Macmillan, 1978)
Chapter 17: The Balance of Payments and its Adjustment.

Index